William Faulkner
A Centennial Tribute

By the same author

Scott Fitzgerald: A Centennial Tribute

William Faulkner
A Centennial Tribute

Edited by
Somdatta Mandal

PRESTIGE

Published by
Prestige Books
3/28, East Patel Nagar
New Delhi 110 008

1999

ISBN: 81-7551-057-9

Photo Typesetting by
Pivot Computers
Delhi 110 006
Ph. 3981867

Printed at
Chaman Offset Printers
New Delhi 110 002

CONTENTS

Fiction: Reassessments

Faulkner Miscellany

I believe that man will not merely endure, he will prevail.

He is immortal, not because he alone among creatures has an inexhaustible voice, but because he has a soul, a spirit capable of compassion and sacrifice and endurance.

The poet's, the writer's duty is to write about these things. It is his privilege to help man endure by lifting his heart, by reminding him of the courage and honor and hope and pride and compassion and pity and sacrifice which have been the glory of the past.

The poet's voice need not merely be the record of man, it can be one of the props, the pillars to help him endure and prevail.

William Faulkner
the Nobel Prize acceptance speech

Foreword

DONALD KARTIGANER

Sherwood Anderson once said to Faulkner: "You've too much talent. You can do it too easy, in too many different ways. If you're not careful, you'll never write anything." As we look back now on Faulkner's life and career, it is abundantly clear that indeed he had talent, enormous talent, and that he might have done it "easy." Instead he became one of the most daring, most innovative writers of his time, in virtually every novel trying something new, something he had not done before, often something no one else had done either. He once wrote, "I'm trying to say it all in one sentence, between one Cap and one period. I'm still trying to put it all, if possible, on one pinhead. I don't know how to do it. All I know to do is to keep on trying in a new way."

Writing was his life; in a strange sense it seems to have been all his life. Regardless of whether one sees his work as the product of his culture or the revision of it, one has the sense that he was a writer whose life outside writing not only has never truly come clear to us, but never existed. It is as if—pace Roland Barthes—it is not the author who disappeared into the text, but the man who disappeared out of it.

A common, indeed nearly unanimous, observation among Faulkner's biographers is his habit of role-playing, a habit so persistent as ultimately to create an impenetrable barrier to the revelation of his personality. The biographical consensus is as well a confession that, whatever the exhaustive accounts of what he did and said and wrote, the subject remains an enigma. Joel Williamson has stated the problem candidly. Among writers of Faulkner's generation, he writes, "none was so deeply unknowable. . . . Virtually no one, it seems, ever knew the real Faulkner." Tracing the long history of poses and posturing—the wounded World War I pilot, the bohemian poet, the town bum, the tough-guy bootlegger, the romantic suitor, the farmer, the gentleman rider—Williamson summarizes: "One of his gifts, perhaps his greatest gift, was that there was no certain Faulkner, nor even a given sequence of Faulkners. It was endless Faulkner. He could be almost anything, take almost any view within the compass afforded him by his culture. In successive phases of his life, he tried very nearly all of them." This sense of the various faces of Faulkner hiding the real man is not merely the conclusion of his major biographers, only one of whom—Joseph Blotner—actually knew him. In an interview with Judith Sensibar in 1986, his daughter, Jill Faulkner Summers, said: "Pappy always—it would be hard for me to say that I could look at him at one point and say, 'this is who he really is,' because, almost always he was playing a part." In life and in death, to his contemporaries and to his biographers, the prevailing theme of his character is its mystery.

Combined with the vividness of Faulkner's poses are the remoteness, the silences, the capacity to withdraw in social situations, that add not only to his unknowableness, but to the suspicion that he was determined to maintain it. In William Faulkner of Oxford, a collection of over forty accounts by people who knew him, many of them over a period of years, there is constant reiteration of this remoteness: "you might speak to him all day long and he wouldn't recognize the fact that you were around. Sometimes he didn't greet his best friends on the street. He didn't mean to be rude—just preoccupied. His friends understood him and knew that he was in no mood to talk. They accepted that fact."

His daughter Jill may have accepted it less easily, yet came to regard it as a given in their relationship: "There was no such thing as the library ever being off-limits. I spent much of my childhood reading on the couch while he was working. I could even talk at him, make comments and such; but I wasn't supposed to ask direct questions, and I wasn't to EXPECT an answer. When Pappy was really concentrating, he didn't hear anything anyway. Nothing could bother him."

Some interpreted that "preoccupiedness" as indifference, possibly even a form of contempt. Albert I. Bezzerides, a screenwriter and friend of Faulkner in Hollywood in the 1940s, recalls: "there was always a kind of distance between us. He always managed to keep himself separate. If he sat with people in the living room, you always had a feeling he was not really there; he was in his head somewhere. He was off thinking about what he was doing. I think we probably bored him to death because he participated very little in conversation or anything." When Bezzerides would occasionally take Faulkner on long drives, "I always talked because he never said a thing; he never said one word. I found the silence a little difficult to stand, so to fill the silence, I would talk about hunting or trucking trips I had made out of Fresno in my youth. Once, during one of my transitions or pauses, Bill said, 'Bud,' and I said, 'Yeah, what is it, Bill?' He said, 'Bud, you're an animal, but I'm just a vegetable.'"

What did he mean? A vegetable because he had nothing to say? or because he required the most attentive cultivation? or because, although forced to exist among animals, he was of another species entirely?

The corollary of his aloofness, for his more sympathetic acquaintances, was that in detaching himself from them he was inhabiting profounder spheres of thought and observation. If he did not seem to see the face before him, it might be because, as Emily Whitehurst Stone said, "his eyes . . . burned through the flesh and bone of everybody in front of him." Missed by those around him, even when he was ostensibily there, he himself missed nothing. He once surprised Emily by commenting on some changes she had made in the furnishings of her home.

> "You surprise me," I said. "Phil says you never see anything."
> "I see everything," he said.

There were those who claimed close friendship with Faulkner, yet recognized, and observed, the inviolable borders he erected. Dr. Felix Linder knew Faulkner since boyhood: "I've been around him every which way you can imagine. I've known him in my practice. I've been hunting with him. I've been fishing with him. I've been on the place with him: he's got a farm out here on Highway 30 East. . . . [But] William never did talk about his writing. Never even spoke to me about it. Never said a word about it to me. I didn't want to ask him."

Dr. Linder was not, of course, the only one. Except when he was asking for advances from his publishers, laying out the plots and time frames of future work, Faulkner—once he was past the apprentice years with Phil Stone—did not discuss his writing with anyone. And yet, what was the friendship made of in which the largest part of a man was utterly off limits? Phil "Moon" Mullen put it succinctly: "Bill Faulkner and I were not what you would call intimate friends. I doubt if he had any."

From these quite representative recollections an image emerges analogous to an iceberg: on the surface a self characterized either by remoteness or by masquerade; beneath, the 90 percent mass, a private, undisclosed being. What was it the masks protected? Was there a self he dared not reveal, or one he did not know and wished in his "preoccupation" to discover? Was it, as Williamson writes, that Faulkner "could never imagine that [the world] would take him as he was"? Or was it, in ways that defy any kind of biographical or psychological evidence, that Faulkner was only, and supremely, an artist? Perhaps it was not only a plea for privacy but a declaration of identity when he wrote Malcolm Cowley that "the sum and history of my life" should simply read: "He made the books and he died."

When I first visited Oxford, at the 1987 Faulkner conference, I heard a story, several versions of which I have heard since—not, as it turns out, describing the same incident, but referring to an incident which happened more than once. A woman at the conference, who had grown up in Oxford but since moved away, remembered how as a four or five-year old in the 1950s she had encountered the famous writer. She was playing on the sidewalk outside her home, probably on South Lamar, when she noticed a man walking toward her—tweed jacket, khaki trousers, pipe—headed for the Square. As he came abreast, she said "Good morning." The man kept on walking without saying a word. She burst into tears and dashed into the house. Upon questioning by her mother, she explained what had happened, the description of the man (and possibly his behavior) left no doubt in the mother's mind as to his identity. Immediately she was on the phone to Maud Falkner, William's mother (who died in 1960 at the age of eighty-eight). "Miss Maud, this is—; you have GOT to do something about that son of yours! He just walked past my little girl in the street without so much as a hello, and she's standing here crying her heart out!"

"That son of yours," was, of course, over fifty years old at the time, and already the recipient of the most prestigious literary honor in the world. Apparently Maud Falkner—who had three sons at the time, two of them living in Oxford—did not have to ask which son had committed the social infraction. "I will talk to Billy," she said, but she urged the mother to tell her daughter that he meant no harm. "He just didn't see her," Maud insisted, "he was writing."

Writing of course is what writers do. If Faulkner seems a unique example of that activity, it is owing, on the one hand, to his enigmatic character, his remarkable inaccessibility even to those closest to him, and, on the other hand, to the quality and enormous output of his writing. During the fifteen-year period 1928-1942 Faulkner wrote ten novels and wrote or revised over seventy short stories. Six or seven of the novels, a score of the stories, are among the indisputably major works of American literature, and virtually all the writing is of compelling interest. As the example of a single writer's sustained excellence, there is nothing to equal it in the twentieth century.

In the midst of it all, he was by no means immune to hardship: to the economic impact of the Great Depression or to devastating personal tragedy. Because of the financial difficulties that dogged him for most of his career, he was forced to do eight different tours of duty, of varying length, as a screenwriter in Hollywood. In 1931 his first child died shortly after her premature birth; in 1935 his youngest brother Dean was killed in a plane crash. His terrible sorrow over daughter and brother are well-known; yet the fact is, nothing could stop him. The year that his daughter died, he published sixteen stories and began *Light in August*, which he completed in six months. Following the death of his brother, he moved into his mother's house, where his widowed sister-in-law was also staying. He was there for several weeks, during which time, working nights on the dining room table, he completed the final chapters of his greatest novel, *Absalom, Absalom!*. Perhaps as much as the books themselves, Faulkner's commitment to them, his dedication, astonishes us and moves us. Asked once about his writing schedule, he simply said, "I write when the spirit moves me, and the spirit moves me every day." As for the real life he wondrously articulated in fiction, it became the necessary arena within which he acted, but outside of which he chose to live. He seemed to stride the world a foot above it, observing, absorbing all of it, even as he passed it by, pursuing what he once called the "dream of perfection."

"He was writing."

Mississippi,
9 September 1997

Introduction

SOMDATTA MANDAL

Born on September 25, 1897 to an old southern family, William Harrison Faulkner was raised in Oxford, Mississippi where he lived most of his life. Faulkner created an entire imaginative landscape, Yoknapatawpha County, with its capital "Jefferson," and found in this small corner of the state of Mississippi, deep in the heart of the South, enough material for a lifetime of writing. Unlike the Fugitives, Faulkner saw the South as a decayed culture; his novels dealt with the stories of several families with interconnections extending back for generations and his characters were often eccentric or grotesque. He re-created the history of the land and the various races—Indian, African-American, Euro-American and various mixtures—who have lived on it. An innovative writer, his social portraits were realistic, yet his prose style was experimental. To show the relationship of the past and the present, he sometimes jumbled the time sequence of his plots; to reveal a character's primitive impulses and social prejudices, he recorded unedited the ramblings of his or her consciousness. If F. Scott Fitzgerald saw the past as a lost, golden age, Faulkner saw it as judgement endlessly handed down. Often he narrated the same incident from different points of view and voices (including those of outcasts, children and illiterates), and in a rich and demanding baroque style built of extremely long sentences full of complicated subordinate parts.

For all that he put down on paper, Faulkner's most protean creation was his own identity. Over the years, he presented himself as a wounded World War I veteran (a lie), an English gentleman (a farce), a bearded bohemian (a phase) and a simple farmer (an evasion). In the 1920s, he wrote pastoral poetry, worked briefly—and badly—as the local postmaster, and published a couple of interesting, uneven novels. He also married a childhood friend, Estelle Oldham, with whom he had a daughter, Jill. Only at the end of the '20s did he figure out what to do with all he had learned from reading Joyce and Balzac and Shakespeare. With *Sartoris* he found his subject matter (suicide, incest, rape, murder) and with *The Sound and the Fury* he found his voice. His publisher's first reaction to the novel *Sanctuary* was that they would both end up in jail. The author's own father told a young woman carrying a Faulkner novel that it wasn't fit for her to read. "This young man was attributing evil to his fellow citizens and that didn't improve his standing, of course. He was resisting this movement to remove evil from the curriculums, from history," says Southern historian C. Vann Woodward. Ernest Gaines, author of *The Autobiography of Miss Jane Pittman* and several other novels had a different explanation to offer. "At first I didn't like Faulkner's work because Faulkner wrote about the kind of things that many people would want to forget. . . . But I began to realize what he was doing. He reminded me of things I saw. I come from the country (rural Louisiana) and I come from the same kind of situation: the grocery store he writes about, the kind of farms, the poor peasants, the broken down wagons and slow mules. I had never seen that in anybody's writing as plainly as I saw it in his. He really makes you pay attention."

Faulkner's most influential works were written in the 1930s, but he didn't become widely recognized until the middle of the next decade. Critic Malcolm Cowley compiled an anthology for the Viking Portable series and Jean-Paul Sartre declared, "Pour les jeunes en France, Faulkner c'est un dieu" ("For the young in France, Faulkner is a god"). In 1945, virtually all of Faulkner's books were out of print and most of his income came from the screen-writing he did for Hollywood. By the end of the decade, he had won the Nobel Prize. "His Nobel Prize acceptance speech espoused faith in the survival of man. This, as many pointed out, is very different from the impression one gets from the great, early novels," says Faulkner friend and biographer, Joseph Blotner. "As time went on, as he grew older, his view changed. He had seen mankind endure. He was not the same young writer, intense as young writers tend to be and very keenly aware of the tragic aspects of the human experience."

Faulkner's career included some teaching at the University of Virginia and some of his family members live in Charlottesville. According to his own point of view, Faulkner admitted that "there's a period in a writer's life when he, well, simply for any lack of word, is fertile and he just produces. Later on his blood slows, his bones get a little more brittle. . . . But I think there's one time in his life when he writes at the top of his talent plus his speed, too." His thinking may have mellowed in his later years, but his way of life was killing him. In the summer of 1962, he was badly injured in a riding accident, drank heavily and was admitted to a sanitarium. White-haired and worn-out, he died of a heart attack two months before his 65th birthday. He was buried in a nearby cemetery at Oxford, on a slightly raised plot of land, where a sign praises him for his "stories about his people" and where mourners have been known to pour whiskey on his grave.

This centennial collection of essays on Faulkner focuses upon various aspects of the writer and establishes him not only as a fine Southern writer in the tradition of Carson McCullers, Eudora Welty and Flannery O'Connor, but also as an internationally acknowledged modern experimentalist to the point where some of his finest fictional explorations of form and consciousness fully compare with those of Joyce, Proust or Virginia Woolf and who "discovered that writing was a mighty fine feeling. You could make people stand on their hind legs and cast a shadow." His work, like many of the best modern American novels, originated amid the decadent despairs and the experimental artistry of the 1920s, and like Fitzgerald's and Hemingway's, it persistently reflects the tragic exposure, the abrasion, the sense of radical discovery through which modern American fiction found itself.

That Faulkner is still read and is quite popular as a writer, albeit quite difficult for some, is also reiterated by the controversial incident which took place a few months ago. Graham Swift, the winner of last year's Booker Prize, has reacted in anger to a suggestion that he "borrowed the storyline and style" of his novel *Last Orders* from Faulkner's 1930 novel, *As I Lay Dying*. "My novel can, understandably be compared to Faulkner's but does not stand comparison to it. It's a different book." It had never occurred to him to include any acknowledgement to Faulkner. There is a ring of truth about what he says next: "If I did such a thing, I would have to acknowledge a great many other writers and a great many other writers would have to acknowledge others. If people haven't read *As I Lay Dying* it doesn't matter and if they have read it the similarities are obvious enough for anyone to recognize them." This is enough evidence to prove that Faulkner's artistic greatness lies in his ability to gradually liberate himself from the outmoded nineteenth century Victorian culture into which he had been born and to accommodate his art to the modernism that was replacing it to such an extent that standing at the threshold of the twenty-first century, his appeal still remains indefatigable. As Richard Moreland aptly states, "Faulkner's work is usually considered modernist and correspondingly critical in its relationship to the social contexts in which and about which Faulkner wrote. But the social criticism elaborated in his work becomes more interesting if we consider how this critical function and modernist periodization remains closely related to a more representational function and realist discourse, and also to a more participatory function of transference, negotiation, and change, in a more obviously multicultural, multitemporal (or non-synchronous) social context." ("Faulkner and Modernism," *The Cambridge Companion to William Faulkner*, Cambridge University Press, 1995, p. 18)

II

This anthology is divided into four sections. The first one, entitled "At the Turn of the Century" is a general overview containing three essays and aptly begins with Thadious M. Davis's assessment of the novelist at the turn of the century as well as looking forward to him in the future. Originally presented as a panel discussion in the C. William Gibson Symposium at Randolph Macon College in Ashland, Virginia, in March 1997, this paper serves as a mouthpiece for the idea plaguing the mind of all serious scholars regarding Faulkner's survival and endurance in the next century. Apart from discussing the affinities of the problem along with Toni Morrison's *Playing in the Dark* and George Kent's *Blackness and the Adventure of Western Culture*, Davis focuses our attention upon four particular areas, namely, Faulkner's location of history and memory, his construction of race, his creation of language and his envisioning of environment along with his general world view. All these make the writer 'confident' that Faulkner 'will survive into the twenty-first century.'

Lothar Hönnighausen begins his assessment by stating how Faulkner, "the great Southerner, is not only an American, but an international phenomenon" and shows how his influence can be felt upon Chinese, Canadian, Japanese, Latin-American writers as well.

This popularity, along with the entry in the *Encyclopaedia Britannica* stating that "more books and scholarly articles have been written about Faulkner than about any other American writer of the 20th century," does not of course mean, argues Hönninghausen, that in this centennial year of his birth, Faulkner is on the verge of becoming a popular author. "He is too subtle and too difficult for that" but his popularity rests with a canon which is "a more ethically and gender conscious criticism that is also more aware of the psychoanalytic and socio-political dimension of style." Discussing his fiction in details, the writer concludes that he will survive as "one of the great fiction writers of all time."

Faulkner's growing popularity from a provincial writer to become the Universal Philosopher, from his "own little postage stamp of native soil" to universal concern with "the problems of the human heart in conflict with itself" is the focus of Tutun Mukherjee's paper. She discusses how this maturity was achieved through a certain basic paradoxical situation, a trait he shared with many other novelists of the inter-war years. This contradiction began when Faulkner, along with other regional Southern writers, searched for a fulfilling cause and an enduring tradition; on the other hand, he also promoted works of art detached from its historical contexts and offered no answers to fundamental questions about society and culture other than the identification of the tension between intellect and emotion crystallized in the form and symbols of a single text. It is probably for this reason that in the later years Faulkner often spoke about his writing and about his concern for humanity's survival.

III

The second section entitled "The Writer and His Art" begins with an erudite essay by Ranu V. Vanikar. Reconsidering Faulkner's writing from a "socio-linguistic perspective," she focuses our attention upon the author's treatment of changing relationships between language and society and how ultimately he reaches a kind of "homogeneity" in which the whole society of Yoknapatawpha County operates. Taking examples from *Light in August, Absalom, Absalom!*, "The Bear," and *Intruder in the Dust*, Vanikar shows how the various communicative modes used by Faulkner constantly change from one work to another. These include Byron Bunch's position vis-a-vis Joe Christmas as per their different perceptions of language and society; the inherent dialogism of sharing ideas with the reader that is framed within the exchange between Quentin and Shreve; a more overtly transactional form in "The Bear"; and how alternating voices combine as Chick Mallison appears to go through a process of accommodation and adjustment.

Talking about language, but in a more traditional sense, Laxmi Parasuram, in her article, discusses the various nuances of Faulkner's style. As the writer himself had confessed in his classroom lectures at the University of Virginia, "the style must change according to what the writer is trying to tell . . . what he is trying to tell in fact compels the style." Most of the novels use different characters to tell parts of the story and demonstrate how meaning resides in the manner of telling, as much as in the subject at hand. The use of various viewpoints makes Faulkner more self-referential, or 'reflexive' than Hemingway or Fitzgerald; each novel reflects upon itself, while it simultaneously unfolds a story of universal interest. The use of imagery with a wide range of connotations and repercussions helps Faulkner to define individual attitudes and moods while an expansive framework in myth and meaning is being created at the same time.

"In explaining the comic side of William Faulkner's fiction, it soon becomes apparent how indivisible it is from the tragic side and how the two are almost inextricably intertwined" begins M. Thomas Inge in "Faulkner as Humorist" and argues that "Faulkner is so thoroughly in the American grain as a comic writer and draws so heavily on the entire body of distinctively American techniques and forms that an understanding of American humor is almost necessary to a full appreciation of his comic talent." Showing us how Faulkner took pleasure in pranks and impish behaviour as a private man, Inge also focuses our attention upon the four masks behind which Faulkner often hid himself, seldom allowing any of them to slip and reveal the man who lurked behind them. "Whoever the real Faulkner was, and whatever he was actually like, certainly the best part of him is to be found in his books, in his saga of the Yoknapatawpha County."

I.R.Draxi's essay on "The Multifarious Variety of Faulkner's Women" concludes this section of the anthology. Taking his cue from Faulkner's own statement that "It's much more fun to try to write about women because I think women are marvellous, they're wonderful, and I know very little about them," the writer tries to show how categorising them is quite a futile task. After a discussion of the merits and demerits of earlier categories of women proposed by critics, Draxi concludes that Faulkner's women can be classified into seven broad categories, namely, nubile women, earth mothers, defeminized women, disreputed women, old women, Negro women and the problem women and admits that done just for convenience sake, these categories often overlap one another but can be used as the stepping stone for understanding the novelist's often ambivalent attitude towards the fairer sex.

IV

The fourteen essays which comprise the long third section of this anthology, entitled "Fiction: Reassessments," deal with individual texts chronologically. Ashis Sengupta examines the four narrative patterns of *The Sound and the Fury* and concludes that the novel "appears to be an anthology of fictional forms, each one of which Faulkner tests in telling the Compson tale and finds wanting" and the book is basically about 'the elusiveness, the multivalence of truth' in a world of individuals cut off from familial and cultural ties. In a different cross-cultural context, Rama Kundu examines *The Sound and the Fury* and Jean Rhys's *Wide Sargasso Sea*, especially comparing the treatment of the black woman servant figure in the American and Caribbean contexts. Both Dilsey and Christophine, in spite of several differences, ultimately represent the marginalized and oppressed victims of racism/sexism/imperialism in two countries, who prove what a woman and an underdog with no power/status/possession could still achieve and thus emerge as the model inspiration for oppressed women anywhere in the world.

In arguing the dialogic relationship of myth, history and narrative which produces the Faulknerian counter-myth of *Light in August*, Manisha Mukhopadhyay stresses the basic dualism that informs Faulkner's work and is postulated by the very creation of Yoknapatawpha County. The counter-myth corresponds to the reorientation of the determinants of the novel as a genre: plot, character development, linear narrative. The writer argues that Faulkner rewrites narrative using polyvocal and polymodal narration, fusing different perspectives and novelistic images to arrive at a reality that is multiple in nature—a reality that can accommodate the antagonistic stories of Joe Christmas and Lena Grove, Percy Grimm and Gavin Stevens, the reality of Hightower and that of Byron Bunch and finds a figurative validation in the triptych conclusion of the novel. This process is what makes writing a cultural act and *Light in August* a cultural document.

Apart from the complicated structure of *Absalom, Absalom!* Rosa Coldfield's character has a unique and interesting role to play, both as a narrator and as an active participant in the unfolding of the Sutpen story and its eventual tragic conclusion. Commenting on the technique of multiple-narrators in the novel, Neerja Jayal Chand argues in her article that Miss Rosa demonstrates this structural principle of re-telling the story, not only by her own sense of inability to penetrate the Sutpen family reality, but also in her apprehension of the fleeting quality of this reality itself. While the motif of child-woman structures Rosa Coldfield's participation in the Sutpen story, the theme of womanhood, on a more general level, carries the figure of Rosa beyond a personal drama and links her narrative to other forms of witness to the Sutpen tale.

"Thomas Sutpen: Ahab of the South" by Amina Amin discusses the diverse features of Faulkner's style in *Absalom, Absalom!*. Locating influences of both American and European writers on the work, similarities between Ahab's character in Melville's *Moby Dick* and that of Thomas Sutpen in Faulkner's novel—both 'failed' heroes—one grants Cleanth Brooks' contention that there is a 'spiritual kinship' between Sutpen and Ahab. Closely elucidating from the two texts, the writer shows how closely Faulkner's portrayal of Sutpen resembles that of Melville's Ahab, in his monomaniac pursuit of his design and how both do not accept any moral responsibility for their actions, neither any purgation transforms them.

The close relationship between *Absalom, Absalom!* and *The Unvanquished* rests upon the fact that Faulkner worked upon both the novels simultaneously, and that both were written at a central moment in his career. John Lowe in "*The Unvanquished*: Faulkner's Nietzschean Skirmish with the Civil War" suggests that it is a far more disturbing book than many readers realize. "Far from being a costumed romp, it moves from comedy to tragedy in a probing examination of issues that also troubled Nietzsche: the will to power, the excesses of virtue, the relationship of justice and revenge, and the dangers involved in distorted perceptions of history." After a detailed analysis of the novel, Lowe shows us how Faulkner and

Nietzsche agree that one cannot totally dismiss collectively perceived history and how finally, it provides the necessary ground, albeit retrospectively, for the World War I edition of Bayard Sartoris, and moves Faulkner even closer to his equally haunted doubles, Quentin Compson, Gail Hightower, Isaac McCaslin, and us.

Faulkner's experimentation with parallel narrative techniques forms part of his general literary style but a significant case study is *The Wild Palms* which has alternated two apparently disparate stories: that of the "tall convict" who is caught in the confusion of a Mississippi flood; and that of Harry Wilbourne, an intern, and Charlotte Rittenmeyer, two lovers "against the world." The two stories seem unrelated, and most critics have refused to consider them as having any significant relationship. In "Faulkner's 'Old Man': A Critique," P.G. Rama Rao even cites two completely contradictory statements by Faulkner himself. At first the novelist gave the impression that he had originally conceived the two stories as separate novels though he found a thematic link between them later. At the Nagano Seminar, on the other hand, he confessed that he needed another story as an antithesis, to counterpoint it. "And I did not write those two stories and then cut one into another." In the face of this controversy, Rama Rao tries to read "Old Man" as an individual work, complete in itself, containing some of Faulkner's thematic pre-occupations and fictional techniques and of his metaphysic of time.

In "Complusive and Revisionary Repetition in 'Barn Burning,'" Richard C. Moreland explicates another aspect of Faulkner's complicated literary style. Faulkner's revisions of his modernism involved an important shift in the function of repetition, both in his own work and also in its historical and literary contexts as he understood them. In order to understand this shift, the notion of repetition with a significant, critical difference, which Moreland calls *revisionary repetition*, should be distinguished from repetition of another kind, which, after Freud, can be called, *compulsive revision*. 'Revisionary repetition repeats some structured event, in order somehow to alter that structure and its continuing power, especially by opening a critical space for what the subject might *learn* about that structure in the different context of a changing present or a more distant or different past.' Discussing in detail this narrative strategy in "Barn Burning," Moreland concludes by drawing clear distinctions between Hemingway's and Faulkner's literary styles.

In the next interesting article, Judy Hen uses the well-known medieval text of *Sir Gawain and the Green Knight* to 'act as a guidebook' for the interpretation of Faulkner's short story "Go Down, Moses." Finding close parallels between the two texts, Hen reveals how the antagonists are presented in far greater detail than the protagonists and how this leads to studied exaggeration and subsequent deflation. Though there is no way we can prove (or dispute) that William Faulkner sat with a copy of the medieval text while he composed his story, nevertheless a connection can be noted and apart from the obvious gap of five hundred years separating the two texts, Hen rightfully assigns the differences to the different cultural milieus in which both these works were composed.

Critics have repeatedly harped upon the manner in which Faulkner uses visual images often in the manner of a 'camera-eye' to strengthen his literary style. Following the modernist and Conradian dictum that the task of a novel is primarily to be 'seen,' Faulkner often combines convergent and divergent vision, thus inducing the reader to record disparate elements of a scene *simultaneously*. Pramod K. Nayar's article entitled "The Poiesis of Description: Imagery in William Faulkner's *Intruder in the Dust*" exemplifies how the novelist adopts three main strategies of image-making: saccades and parataxis, gestural and translocal imagifying and visual deficiency and gives ample references as to how 'imagifying in the novel consists of at least two of these strategies working in tandem.' In a suspense story, Faulkner's use of visual deprivation also creates an intense atmosphere, where events are waiting to happen.

Discussing *Intruder in the Dust* in a totally different perspective, Isaac Sequeira analyses the novel as 'The Initiation of Chick Mallison.' Though the book has been called by Edmund Wilson "William Faulkner's Reply to the Civil Rights Program," the writer argues that the novel is primarily an account of the heart of Chick Mallison, the young protagonist, in conflict with itself, and in conflict with his society. This conflict, an important part of his painful maturation process, results in Chick's decisive initiation. Coming up against the dual standards of the South in its attitude towards race, Chick at first responds like a typical Southern white adult but changes when he comes in contact with the essential humanity and individual dignity of a man like Lucas Beauchamp.

When Faulkner's collection of four hunting stories namely, "The Bear," "The Old People," "A Bear Hunt," and "Race at

Morning" (all previously published), appeared in 1955 as *Big Woods*, most reviewers criticized it as a lesser effort, one which lacked the power and range of Faulkner's earlier works from which parts of it were drawn. Yet David Paul Ragan argues in his article that Faulkner considered the volume a serious artistic project, one in which he advanced some of the most important and moving themes he dealt with in the final decade of his career. It was undertaken to give his moral concerns artistic form. His concern with the artistic integrity of the book is even more evident in the careful orchestration of the prologue, the interludes between the stories, and the epilogue. (Faulkner himself termed the five short prose pieces "interrupted catalysts" that linked the stories to each other and also tied them to the history of Yoknapatawpha.) Moreover, the themes of *Big Woods* reverberates beyond the individual situation of Isaac McCaslin because with the passing of the woods passes much of the nobility and heroism man can achieve in them. Thus the book should be read as 'a complex study of man's struggle to function successfully in his world, to cope with the circumstances of his life and with the changing forces of his environment.'

Andrew Hook's premise that he does not consider the late trilogy about the sharecropping predatory Snopes family—*The Hamlet, The Town, The Mansion*—one of Faulkner's very great achievements is justified with various explanations. 'What any analysis of the writing history of the Snopes trilogy reveals is the astonishing degree to which it represents a rewriting of Faulkner's own writing history. The origins of the Snopes as a potential subject for Faulkner lie back in the early 1920s at the very start of his writing career and he never stopped writing about the Snopes throughout his entire life.' According to David Minter, *The Hamlet* includes more social history, economics and politics than any of Faulkner's earlier novels. Morally Flem Snopes is terrifying, as Faulkner several times remarked. But he is free in ways that were for Faulkner liberating: no traditions, patterns, or models hound him. His grossest failings, including sexual impotence, scarcely trouble him. Even when he repeats man's oldest games and vices, he does not know it. In this connection, Faulkner's remarks at the University of Virginia are relevant. Speaking of Flem's desire for respectability in *The Town*, he said that "rapacious people—if they're not careful—they are reduced away and decide that what they've got to have is respectability, which destroys one, almost anybody." A first-rate scoundrel, "like a first-rate artist, he's an individualist, and the pressure's all against being an individualist." (*Faulkner in the University*, 32, 33) But later he pointed out: "I never did feel sorry for him any more than one feels sorry for anyone who is ridden with an ambition or demon as base as simple vanity and rapacity and greed. I think that you can be ridden by a demon, but let it be a good demon." (120) Hook concludes very emphatically that though the volume may have no larger meaning, perhaps, at least 'life is permanently enriched by Faulkner's art.'

When Faulkner died of a heart attack on 6th July 1962, he left a final novel *The Reivers* published just a few weeks before and which was awarded the Pulitzer Prize posthumously in 1963. Earlier he had told Jean Stein in 1956 that "my last book will be the Doomsday Book, the Golden Book of Yoknapatawpha County. Then I shall break the pencil and I'll have to stop." (*Three Decades*, 82) According to Frederick J. Hoffmann (115), the novel is a secondary "grace note" on the lives of County people, an adventure story that has reflections of the young boy's initiation into the ways of the world, a comedy with sentimental overtones. In the last essay of this section, "On *The Reivers*: From the Last Chapter to the First," Amitabha Sinha contends that apart from the novel being 'a comic pastoral,' it is unique in the sense that 'it deviates from the *Faulkner canon as a whole*, a novel without the sense of decay, with no tortured, anguished mind within it.' Referring to the sub-title, *A Reminiscence*, Sinha argues that though the novel is one of the past, with memory, indisputably Faulknerian; that reminiscence is nevertheless re-enacted as though the narrative were of the present. This has indeed 'reived' familiar Faulknerism, has de-Faulknerized Faulkner, so to say, has produced a non-Faulknerian Faulkner and he concludes with a wish that Faulkner should have lived longer 'just to write a few such novels.'

V

The last section aptly entitled *Faulkner Miscellany* begins with a very brief paper by Howard Wolf, who narrates his practical experiences as a teacher trying to teach Faulkner to overseas students. Apart from coming from different socio-economic backgrounds and therefore interpreting the novelist with separate culture-specific values, foreign students, especially in Asian countries, still approach literature for better or worse, with an essentially 19th century perspective, expecting it to be a 'reflection of life' and though there are apparent parallels between Faulkner's 'genealogical' stories with the family constellations of traditional oriental cultures, Faulkner still remains, according to Wolf, a difficult writer for the classroom.

My own article deals with the most neglected genre of Faulkner's writing, namely, the film scripts he wrote for Hollywood. Unlike F. Scott Fitzgerald, who encompassed his entire literary world with the myth of Hollywood, William Faulkner's ambivalent attitude towards the sunny Californian town and the film industry is more interesting because in spite of spending so many years as a script-writer there (from 1933 to 1945 he made several visits there, some of them lasting even a few months or less), he produced only one short story "Golden Land" based entirely on his sojourns in the film colony. His abiding dislike of the "Tinsel Town" has led some commentators of his life and work to surmise that he carried out his studio assignments hastily and carelessly, just to "take the money and run." Yet there is great deal of evidence that Faulkner did conscientiously try to give the studios that hired him an honest week's work in return for his weekly wages. In fact, the sheer number and variety of the more than forty scenarios to which he applied his creative energies over the years attest to the seriousness with which he viewed his obligations to his employers. Another paradox about the novelist's relationship with Hollywood remains that it was his script writing assignments for various studios and his sale in 1938 of the movie rights to *The Unvanquished* that had sustained him financially during the decade of his most impressive fiction writing.

William Faulkner stayed for two semesters as Writer-in Residence at the University of Virginia at Charlottesville from February to June 1957 and February to June 1958. Apart from the collection of his talks edited and published by Fredrick L. Gwynn & Joseph Blotner as *Faulkner in the University: Class Conferences at the University of Virginia, 1957-1958* (Charlottesville, Univ. Press of Virginia, 1959), it is interesting to know how local people and the local media reacted to the writer and his work. Subsequently, I had approached Arnold and Marianne Jensen, senior citizens and long time residents of Charlottesville, to locate whatever they could, apart from the regular serious material available to scholars. After painstaking search at the local libraries, and especially at The Albemarle County Historical Society located at 200, 2nd Street NE,

Charlottesville, VA 22902, the Jensens unearthed a variety of articles from local newspapers and magazines, including book reviews, memoirs and criticism. These range from publications in *The Cavalier Daily*, the student-operated newspaper of the University of Virginia, *The Charlottesville Daily Progress*, the women's fashion magazine, *Vogue, The Albemarle Monthly, The Observer,* and *Richmond Times-Dispatch*. Certain excerpts from this multifarious collection are included in the section, entitled "Faulkner. Charlottesville and the Media" and though serious Faulkner scholars might find these articles warmed-up fare, nevertheless, the average reader will find it interesting to read about the Virginian jaunt of the Mississippi man—a place which he loved for fox-hunting and for its 'snobs.' Incidentally, my letter to Jill Faulkner Summers, daughter and executrix of the Faulkner Estate and who resides in Knole Farm, just near Charlottesville, asking her for her comments on the celebration of the centenary of her father's birth, remained unanswered.

VI

Now about the news of some of the events that took place all around the world celebrating Faulkner's birth centenary. This ranged from places like Russia to Japan and Europe. The University of Mississippi celebrated the 24th Annual "Faulkner and Yoknapatawpha" Conference at Oxford, Mississippi from July 27th to August 1st, 1997. Entitled "Faulkner at 100: Retrospect and Prospect," this was a big jamboree of almost all Faulknerians from around the world. Apart from the more serious literary sessions, this conference was interesting because of other events too. These included a picnic at Rowan Oak, walk through Bailey's Woods, guided tours of several areas in North Mississippi like Oxford and Lafayette County, Columbus, Holly Springs, New Albany, Ripley, Pontoc and the Mississippi Delta. Though Faulkner's landmarks are everywhere in and around Oxford, the place he knew and wrote about, it was, according to a newspaper reporter (Hillel Italie of Associated Press) no longer the 'rural, segregated community.' "Oxford is now a modern college town, where students, black and white, use ATM machines on campus and drink cappuccino on the square. . . . One wonders what he [Faulkner] would say about Rowan Oak, now an air-conditioned museum where a Xerox machine sits atop the old kerosene stove." There was also a book exhibition on display titled *A Faulkner 100: The Centennial Exhibition*, accompanied by a catalogue. Another interesting feature was the two exhibitions of Faulkner's photographs entitled *Faulkner's World: The Photographs of Martin J. Dain* and photographs by Colonel J.R. Cofield and his son Jack.

Apart from the Ole Miss Conference, the Faulkner Symposium in Rennes followed by the Faulkner celebrations in Paris are now behind us. The Rennes meeting was one in the series of International symposia organized by European Faulkner scholars. Professor Lothar Hönnighausen, eminent Faulkner scholar at the University of Bonn, reports that "the Paris event was a very glamorous affair with a luncheon in the Victorian stucco hall of the Muséé D'Orsay, followed by a session in M. Chirac's residence, the Palais du Luxembourg (Carlos Fuentes was one of the speakers)." This was followed by a walk across to the Rue Servandoni where a plaque commemorating Faulkner's stay there in 1925 was unveiled, followed by refreshments at Gallimard.

Before concluding it must be mentioned that this anthology comprises Faulkner lovers from all around the world. Hence, I thought it fit to retain both American as well as British spellings of certain words, giving freedom to the paper-writers in a way. Faulkner had always been interested not simply in the onerous pains of Southern history and its relation to the crises of the modern psyche, but in the plenitude of human nature, the lyrical and transcendental aspects of the natural world and the feeling that creativity and hope can be relived and passed from generation to generation, so becoming timeless. Early in his life as an artist, he had begun to dread the moment "when not only the ecstasy of writing would be gone, but the unreluctance and the something worth saying too" (cf. "An Introduction to *The Sound and the Fury*" [1973], pp. 410-15). But his belief in man's "endurance" has prevailed so successfully that we can surely assert that William Faulkner, one of the most significant Modern experimentalist American writers, will "endure" even in the twenty-first century.

Survival and Endurance: Faulkner in the Future

THADIOUS M. DAVIS

There are, of course, multiple possibilities for speaking about Faulkner's achievement and his endurance. I am concerned here with four particularly noteworthy areas.

1. Faulkner's location of history and memory as major sites of American fiction, his sites of memory—"les lieux de memoire" in Pierre Nora terminology; Faulkner's achievement in this regard is like Proust's in France because he is our first major American novelist of memory.
2. Faulkner's construction of face as central to his representation of characters, specifically his construction of whiteness; his achievement is remarkable for its insistent race-consciousness and for its enabling discourses on race and racial taboos in the United States.
3. Faulkner's creation of a language of loss, longing, and desire as the articulation of a modern American sensibility, a practical of poetry in prose; his achievement is the painful beauty and elastic richness of his writing styles over the course of his entire career.
4. Faulkner's envisioning of environment, both ecological and social, at the center of his fiction, in particular his Yoknapatawpha landscape of Mississippi and the South as natural world and social world, but in general his world view as manifested in his concern about the destructive potential of the Second World War, the Atomic Bomb, and their aftermath in the Nuclear Age.

These four constitute what I would term Faulkner's primary assets for the next century and new generations of readers, and I do want to suggest that they are interconnected and not easily separable items. All four are linked to and by an ethical humanism that Faulkner increasingly articulated late in his career, and perhaps because of my own interests, I also connect all four to the matter of race and its importance in Faulkner's canon.

In the preface to *Playing in the Dark: Whiteness and the Literary Imagination* (1992), Toni Morrison delineates her project in a few deft sentences:

> [U]ntil very recently, and regardless of the race of the author, the readers of virtually all of American fiction have been positioned as white. I am interested to know what that assumption has meant to the literary imagination. When does racial 'unconsciousness' or unawareness of race enrich interpretative language, and when does it impoverish it? What does positing one's writerly self in the wholly racialized society that is the United States, as unraced and all others as raced entail? What happens to the writerly imagination of a black author who is at some level *always* conscious of representing one's own race to, or in spite of, a race of readers that understands itself to be 'universal' or race-free? In other words, how is 'literary whiteness' and 'literary blackness' made, and what is the consequence of the construction? How do embedded assumptions of racial (not racist) language work in the literary enterprise that hopes and sometimes claims to be 'humanistic'? When, in a race-conscious culture, is that lofty goal actually approximated? When not and why not? (xii-xiii)

Morrison, being Toni Morrison and unabashedly a lover of language, necessarily complicates her articulation of project with a series of revelatory questions; however, she does not obscure her focus: her interest in knowing what the positioning of readers of American fiction as white has meant to the literary imagination. Moreover, she does not problematize her project with concessions to majority opinion. She asks, for instance: "In what public discourse does the reference to black people not exist? It exists in every one of this nation's mightiest struggles." (65) And that answer consolidates her insistence on the importance of her project, and her understanding that "[t]he fabrication of an Africanist persona [by white American authors] is reflexive; an extraordinary mediation on the self; a powerful exploration of the fears and desires that reside in the writerly conscious. It is an astonishing revelation of longing, of terror, of perplexity, of shame, of magnanimity. It requires hard work *not* to see this." (17)

Until the publication of *Playing in the Dark*, few readers of Morrison's fiction had access to her abiding concern with constructs of racialization in American literary studies, though some readers did know that her masters thesis included a treatment of William Faulkner. I take this fact as a point of confluence and of departure. Morrison's project enables me to reflect on William Faulkner's achievement as the major twentieth-century writer who follows Melville in a serious confrontation of race in American life. Early in his career, Faulkner accepts a notion articulated by W.E.B. DuBois at the start of the century: "the problem of the twentieth century is the Color Line." With more insight, clarity, and artistry than any other writer of his generation, specifically Hemingway and Fitzgerald (the latter being vocally racist), Faulkner represented issues of race, racialization, racial construction and racial division. Most impressive about his achievement is not that he created black characters and positioned them within his fictional Yoknapatawpha, but rather that he envisioned what Melville represented as "the whiteness of whiteness." That is to say, Faulkner constructed characters who are consciously white, racialized as white, and he depicted the construction of whiteness within Southern and, by extension, American society. This treatment of white people, with the normalizing, universalizing elision of racial identity, but with the complexity of the burden of racial subjectivity is an extraordinary achievement, unequaled in the first half of the century and unparalleled in the second.

When we examine how and where American critics, both black and white, participated in discourse on race during the middle of the twentieth century, we may find that one answer lies in the writing of William Faulkner. Faulkner's texts, *The Sound and the Fury*, *Light in August*, *Absalom, Absalom!* and *Go Down, Moses*, for instance, provide access to talking about race, race formation and race politics. To this end, Morrison's conceptualization of *Playing in the Dark: Whiteness and the Literary Imagination* speaks both to the significant subject of race in American literature, but also to Morrison's own intellectual engagement with race and with Faulkner's texts as well. For Morrison, in her "serious" study of literature as a graduate student at Cornell, it was William Faulkner who provided an entre into the concerns that more properly would result many decades later in her discourse on race and the literary imagination—on not blackness, but whiteness and the literary imagination.

Moreover, Morrison's case is not unique. The late George Kent's 1972 *Blackness and the Adventure of Western Culture* provides another example of the access to racial discourse Faulkner's texts represent. Kent, a tenured professor at the University of Chicago, produced his book within the developing nationalist movement in Chicago; one jacket blurb announced that *Blackness and the Adventure of Western Culture* was "the first book of literary criticism by a black scholar to be published by an independent black publishing company," Third World Press. Kent's table of contents lists chapters on Claude McKay, Langston Hughes, Richard Wright, Gwendolyn Brooks, James Baldwin, and—bringing up the rear—William Faulkner.

In Kent's nationalistic critical project, the inclusion of Faulkner is not a gesture toward interracial intertextuality. Kent entitles the chapter "Faulkner and the Heritage of White Racial Consciousness: Notes on White Nationalism in Literature," and proceeds to interrogate Faulkner's iconic presence in the modern American literary landscape. Beginning with the observation that "[w]hen confronting Blackness, white writers are free to take a variety of attitudes toward . . . cultural drives, but they cannot escape from the fact that, as much as skin color, the cultural drives are transmitted by cultural instruments as the definition of whiteness," (166) he moves to the conclusion that for white writers such as Faulkner, "Blackness" becomes both "a proliferation of racial myth and ritual" and a "validation of whiteness." (167) Kent's project engages the larger American cultural landscape, though he is acutely aware of the specificity of region: "[I]f Faulkner overcame aspects of Southern white consciousness, he was still a part of the general American white consciousness and its symbolic needs. The South simply exemplified more concretely the economic and psychological rituals that arise in the confrontation of the white consciousness with Blackness." (167) While I will not venture into Kent's own lapses into essentialism, I will point out that like Morrison's, Kent's discourse on race in American literature situates as its originary modern Southern literature and positions William Faulkner as the "official text" to decode racial discourse (perhaps I might even say here that Faulkner's positionality is as the "*master* text").

Twenty years separate Morrison's and Kent's texts. The intellectual climate for Morrison in the 1990s is a quite different one from that Kent experienced in the 1970s. Racial discourse has become a given; Henry Louis Gates, Jr.'s *Thirteen Way of Looking at a Black Man* (essays first published in *The New Yorker*, Cornel West's *Race Matters* or Michael Dyson's *Making Malcolm* or Bell Hooks' *Black Looks*, all participate in larger conversations about race that command readerly attention, as well as media play. Thus, we may forget what lapses and absences or silences there were regarding matters of race only a very few decades ago. Morrison can produce in these current times an entire volume, albeit a slim one, on the effects of race/whiteness on the literary imagination, a volume whose antecedents are in her thesis on Faulkner, and Kent can openly interpolate one essay on Faulkner and whiteness into his volume on blackness. For Morrison in the 1990s, the intellectual climate is such that her effort is neither surprising nor unfamiliar, and she does not have to enter into her expansive discourse through a narrower, author-specific lens. In fact, *Playing in the Dark* made the New York *Times* bestseller list, which marked it as an acceptable American commodity. For Kent, however, in the 1970s, racial discourse was not considered a proper aspect of humanistic studies, of sociological studies perhaps, but not of literary studies, yet he makes his study "legitimate" intellectual work with the inclusion of Faulkner, who was, ironically, not always so respectable or acceptable as subject matter, but that is another story.

To speak of race, whether to forward theories of the construction of race in literature or to observe relationships of power across race lines, was neither acceptable or expected within much of the academic and literary community. But Kent found, as critics had before and after him, that there did exist, a proverbial "back door," through which to enter into the interrogation of race in American literature of the twentieth century: Mr. William Faulkner. It should be observed that the canonized literature of nineteenth-century American authors presents an alternative case, one in which racial representation, racial difference, and racial thematics more often occupied the attention of the authors, and thus, acceptably, of the critics, possibly because of the cultural work performed by Harriet Beecher Stowe's *Uncle Tom's Cabin* and its numerous stage versions, and possibly because of the relentless political work of abolitionists, both black and white, throughout the middle of the century in particular. Mark Twain's *Adventures of Huck Finn* add

Pudd'nhead Wilson, and also Melville's *Moby Dick* and *Benito Cereno* are several of the nineteenth-century titles that come to mind for their performance of race. Notice, however, that when Kent shifts gears from the construction of blackness and racial subjectivity by black authors to the production of blackness as racial object in the twentieth century, he necessarily relocates his attention to William Faulkner. Faulkner's blacks and people of mixed race—Dilsey Gibson, Sam Fathers, Lucas and Molly Beauchamp, Joe Christmas—as well his whites who engage in the social construction of racial identities—Ike McCaslin, Quentin Compson, Thomas Sutpen, Rosa Coldfield—all forever changed the landscape of modern American writing and expanded the possibilities for racial discourse within American criticism, and they did so for critics as different as Irvin Howe and Ralph Ellison.

These critics and their numerous students, including myself, interested in race knew that there was "no other game in town." Faulkner provided *the* access route to discourse on race. We can think of the work of Charles Nilon, Blyden Jackson, Leslie Fiedler, and many more who wrote on Faulkner and taught him within the academy and across the racial divide; these teachers helped to promote Faulkner as much as they utilized Faulkner for their own specific interests. Despite Faulkner's naturalization of whiteness and his othering or objectifying of blacks, his fiction did, at the very least, accommodate self-conscious and self-reflexive treatments of race, usually in some form of racial difference or of interracial relations. While this small point may seem an odd way to celebrate Faulkner's achievement, it remains for me one of his signal contributions to the intellectual life of our century and one of the main reasons why I am confident he will survive into the twenty-first century.

Faulkner's Achievement

LOTHAR HÖNNIGHAUSEN

William Faulkner, the great Southerner, is not only an American, but an international phenomenon. His influence on leading Japanese writers has been as well documented as that on the Chinese novelist Mo Yan and the Canadian Aritha Van Herk.[1] Before he had become the mark by which American writers from Flannery O'Connor and Eudora Welty to Toni Morrison measured themselves, he had already been made an international hero by Jean-Paul Sartre, André Malraux, and Albert Camus. He was the dominant figure among the new American novelists of "l'age du roman américain," and, he has proved a source of inspiration to German writers from Hermann Hesse and Gottfried Benn to Siegfried Lenz, Ingeborg Bachmann, Helmut HeiBenbüttel, and Peter Handke.[2] The Italian novelists Cesare Pavese and Elio Vittorini have translated him and in their own work learned from his example. In his Nobel Prize speech, Gabriel Garcia Márquez refers to that of "his master William Faulkner." Like Mário Vargas Llosa and Carlos Fuentes, Jorge Edwards acknowledges a specific relevance of Faulkner: "The reading of Faulkner showed me, for the first time in my life, that there is a kind of poetry that can go into narrative fiction."[3]

In view of this response from creative writers, it is not surprising to find the entry on Faulkner in the *Encyclopedia Britannica* opening with the statement: "More books and scholarly articles have been written about Faulkner than about any other American writer of the twentieth century" and this year's centennial of his birthday means a boomtime for the Faulkner industry. However, the activities of Faulkner scholars the world over must not deceive us into believing that Faulkner is on the verge of becoming a popular author. He is too subtle and too difficult for that, and the danger with Faulkner, as with other classics, will always be that they are more admired than read. Where does Faulkner's achievement lie? He wrote nineteen novels of which eleven are major works of fiction, four are among the masterpieces of twentieth century fiction: *The Sound and the Fury, Light in August, Absalom, Absalom!*, and *The Hamlet*. Of his short stories "Barn Burning," "Red Leaves," "Dry September," "That Evening Sun" and "Pantaloon in Black" belong to the short story classics of world-literature. However, like Shakespeare he wrote not only masterpieces. *Soldiers' Pay* and *Mosquitoes* are apprentice works and *Pylon, Intruder in the Dust* and *A Fable* can hardly be called strong novels and many of his short stories are just potboilers. On the other hand, some of his works have been rediscovered or upgraded, and today only very innocent Faulkner readers continue to regard *The Unvanquished* and *The Reivers* as nothing more than slight and superficial reprises. Most critics have learned to appreciate *The Hamlet* and some understand that the last three novels *The Town, The Mansion* and *The Reivers* mark a new turn in his writing rather than a return to the old.

What has led to this and other readjustments of the Faulkner canon is a more ethnically and gender conscious criticism that is also more aware of the psychoanalytic and socio-political dimension of style. It has replaced Cleanth Brooks's vision of Faulkner's South as essentially whole and healthy and of his art as a "well-wrought urn." Today, we see Faulkner as a liberal but one with conservative yearnings, as an ameliorist rather than a radical reformist, in any case as a white, male Southerner of the first half of the twentieth century. Many Faulknerians continue to be puzzled by the incongruities between his nonchalant "lynching"-letter, the embarrassing Howe-interview and his advocacy of a "Go slow policy" for racial integration, on the one hand, and his courageous racial views in "Dry September," "That Evening Sun," "Pantaloon in Black," and *Intruder in the Dust*, the soul-searching and work of mourning in "The Bear" (*Go Down, Moses*) and *Absalom, Absalom!*, on the other. Meanwhile, Arthur Kinney and other critics have reminded us how important it is in this matter to "contextualize" Faulkner and to see his attitudes as conditioned by the socio-cultural patterns of his time and place, the pre-civil rights South where he was ostracized as a "nigger lover."[4]

Connected with Kinney's approach is a new understanding of Faulkner's biography that is inspired by sociological models of role-play and allows us to dispense with the unsatisfactory impostor-theory. From this perspective, Faulkner's bewildering "lies," his impersonations as World War I fighter pilot and as bum, as dandy and as Mississippi farmer, are strategies of assimilating material and thus an integral part of his creative life. In connection with his own suicidal temptations, Faulkner's shrill insistence, in the Nobel Prize speech, that "man will not only endure but prevail" and "that the basest of all things is to be afraid" takes on a more complex meaning.[5] One comes to respect his gigantic work not only as attesting to his amazing creative gift and vitality but also to his moral achievement.

Related to Faulkner's peculiar brinkmanship evident in his apocalyptic scenario of the writer ("he will write as though he stood among and watched the end of man") is Faulkner's readiness to take both great personal and artistic risks. The personal side of this desperate courage is embodied in *Flags in the Dust* in Bayard Sartoris's drunken stallion ride, his hazardous driving, and his death-courting test-flights. The artistic side of it manifests itself most poignantly in his peculiar aesthetic of risk-taking and "the splendor of failure." From this perspective, Faulkner is a greater writer than Hemingway because he deals with much more radical forms and with a much greater area of human experience.

His world extends from the pre-rational minds of the idiots Benjy in *The Sound and the Fury* and Ike in *The Hamlet* to the sophisticated dilettantes Horace Benbow and Gavins Stevens, from the haunted imagination of Joe Christmas to the placid ruminations of Lena Grove, from the lonely suffering of Rider in "Pantaloon in Black" to the humorous sociability of Ratliff in *The Hamlet*, from the frustrated Rosa Coldfield in *Absalom, Absalom!* to Eula, the avatar of the female principle, in *The Hamlet*, from history-conscious Quentin in *Absalom, Absalom!* to the slave-holding Choctaw Indians in "Red Leaves," from the deprived Thirties hobos in "Pennsylvania Station" to the spoilt children of hardworking immigrants in the California of "Golden Leaves."

Connected with Faulkner's aesthetic brinkmanship and willingness to always start anew is a narrative and stylistic originality, reminding one of Picasso's continuous self-renewal. He re-writes, or rather, re-conceives the Quentin of *The Sound and the Fury* in *Absalom, Absalom!*, the complicated Freudian relationship of the Benbow siblings Horace and Narcissa of *Flags in the Dust* in

Sanctuary, the relationship of Narcissa and the voyeurist Snopes of *Flags in the Dust* in "There was a Queen," the Compson children of *The Sound and the Fury* in "That Evening Sun." Only a year after *The Sound and the Fury*, he publishes *As I Lay Dying*. Artistically, the new novel constitutes a continuation but at the same time a considerable modification of his point of view technique. Instead of the far-ranging and deep searching sections presented from four viewpoints, we get shorter segments presented from many viewpoints. They are more accessible to readers but challenge them by the quick changes and careful orchestration of their more developed polyphony. Even so, the difference in social milieu, psychology, and language of the two novels could not be greater, Faulkner capturing the streams-of-consciousness of the rednecks as authentically as those of the decadent plantation aristocrats.

After his rather long apprenticeship occurs the first big bang; he publishes within the four years 1929 to 1932, and in addition to a host of short stories, five great novels: *Sartoris* (*Flags in the Dust*) and *The Sound and the Fury* (1929), *As I Lay Dying* (1930), *Sanctuary* (1931) and *Light in August* (1932). None of them has the symptoms of hasty and sloppy writing, of repetitiveness, of stereotypical characterization, of insufficient visualization. Instead, these five novels have each a strong thematic and aesthetic individuality. It is not only that all five deal with different themes or present different characters. The thematics of each novel also has engendered a different mode of plotting. The diverse characters emerging in these plots have their own voices and, as a consequence, all of these novels radiate their own atmospheres.

The scope of Faulkner's wide world is marked by his great number of very different characters and by his concreteness in rendering them. Mr. Compson, the nihilistic scion of tradition ("victory is an illusion of philosophers and fools"),[6] his selfish wife, and their very different but equally unhappy children, Benjy, Quentin, Caddy, and Jason, and Dilsey, the black cook, who keeps the family going and who draws sustenance from poor Rev. Shegog's powerful Easter sermon. The same author, who in *If I Forget Thee, Jerusalem* (*The Wild Palms*) conceives the lovers Harry Wilbourne and Charlotte Rittenmeyer and their modernist malaise, invents characters like the dwarfish revengeful Mink Snopes in the trilogy or Reba Rivers, the madam of the Memphis brothel, in *Sanctuary, The Mansion*, and *The Reivers*. Other characters reflect more specific socio-economic conditions. Temple Drake, the spoilt society girl, who, as both victim and victimizer reveals the corruption of the old regime; Thomas Sutpen, the megalomaniac redneck, social climber and would-be aristocrat in *Absalom, Absalom!* whose Faustian plans of a plantation-dynasty prove abortive because his racist design defeats itself; and Flem Snopes whose new system of expropriation replaces the older rural exploitative system of Will Varner. Their thematic counterweight, in *The Hamlet,* is Eula, Faulkner's male projection of mythic womanhood contrasted with the frustrations of men like Labove and Jack Houston.

While Faulkner's novels up to *Absalom, Absalom!* (1936) are tragic in the sense that many of their heroines and heroes appear as doomed pawns in the hands of a divine Player, with *The Hamlet* (1940) Faulkner's humor, already announcing itself in *Flags in the Dust* and *As I Lay Dying*, gains in ascendance. The sexual neurosis that in *The Sound and the Fury* had led to Quentin's suicide, in *The Town* and *The Mansion*, produces Gavin Stevens's comic figure. But then Faulkner's comic figures often have a tragic dimension and Miss Reba Rivers has different thematic functions in *Sanctuary, The Mansion*, and *The Reivers* and is not only hilariously funny but like Mrs. Over-done in Shakespeare's *Measure for Measure* metonymic of the general malaise.

In Faulkner's world coexist wheat and weeds, Caddy's love for Benjy and Mrs. Compson's selfishness, Dilsey's humaneness and Jason's bitter frustration. He lets Quentin die and Rider suffer, Lee Godwin be lynched and Temple Drake escape scot-free, Flem Snopes exploit the hamlet and the town and Gavin Stevens, the idealist, make a fool of himself. He registers with the kind of objectivity Lukácz praised in Balzac the take-over of the South by the Snopeses, although his aesthetic and emotional sympathies are with plantation aristocrats like the Percys rather than with redneck demagogues like Bilbo and Vardaman. He admires the cultural achievement of the noble plantation house that the French architect in *Absalom, Absalom!* creates and that the rednecks, in *The Hamlet*, dismantle. Nonetheless, he relentlessly traces and explodes the inhuman racism of Sutpen's dynastic "design" in *Absalom, Absalom!*, the decay and failure of the ruling class in *Flags in the Dust, The Sound and the Fury*, and in *Sanctuary*. He lets the potential he has invested in his characters and his plots play itself out, using his enormous narrative and stylistic powers to register minutely these processes within their given socio-political and cultural contexts.

While the spirit of objectivity and openness, resulting from role-play and perspectivism, was part of Faulkner's late nineteenth and early twentieth century heritage, his amazing narrative and linguistic genius in expressing this philosophy in concrete artistic terms was his own. Helping him in this was his capacity to eclectically absorb the most heterogeneous materials and methods, Keats's aesthetics and A.E. Housman's pessimism, Beardsley's sophistication and Sherwood Anderson's Western regionalism, Balzac's panoramas and Joyce's stream-of-consciousness, Swinburne's sound effects and Eliot's verbal skill. Just as great as the scope of his assimilation was his integrative power enabling him to fuse all these foreign elements with the inspiration from his own Southern oral tradition.

The result is an immensely pliable and rich new prose that can easily accommodate the wide stylistic range demanded by his wide ranging thematics. In *Flags in the Dust* the sardonic voice of the old aristocrat Aunt Jenny amuses us till she suddenly shocks us with her revelatory identification with J.L. Vardaman's racist evangel ("who thought of putting niggers into the same uniforms with white men. Mr. Vardaman knew better").[7] In the same novel, we see a subtle symbolist leitmotif technique transform a realistic stallion into an aesthetic icon of *motion in stasis* before he explodes and becomes a symbol of uncontrolled power ("The stallion stood against the yawning cavern of the livery stable door like a motionless bronze flame and along its burnished coat ran at intervals little tremors of paler flame, little tongues of nervousness and pride" [137]). In *Sound and the Fury* we encounter, besides the widely differing streams of white consciousness, Benjy's pre-rational syntax, Quentin's synaesthetic *glissando*, Jason's sarcastic bonmots, the very complex impact of black culture on Faulkner, the moving vernacular of Rev. Shegogg's Easter sermon ("Breddren! Look at dem little chillen settin dar" [296]), and Dilsey's monumental portrait: "until only the indomitable skeleton was left rising like a ruin or a landmark." (266) The stylistic amplitude of *Sanctuary* reaches from the cubist caricature of Popeye's ("like a mask carved into two simultaneous expressions")[8] down to the psychoanalytic deep-structure of Temple Drake's sexual ecstasy and gender change: "I'd try to make like I was a boy . . . could see myself in the coffin. . . . So I was an old man, with a long white beard." (216-20) *Light in August* comprises the calvinistic interieur of the McEachern's ("The clean, spartan room . . . In the windows the clean, darned curtains . . . The boy sat in a straight chair . . . an enormous Bible . . . He wore a clean white shirt")[9] as well as the surrealistic nightmare embodying Joe Christmas' fear of female sexuality ("in a cave he seemed to see a diminishing row of suavely shaped urns in moonlight, blanched. Each one was cracked and from each crack there issued something liquid, deathcolored, and foul" [189]) and, finally, the prose poem of his castration and apotheosis: "the pent black blood . . . seemed to rush out of his pale body like the rush of sparks from a rising rocket; . . . soaring into their memories forever and ever." (465)

The stylistically subtle probing, in *Absalom, Absalom!,* of a guilty past, of the Southern denial of its biracial reality, and of its nostalgic and narcissistic preoccupation with an anachronistic self-image, naturally have a special appeal for German readers of my generation for whom the reading of history continues to be a work of mourning. But no less fascinating is Faulkner's artistic exploration of what for a man of his generation were remote areas of experience. The mannerism of Rosa's high-flown diction, awkwardly teetering on the brink of blank verse, authentically renders her tragic isolation and her frustration at her stunted development as a woman. She reveals the conscious and halfconscious aspects of her painful puberty and also her considerable sophistication by employing prenatal imagery.

> That was the miscast summer of my barren youth which (for that short time, that short brief unreturning springtime of the female heart) I lived not as a woman, a girl, but rather as the man which I perhaps should have been. I was fourteen then, fourteen in years if they could have been called years while in that unpaced corridor which I called childhood, which was not living but rather some projection of the lightless womb itself; I gestate and complete, not aged, just overdue because of some caesarean lack, some cold head-nuzzling forceps of the savage time which should have torn me free, . . .[10]

In the realistic ruralism of *The Hamlet*, we are overwhelmed by the manneristic imagery which Faulkner uses to turn the Mississippi schoolgirl Eula into an avatar of love and the sodomitic relation of the idiot Ike Snopes's into a new myth of man's reconciliation with nature. In the same novel we enjoy the narrative gusto with which Ratliff retells Southern tall tales. But Faulkner's comedy rarely remains without a tragic dimension. The horse-swapping motif in *The Hamlet*, which in the old Southwestern humorists remained entirely comic, in Faulkner's creative re-use, becomes tragic-comic when Mrs. Snopes weeps over her husband's foolish deal with Pat Stamper and the loss of the money she had so painfully and proudly saved for a new separator:

> She looked like the kind of somebody that never had done much crying to speak of nohow, because she cried hard, like she didn't know just how to do it, like even the tears never knowed just exactly what they was expected to do, standing there in a old wrapper, not even hiding her face, saying, "Fool about a horse, yes! But why the horse? why the horse?"[11]

An artist's ability to continually reinvent himself and his modes and forms of expression is a distinctive mark of his genius: in *A Fable*, where the spirit of the Thirties and Forties forces Faulkner to artistically engage the experience of masses, the enormousness of the military industrial complex, and above all, the absoluteness and absurdities of anonymous power, he uses the gift of his manneristic language for satiric purposes. Associating the leitmotif of the three flags with the Roman triumvirate and the Christian trinity, the movement proceeds downwards from the images of stars and consecration at the peak of this hierarchy downward to the minor military altarboys. The ironic pattern of the imagery gleefully combines "cardinals and Brahmins," "acolytes and colonels," and through three-fold repetition transforms "portfolios" into ritualistic objects like "monstrance, host, and censer."

> First and topmost were the three flags and the three supreme generals who served them: a triumvirate consecrated and anointed, a constellation remote as planets in their immutability, powerful as archbishops in their trinity, splendid as cardinals in their retinues and myriad as Brahmins in their blind followers; next were the three thousand lesser generals who were their deacons and priests and the hierarchate of their households, their acolytes and bearers of monstrance and host

> and censer: the colonels and majors who were in charge of the portfolios and maps and memoranda, the captains and subalterns who were in charge of the communications and errands which kept the portfolios and maps up to date, and the sergeants and corporals who actually carried the portfolios and mapcases and protected them with their lives and answered the telephone and ran the errands, . . .[12]

The reflections on "Faulkner's achievement" are to make readers curious and stimulate their own re-discovery of Faulkner. Even a brief encounter with a few specimen of his styles shows that his creation of a new poetic language in fiction is as important a contribution to the history of the twentieth century novel as his new narrative perspectivism, making him one of the great fiction writers of all time.

NOTES

1. See *Faulkner Studies in Japan*, compiled by Kenzaburo Ohashi and Kiyoyuki Ono, ed. Thomas L. McHaney (Athens: Univ. of Georgia Press, 1985); Kenzaburo Ohashi, "'Native Soil' and the World Beyond: William Faulkner and Japanese Novelists," *Faulkner: International Perspectives*, ed. Doreen Fowler and Ann J. Abadie (Jackson: Univ. Press of Mississippi, 1984), pp. 257-75; M. Thomas Inge's article, "Mo Yan and William Faulkner: Influences and Confluences," *The Faulkner Journal*, VI (Fall 1990): 15-24.
2. In Peter Handke's recent book, *My Year in No-man's Bay*, a painter turns Faulkner's *As I Lay Dying* into a film. See also Handke's biographical remarks: "Und diese Geschichte stand längst schon im Buch, einem fur den jungen wie auch den inzwischen fast alten Maler, entscheidenden, William Faulkners 'Als ich im Sterben lag.' Immer neu war er darüber ins Wundern gekommen, daB in den fast siebzig Jahren des Durch-die-Welt-Ziehens der Farmerfamilie aus Mississippi, abenteuerlich unterwegs mit dem Sarg der toten Mutter, um sie auf ihren Wunsch in deren Heimatort unter die Erde zu bringen, scheint's noch niemand dazu den Film erzählt hatte. Ihn jedenfalls verlangte es nach dem" (*Mein Jahr in der Niemandsbucht*, Fft. 1994, pp. 524-32). I would like to thank Peter Pütz of the University of Bonn for kindly drawing my attention to this.

3. Jorge Edwards, "Yoknapatawpha in Santiago de Chile," *Faulkner: International Perspectives*, p. 64.
4. See Arthur Kinney, "Faulkner and Racism," *Connotations: A Journal for Critical Debate,* 3.3 (1993-94): 265-78; Noel Polk, *Children of the Dark House* (Jackson: Univ. Press of Mississippi, 1996); Thadious Davis, *Faulkner's "Negro": Art and the Southern Context* (Baton Rouge: Louisiana State Univ. Press, 1983); Eric Sunquist, *Faulkner: The House Divided* (Baltimore: Johns Hopkins Univ. Press, 1983). On the impact of the Howe interview and of Faulkner's roleplaying in interviews and public letters (as opposed to his literary masks), see Lothar Hönnighausen, *Masks and Metaphors* (Jackson: Univ. Press of Mississippi, 1997).
5. "Address upon Receiving the Nobel Prize for Literature," *Essays, Speeches and Public Letters by William Faulkner*, ed. James B. Meriwether (New York: Random House, 1965), p. 120
6. William Faulkner, *The Sound and the Fury: The Corrected Text* (New York: Vintage, 1990), p. 76.
7. William Faulkner, *Flags in the Dust*, ed. Douglas Day (New York: Random House, 1973), p. 57.
8. William Faulkner, *Sanctuary: The Corrected Text* (New York: Vintage, 1993), p. 56.
9. William Faulkner, *Light in August: The Corrected Tex*t (New York: Vintage, 1990), p. 146.
10. William Faulkner, *Absalom, Absalom!: The Corrected Text* (New York: Vintage, 1990), p. 116.
11. William Faulkner, *The Hamlet: The Corrected Text* (New York: Vintage, 1991), p. 48.
12. William Faulkner, *A Fable: William Faulkner Novels,* 1930-1935 (New York: Library of America, 1994), p. 887.

A Provincial Writer becomes the Universal Philosopher: Faulkner's Address upon Receiving the Nobel Prize in 1950

TUTUN MUKHERJEE

> I feel that this award was not made to me as a man, but to my work—a life's work in the agony and sweat of the human spirit, not for glory and least of all for profit, but to create out of the materials of the human spirit something which did not exist before.
>
> Stockholm, December 10, 1950

Faulkner's work has been the subject of vast and still growing body of scholarship. It has been interpreted, explicated, and analyzed; or condemned, praised, and exalted in numerous articles, dissertations and books. His popularity continues to grow. Today he is considered by many to have been the greatest writer of fiction that the U.S. has yet produced. His recognition in the U.S. and by the world came late in life. In fact only after the World War II was there a dramatic rise in his literary reputation. Ironically, the Nobel Prize was awarded for works that had been written years before and were so little acclaimed at the time of their publication that most of them were out of print by 1944. The only Faulkner novel still available was *Sanctuary*, a book more famous perhaps for its shock value than for its literary quality (though it received high praise from André Malraux for having achieved the intrusion of Greek tragedy into a detective story by setting the characters face to face with the horror of their own obsessions).

After he received the Nobel Prize, Faulkner's reputation and influence spread to every part of the world. Scholars and critics argued that Faulkner was a great writer whose greatness had been ignored and the literary situation after the war provided the right context for a reconsideration and that the Nobel Prize and the consequent literary fame were the just rewards after years of obscurity and neglect because his work was simply the best.

Born to an old southern family, William Faulkner was raised in Oxford, Mississippi, where he lived most of his life. Faulkner created an entire imaginative landscape which he called the Yoknapatawpha County and mentioned in numerous novels along with several families with interconnections extending back for generations. The Yoknapatawpha County with its capital "Jefferson" was closely modeled on Oxford, Mississippi and its surroundings. Faulkner recreated the history of the land and the various races like the Native Americans, the African Americans, the European Americans who lived on it. As he later said, he discovered that "my own little postage stamp of native soil was worth writing about and that I would never live long enough to exhaust it and that by sublimating the actual into the apocryphal I would have complete liberty to use whatever talent I might have to its absolute top. It opened up a goldmine of other people so I created a cosmos of my own" (McMichael 1759). His central themes, however, were not Oxford, Mississippi, or even America. It was, as he many times emphasized, the universal concern with "the problems of the human heart in conflict with itself." (Faulkner 723)

This paper attempts to gain some perspective on the post-World War II changes in aesthetics and the interpretation of Faulkner's value. It is therefore necessary to first summarize the general estimation of Faulkner's work in the early decades of the century.

It would be safe to state that Faulkner was little appreciated in the twenties and the thirties. Even Malcolm Cowley, to whom must go the credit of initiating the revival of interest in and the reappraisal of Faulkner's work in the 1940s, was then merely one of the very few reviewers responding favourably to Faulkner's novels. Most of the other critics—like Clifton Fadiman, Bernard De Voto, Granville Hicks—did a fairly thorough job of sealing Faulkner's publishing prospects. They were either scathing about his style and narrative technique: "First we have the Non-stop or Life Sentence. . . . Then we have what may be called the Anti-Narrative or a set of complex devices used to keep the story from being told . . . confusing the reader and otherwise enabling Mr. Faulkner to demonstrate that as a technician he has Joyce and Proust punch-drunk!" (Fadiman 78) or, found no value in the exploration of 'primitive violence of the unconscious mind' and the so-called 'fondness' for rape, mutilation, castration, incest, patricide, lynching and necrophilia. Hicks wrote that the Faulknerian world echoing with "the hideous trampling march of lust and disease, brutality and death" aroused in the reader only loathing. (266) In his analysis of modern American fiction (1934), Harry Hartwick titled the chapter on Faulkner "The Cult of Cruelty," obviously subscribing to the view that Faulkner's preoccupation with horror, cruelty and pessimism left no positive impact but showed him as a nihilist who had missed the best spirit of naturalism and had drifted into his own blind alley. (166) Maxwell Geismar was slightly more charitable. He called *The Sound and the Fury* a magnificent novel and Faulkner "perhaps in sheer craft, the best American writer of his generation." (167) But he traced a gradual decline of the great virtuoso talent and found that Faulkner had "moved steadily toward the perverse and the pathological and the denial of humanity. . . . From the touching drama of innocence, he had advanced to that of corruption." (167) Even Malraux and Sartre who admired Faulkner's style, rejected his worldview as too despairing.

The vehemence of the negative response from such respected critics can be neither ignored nor set aside as lacking in foresight. Such criticisms in fact make the examination of their ideological bases imperative. It would be worthwhile to investigate the conditions that made Faulkner a representative of his time yet his art and worldview so much at odds with it?

Many historians have characterized the period between the two world wars as the United States' traumatic coming-of-age, despite the fact that U.S. direct involvement was relatively brief and its casualties fewer than those of its European allies and foes. John Dos Passos expressed the post-war disillusionment in his novel *Three Soldiers* (1921) and described the civilization as a "vast edifice of sham, and the war, instead of its crumbling, was its fullest and most ultimate expression." Shocked and permanently changed, Americans returned home but never regained their innocence.

During the years between the first and the second world wars, which included a decade of wild prosperity and another of unrelenting depression, the ideology of culture crumbled. The word that had been imbued with more potent magic than any other was "culture"—a vague quality of an educated and idealistic stratum in a society concerned about class division and materialistic habits. It is of particular significance that "Culture" was extensively re-examined. Nothing seemed plainer than the dependence of great systems and institutions of faith and reason on hidden agendas and irrational fetishes and motives.

The writers who came to maturity in the inter-war years of intellectual contestation recorded in their work the curious interplay of the forces of historical and social changes and individual quest. Often they echoed Santayana's complaints about the discrepancy between pretentious idealism and vital realities of social life. Their suspicion of old sentiments and moralities was personified, for instance, by Hemingway's hero in *A Farewell to Arms* (1929) who said, "I was always embarrassed by the words *sacred, glorious* and *sacrifice* and the expression *in vain.*" Van Wyck Brooks decried the lifeless "highbrow" and "lowbrow" cultures in his essay, "America's Coming-of-Age" (1915); Randolph Bourne attacked unquestioned prejudices in "This Older Generation" (1920); Lewis Mumford criticized the "blankness" and "boredom" of American culture in *The Golden Day* (1926). In his Nobel Prize Acceptance Speech, the first American to win the prize, Sinclair Lewis bitterly pointed out "the divorce in America of intellectual life from all authentic standards of importance and reality."

But where could authentic standards be found and how would they be enforced? Such preoccupations engaged a group of intellectuals or the Modernists whose endeavours can only be defined in negative terms. Modernism took for granted the impossibility of permanent consensual answers to such questions and cultivated: a repudiation of nineteenth century regularities and verities; a critical attitude to life and conventional morality; a probing of the sexual and 'animal' instincts of human being. The Modernists took pride in their openness and cosmopolitanism. Malcolm Cowley tries to explain these new aspirations of American literature in his book, *After the Genteel Tradition* (1937).

In the American South, Modernism received as sharp an expression as in New York. Though it had none of the cosmopolitan advantage of Proust's and Joyce's Paris and little of the ethnic bohemianism of New York, yet nowhere else were the sociological, anthropological and psychological enquiries turned so relentlessly to self criticism. It is indeed remarkable that that part of the country often considered by the North as the economically and culturally backward land of horrid violence should have produced so many of the most accomplished writers and critics of the modernist movement. (H.L. Mencken called the South the "Sahara of the Bozart"; Henry Adams wrote in the *Education* that "the Southerner had no mind, he had only temperament!") The general attitude towards the South was also responsible for fostering the stereotype of the Southern writer as a solitary genius writing in an oppressive climate of primitivism and decadence about the loneliness and tragedy of the region.

A significant aspect of the regionalism of the South was the tenacious hold upon it of Victorian culture creating the atmosphere of "evasive idealism," to use the words of Ellen Glasgow, in which conventions of respectability blended with "the myths of cavalier gentility" and "visions of an industrialized future" combined with inescapable historical hypocrisy and unacknowledged evil. (Perry 337) It was not that the South lacked imaginative writers but much of their writing was directed toward the justification of their way of life that was actually a situation overwhelmingly rural, isolated, under-educated, with its peculiar institution of chattel slavery and racial segregation. A phenomenal evolution after the First World War in the shape of Southern Renaissance saw the southern writers moving beyond the narrow regional issues to confront more pervasive and disturbing loss of faith that followed the shattering of Victorian culture.

There prevailed, however, a strange paradox. On the one hand these writers searched for a fulfilling cause and an enduring tradition; on the other hand, some of them promoted a literary theory (i.e. "New Criticism") that advocated the study of the work of art detached from its historical contexts and offered no answers to fundamental questions about society and culture other than the identification of the tension between intellect and emotion crystallized in the form and symbols of a single text. It seemed that only snatches of meanings could be grasped in an ethos devoid of all verities and values of Western civilization.

Though Faulkner's fictional world cannot be reduced to capsulized meanings, yet when his novels first appeared, they were taken to merely reflect the transition of the traditional agrarian world into an uncertain New South. Along with writers like J.C. Ransom, Allen Tate, Robert Penn Warren, Donald Davidson,

Thomas Wolfe, T.S. Stribling and Erskine Caldwell, Faulkner too was considered a creator of a new image of a savage benighted South. If in his first four Yoknapatawpha novels Faulkner was seen as a dispenser of Southern gothic, a chronicler of a primitive and frightening South, his later tragedies *Light in August* (1932) and *Absalom, Absalom!* (1936) merely enhanced that reputation. In fact not only did Faulkner reveal an allegiance to certain elements of the southern past but he was also, in some ways, very much within a southern literary tradition. Moreover, the southern writer was often discredited for his love of language, sentimentality and rhetorical flourishes. Faulkner too was given to long flowing sentences and excessive adjectives. His professed compulsion "to say everything in one sentence" in combination with heavy moral purpose made his novels difficult to read and too complex. Though critics like Malcolm Cowley and Robert Penn Warren emphasized Faulkner's modernist endeavour to observe from many angles of vision, the complexities of achieving a human sense of identity amid a history mingling great evil with moments of honour, in an era celebrating the apotheosis of neo-naturalism in the writing of Crane, Norris, London, Dreiser, Upton Sinclair, Sinclair Lewis, Dos Passos, Farrell, Steinbeck and Hemingway, Faulkner was marginalized as "a traditional moralist in the modern south. According to Hartwick:

> the vital tradition of naturalism, which is at heart broad in its sympathies and warm in its passionate recognition of life, cannot rest upon such a specialized, reptilian art as that of Faulkner's; it requires thought to justify its style and meaning to adorn its emotion. It should be a . . . source of inspiration for all those who draw their values from Nature rather than Man, not a haunted house, dark and cold, inhabited only by spiders and morons. (166)

Thus, critics sympathetic to the realist tradition and also to the leftist ideology, found Faulkner wanting in universal appeal. Faulkner like his nineteenth century counterparts—Melville, Hawthorne and James—was a writer in "collision" with his culture, a writer whose works were rejected as too difficult, obscure and idiosyncratic. He was considered a minor writer and would have remained one had not Cowley, Conrad Aiken and Southern Agrarians made a concerted effort to revise the critical evaluation of Faulkner's work.

In 1939 Aiken described Faulkner as disconcerting, distracting and demanding; a genius of form and of inventiveness like James and Balzac. He said that Faulkner's inventiveness was "of the richest possible sort—a headlong and tumultuous abundance, an exuberant generosity and vitality, which makes most other contemporary fiction look very pale and chaste indeed" (Hoffman and Vickery 138). Aiken added:

> What sets him above . . . all his American contemporaries, is his continuous preoccupation with the novel as form. . . . He wanted a medium as a continuum without stops or pauses, a medium which is always of the moment yet is as fluid and undetectable as life itself. (Hoffman and Vickery 139)

Faulkner's preoccupation with form, technique and language governed not only the length and elaborateness of the sentence structure but the repetitiveness of the language as well.

In 1942 Cowley declared that there was no American writer who had been so consistently misrepresented by his critics and that he deserved to be rehabilitated among the most distinguished talents. He argued that Faulkner's artistic power, like that of Hawthorne's or James's, mesmerizes the reader with richness of story and detail. He maintained that Faulkner had performed a labour of imagination that had not been equaled: "a double labour: first, to invent a Mississippi county very much as children invent a mythical kingdom and to work over it until it becomes lifelike and consistent in all its parts; second, to make the story . . . stand as a parable or legend of the Deep South as a whole." (see Schwartz 229-42) He insisted that Faulkner be appreciated as an idealist and a moralist who, seeing little hope in the future, returned again and again to the past where he hoped to discover a legendary and recurrent pattern that would illuminate and lend dignity to the world about him. Cowley traces this underlying pattern through the stories rearranged for Viking's *The Portable Faulkner* (1946), the volume solely responsible for renewing the world's acquaintance with Faulkner.

Cowley's goals were clear. He wanted to end the critical neglect and to offer a base from which to confront the entirety of Faulkner's work by stressing the coherent design that held the stories together. If he had hoped to force a serious reconsideration by the other critics, he succeeded beyond all moderate expectations.

But to be absolutely fair, it was the collective effort of several individuals and institutions that gave fresh life to Faulkner's work and launched his career anew. In his well-researched book *Creating Faulkner's Reputation* (1988), Lawrence H. Schwartz explores the linkage between Cowley—the New Critics—the New York intellectuals—Viking Random publishing house—the Humanities Division of Rockefeller Foundation that was responsible for *re-presenting* Faulkner to the world. Schwartz also argues that in the radically altered post-World War II political environment with the restructured zeitgeist, Faulkner's work integrated into the new liberalist order. Moreover, as a writer who had refused to compromise with popular taste, he could be projected in the global arena as a representative of cultural democracy from a country which had now emerged as the protector of Western civilization from fascist forces. So, what had been denounced earlier as immorality, as morbid interest in lust, rape, incest, patricide etc., as barbarism and decadence was, after World War II interpreted as an individual's struggle against moral and social decay. His individualism was applauded as resistance to domination, as desperate fight for personal values.

Robert Penn Warren lent strength to this perspective when he said that Faulkner writes of two Souths: he reports of one South and creates another. But he added that Faulkner's work should not be regarded in terms of the South against the North, but in terms of the issues concerning the modern civilization. The Faulknerian legends were not merely the legends of the South; they were also the stories about the general plights and problems of the world. He was far more than a regionalist. His message was universal, transcending all parochial parameters. In fifteen novels and a great many short stories his legendary Yoknapatawpha County, rooted in actual history, emerges as the locus of the national consciousness bearing unexpiated guilt often delineated through myths and legends of ancient tragedies. Past and present history, the state and the family, are inextricably bound by an inherited curse on the land and its habitants. In Faulkner's fiction the violations which brought down such curse on generations are the abuse of the land and the enslavement of fellow human beings. As in ancient tragedy, individual acts of violence also follow a pattern of inherited human destiny.

In the 1940s the arbiters of literary taste declared that the Naturalists' protest had served its purpose. Their style and their use of language was found to be, in the changed cultural scenario, superficial, crude and didactic, deriving from narrow life experiences. In contrast to them, Faulkner was mythologizing the drama of human destiny in an increasingly anarchic and horrifying world. His complex style was adjudged to be commensurate with his theme. If the need of the times was literature that was democratic, value-based and universal, then who could better represent the existential angst, artistic freedom and unrelenting struggle than William Faulkner?

By 1946-47 Faulkner had come to be regarded as the universal philosopher. He was awarded the Nobel Prize for literature in 1949. In the later years Faulkner often spoke about his writing and about his concern for humanity's survival. For him the two were inextricably interconnected. Beginning with his Nobel Address in 1950, he always reflected upon the writer's role in the world. He said:

> I believe that man will not merely endure, he will prevail. He is immortal, not because he alone among creatures has an inexhaustible voice, but because he has a soul, a spirit capable of compassion and sacrifice and endurance. The poet's, the writer's, duty is to write about these things. It is his privilege to help man endure by lifting his heart, by reminding him of the courage and honor and hope and pride and compassion and pity and sacrifice which have been the glory of his past. The poet's voice need not merely be the record of man, it can be one of the props, the pillars to help him endure and prevail. (Faulkner 724)

The repeated use of the word "poet" is significant. It is not a reference to an unfulfilled desire for another role nor a comment in general terms. It goes to show Faulkner's deep investment in language and his lasting faith in its power. As he endeavoured to communicate his personal vision to an international audience, he sought the resonance of poetic utterance. The words that he spoke or wrote were loaded with his belief that the writer must set the "truth on fire" and make the reader the receptor of declared truth. The writer's responsibility was to chronicle human history. Since he was empowered by his mastery of language to articulate and order human experience, he could influence human behaviour. This he must understand and accept as his role and therefore "leave no room in his workshop for anything but the old verities and truths of the heart—the old universal truths lacking which any story is ephemeral and doomed—love and honor and pity and pride and compassion and sacrifice." (Faulkner 724)

The contemporary state of the society was that of confusion, suffering from the lack of discipline and the loss of values and the sense of mission. To such a confused world, Faulkner's work seemed to offer a steadiness of vision; his quest for eternal verities sounded the note of hope. Warren had said that he had found in Faulkner's fiction "a release into life, into the sense of a grand and disturbing meaningfulness beneath the crust of life, into a moral reality beneath the crust of history." (Hoffman and Vickery 113) Faulkner confronted the past with its historical burden, dealt with the collective inheritance of sin and guilt, pride and shame, and in so doing left the world the enduring legacy of an inexhaustible voice.

Works Cited

Fadiman, Clifton. "Faulkner, Extra Special, Double-Distilled," *New Yorker*, Oct. 31, 1936, pp. 78-80.

Faulkner, William. *The Portable Faulkner*. Ed. Malcolm Cowley. New York: Viking, 1946; 1988.

Geismar, Maxwell. *Writers in Crisis: The American Novel 1925-1940*. New York: 1942; Hill and Wang, 1961.

Hartwick, Harry. *The Foreground of American Fiction*. New York: American Books, 1934.

Hicks, Granville. *The Great Tradition: The Interpretation of American Literature since the Civil War*. New York: Macmillan, 1935.

Hoffman, Frederick J. and Olga Vickery, ed. *William Faulkner: Three Decades of Criticism*. New York: Harcourt, 1960.

Perry, Lewis. *Intellectual Life in America: A History*. New Delhi: Asian Books, 1988.

Schwartz, Lawrence. "Malcolm Cowley's Path to Faulkner," *Journal of American Studies*, 16 (Aug. 1982), pp. 229-42.

———. *Creating Faulkner's Reputation*. Knoxville: Univ. of Tennessee Press, 1988.

Vision and Voice: A Study of Communicative Modes in the Novels of Faulkner

RANU V. VANIKAR

Andre Gide held Lessing's Laokoon to be a work of art that compels review and reinterpretation every thirty years. Over the years criticism on Faulkner's works has undergone changes in approach. This paper calls for a reconsideration of Faulkner's writings from a sociolinguistic perspective, on an assumption that the author's primary concern is with language and society. Most critics have focused on the thematic aspects (Robert Penn Warren, Malcolm Cowley, Olga Vickery, John Hoffman, W. Brylowski) while others have drawn attention to experimentation with genre and language (W. Beck, P. Swiggart, C. Brooks, J.P. Sartre, H. Waggoner). In this review of Faulkner's contribution to the American novel, the major concern is with the author's treatment of changing relationships between language and society.

Faulkner's novels show how the "postage stamp" of Yoknapatawpha County is transformed into varying representations of a world characterized by activities and states and values. These representations are perhaps best accessed from an analysis of communicative modes. Leech and Short refer to "conversation" as the strategy used by an author to convey ideas to the reader either directly or via dialogue between characters. A scrutiny of Faulkner's writings reveals ways in which voices are modulated and readjusted to convey a transformed vision. Excerpts from the novels considered for analysis include *Light in August* (1932), *Absalom, Absalom*! (1936), "The Bear" (1942) and *Intruder in the Dust* (1948). "Conversations" in these novels appear to address themselves to that "process of very imperfect sharing, each participant both creatively and conventionally structuring and restructuring his own view of things." (Pride) It is contended that the process of imperfect sharing problematises the pursuit of authenticity of language to convey authenticity of experience. In *Light in August* the exchange between the writer and the reader is projected as a point of view, that of Byron Bunch. *Absalom, Absalom*! being a multilayered novel, the communicative mode between the narrator and the narratee is farther distanced, framed in the dialogue between Quentin and Shreve. The conference in the commissary between Ike and his cousin Cass, though generally regarded as an appendage, holds a central position in "The Bear" tale. The ongoing debate between Chick and his uncle Gavin Stevens is what structures and provides direction to *Intruder in the Dust*.

Exchanges in Faulkner's novels appear to cover a range of communicative modes; the form is derived from the notion of a common shared ground. What seemingly stands as talk between two characters, apparently reflects an inherent dialogism as it enters into a sharing and reshaping of views (Fowler; Leech and Short). The study of shared points of view between author/narrator and reader/narratee calls for a distinction in the frame-interactional versus transactional. Brown and Yule claim that the interactional has a listener orientation, serves a social purpose and tends to be perfunctory on account of greater common shared knowledge; transactional on the other hand is message oriented, the purpose is idea generation, and is far more elaborate as speakers go to considerable trouble to make what they are saying clear. Conversations under scrutiny from the four novels underline Faulkner's preoccupation with how vocabulary over a period of time tends to become stereotypical and reductive; it is the individual's striving to articulate insights and apprehensions that assigns meaning and value to language.

In *Light in August* apart from the silence and stillness that envelopes Joe Christmas, the entry and positioning of Byron Bunch in the wings provides yet another perspective on language and society. Unlike Joe who by virtue of being black is seen in the role of scapegoat, and then being the killer of a white woman, seen in the role of an exile, Byron's status as one of them, and yet on the periphery of the same community poses a more complex issue. The fact that his profile does not merge, but is silhouetted against the backdrop of a sea of faces compels the reader to examine the features that distinguish him from the crowd.

As Byron stands outside the sheriff's office, he notices "the wagons and the dusty cars in which they had come to town were ranked about the square, and along the streets and in and out of the stores the wives and daughters who had come to town with them moved in clumps, slowly and also aimlessly as cattle or clouds." What is striking is the distancing of Byron from the community as he views them standing motionless and with a "grave purposelessness." Byron's beliefs in his own people are somewhat dispelled as he realizes the lack of sanctity in their posture. He sees them "talking to one another from the sides of their mouths," and "speaking quietly among themselves of money and crops," showing utter unconcern for the man under trial, and justly or unjustly, about to be hanged. The reference to their manner of speech as well as the subject of their talk underlines Byron's place on the periphery. This position is endorsed further in the description of Byron provided to the reader as "a small man who had lived in the town seven years yet whom even fewer of the country people knew . . . by name or habit."

What distinguishes Byron from Christmas is perhaps their perceptions of language and society. For Christmas withdrawal from society and silence is an act of will; whereas for Byron his attempts to relate and integrate with the community at every stage fail to generate an appropriate response. Till the close of the novel, Byron is haunted by his inadequacy to articulate his emotions and ideas. At the end Byron remains in the wings unnoticed, and his gesture of generosity towards Lena unrecognized or misinterpreted. On return to the boardinghouse, and on being greeted by the landlady Mrs. Beard, his impoverished language does not take him beyond "Yessum." He is unable to explain to her his act of charity towards Lena, as he "could not think of the word that Hightower would know, would use without having to think of it." The man stands at the door "not even able to tell her that he had come to say goodbye," incapacitated not by the lack of courage, but by the paucity of language.

In *Absalom, Absalom!* the inherent dialogism of sharing ideas with the reader is framed within the exchange between two friends Quentin Compson and Shreve McCannon. As participants they are engaged in role play, and in alternating voices they together reconstruct the tragic tale of Sutpen. Though this exchange takes place in a room in the hostel at Harvard, the frame shifts time and space zones to assemble the rag and bobtails of the Sutpen story. Pieced together from hearsay, tall tales, face to face encounters, rumour and gossip, the history of the rise and fall of Sutpen emerges. While the two young scholars engage in a game of delving into the past, their responses remain distinct. For Shreve, who is Canadian, the exercise is play in pursuit of one's roots; whereas for Quentin there is pain in the discovery of his personal involvement and commitment to the South. In this retelling borders between fact and fiction are blurred, and the sanctity of history as a record of the past is challenged, from every retelling, new truths surface, and so many versions of truth appear to evolve. The exchange closes on a note of anguish as Quentin is faced with the utter ineffectuality of words when he finds himself trying to explain to an outsider the story of not only Sutpen, but of my family, my race, explain "the South." What is foregrounded in this frame is the author's projection of language, as caught in the words "trying to explain," as it creates/crosses boundaries of class/caste, North/South, America/Canada. The author deliberately uses role play as the communicative mode as it combines registers, dialects and sociolects, and at the same time exposes the gaps in the common shared ground between author/narrator and the reader/narratee.

The communicative mode shifts to a more overtly transactional form in "The Bear" and in *Intruder in the Dust*. Section iv in "The Bear," in which the debate on the inheritance between Ike McCaslin and his cousin Cass is presented, has been viewed as a structural flaw that disrupts the mood and tension of the hunting tale. However in the context of Faulkner's preoccupation with the dialectics of language and society, the conference in the commissary acquires significance. Ike challenges the efficacy of the erratic incomplete entries in the old ledgers and decides to abnegate his rights on the land that "his grandfather had bought with white man's money from the wild men whose grandfathers without guns hunted it, and tamed and ordered. . . ." Ike's dilemma and his decision to repudiate the land are incomprehensible to his cousin. The argument centres around Ike's attempts to vindicate his stance as, although they speak the same language, there are apparent gaps in the common shared ground. Multiaccentuality of words (Bakhtin) generates a crisis as Cass exclaims "Relinquish. You the direct male descendant of him who saw the opportunity and took it, bought the land, took the land, got the land no matter how, held it to bequeath, no matter how, out of the old grant, the first patent"; he finds himself even more at a loss when Ike responds with these words "I cant repudiate it. It was never mine to repudiate. It was never Father's and uncle Buddy's to bequeath me to repudiate because it was never Grandfather's to bequeath them to bequeath me to repudiate because it was never old Ikkemotubbe's to sell to grandfather for bequeathment and repudiation."

What distances Ike from his cousin is that though from a common background, their divergent interpretations of the legitimacy of the old records, and perhaps of even what constitutes the truth. This debate assumes greater prominence when analyzed in the context of multiaccentuality, as the register of legal texts are interspersed with rhetoric from the Bible. Official discourse is combined with ordinary speech in Ike's effort to communicate his insights and apprehensions. This exchange is used by Faulkner to show how "in ordinary speech, more so in official discourse, there is a tendency to use words as if they had only one meaning: to suppress critical and paradoxical values in favour of the meaning convenient for the ideology of the current discourse." (Bakhtin) Differences between Ike and Cass remain irreconcilable, as one operates within the constraints of a given framework, while the other strives to create a lexicon that is intensely personal. The transactional form of this communicative mode is evident in Ike's utterance: "I am trying to explain to the head of my family something which I have got to do which I don't quite understand myself, not in justification of it but to explain it if I can." As with Byron Bunch and with Quentin Compson, the frame of the debate in the commissary is used to highlight the lack of authenticity of language to convey authenticity of experience.

In *Intruder in the Dust* the transactional overtones are more apparent. The frame of an ongoing dialogue between Chick Mallison and his uncle Gavin Stevens is a strategy for the process of disclosure and concealment, as Faulkner explores the genre of a detective novel. Chick, a sixteen-year-old on the trail of a murderer represents the quest of an individual to restore a community threatened by degeneration and loss of a sense of humanity. Lucas, for him, symbolizes the ability in a few to endure and prevail, and the pursuit for release of Lucas stands as an act of assertion.

As Chick takes position from his vantage point, at the Square, his vision is bound by configurations of a faceless mob reduced to stereotyped and trite responses. The novel opens and closes with projections of the view from the Square and is used to shape the young boy's changing perspectives. As Chick undertakes the unravelling of the plot, the image of the pines as backdrop is run parallel to the trail that he follows "till the boundaries of the South move away to the uttermost rim of the earth itself." Simultaneously along with the shifting boundaries, Chick is confronted with the essence of his personal pursuit "not north but North, outland and circumscribing and not even a geographical place but an emotional idea."

The narrative unfolds as commentary and the exchanges between Chick and his uncle are used to contextualize the commentary in terms of space and time. The exchanges demonstrate how the two interlocutors shift position from one of divergence to one of unison. At the entry, Gavin Stevens is an unsympathetic listener, and Chick finds himself in despair as he attempts to convey to his own uncle the compulsion to take on the responsibility of investigating the scene of the crime. It is during his uncle's interventions that Chick confronts "the paucity, the really almost standardized meagreness not of individual vocabularies, by Vocabulary itself." The boy is faced with the lack of power in language to communicate in effective terms the force of his pursuit. He finds the doubts expressed by his uncle hard to dispel "because thinking it into words even only to himself was like the struck match which does not dispel the dark but only exposes its terror." Chick's struggle for an appropriate lexicon is run parallel with his pursuit of the murder trail. His success in identifying the culprits and exposing the conspiracy provides the confidence to share the experience with his uncle. The move towards integration of ideas is endorsed as the novel nears the close "whereupon once more his uncle spoke at complete one with him and again without surprise he saw his thinking not be interrupted but merely swap one saddle for another."

In the exchange between the two interlocutors at the end, in which the communicative mode assumes the form of a chorus, the focus falls on the words "our homogeneity." The use of "our" in this context, is assigned a depth and value which was lacking in the earlier reference to "our politics or beliefs or even our way of life." Its depth and value may be gauged from a closer examination of the term "homogeneity." The perspective suggested by Del Hymes appears to have specific relevance: "if one analyses the language of a community as if it should be homogeneous, its diversity trips one around the edges. If one starts with the diversity, one can isolate the homogeneity that is truly there." The shift in the communicative mode from the dialogue between the boy and his uncle to one of chorus dramatizes for the reader the dynamics of the relationship between language and society. The closer alignment of voice between Chick and Gavin, one tentative, probing, the other cultivated and suave is endorsement of a transformed vision appropriately captured in the utterance "we-he and us-should confederate." Homogenization is presented not as product, but as a process "eating it into to be annealed, the proud vainglorious minuscule which he called his memory and his self and his I-Am into that vast teeming anonymous solidarity of the world." The impact of integration of self with that vast teeming anonymous solidarity is achieved by assonance of voice. A sense of unity is derived from echoing of earlier reflections on time. The view earlier expressed by Gavin as "yesterday today and tomorrow are: Is Indivisible One" is once again reiterated at the end. However the retelling is assigned a control that can only come from the rediscovery of the power of language expressed thus: "Its all now you see. Yesterday won't be over until tomorrow and tomorrow began ten thousand years ago."

The integration of the self with the anonymous solidarity of the world is projected in ironic inversion in the exchange between Lucas Beauchamp and Gavin Stevens which provides an apt closure for the narrative. The communicative mode explores a subtle interplay of the interactional and the transactional. On his release, Lucas visits the office of his lawyer to pay his fees. Ever since Lucas had been a suspect and in custody, the roles of lawyer and client had been defined. What remains unstated is the transformation in the redefined relationship. The crisp exchange between Lucas and Gavin compels a reconceptualization of the presence of language in society. As Lucas lingers after paying his fees, the reader's belief is held in suspense briefly. What follows is an understatement:

> "Now what?" his uncle said. "What are you waiting for now?"
> "My receipt," Lucas said.

This exchange underlines the redefined role of Lucas from Lucas: Sambo to that of a client who is invested now with the authority to ask for what is legitimately his "my receipt." This closure effectively captures through the metaphor of transaction the rewritten roles and functions envisioned and emphasized in the chorus voiced by Chick and Gavin "to save the South and to save the United States, to present a front not only impregnable but not even to be threatened by a mass of people who no longer have anything in common save a frantic greed for money and basic fear of a failure of national character which they hide from one another behind a loud lipservice to a flag." The loud lipservice to a flag echoes the mechanical outpourings of stereotypes and clichés. Against the setting of the lawyer's office Gavin Stevens is now positioned in the role of servicing his client, and Lucas is now seen in the role of the Client, now noticed for his capacity to endure and prevail.

Intruder in the Dust stands as one of Faulkner's most poignant accounts of the dynamics of language and society. What makes this narrative more significant is the combination of communicative modes. In *Light in August*, *Absalom, Absalom*! and in "The Bear" the use of talk between two characters serves as strategy for exploring the extent of common shared ground. The voice of the speech community in *Light in August* defines the parameters of language use. As in the case of Byron Bunch, Joanna Woodward, Joe Christmas or even Hightower, inability to articulate emotions/assertions remain as personal tragedy, by choice or by coercion. Voices in *Absalom, Absalom!* are multilayered and cross time and space zones. Through each version of the retelling of the Sutpen tale the reader is taken perhaps closer or probably farther from the truth, on the assumption that the common shared ground covers generations and regional boundaries. "The Bear" if merely considered as a hunting tale would be to set aside the conference in the commissary as irrelevant. On the other hand it is possible to view the debate as central to the narrative. It appears more likely that the backdrop of the woods and the motif of pursuit provide an appropriate context for not just Ike's act of abnegation, but the "trying to explain to the head of my family . . . not in justification of it but to explain it if I can." Unlike Ike who remains in isolation, in *Intruder in the Dust* alternating voices combine as Chick appears to go through a process of accommodation and adjustment. The backdrop of the pines on the hills and the motif of pursuit once again provides an appropriate context for foregrounding a common shared ground that crosses barriers of age, class and colour. Participants in Chick's quest directly/indirectly are Gavin Stevens, Lucas, Miss Habersham and the nigger boy. With the merging of voices, and sharing of experiences representative of moving towards "that vast teeming anonymous solidarity of the world," *Intruder in the Dust* ends on a note of affirmation.

References

Adams, R.P. *Myth and Motion.* Princeton: Princeton University Press, 1968.

Bakhtin, M. *The Encyclopedia of Language and Linguistics.* Oxford: Pergamon Press, 1994.

Beck, W. *Man in Motion: Faulkner's Trilogy.* Madison: University of Wisconsin Press, 1961.

Brooks, C. *William Faulkner, The Yoknapatawpha County.* New Haven: Yale University Press, 1963.

Brown, G. and G. Yule. *Discourse Analysis.* Cambridge: Cambridge University Press, 1983.

Brylowski, W. *Faulkner's Olympian Laugh: Myth in the Novels.* Detroit: Wayne State University Press, 1968.

Cowley, M., ed. *Writers at Work: The Paris Review Interviews.* New York: Viking Press, 1956.

Faulkner, W. *Light in August.* New York: Random House, 1932.

______. *Absalom, Absalom!* New York: Random House, 1936.

______. *Go Down, Moses.* New York: Random House,1942.

______. *Intruder in the Dust.* New York: Random House, 1948.

Fowler, R. *Linguistic Criticism.* Oxford: Oxford University Press, 1996.

Giglioli, P. ed. *Language and Social Context.* Harmondsworth: Penguin, 1972.

Halliday,, M.A.K. *Explorations in the Functions of Language.* London: Edward Arnold, 1973.

Hoffman, F.J. *William Faulkner.* Twayne, 1961.

Holquist, M. *Dialogism: Bakhtin and his World.* London: Routledge, 1990.

Howe, I. *William Faulkner: A Critical Study.* New York: Random House, 1951.

Leech, G. and M. Short. *Style in Fiction.* London: Longman, 1981.

Pride, J.B. and J. Holmes, ed. *Sociolinguistics: Selected Readings.* Harmondsworth: Penguin, 1972.

Richardson, K. *Force and Faith in the Novels of William Faulkner.* Paris: Mouton, 1967.

Romaine, S. *Language in Scoiety.* Oxford: Oxford University Press, 1994.

Slatoff, W. *Quest for Failure: A Study of William Faulkner.* Ithaca: Cornell University Press, 1960.

Swiggart, P. *The Art of Faulkner's Novels.* Austin: University of Texas Press, 1962.

Vickery, O. *The Novels of William Faulkner.* Louisiana: Louisiana State University Press, 1959.

Warren, R.P. *Selected Essays.* New York: Random House, 1941.

Widdowson, H.G. *Stylistics and the Teaching of Literature.* London: Longman, 1975.

Faulkner's Use of Language

LAXMI PARASURAM

Faulkner's use of language has been the subject of much enlightening discussion on the very nature of language and its function. While there has been general agreement in critical circles about the modernity and relevance of his major themes and techniques, critics of his language have tended to take widely divergent stands on its effectiveness and communicability. Thus, Alfred Kazin, speaking of 'The Rhetoric and the Agony' in his *On Native Grounds* comments on Faulkner's rhetoric as a power almost grotesque in its lack of relation to situation or characters.[1] According to Kazin, Faulkner's handling of language shows at times an inability to choose between Dostoevsky and Hollywood Boulevard, and its overwhelming imaginative energy often becomes a nervous magnificence suspiciously grandiose in application. Martin Green in *Reappraisals* calls Faulkner's language 'rhetoric in vaccuo' and analyses its drawback as one arising from a lack of normal interplay between critical intelligence and passionate experience.[2] Warren Beck writing on Faulkner's style raises question as to where to place Faulkner's style within the main tendencies of modern fiction writers.[3] Walter Slatoff in *Quest for Failure* says that Faulkner's oxymorons, synesthetic images, mixed metaphors, pseudo-syntax, noncoherent explanations and alternate and multiple suggestions prevent the substitution of language and logic for feelings.[4] F.C. Riedel commenting on Faulkner as stylist points out that Faulkner's sentences suffer not only from something like varicose, if not broken veins; but also from a kind of thrombosis in the form of abnormally distended parenthesis.[5]

Speaking at the Virginia interview, Faulkner himself touched on the problem of style. "The style must change according to what the writer is trying to tell," says he, "What he is trying to tell in fact compels the style."[6] This surely is a very functional concept of style, and this means that Faulkner has consciously opted for the kind of style in which he has rendered the workings of modern southern consciousness and has considered it an apt vehicle for whatever he was trying to say through his tormented and passionate people.

As stated earlier there has been general critical consensus on Faulkner's major themes and preoccupations. The defeat of the south in the Civil War and the subsequent inroads of alien ways of life into the frustrated lives of southerners set in motion the tenuous working of consciousness depicted in Faulkner's novels. It is an oversubtle awareness of the minute variations in tones and rhythms of the manifold types of such consciousness that guides and dictates the use of Faulkner's language.

A great deal of the material in Faulkner's novels is presented as though it is being retrieved from the past through a process of creative recollection. Although Faulkner may be cited as adopting Bergson's precepts on cumulative memory and eternal duree, his handling of memory is not exactly the same as what we find in stream-of-consciousness novels. Faulkner adds a totally mythic or unsubstantial quality to memory which we may call super-Bergsonian and post-Proustian. Thus Miss Rosa in Faulkner's *Absalom, Absalom!* says, "There is no such thing as memory, the brain recalls just what the muscles grope for: no more, no less, and its resultant sum is usually incorrect and false and worthy only of the name of a dream."[7] It is this concept of memory freed from all trammels and solidity of reality that Faulkner applies to the contents of the consciousness of his characters and hence their language partakes of the quality of a dream or "mythic thinking" as Warren and Welleck call it.

The infinite range of the linguistic problems that are confronted by Faulkner in a book such as *Absalom* can now be understood. His focus in the book is on the consciousness of Quentin and Shreve as they dramatically interact to recall and reconstruct the history of the House of Sutpen. As this history evolves through the labyrinthine channels and multiple layers of Quentin's consciousness assisted by Shreve's speculations and dramatic stimulus, it becomes a cumulative continuum constantly modified, reinterpreted, varied, contradicted and mythicized. The language in *Absalom*, therefore, has to explore into vast unknown areas created by pure myth, speculation, ambiguity, conflicting notions and uncertainties.

Similar as well as different needs arise in Faulkner's handling of language in his other books. The past of Sartoris family sets Faulkner to florid rhetoric in his *Sartoris*, and the multiple layers of time and understanding in the consciousness of Compsons are brought to light in his *The Sound and the Fury*. A weird and complex tale of uncertain motives and action is unfolded through the interior monologues of fifteen characters in *As I Lay Dying*, and folkways and language are shown in mythic purity and expansiveness in *The Hamlet*. In almost all of Faulkner's novels and short stories, language finds itself confronted with special cases of challenge and responsibility.

Martin Green has noted that almost every character in Faulkner demands his/her own rhetoric. It is also true that most of Faulkner's characters, driven as they are by their obsessive memories and changing interpretations of the past have made increasing demands on Faulkner's language to express their differing and distorted modes of perception. In dealing with the nervous and intense vitality of his characters, Faulkner has kept omniscient interpretation to minimum and this has further added to the load on Faulkner's language.

The use of imagery with a wide range of connotations and repercussions helps Faulkner to define individual attitudes and moods while an expansive framework in myth and meaning is being created at the same time. Thus Miss Rosa in *Absalom*, being an old spinster brought up in a grim mausoleum air of Puritan righteousness and outraged female vindictiveness, can see Sutpen only as a demon—the evil's source and head pushed down the throat of her poor sister Ellen. (60) Shreve to whom Miss Rosa's demonising is more an imaginative concept rather than a stark reality freely mythicized this demon picture with his "Faustus, this demon, this Beelzebub scuttling into respectability like a jackal into a rockpile." (178) To Quentin, listening to Miss Rosa's tale in the closed room, Sutpen becomes a ghostly presence who erupts out of "the Soundless Nothing creating the Sutpen's Hundred the Be Sutpen's Hundred like the olden time Be Light." (2) Faulkner's subtle variations of imagery, while suggesting individual types of responses, builds up Sutpen to mythic grandeur. However, when Quentin's grandfather, listening patiently to Sutpen's mistake from Sutpen himself, hits on the everyday imagery to describe his type of innocence, Sutpen becomes one who believed that the ingredients of morality were like the ingredients of pie or cake, and once you had measured them and balanced them and mixed them and put them into the oven it was all finished and nothing but pie or cake come out. (263) The inflation and deflation of the Sutpen myth achieved here through imagery are very clear.

The individual colouring that Faulkner's imagery imparts becomes clearly expressionistic when Faulkner wants to register abnormal perceptions. The Benbow idealism in *Sanctuary* sees the vicious depthless quality of stamped tin in Popeye even at the first glance, and to Horace's outraged moral sense, even the insect buzz sounds like the chemical agony of a world left stark and dying above the tide ridge of the fluid in which it lived. (160) Sutpen, who wanted to rear a progeny as from the sowing of dragon's teeth, was himself swallowed by the public's stomach out of which he walked away unharmed with the help of two of the citizens who should have made two of the teeth in the outraged jaw, but who actually served only as props to hold the jaw open. (52) These unusual and expressionistic descriptions form essential part of the flow and clash of perception; they contribute those special flavours and abnormal twists which are so much a part of Faulkner's rare gallery of characters.

The composite elements of the imagery in Faulkner reveal the kinetic forces operating through Faulkner's language. Thus motion and immobility, sound and silence, quiescence and turbulence and various other types of dramatic and psychological conflicts and tensions are incorporated into Faulkner's use of language. There are innumerable images of movement and stasis in Faulkner; and words such as *motionless*, *arrested*, *frozen*, *carven*, *suspended*, *immobile* and so on are frequently used by him to denote the deadrock against which his restless characters face their helplessness. The last worthless rock of the Stockholm address, the dying star, the clock's blank face, the empty globules of a dead child's eye in *Sanctuary*, the poised gull of *The Sound and the Fury*, the immobile wagon and mules in *Light in August* are basic to the inner tensions of his language. As against the frustration of immobility come images of motion, and of antithesis between movement and immobility. The figure of the empty carcasses immobilised by the heels in attitudes of frantic running in *Intruder in the Dust* illustrate the concept of antithesis between flow and stasis. A dance interpretation of the imagery of movements in *As I Lay Dying* has been done by Truman

Capote in "Faulkner Dances."[8] Faulkner is here shown as emphasising motion as choreography—"a dance not only of humans, but of mules, buggies, planes and trains and even involving entities like vernal equinoxes which come with galloping fury, and winds which run back and forth like a drove of bridleless horses in an empty plain and including even the earth itself, spinning, slowing or racing toward destruction."[9]

Sounds of various blends and velocities cling and clang through Faulkner's rhetorical imagery. Even silence speaks in Faulkner through Benjy's crying nothing, silence becomes space in *Light in August* when the shocked silence around McEachern becomes the peaceful moonlit night of a young summer. Symbolic motifs are spun around sounds such as a ticking clock and Dilsey's singing in *The Sound and the Fury.* Sound and silence are in a permanent struggling deadlock in Faulkner's style, at once intensifying each other by contrast and negating one another by contradiction, says Slatoff.

Faulkner also uses several visceral and kinesthetic imagery to call forth the active neurological responses of his readers. Images drawn from respiratory and circulatory processes are also frequent. The tormented lives of most of Faulkner's characters stand revealed as vital, violent and elemental by means of these images.

Apart from these qualities evoked by imagery, Faulkner's language tends to follow a course of abstract emphasis and subject its concrete world to a process of profound transformation. Warren Beck quotes two parallel passages from Faulkner's earlier and later versions of *The Hamlet* and points out Faulkner's increasing tendency to transmute the factual objective into the descriptive definite. The earlier sentence, "Texas man's bootheels like a couple of walnuts on two strings" becomes later "a kaleidoscope of inexorable and incredible violence on the periphery of which the metal clasps of the Texan's suspenders sunglinted in ceaseless orbit with terrific slowness across the lot." The difference, as Beck points out, is like evolution here towards a more subjective abstraction, and it does not merely rest on the use of abstract words. (146) What Faulkner has done is to invest the concrete facts with expansiveness of a brooding consciousness which has a characteristic mode of perception. Jean Jacques Mayoux notes that the bizarre and instantaneous perceptions of the consciousness in Faulkner are always on the point of transforming the details of the physical world to unearthly absolutes.[10]

The long and winding structure of Faulkner's sentences with their many stylistic intransigences add an extra dimension to his meaning. Conrad Aiken calls attention to their calculated system of screens and obtrusions, of confusions, ambiguous interpolations and delays which guard the enigma of their meaning until the falling of the last syllable.[11] Robert H. Zoellner, in his elaborate examination of Faulkner's prose style in *Absalom, Absalom!* tries to prove how Faulkner's sentences composed of massive doses of simultaneous and suspended perceptions establish the thematic preoccupation with a cumulative continuum of experience transcending Time and Space.[12] F.C. Riedel draws our attention to the various devices that Faulkner uses to amplify a five line sentence to 800 words and these include appositives, lengthy parentheses, delayed modificators, parallelisms, synonyms grouped together, subordination with dependent clauses extending to the order of four degrees, lack of predication and so on. Faulkner's sentences effect a calculated attack on the readers' time sense and invite them to apprehend the total meaning simultaneously with no sequential division into morsels.

Faulkner's variations and juxtapositions of different tones and rhythms of speech are also part of his functional use of the language. The rich monolithic presentation of materials in most of his books is accompanied by realistic colloquialisms which abound in regionalisms and idiosyncracies of character and mood. His skill in the manipulation of verbal rhythms should certainly absolve him of the charge of mere romantic prolixity in style.

However, it may be true to say that Faulkner's concern for poetic truth often tends to give the scope and pitch of lyric style to the voices of all his characters. Even his folk characters do not always speak in their own natural idiom—Faulkner often wants to put an inflated expression of his narrative's meaning or subtlety of perception in their simple mouths. There are also some awkward passages of description and discourse in some of his earlier books which may not be able to justify in terms of imagination or meaning (One such passage is the rhapsodic description of the mule in *Sartoris*).

In conclusion, it may be stated that it is the very nature of language—its sequential and spatial qualities, its inadequacy to communicate the essence of experiential reality that Faulkner really comes to grip with in his use of language. In this sense, Faulkner's problems with the use of language are the same as those of any modern writer. He was conscious that an author with whatsoever an effort will be able only "to spin that meager and fragile thread by which the little surface corners and edges of men's secret and solitary lives may be joined for an instant now and then before sinking back into the darkness." (251) It is the persistent sense of grouping and searching for the right word to express the intensely personal and non-verbal quality of experience that we get in Faulkner's use of language.

NOTES

1. (N.Y., 1942), pp. 453-85.
2. *Reappraisals* (London, 1963), p. 190.
3. "Faulkner's Style," *Three Decades of Criticism*, ed. Vickery and Hoffman (Michigan, 1960), p. 143.
4. *Quest for Failure: A Study of William Faulkner* (N.Y., 1961), p. 23.
5. "Faulkner as Stylist," *The South Atlantic Quarterly*, LVI, p. 462.
6. Qtd. R.P. Adams, *Faulkner: Myth and Motion* (Princeton, 1968), p. 108.
7. William Faulkner, *Absalom, Absalom!* (Modern Library), p. 143.
8. Qtd. Walter Slatoff, p. 23.
9. *Ibid.*
10. Jean Jacques Mayoux, "The Treatment of the Real in Faulkner," *The Three Decades*, pp. 157-73.
11. "William Faulkner: The Novel as Form," *The Three Decades*, p. 135.
12. "Faulkner's Prose Style in *Absalom, Absalom!*," *American Literature*, Jan. 1959, p. 486.

Faulkner as Humorist

M. THOMAS INGE

In explaining the comic side of William Faulkner's fiction, it soon becomes apparent how indivisible it is from the tragic side and how the two are almost inextricably intertwined. Early critics who mistook Faulkner for a naturalist obviously overlooked his comic vision. It also becomes evident that Faulkner is so thoroughly in the American grain as a comic writer and draws so heavily on the entire body of distinctively American comic techniques and forms that an understanding of American humor is almost necessary to a full appreciation of his comic talent. We have only recently come to realize that the entire canon of Faulkner's works—from the sophisticated, subtle, ironic, and smug humor of *Mosquitoes* (1927) through the wild, raucous, bawdy, and vulgar humor of *The Reivers* (1962)—is invested with the spirit of American comedy.

In his private life, as well as his public fiction, Faulkner practiced the hyperbole and comic exaggeration that have characterized American humor from William Byrd to John Barth. When asked to prepare a brief biography to appear with his first nationally published story, "A Rose for Emily," in *The Forum* magazine for April 1930, Faulkner submitted the following: "Born male and single at early age in Mississippi. Quit school after five years in the seventh grade. Got job in Grandfather's bank and learned medicinal value of his liquor. Grandfather thought janitor did it. Hard on janitor. War came. Liked British uniform. Got commission R.F.C., pilot. Crashed. Cost British gov't £ 2000. Quit. Cost British gov't $ 84.30. King said, 'Well done.' Returned to Mississippi. Family got job: postmaster. Resigned by mutual agreement on part of two inspectors; accused of throwing all incoming mail into garbage can.

How disposed of outgoing mail never proved. Inspectors foiled. Had $ 700. Went to Europe. Met man named Sherwood Anderson. Said, 'Why not write novels? Maybe won't have to work.' Did. *Soldier's Pay*. Did. *Mosquitoes*. Did. *Sound and Fury*. Did. *Sanctuary*, out next year. Now flying again. Age 32. Own and operate own typewriter." In general, the facts are not far wrong.

He was first of four sons born to Murry Cuthbert and Maud Butler Falkner. When William later added a "u" to the family name, he was, he said, simply restoring the original spelling, which was said to have been simplified by his great-grandfather, Col. William Clark Falkner, prominent Mississippi Civil War officer, post-war railroad builder, and author of a successful novel called *The White Rose of Memphis* (1882)—a figure who served as a prototype for the Col. John Sartoris of his great-grandson's fiction. According to his own testimony, William added the "u" again so as to distinguish himself from his great-grandfather as an author and to bring the spelling into accord with its pronunciation.

In 1902, the Falkner family moved from New Albany to Oxford, Mississippi, where Murry C. Falkner first tried several unsuccessful ventures, finally settling into the position of secretary and business manager of the University of Mississippi. Young William attended school with little enthusiasm and stayed in high school for only a couple of years, so his father got him a job as a bookkeeper in the First National Bank of Oxford, which his grandfather, John Wesley Thompson Falkner, had helped establish and had served as its first president. But Faulkner's education did not cease; he became friends with a young Oxford lawyer named Phil Stone, a graduate of Yale University and a man of somewhat cultivated literary taste, who would provide him with some of the first reading matter which would help shape his talent—copies of *Poetry, Dial* and other little magazines, *Moby-Dick*, *The Education of Henry Adams*, Fitzgerald's *The Beautiful and the Damned*, and the work of Aldous Huxley, D.H. Lawrence, and Willa Cather, among others. With Stone's encouragement, Faulkner did some of his earliest creative writing, but in verse, which was later to be abandoned for the more congenial genre of fiction.

In 1918, Faulkner traveled to Canada to enlist in the Royal Air Force after having been rejected by the aviation branch or the U.S. Signal Corps. World War I was concluded, however, before he completed training as a pilot, but not soon enough, according to some reports, to prevent the novice flyer from wrecking a plane in an accident. He returned to Oxford and enrolled as a special student at the University of Mississippi for the 1919-1920 academic year, where he excelled in French and Spanish but performed poorly in English. During this period he published his first poem in the August 6, 1919, issue of the *New Republic* and contributed other poems and his first short story, "Landing in Luck" (based on his experience in the Canadian Royal Air Force), to the student newspaper the *Mississippian*. Tiring again of formal education, Faulkner went to New York City for a brief stay at the invitation of Stark Young, a former Mississippian then trying to earn his living as a dramatist. He lived with Young while he worked in the Doubleday Bookshop, managed by Elizabeth Prall, who later became the wife of Sherwood Anderson. Then Faulkner decided to return to Oxford to serve as postmaster at the university, a position he held from December 1921 to October 1924. He was reputedly the worst person ever to fill the job, as evidenced by customers' complaints and an official government reprimand. He may have neglected his duties to spend his time writing, as he continued to work at his poetry during this period and wrote as well a quantity of unpublished short stories.

It was through the financial patronage of his friend Phil Stone that Faulkner's first book saw print in mid-December 1924. *The Marble Faun*, a pastoral cycle of nineteen poems, marked an undistinguished beginning for perhaps this century's finest literary talent. The book was barely out when he left Oxford to settle temporarily in New Orleans, which was the gathering place of a host of young writers and intellectuals who clustered around two centers of attention—Sherwood Anderson, then the most influential figure on the American literary scene, and the offices of the *Double Dealer* magazine (which had accepted three pieces from Faulkner). In this rich milieu of contemporary intellectual conversation, dominated by the influences of Sigmund Freud, Sir James Frazer and James Joyce, Faulkner undertook to write his first novel while contributing prose pieces to the *Double Dealer* and the *Times-Picayune* and becoming involved in a variety of activities, such as flying with a "barnstorming" group which passed through the city and reportedly working for one of the many local bootlegging outfits. When the manuscript was completed, his friend Mrs. Sherwood Anderson prevailed upon her husband to give Faulkner literary advice. The story goes that Anderson agreed to recommend it to his publisher, Horace Liveright, provided he did not have to read it. Before Liveright accepted the manuscript, Faulkner shipped out for Europe with an artist friend, William Spratling, in July 1925. He landed in Genoa and passed through Switzerland to settle in Paris, where he frequented the busy cafes, studied the paintings of Cezanne, Degas, Matisse and Picasso, but had few contacts with the expatriate writers inhabiting the city, going only so far as to view Joyce from a distance.

Faulkner was back home in Oxford in time for the publication of his first novel, *Soldier's Pay*, in February 1926. This story of a returned Southern veteran of World War I is an ineffectively synthesized imitation of F. Scott Fitzgerald and Aldous Huxley, as well as some of the flippant, satiric, melancholy authors of the jazz age; it was reviewed favorably but sold poorly. He was already at work on other projects, including a second novel, completed in the fall of 1926 and based on his experiences and acquaintances in New Orleans. *Mosquitoes* was published in April 1927, and it proved to be a *roman á clef* even more imitative of the sophisticated satiric novels of the twenties than *Soldier's Pay*. Clearly Faulkner had not yet found his proper style or subject matter, and his royalty account showed it. In the composition of his third novel he began to draw upon his knowledge of local Mississippi history and experience of members of his own family. With *Sartoris*, published in January 1929, Faulkner said, "I discovered that my own little postage stamp of native soil was worth writing about and I would never live long enough to exhaust it." He had found his subject matter and now had but to give free reign to the marvelous range of his natural stylistic ability. Accidentally at first, but later in a more methodical fashion, he began to construct his fictional chronicle of Yoknapatawpha County, often based directly on the history of his own Lafayette County; all but three (*Pylon*, 1935; *The Wild Palms*, 1939; and *A Fable*, 1954) of his next thirteen novels are set in that region. Living in Oxford for the largest part of the remainder of his career, Faulkner married his recently divorced childhood sweetheart, Estelle Oldham Franklin, on June 20, 1929. He was already settled into the most productive period of his life. The manuscript of his technically finest and most profoundly brilliant novel, *The Sound and the Fury*, had been completed in September 1928, and by the time it was published in October 1929, he had finished the first version of *Sanctuary* and was well into *As I Lay Dying*, published in

October 1930. While *The Sound and the Fury* and *As I Lay Dying* brought Faulkner warm critical praise, they did little to alleviate his poor financial condition, which he decided somehow to improve. One part of his program was to construct an intentionally shocking novel which would surely satisfy the most violence-thirsty of American readers; *Sanctuary,* published in a revised version in February 1931, proved to do the trick and was a commercial success. A more important part of the program was to ply the large-circulation and well-paying magazines with his short stories, a large collection of which he had accumulated over the previous decade. The reputation of his innovative fiction, and later his notoriety as author of *Sanctuary*, opened the way for him. Beginning with "A Rose of Emily," published in *The Forum* in 1930, the best magazines, such as the *Saturday Evening Post* and *Scribner's,* paid generous fees for his work. He continued to contribute stories to national magazines and bring them together subsequently in collected volumes while he labored at further chapters in his golden book of Yoknapatawpha County: *Light in August* (1932), *Absalom, Absalom!* (1936), *The Unvanquished* (1938), *The Hamlet* (1940), and *Intruder in the Dust* (1948). The several short-story collections—*These 13* (1931), *Doctor Martino and Other Stories* (1934), *Go Down, Moses and Other Stories* (1942), and *Knight's Gambit* (1949)—were capped in August 1950 by the publication of the *Collected Stories of William Faulkner*, which won the National Book Award. Less than four months later he flew to Stockholm, Sweden, to accept the 1949 Nobel Prize for Literature. Most critics feel the work completed after the Nobel Prize—a play, *Requiem for a Nun* (1951), and four novels, *A Fable* (1954), *The Town* (1957), *The Mansion* (1959), and *The Reivers* (1962)—does not match his achievement of the two decades before it. But few will dispute that his total life's work is unmatched in the annals of American fiction.

Faulkner was a private man who took pleasure in pranks and impish behavior, especially if they served to fend off the intruding public. He addressed this point in a speech written in 1955 and later published in *Harper's*: "About ten years ago a well known literary critic and essayist, a good friend of long standing told me that a wealthy widely circulated weekly pictorial magazine had offered him a good price to write a piece about me—not about my work or works, but about me as a private citizen, an individual. I said No, and explained why: my belief that only a writer's works were in the public domain, to be discussed and investigated and written about, the writer himself having put them there by submitting them for publication and accepting money for them; and therefore he not only would but must accept whatever the public wished to say or do about them from praise to burning. But that, until the writer committed a crime or ran for public office, his private life was his own; and not only had he the right to defend his privacy, but the public had the duty to do so since one man's liberty must stop at exactly the point where the next one's begins; and that I believed that anyone of taste and responsibility would agree with me." This request sounds reasonable, and our tendency is to sympathize and agree with it. But then it is wise to remember what someone has said about historians: that they consider privacy their enemy and vulgar curiosity their chief ally.

It seems fairly certain, in any case, since Faulkner succeeded so well in maintaining his personal inaccessibility, that we can never fully know Faulkner the man. To protect himself, he employed throughout his life a particular technique, a device which might be termed *comic*. He assumed at various times different masks, mythical faces purposely created for the sake of divertissement and illusion, to cover up the precocious man hiding behind them. He had essentially four public faces: the aristocratic poet, the drunken genius, the ignorant farmer, and the scholarly lecturer.

The fellow citizens of Oxford, Mississippi, where Faulkner grew up, reportedly considered the Falkner family to be proud and even somewhat snobbish. And true to the nineteenth-century form of the sensitive young aristocrats who sought literary distinction of the proper sort, he first determined to be a poet. He began composing verses as an adolescent and imitated the conduct expected of the melancholy, lovelorn, romantic poet; he became shy, withdrew from neighborhood scraps and sports, and shirked his schoolwork to the point that graduation from high school was denied him.

The mask of the aristocratic poet took more solid lines when Faulkner returned from his brief stint as a pilot trainee in the British Royal Air Force, nattily decked out in his trim uniform, with a jauntily held walking stick in his hand. The uniform was soon exchanged for the very latest in fashionable clothing, and the distinctive appearance he made soon earned him the nickname "Count." Nothing could have pleased Faulkner more.

This was a mask which Faulkner was soon forced to abandon,

however, simply because he was unable to succeed in his first chosen literary form. No matter how he tried, his poetry remained uninspired, imitative, and barely third or fourth-rate. He was always to cherish this dream of becoming a poet, and as late as 1957 he told a group of students of the University of Virginia, with understatement and a sense of nostalgia, "I wanted to be a poet, and I think myself now as a failed poet, not as a novelist at all but a failed poet who had to take up what he could do."

The mask of the drunken artist, the rude, careless, temperamental bohemian genius, was one Faulkner actually maintained most of his career. As his early years of poetic effort passed without recognition, he paid less attention to his appearance, loafed around Oxford unshaven, and wore dirty clothes and went without shoes, lost in a state of reverie. The town wits who earlier found amusement in his aristocratic bearing now dubbed him with a second nickname, "Count No Count." The lack of attention given to his volume of verse, *The Marble Faun* (1924), brought about two decisions: first, he had better reconsider his aims and try his hand at another form of writing; second, he had better get out of Oxford and make a more active effort to launch his literary career on a greater scale. The last decision ultimately led him to the French Quarter in New Orleans, where Sherwood Anderson was directing his little bohemia for young artists and writers, among whom at one time or another were Roark Bradford, Oliver LaFarge, Carl Sandburg, John Dos Passos, and Sinclair Lewis. Once accepted as a member of the group and inspired by Sherwood Anderson's example, Faulkner wrote his first two novels. Both were directed at the popular reading public and therefore lacked those innovative techniques to be found so distinctly in his later work.

But at least his career was underway. Phil Stone advised him that he should stop trying to cater to the public taste and write instead for "the discriminating few." He should write only to please himself and hope that the ages would discover him. It was then that he produced *The Sound and the Fury* and *As I Lay Dying*, but this enforced isolation and the small notice given these masterpieces may well be one of the roots of Faulkner's later bitterness and reticence. It may have made him more determined than ever to maintain a frequently satirical and disdainful mask toward the world.

It was during this time that alcohol apparently became a permanent fixture in his life. Perhaps it was one refuge from reality and the hardships of attaining success, and perhaps he never drank as much as the stories say he did, but certainly it was an easy way to maintain a scandalous guise in the world's eye. Many of the drinking stories about Faulkner originated in Hollywood, where he forced to work periodically to support his more serious endeavors. For example, there is a story that he hired a male nurse to follow him around carrying a bottle in a small black bag, producing it when needed, and making sure that Faulkner made it to work the next day.

The most widely circulated drinking tale had to do with the Nobel Prize award. At first, the story goes, Faulkner did not want to go to Stockholm to receive it, but his family persuaded him to make the trip. He entered, however, one of his drinking marathons which the family feared would not end in time to get him off, so they set the calendars in the house ahead. One Saturday (the calendars said Tuesday, the day before the date of departure) he asked for a male relative and someone said that he was at the high school football game. Faulkner sat up in bed, it is reported, and exclaimed. "Somebody's been deceivin' me! They don't play football on Tuesday, I got three more days to drink." And perhaps he did, but he made it to Stockholm, graciously accepted the award, and made what many consider one of the finest acceptance speeches ever de-livered.

Another facet of his second mask was the eccentric things he did, all obviously directed toward a calculated image of an erratic, arrogant artist. There was, for example, the famous Hollywood story about the time Faulkner grew tired of working in a cramped little office and asked his employers if he might be permitted to work at home. They said yes, of course, and several weeks later were unable to find him anywhere in the city. Their perplexity was soon resolved, however, when to their horror and surprise a postcard arrived from Oxford, Mississippi, the home Faulkner had meant.

His third mask was assumed after Faulkner had finally reached the level of distinction and recognition he had once so earnestly desired. But now success was almost bitter to his taste, and his scorn for his sudden adulators deepened as he tried to assume the appearance of being anti-intellectual. This was the mask of the ignorant farmer, a crude joke he tried to play on the world. When he had tried to be a serious, dedicated artist, the world had paid him no heed. He now refused the role of the newly discovered artist, grateful, genial, and brilliant, and played instead the part of an ignorant, redneck land tiller, who only wrote as a sideline. Thus he would force the intellectuals to venerate and praise their antithesis, the lowliest and most common member of society. When his publishers bought and sent him a full dress suit to wear at the Nobel Prize ceremonies, he said, "I'm just a farmer. I never had on one of these monkey suits." Faulkner conveniently forgot his early days in Oxford as a neatly dressed young dandy, when he was called the "Count." Throughout most of his later years, when literary critics and graduate students cornered him with literary questions, he would repeat, "I'm not a literary man. I'm just a farmer who likes to tell stories." This was the most obvious false face of all. He and the world now knew that he was a man of literary genius, all his protests to the contrary, and his farm in Oxford gave him neither independence nor income; in fact, it barely supported the tenant family who operated it.

The last mask Faulkner assumed was the most surprising of all, because it led him to become something of a public figure. His daughter Jill seems to have been somewhat responsible for it, as it seems to have developed as she grew up. The first steps were the commencement speeches he delivered at Jill's graduation first from high school and later from Pine Manor Junior College. All his life Faulkner had scorned literary events and writers's conferences, especially if he was to be the main attraction, but in February 1957 he accepted a position as writer-in-residence at the University of Virginia. For the student who wished to make the trip, here Faulkner could be found reading from his books, answering the questions of young writers and interested students of literature, and explaining even to the most pedantic scholars the meanings, themes and symbols in his writings. But for one who saw him there, it was quite evident that even this was not the real Faulkner. He was too obliging. He made the answers too easy. And there was always a touch of disdain in the way he would look through a person with his steely eyes and preface each answer to a question with a "Yes, sir" or "Yes, ma'am." This is what Allen Tate was talking about when he wrote in a memoir of Faulkner shortly after his death that "he seemed to me arrogant and ill-mannered in a way that I felt qualified to distinguish as peculiarly 'Southern': in company he usually failed to reply when spoken to, or when he spoke there was something grandiose in the profusion with which he sprinkled his remarks with 'Sirs' and 'Ma'ams.'"

At any rate, despite his attitude, here was Faulkner under the guise of the scholarly lecturer, and it was no mere coincidence that his daughter Jill, married to a lawyer, Paul Summers, Jr., was resident in Charlottesville. There was another attraction, however. Faulkner liked the aristocratic atmosphere of Virginia, a place where the concepts of the Virginia gentleman and the First Families of Virginia are not ephemeral things of the past but living traditions of the present. (It will be recalled that in *Requiem for a Nun*, Gowan Stevens, a graduate of the University of Virginia, has married Temple Drake, the girl he was responsible for having started on a career of corruption through his careless conduct, in order to live up to his standards as a Virginia gentleman.) He enjoyed riding Virginia thoroughbreds at the country club, sipping drinks on the veranda during the evenings, and living the slow-paced life of a gentleman of leisure. He summed it up well enough himself in a sarcastic reply to a Virginia newspaperman who asked why he accepted the invitation to come to the university: "It was because I like your country. I like Virginia, and I like Virginians. Because Virginians are all snobs, and I like snobs. A snob has to spend so much time being a snob that he has little left to meddle with you and so it's very pleasant here."

Faulkner seldom allowed any of his four masks to slip and reveal the man who lurked behind them. Whoever the real Faulkner was, and whatever he was actually like, certainly the best part of him is to be found in his books, in his saga of Yoknapatawpha County, where was enacted in such brilliant style the drama of the "human heart in conflict with itself," which he said was the only thing "worth writing about."

Faulkner's final novel, *The Reivers*, began with two highly significant words, "Grandfather said." From that point on, the entire narrative is one monologue, a fantastic tall tale about a motorized Huckleberry Finn who takes an automobile ride to Memphis rather than a raft down the Mississippi and in the process is initiated into the pleasures, pains, and responsibilities of adult existence—the whole being passed on by grandfather Lucius Priest to his grandson as an important part of his legacy and heritage as a Southerner. The narrative situation itself, though drawing heavily from southwestern humor, Mark Twain, and Joseph Conrad, pretty much defines the relationship between Faulkner as author and his readers—that is, the relationship which exists between the grandfatherly tale-teller and the children who sit at his feet to witness the elaborate verbal creations of his imagination. For those who prefer to think of Faulkner as a social historian, it is important that they recognize finally that he was a creator of fiction and that while he dealt tellingly with all the darker and tragic implications of social disorder the Southern past has witnessed, he also dealt wittily and playfully with life and remains the most masterful trickster and fabricator in American literature since Mark Twain, especially in the art of the tall tale.

Anyone who studies the full canon of his works will soon discover that the way a story is told, who narrates it, or the importance of point of view was one of Faulkner's major concerns as an artist. He was aware of the early experiments of the Southwestern humorists who permitted skillful raconteurs to tell of their fantastic exploits in their own metaphorically rich vernacular; Mark Twain's masterpiece in the first person narrative tradition, *Adventures of Huckleberry Finn*; and Joseph Conrad's brilliant use of the narrator Marlow as witness to the heroic actions of darkly romantic figures. Faulkner decided to build upon this impressive tradition by carrying the technique a few steps further. What he achieved were some of the most impressive experiments in point of view to be found in modern literature.

In *The Sound and the Fury* Faulkner charted the decline and fall of an aristocratic Southern family through incest, insanity and greed, by telling their story through the consciousness of three of its members before speaking as narrator. The remarkable and audacious thing is that one of the consciousnesses is that of Benjy, an idiot, a tour de force which demanded a brilliant leap of the imagination. In recounting the history in *Absalom, Absalom!* of Thomas Sutpen, a nineteenth-century Faustus who sells his soul in order to establish a Southern dynasty fated at its very inception to be a tragic failure, Faulkner uses at least four tale-tellers. None of them has all the facts, however, and the reader must piece together the full story for himself, the point being that history as truth is ultimately beyond man's grasp, and as an author, Faulkner does not wish to perpetuate the notion that the function of the artist is to find the truth for us.

Perhaps his most elaborate experiment with tale-tellers, however, is *As I Lay Dying*, in which he uses no less than fifteen narrators to chronicle the manners in which a poor white family surmounts enormous physical and natural disasters to see that the deceased mother is buried in her native soil. One is tempted to consider this particular novel a hoax in the Southwestern humor tradition when the reader learns at the very end that the father, Anse Bundren, made the epic journey less out of devotion to his wife and her wishes than because of his need for a new set of false teeth and his desire to acquire a pop-eyed, duck-shaped woman, who owns a phonograph, as a new wife. Perhaps here Faulkner's deadpan, suitable for the chronicling of tragic occasions, slips, and we glimpse the wry face of the trickster beneath.

That Faulkner may be putting us on much of the time is a suspicion that lurks in the reader's mind throughout his stories and novels. Sometimes, in fact, he stops the progress of the serious business at hand to divert the reader with an unabashedly obvious piece of humor which matches anything in a similar vein by the literary comedians from America's past. Perhaps the finest comic episode in Faulkner is that marvelous fantasy in *The Hamlet* about what would happen if Flem Snopes, the master sharper and consummate conman of American literature, went to hell and confronted that other great degenerate of world literature, Satan himself. The journey through hell, of course, is one of the most honorable events in Western literature, a topic which brought Milton and Dante to their most poetic and inspired heights. Faulkner, however, as the master satirist that he is, debunks the whole tradition by putting it in the language of an itinerant sewing-machine salesman and finally turning the whole Judeo-Christian cosmogony upside down. When Faulkner had a mind to draw the longbow, he could tell a tall tale which only Davy Crockett might have matched in its exaggeration and sheer comic genius. Several were drawn directly from the literature of frontier humor. The horse swaps by Pat Stamper in *The Hamlet* borrows from Augustus Baldwin Longstreet's *Georgia Scenes* (1835); the wild pony episode in the same novel appears stylistically to have been inspired by the animal stampedes in *Sut Lovingood's Yarns* by George Washington Harris (1867); and "The Bear" was influenced by Thomas Bangs Thorpe's classic tale "The Big Bear of Arkansas." (1841) While Faulkner's familiarity with his material can be documented, to do so would be beside the point, because finally he was drawing from the same source the early humorists did—the oral tradition.

Faulkner's use of the oral tradition accounts for the numerous tales without literary analogues, a type of humor characteristic of the bawdy backwoods masculine society of the nineteenth century: the Snopes boys who board in a Memphis bordello in *Sanctuary* under the impression it is a rooming house, while they secretly attempt to find elsewhere what is already at hand; Dewey Dell (of the remarkably comic/erotic name) in *As I Lay Dying*, who gives herself to the drugstore clerk under the impression that it will reverse or undo her pregnancy; and Eula Varner of *The Hamlet*, the fecund earth goddess whose human odor and sensual presence in the one-room school inspire the teacher to remain after class to smell the bench where she sat. In *Light in August*, we are told that Lena Grove's pregnancy is attributable to her having learned to raise her window and raising it once too often; and her relentless pursuit of Brown and his final escape out the window once more are the stuff of many a backwoods dirty joke. In the remarkable passage about Ike Snope's sexual intercourse with a cow in *The Hamlet*, Faulkner achieves a tour de force by investing the subject matter of hundreds of vulgar pornographic jokes with the rich, ornate diction of Renaissance love poetry. While the content repels the reader, the style gently seduces us into accepting the liaison as a tribute to love. Then the whole affair is wrenched into a rude perspective when Lump Snopes sells tickets to watch Ike enact his love.

Perhaps the most clever use of understatement in American literature, outside of Mark Twain, occurs toward the conclusion of the story "Old Man," which forms one-half of the book published as *The Wild Palms*. The story is set during the worst flood in the history of the Mississippi River in 1927. In six weeks the rising river has put more than twenty thousand square miles under water and has driven six hundred thousand people from their homes. A tall convict is ordered out in a rowboat to find a woman spotted in a cypress snag and a man seen on the ridgepole of a cottonhouse. He has an incredible series of adventures which includes helping the rescued woman give birth, surviving several natural disasters attendant to the flood, and learning how to trap alligators from a Cajun alligator hunter near New Orleans. Somehow he makes it back up the Mississippi after seven weeks and greets the deputy with the simple report, "Yonder's your boat, and here's the woman. But I never did find that bastard on the cottonhouse."

The master of irony and sarcasm in Faulkner's fiction may be Jason Compson, the coldly pragmatic brother of the romantically impractical Quentin. At the beginning of the section of *The Sound and the Fury* narrated by Jason, he establishes a caustic attitude in telling his mother about his niece: "Once a bitch always a bitch, what I say. I says you're lucky if her playing out of school is all that worries you. I says she ought to be down there in that kitchen right now, instead of up there in her room, gobbing paint on her face and waiting for six niggers that can't even stand up out of a chair unless they've got a pan full of bread and meat to balance them, to fix breakfast for her." From this first paragraph to the last, where he says of the idiot Benjy, "I could hear the Great American Gelding snoring away like a planing mill," Jason maintains a steady stream of sardonic one-liners and wisecracks. While Jason's cruel logic and materialism have led critics to consider him a villain, his darkly humorous sarcasm suggests that Faulkner meant for us to find him human if not admirable for his stability and unillusioned acceptance of the Compson insanity surrounding him. Faulkner once described him as "The first Compson since before Culloden and (a childless bachelor) hence the last," and of both Jason and Dilsey, his enemy, it may well be said, "They endured."

As if in anticipation of the theories of the absurd and the black humor which would engulf American literature in the late 1950s and early 1960s, Faulkner frequently used alienation, sadism, and cruelty as the bases for humor in his work. Probably the best-known example of this tendency is the macabre funeral scene of the gangster Red in *Sanctuary*. In a parody of tradition funerals, the event occurs in a nightclub, attended by criminals and prostitutes, with a bootlegger officiating. The whole is brought to a repellent conclusion when a drunken brawl leaves Red's body thrust out of the coffin on the floor. While the cruel humor of this passage is evident, it is less so in "A Rose for Emily." Nevertheless this story, Faulkner's best known, partakes of this tradition in its exaggerated treatment of a Southern lady who resorts to necrophilia as a means of protecting her genteel reputation. While critics have labored at the serious and symbolic meanings of the story, perhaps Faulkner finally meant for it to be another of his outrageous tricks on his gullible readers.

To read Faulkner's fiction is to witness him ring the changes on every conceivable technique and device available to the literary humorist. To understand this is to put his entire canon in a helpful perspective. Fauklner best summarized his comic vision in the Nobel

Prize acceptance address, where he affirmed the possibility of salvation and noted the writer's duty "to help man endure by lifting his heart." Few American writers have so effectively lifted hearts as Faulkner through the saving grace of comedy.

The Multifarious Variety of Faulkner's Women

I.R. DRAXI

William Faulkner is one of the most successful novelists of this century because of the sheer imaginative wealth of the fictional world he has created. He wrote nineteen novels, seventy-five short stories, and a few poems. The families which prominently figure in his novels are—the Chickasaws, Habersham, Holston, Grenier, Benbow, Stevens, Sartoris, Compsons, Mc Caslin Edmonds, Priest, Sutpen, Mc Callum and Snopes. There are many families of Negroes that appear mostly in the novels such as *Sartoris, The Sound and the Fury, Light in August, Absalom, Absalom!* and *Go Down, Moses.*

A close and diligent study and arduous efforts would reveal the fact that Faulkner depicts "a wide range of female characters" in his novels. Patricia E. Sweeney's *William Faulkner's Women Characters: An Annotated Bibliography of Criticism, 1930-1983* is a monumental work which enlightens us with rich and profuse information about Faulkner's women characters. No other American novelist has brought to literature such an abundance and variety of women characters.

Faulkner repeatedly maintained that the main concern of his writings was the human being. During the Class Conferences at the University of Virginia in 1957-58 he stated the case in terms that have become classic: "I'm interested in people.—I'm interested primarily in people, in man in conflict with himself, with his fellow-man, or with his time and place, his environment."[1] This rings very true in relation to most of Faulkner's fiction, in which he has portrayed a number of human beings. His fictional women are as rich as his men. Whenever there is a debate about Faulkner's portrayal of women, his following remark serves as an evidence that his fictional women are as richly portrayed as his men: "It's much more fun to try to write about women because I think women are marvelous, they're wonderful, and I know very little about them, and so I just—it's much more fun to try to write about women than about men—more difficult, yes."[2]

In *Soldiers' Pay*, Julian Lowe and Joe Gilligan pursue Margaret Powers, Donald Mahon courted both Emmy and Cecily Saunders, and George Farr lustfully dreams of Cecily throughout the novel. In *Mosquitoes*, Mrs. Maurier pursues Mr. Talliaferro; Miss Jameson, Pete and Mark Frost; Gordon and David pursue Pat Robyn; Mr. Talliaferro pursues Jenny, and at the end of the novel Dawson Fairchild, the Semitic man, and Gordon seek out their respective prostitutes. In *Sartoris*, the main plot deals with the married life of Bayard and Narcissa; the two sub-plots grapple with Horace Benbow and Belle Mitchell, Narcissa and Byron Snopes. It is Miss Jenny who represents all that is most genuinely valuable. Strong, sensible, and eminently capable, she is able to reflect the best qualities of bygone days without living in the past or letting the past dominate the present. *The Sound and the Fury* is what Faulkner says "the tragedy of two lost women: Caddy [Candace] and her daughter [Miss Quentin]."[3] Dilsey Gibson "represents a moral norm in the decadent Compson world and her actions set a standard of human behaviour."[4] Mrs. Compson is quite contrary to Dilsey Gibson. In *As I Lay Dying*, there are thoughts and feelings of fifteen characters—the seven Bundrens and eight "outsiders"—each of whom narrates one or more short sections describing Addie's death or funeral journey. Addie Bundren is one of Faulkner's most fully rounded female figures. Dewey Dell is much like Addie in her intense response to the physical sensations of pregnancy. Cora Tull, whose life is composed only of words, "could never even cook."[5] In *Sanctuary*, there are a number of women characters. Temple Drake, who is the most complex character of Faulkner, causes the death of two persons, the innocent Lee Goodwin, and the invalid Tommy. Ruby Lamar who is a faithful woman to Lee Goodwin is the most attractive character. There is a sub-plot dealing with the family life of the lawyer, Horace Benbow and his wife, Belle Mitchell, Little Belle, a step-daughter, Narcissa Benbow, a sister. There are many minor women working in the brothel of Miss Reba.

Light in August reveals a number of women—Lena Grove, Joanna Burden, Miss Atkins, Allen Bobbie, Mrs. Mc Eachern, Mrs.

Hines, the wife of Hightower and a number of prostitutes. Lena Grove, who symbolises the possibility "for fertility, creativity, serenity, and abundance which human life offers to mankind," represents "Helen and Diana" who were originally goddesses of vegetation. In Joanna Burden, Faulkner "suggests that a woman is just as susceptible to the destructive forces of the past as a man. He also shows that even a woman as warped by these forces as Joanna Burden can attain tragic stature through the courage and tenacity of her will to struggle against the dark forces that threaten her identity."[6] There are a number of minor women characters—Mrs. Armstid, Mrs. Beard, Milly Hines. Laverne Shumann of *Pylon* is, like Lena Grove, a kind of earth- goddess, a personification of fertility in a sterile and death- imbued world. In *Absalom, Absalom!* there are three main female characters. Rosa Coldfield is suffering from neurotic attachments which have distorted her. Perhaps she is a more complex person, because Faulkner tries to show us both her early and later years; we know more about the reasons for her grim determination. Judith is one of Faulkner's finest characters of endurance—and not merely through numb, bleak stoicism but also through compassion and love. Clytie, instead of fleeing, remains behind at Sutpen's Hundred, but she does so out of filial devotion and as an equal with Judith and Rosa. Ellen Coldfield, the sister of Rosa Coldfield and wife of Thomas Sutpen, is a minor character. Rosa Millard and Drusilla Hawk appear in *The Unvanquished.* Rosa Millard is, like the other three old women, Aunt Jenny Du Pre, Rosa Coldfield and Miss Habersham, a religious person who realizes the nature of her sins and tries to confess them to a Calvinist Lord. Of all Faulkner's characterizations of old Southern women, Rosa seems the most romantic. Drusilla Hawk who believes whole-heartedly in the Confederate cause, not considering its fundamental inhumanity, discovers that she must act like a man to defend it. Drusilla adopts masculine attire, speech and means of action; she engages in active combat along with her husband-to-be, John Sartoris, against the invading Union forces. Charlotte Rittenmeyer, the heroine of *The Wild Palms*, is a character much like Addie Bundren; she possesses a great sensitivity to life's limitations and possibilities and, like Addie, she is a woman of courage and integrity. But also, like Addie, Charlotte has the fatal flaw of devotion to idealism. In glaring opposition to Charlotte, the pregnant woman in the "Old Man," narrative survives various disasters and gives birth successfully, albeit in horrific conditions and with the unwilling help of the tall convict whose famous last expletive 'Women—!' contains a good deal of the narrator's and Faulkner's ambivalence. The trilogy—*The Hamlet, The Town,* and *The Mansion*—tells the story of the Snopeses who take over the hamlet of Frenchman's Bend and then graze up the town of Jefferson and the positions of conservative power and respectability: the bank president and the U.S.A. senator. Flem Snopes makes his move from hamlet to town with the wealth he acquires by marrying the pregnant Eula Varner, a "loose girdled bucolic Lilith."[7] When the child Linda is nineteen, Eula kills herself in an effort to protect her daughter from the shame of illegitimacy. Nineteen yeas later Linda petitions for the release of a relative, Mink Snopes, from the penitentiary where he has spent thirty-eight years because his kinsman Flem would not help him; she accepts the moral responsibility for what she knows he will do—kill Flem. The women that do matter in *Go Down, Moses* are black. These women—Eunice, Tonnasiana, Fonsiba and especially Molly—are portrayed with dignity and pathos. Moss Eunice Habersham, who plays a key role in *Intruder in the Dust*, is a spinster of nearly eighty. She is the last descendant of one of the original founders of Jefferson. When Lucas Beauchamp is threatened with lynching for the murder of a white man, Miss Habersham helps young Chick Mallison and his Negro companion Aleck Sander prove Lucas innocent. Nancy Manningoe appears in *Requiem for a Nun*. Like many of Faulkner's female Negro characters, Nancy, the "Nun" of the title, is deeply perceptive, sacrificing, and loyal; she murders Temple's baby—and thus knowingly sacrifices her own life—in order to force Temple to face the truth about herself and, in so doing to achieve some kind of moral salvation. Marthe and Marya are the two female characters in *A Fable*. Marthe is the 'corporal's half-sister'; Marya is Marthe's feeble-minded older sister. According to Noel Polk, Marthe "bears many resemblances to Rosa Coldfield."[8] *The Reivers,* the last novel of Faulkner, recalls many familiar inhabitants of Yoknapatawpha county—the Sartorises, the Sutpens, the McCaslins, with fragments of their histories. *The Reivers* is aptly subtitled "A Reminiscence." There are several elements in the novel connecting it with the earlier Yoknapatawpha County books, notably the senses at Miss Reba's brothel (cf. *Sanctuary*, and *The Mansion*), the connection of the Priest family with the McCaslin family of *Go Down, Moses*, and the episode of the horse that will run only for one man, which is reminiscent of the horse stolen by the Cockney groom in *A Fable*. The madam of a Memphis brothel, Miss Reba, is fat, warm-hearted and inclined to be maudlin after too much gin. Everbe Corinthia is a good-hearted prostitute who reforms and marries Boon Hogganbeck. There are a number of minor female characters in all these nineteen novels too which I have left out of the purview of this essay.

Considering the impressive gallery of women, Linda W. Wagner opines, "Faulkner . . . was always bemused, and astonished by the infinite variety of women . . . (he) gave Western literature some of its most memorable women since Shakespeare."[9] According to Alice Hall Petry, "Faulkner created some of the most appealing, appalling, but ultimately unforgettable female characters in fiction."[10] The variety of women appeals so much to the critics that they begin to raise innumerable questions. Cleanth Brooks maintains that "one of the most difficult of all questions in Faulkner is Faulkner's attitude toward women."[11] This has continually perplexed his readers and provoked an abundance of critical attention. The call for the papers at the twelfth annual "Faulkner and Yoknapatawpha Conference" on the subject of "Faulkner and Women" is quite provocative and has generated considerable and lively critical debate.

Having seen the portrayal of women in his nineteen novels, let us have a look into different critics who seek categories in order to analyse them. Brooks, while observing Faulkner's women in *Light in August* and *The Hamlet*, points out that Faulkner has "full range of female types: strong-minded women, some of heroic proportions; women who are cowed and victimized by their husbands; women who are in the full bloom of their first beauty; and women who are beaten down after a life of heavy toil."[12] Kenneth E. Richardson categorises Faulkner's women into "the earth mother," "the foster mother," or "the grandmother."[13] Irving Malin studies Faulkner's women from the point of view of sex: "His women fall into two large groups: the sexual and the asexual."[14] "The sexual" category consists of Cecily Saunders, Patricia, Jenny, Temple Drake and Miss Burden. "The asexual" group refers to Aunt Jenny Du Pre, Rosa Coldfield, Rosa Millard, Miss Habersham, Emmy, Mrs. Margaret, the unnamed woman of *The Wild Palms*, Lena Grove, Dewey Dell and Eula Varner Snopes. Leslie Fiedler classifies them into "mindless daughters of peasants" who resemble "beasts in heat or sexually insatiable daughters of the aristocracy."[15] Irving Howe divides all of Faulkner's women into two groups—the splendid old ladies like Miss Rosa Millard, Aunt Du Pre and Dilsey who are "beyond the age of sexual distraction —they are beyond the magical powers of sexuality." The second group is known as "the young American bitches," consisting of Cecily Saunders the "papier-mache Virgin" of *Soldiers' Pay*, Patricia the "sexless yet somehow troubling" flapper of *Mosquitoes*, and that abomination of "castrating femaleness, Temple Drake,"[16] Belle Mitchell, Laverne Shumann and Lena Grove are some of the young bitches. Howe divided the women into two types without any acknowledgement of the vast differences in their characters. Similarly, in order to place the women into his two categories of "earth mothers" and "ghosts," David Miller is led to group together indiscriminately such diverse characters as Jenny Du Pre, Judith Sutpen, Addie Bundren, Margaret Powers and Joanna Burden without indicating the tremendous differences in the nature and meaning of their roles in the separate works.[17] Elizabeth M. Kerr concludes that "Faulkner's rejection of the Southern ideal or what she calls Southern gyneolatory accounts for his two attitudes toward women: rejection of those who personify it and sympathy for those who rebel against it or live naturally outside it."[18] Naomi Jackson's categories are "Demon-Nun and Angel-Witch."[19] Irene Kae Parks categorized into two types—"feminine or feminized."[20] "Faulkner's women, we have been told are either 'creative' or 'destructive.'"[21] Doreen Fowler puts women into two categories—women who "'lack intellectual awareness' and women who are 'introspective.'"[22] Joseph Blotner presents a division of five kinds of women: "admirable, virginal young women, voluptuous, the mature temptress, and the matron."[23] Olga W. Vickery presents six types: "the earth mothers, the wives, the indomitable, the sexual, the older and the Negro."[24] V.R.N. Prasad classifies Faulkner's women into "archetypal mother, the adventurous feminine prototypes, the immoral and amoral heroines."[25] Kny Francis Basco presents three divisions—"women as ghosts of the past, women of the new order and Negro women."[26] Nancy Mc Fadden classifies women characters as weak, 'relief figures,' promiscuous, calm and serene, strong and enduring.[27] Samuel A. Yorks observes: "she may be sexually tempting, and so morally destructive (Candace, Charlotte, Joanna); she may be a mindless and amoral force (Eula Varner Snopes, Lena Grove). Old—a monument of endurance (Aunt Jenny Sartoris, Miss Rosa Coldfield, Dilsey.)"[28] Gail L. Mortimer presents them into four divisions: "sexually intense, desiccating spinsters, faded housewives, or venerated old ladies."[29] Wagner classifies women into two groups: "in the early novels women who 'endure'; in the later novels women who not only 'endure' but are also 'coping and responsibility.'"[30] Myriam Diaz-Diocaretz presents a division of five kinds of women in Faulkner: admirable, virginal young women, voluptuous, the mature temptress, and the matron. There are critics who do not approach Faulkner's women by categorization or by classification. David Williams approaches the female characters as "Jungian archetypes."[31] David L. Minter approaches the female characters as projections of "Faulkner's disease with female sexuality."[32] John N. Duvall pays no attention to the categorization of women. He assumes two voices of the community: "Nearly every woman in Faulkner's novel has violated the existing moral code—and the second voice is that woman is the source and sustainer of virtue and also a prime source of evil."[33] Carvel Collins, Richard P. Adams, Walter Brylowski and Mimi R. Gladstein approach Faulkner's women in the light of the Demeter/Persephone myth.

Obviously the question of how Faulkner viewed women will not be answered by arriving at any number of categories, no matter how useful and interesting those approaches might be. Nor is the type of the 'indestructible' woman meant to be used as a touchstone by which to judge Faulkner's attitude toward all women. The women in his works are diverse and his attitudes toward them are by no means monotypic. The delineation of such a type in his works is meant, among other things, to suggest one way in which the articulated optimism of Faulkner's Nobel Prize speech is communicated in his fiction, to identify a type which personifies one of Faulkner's dominant attitudes toward women and to suggest the similarities between his attitudes and those of two of his distinguished peers.

Not to confuse with these categorization of Faulkner's women, it is, like a layman, better to admit that there are hordes of mothers, daughters, sisters, old maids, wives, governesses, prostitutes, virgins, grandmothers, big and little girls. Wagner observes aptly: "Generalizing about kinds of characters in Faulkner's fiction is nearly impossible because each character is distinctive. There is little danger of confusing even the same kinds of characters, Jenny Du Pre with Rosa Millard, for example, or Dewey Dell Bundren with

Eula Verner. For that reason, any generality must be understood as a convenience, a categorization that will fit at sometimes and miss at others."[34] Ilse Dusoir Lind feels the same as Wagner. She observes: "Generalizing about Faulkner's women seems to me as fruitless as generalizing about Faulkner's men, or about women or men in general or about the human race."[35] Asked about the generalization of women, Faulkner answered: "I don't think that I would make any generalization about an opinion of men—some of the best people are women, and I am inclined to think that every young man should know one old woman, that they can talk more sense—they would be good for any young man—well, an old aunt, or an old school teacher, just to listen to."[36]

Quoting Judith B. Wittenberg and Carol Ann Twigg, Minrose C. Gwin comments: "Most recently we have been warned, convincingly, that generalizations about Faulkner's female characters are clearly problematical and may lead to "transtextual exercises" that inevitably distort and oversimplify single texts. Yet we persist. As the length of Sweeney's bibliography suggests, these female voices of Yoknapatawpha continue to fascinate and, I believe, elude us."[37]

It has been observed by most of the critics that Faulkner's major female characters often present problems of interpretation because they exist in several dimensions, not necessarily closely integrated. What has been said of Temple Drake by Polk may apply to most of the major female characters: "She is one, but she is also many."[38] Sally R. Page who classifies Faulkner's women into two broad categories of "creative" and "destructive" realises that any attempt at categorization of Faulkner's women is quite unrewarding. She further observes: "Most of Faulkner's women are too original to be regarded as replicas of other characters or of some stereotyped view of woman. None of those whom Miller and Howe group together as common types are really very much alike either in terms of their individual personalities or in terms of the roles they play in the structure and meaning of the novels in which they appear. Though it is possible to group the characters into the two broad categories of creative and destructive types, this kind of analysis is quite unrewarding apart from the exploration of the relationship between characterization and narrative purpose. When Faulkner's women are examined in the context of the form and meaning of the works in which they appear, their uniqueness and their effectiveness as fictional characters are readily apparent."[39]

His female characters, or characters in the works of any author for that matter, are usually so complex that categorizing them seems a futile task.

It is to be mentioned, of course, that any classification or categorization leads to oversimplification and jeopardy. Moreover, critics are beginning to move outside these categories. Myriam Diaz-Diocaretz,[40] John N. Dull,[41] Judith L. Sensibar[42] and James A. Snead[43] are some of the critics who seem to defy the earlier categorizations. The views of Gwin represent "a great step forward from the traditional reading of Faulkner's women as bitches or goddesses, archetypes or nonentities."[44] However, the women characters in Faulkner's novels can make an interesting subject of study under a classification such as Nubile women, Earth mothers, Defeminized women, Disreputed and Negro women. This classification is not very rigid and overlaps another. Done rather for convenience, it helps the readers of Faulkner to understand more and more of his ambivalent attitude towards the women of the Old South and the New and may kindle interest or create the desire to delve deep into his fiction. The list of the classification is as follows:

(A) Nubile Women: 1. Cecily Saunders (*Soldiers' Pay*); 2. Pat Robyn (*Mosquitoes*); 3. Jenny Steinbauer (*Mosquitoes*).

(B) Earth Mothers: 1. Emmy (*Soldiers' Pay*); 2. Narcissa Benbow (*Sartoris*); 3. Caroline Bascomb (*The Sound and the Fury*); 4. Candace, "Caddy," Compson (*The Sound and the Fury*); 5. Addie Bundren (*As I Lay Dying*); 6. Dewey Dell Bundren (*As I Lay Dying*); 7. Cora Tull (*As I Lay Dying*); 8. Temple Drake (*Sanctuary*); 9. Lena Grove (*Light in August*); 10. Laverne Shumann (*Pylon*); 11. The unnamed Woman (*The Wild Palms*); 12. Eula Varner Snopes (*The Hamlet*).

(C) Defeminized Women: 1. Joanna Burden (*Light in August*); 2. Judith Sutpen (*Absalom, Absalom!*); 3. Drusilla Hawk (*The Unvanquished*); 4. Charlotte Rittenmeyer (*The Wild Palms*); 5. Linda Snopes (*The Town*).

(D) Disreputed Women: 1. Ruby Lamar Goodwin (*Sanctuary*); 2. Bobbie Allen (*Light in August*); 3. Everbe Corinthia, 'Corrie' (*The Reivers*); 4. Miss Reba Rivers (*The Reivers*).

(E) Old Women: 1. Virginia Sartoris Dupre, "Miss Jenny" (*Sartoris*); 2. Mrs Rosa Millard, "Granny" (*The Unvanquished*);

3. Miss Eunice Habersham (*Intruder in the Dust*); 4. Rosa Coldfield (*Absalom, Absalom!*).

(F) Negro Women: 1. Dilsey Gibson (*The Sound and the Fury*); 2. Nancy Manningoe (*Requiem for a Nun*); 3. Molly Beauchamp (*Go Down, Moses*); 4. Clytie Sutpen (*Absalom, Absalom!*).

(G) Problem Women: 1. Rosa Coldfield (*Absalom, Absalom!*).

NOTES

1. *Faulkner in the University*, ed. Frederick L. Gwynn and Joseph L. Blotner (New York: Vintage Books, 1965), p. 19.
2. *Ibid*, p. 45.
3. Cynthia Grenier, Interview, 1955, *Twentieth Century Interpretations of "The Sound and the Fury,"* ed. Michael H. Cowan (Englewood Cliffs, N.J.: Prentice-Hall, 1968), p. 18.
4. Philip Dubuisson Castille, "Dilsey's Easter Conversion in Faulkner's *The Sound and the Fury*," *Studies in the Novel*, vol. 24, No. 4 (Winter, 1992), p. I.
5. William Faulkner, *As I Lay Dying* (Harmondsworth, Middlesex: Penguin Modern Classics, 1967), p. 138.
6. Susan Hayes Tully, "Joanna Burden: It's the dead folks that do him the damage," *Mississippi Quarterly*, Vol. XL, No. 4 (Fall, 1987), p. 371.
7. William Faulkner, *The Town* (New York: Random House, 1957), p. 319.
8. Noel Polk, "Woman and the Feminine in *A Fable*" in *Faulkner and Women*, ed. Doreen Fowler and Ann J. Abadie (Jackson: Univ. Press of Mississippi, 1986), p. 189.
9. Linda W. Wagner, "Faulkner and (Southern) Women" in *The South and Faulkner's Yoknapatawpha: The Actual and the Apocryphal*, ed. Evans Harrington and Ann J. Abadie (Jackson: Univ. Press of Mississippi, 1977), p. 146.
10. Alice Hall Petry, "Double Murder: The Women of Faulkner's 'Elly'" in *Faulkner and Women*, p. 220.
11. Cleanth Brooks, *William Faulkner: The Yoknapatawpha County* (New Haven: Yale Univ. Press, 1963), p. 40.
12. Cleanth Brooks, *On the Prejudices, Predilections, and Firm Beliefs of William Faulkner* (Baton Rouge: Louisiana State Univ. Press, 1987), p. 81.
13. Kenneth E. Richardson, *Force and Faith in the Novels of William Faulkner* (The Hague, Paris: Mouton, 1967), p. 91.

14. Irving Malin, *William Faulkner: An Interpretation* (California: Stanford Univ. Press, 1957), p. 31.
15. Leslie A. Fiedler, *Love and Death in the American Novel* (New York: Criterion Books, 1960), p. 309.
16. Irving Howe, *William Faulkner: A Critical Study* (New York: Vintage Books, 1962), p. 119.
17. Sally R. Page, *Faulkner's Women: Characterization and Meaning* (Deland, Florida: Everett/Edwards, 1972), p. xxiv.
18. Elizabeth M. Kerr, "William Faulkner and the Southern Concept of Woman," *Mississippi Quarterly*, XV, Microfilm (Winter, 1961-62), p. 83.
19. Naomi Jackson, "Faulkner's Woman: 'Demon-Nun and Angel-Witch,'" *Ball State Univ. Forum*, VIII (Winter, 1967), p. 350.
20. Minrose C. Gwin, *The Feminine and Faulkner: Reading (Beyond) Sexual Difference* (Knoxville: Univ. of Tennessee Press, 1990), p. 22.
21. Sally R. Page, pp. xxiii-xxiv.
22. Doreen Fowler, "Introduction" in *Faulkner and Women*, p. viii.
23. Joseph L. Blotner, "William Faulkner: Life and Art" in *Faulkner and Women*, p. ii.
24. Olga W. Vickery, *The Novels of William Faulkner: A Critical Interpretation* (Baton Rouge: Louisiana State Univ. Press, 1964), pp. 287-89.
25. V.R.N. Prasad, *William Faulkner: The Southern Syndrome and the Eternal Verities* (Aurangabad: Parimal, 1978), p. 15.
26. Elizabeth M. Kerr, p. 18.
27. *Loc. cit.*
28. Samuel A. Yorks, "Faulkner's Woman: The Peril of Mankind," *Arizona Quarterly*, Vol. XVII, No. 2 (Summer, 1961), p. 119. Microfilm.
29. Gail L. Mortimer, *Faulkner's Rhetoric of Loss: A Study in Perception and Meaning* (Austin: Univ. of Texas Press, 1983), p. 124.
30. Linda W. Wagner, p. 129.
31. Minrose C. Gwin, p. 157.
32. Gail L. Mortimer, pp. 97-125.
33. John N. Duvall, "Faulkner's Critics and Women: The Voice of the Community" in *Faulkner and Women*, pp. 42-43.
34. Linda W. Wagner, p. 146.
35. Ilse Dusoir Lind, "Faulkner's Women" in *The Maker and the Myth: Faulkner and Yoknapatawpha Conference 1977*, ed. Evans Harrington and Ann J. Abadie (Jackson: Univ. Press of Mississippi, 1978), pp. 90-91.
36. Robert A. Jelliffe, ed., *Faulkner at Nagano* (Tokyo: Kenkyushu, 1956), p. 24.

37. Minrose C. Gwin, pp. 22-23.
38. Noel Polk, "The Dungeon was Mother Herself: William Faulkner: 1927-1931" in *New Directions in Faulkner Studies*, ed. Doreen Fowler and Ann J. Abadie (Jackson: Univ. Press of Mississippi, 1984), p. 66.
39. Sally R. Page, p. xxv.
40. Myriam Diaz-Diocaretz, "Faulkner's Hen House: Woman as Bounded Text" in *Faulkner and Women*, pp. 235-69.
41. John N. Duvall, pp. 41-57.
42. Judith L. Sensibar, *William Faulkner: Criticism and Interpretation* (Austin: Univ. of Texas Press, 1984), pp. 174-237.
43. James A. Snead, *Figures of Division: William Faulkner's Major Novels* (New York: Methuen, 1986), pp. 1-10.
44. Deborah Clarke, "Faulkner and His Critics: Moving into the 90s," *Arizona Quarterly*, Vol. 47, No. I (September 1991), p. 128.

The Sound and the Fury: Faulkner's Grope for Meaning

ASHIS SENGUPTA

It is customary to look on *The Sound and the Fury*, the first of Faulkner's major novels, as a socio-economic study of the decline of a post-bellum Southern family. But such an interpretation is not adequate. For the book is basically about "the elusiveness, the multivalence of truth" in a world of individuals cut off from familial and cultural ties. Every man is prisoner of his own private consciousness, and Faulkner seeks to show in his novel the individual's persistent tendency to make of truth a personal thing. Each of the major characters interprets the given situation in his own way and apprehends some fragment of the truth which he elaborates into "a total vision of the world." What he seizes upon as the whole truth is "rigidly exclusive and hence utterly fallacious"(Millgate 298-99). This explains Faulkner's use of interior monologues in the novel's first three sections. The Compson story is told through one obsessed consciousness after another: we pass from Benjy's intensely private world to Quentin's obsessed mind and then to the very differently obsessed mind of Jason. The fourth section is not passed through any character's mind as such, though it is dominated by the Negro servant Dilsey who was intended to be the one unifying and sustaining force in the crumbling Compson household. But even the last section, narrated entirely from without, fails to add any meaning to what has gone before. Thus the "atomized Southern family," Kartiganer correctly maintains, "becomes Faulkner's impassioned metaphor for the modern crisis of meaning." (328) The novel is a collection of separate perspectives, each presenting at best a tentative pattern of significance, a lonely truth.

The Sound and the Fury is in a sense Caddy's story. Her sexual maturation, and what she makes of it, is the core of the novel. It is her surrender to Dalton Ames which serves "both as the source of dramatic tension and as the focal point for the various perspectives." However, the sequence of events is not caused by her act as such but by the significance which each of her brothers individually attaches to it. Her loss of virginity means something different to each of the narrators. And as a result, the four sections appear unrelated and inconsistent even though they are concerned with the same problem of Caddy's encounter with reality. The novel thus seems to probe "the relation between the act and man's apprehension of the act, between the event and the interpretation." (Vickery 279-80) As individual consciousness assumes an extreme freedom, truth becomes a purely subjective matter. No wonder the tale Faulkner is trying to narrate in different ways is a tale that refuses to come clear. And this he admitted in an interview:

> I had already begun to tell it through the eyes of the idiot child Benjy since I felt that it would be more effective as told by someone capable of knowing what happened, but not why. I saw that I had not told the story that time. I tried to tell it again, the same story through the eyes of another brother. That was still not it. I told it for the third time through the eyes of the third brother. That was still not it. I tried to gather the pieces together and fill in the gaps by making myself the spokesman. It was still not complete. . . . I never could tell it right, though I tried hard and would like to try again, though I'd probably fail again. (Qtd. in Minter 233)

Each of the first three sections presents an isolated world built around one of the splinters of truth. The novel opens with Benjy's monologue simply because Benjy, of all the narrators, cannot lie. Being an idiot, he lacks intelligence which is a prerequisite to ordering and interpreting events. As he cannot interpret, he does not distort the real. Again, he cannot recall the past as he lacks memory; he just relives it. Time, for him, is a recurring present, and so he, of all the Compsons, does not suffer the past in conscious experience. But the irony of such extreme objectivity is that Benjy's reliving of discrete images from the past, in turn, demands *our* organization and interpretation, thus eliciting from us "simplistic evaluations empty of deep moral insight." (Kartiganer 331) On the other hand, Benjy's "mind," which does not select or condition what it projects, automatically moves around his purely private feelings and sensations which inevitably limit the truth his monologue reveals.

Not merely Caddy but Caddy and Benjy are at the centre of Benjy's perceptual life. His visions "revolve not around her, but around his relations with her and her absence from him." (Kinney 300) Caddy is devoted to her "baby" brother. Benjy feels secure in his world because she is always there to protect him. Every change in Caddy, therefore, destroys his sense of security and order, evoking "a howl of protest." At the age of fourteen, the girl begins to use perfume. Benjy howls. The clean smell of trees he associates with his sister is smothered. Benjy calms down after Caddy has washed off the perfume. There are numerous instances of this sort in the novel. But when she loses her virginity, she can never again smell like trees. And her marriage completes the process that her affair with Dalton started. Benjy's world no longer has a centre. After Caddy's wedding he keeps on waiting for his sister, though he does not know precisely what he waits for.

Benjy's adult life consists of routines that reveal the way he has adapted to his losses. His routines are very important to him because they substitute another inflexible pattern for his rigid world with Caddy as its nucleus. Even some of his present activities, like the objects in which he senses Caddy, connect him with his sister who is now physically away. Benjy defends his private world against further changes because they would destroy whatever order still sustains him. The Compson pasture has become a golf course. Benjy enjoys watching the players on the green and hearing their shout—"Caddie"—a sound which, for him, means only one thing and evokes only one response. He is also fond of playing with what Dilsey calls his graveyard—two empty bottles of blue glass holding withered stalks of jimson weed. A stink weed, which it is, "reminds" him of Caddy who smelled like trees. Luster's removal of one of the bottles, therefore, provokes Benjy's protest. The fixed route to the graveyard is equally sacred. When Luster takes the wrong turn, Benjy howls. His agony ceases only when the mistake is corrected. The smooth shapes of the fire and the shapes he sees while going to sleep continue to provide him comfort. So do the smooth shapes the trees form as the carriage travels along the road towards the cemetery.

Thus Caddy is identified with the rigid order of Benjy's private world in two interrelated ways: first in terms of his complete dependence on her when she is physically present and then through his strict adherence to anything that reflects her image in her absence. However, Caddy is simultaneously identified with the disorder of Benjy's adult experience. What the brother instinctively wants from his sister is the kind of love that must defy time. But Caddy, unlike Benjy, is in time and hence cannot keep herself or his world from change. That is why Benjy's visions of Caddy lead him to impressions of privation and loss. Whether he would moan or smile depends on how he "sees" Caddy at the moment. Benjy's perceptual response to the Compson situation constitutes one of the four quartets of truth in the novel.

Quentin's world also revolves round Caddy. But his order is "based on emotions rather than sensations, on concepts rather than physical objects." (Vickery 283)) Again, while Benjy is free from time, Quentin is tyrannized by his excessive awareness of it. With the former, both the pattern and its destruction are "eternally present," as his vacillation between moaning and smiling indicated. For the latter, the pattern has become a buried past and disorder reigns the present which drives him to total despair. Reality, to Quentin, is primarily change, and interpretation is "the created ground of permanence" in which that change is vainly sought to be eliminated. (Kartiganer 333) It is not easy to identify precisely the object of his obsession; yet it is Caddy's maturation culminating in her loss of virginity which, as it epitomizes change, is the essence of his confusion.

The order which Quentin once associated with Caddy is as rigid as Benjy's. The difference, then is a difference of perspective. Quentin demands that everything conform to his system which he seeks to uphold in defiance of experience. Benjy instinctively feels the loss of love and mourns; but Quentin *thinks* that he is troubled by Caddy's neglect of chastity. In the traditional social code and in the religious code, which is a significant element in Quentin's background, female purity is an important concept, associated with virtue and honour. As he finds it physically present in Caddy, her promiscuity shakes his moral beliefs. However, the intensity of Quentin's reaction, which leads to suicide, suggests that "his ideals are allied to the emotional ties of his early years" and it is emotional security that he ultimately seeks. Quentin makes much of sexual innocence, of Compson honour; but "it is not merely sexual innocence" that he wants. He finds real comfort in the thought of "childhood sexlessness." (Volpe 108) Caddy's loss of virginity strongly affects Quentin's childhood vision and, therefore, precipitates his emotional and moral crisis. Like Benjy, he also fights to stave off the intrusion of reality into his world with Caddy at its centre, but in his own reflective manner. While one only howls at the loss, the other attempts to deal with it. Quentin thinks that he can repair the loss only by retrieving Caddy from time to which she has been forfeited.

In the past, Caddy supplied the love that Mrs. Compson denied Quentin and Benjy. And Quentin would try to keep up his intimacy with Caddy at all cost. Since sex threatens it with change and disorder when they grow up, he struggles to keep himself and his sister from all its advances. After Quentin has hugged the adolescent Natalie, he throws himself into the pig trough. His revulsion at his own sexual urge is ascribable more to his fear of losing his childhood relationship with his sister than to his moralistic and religious training. Quentin reacts in the same way to each manifestation of Caddy's sexual maturity. The fifteen-year-old girl's kissing a boy, however trivial an incident, is the first jolt to Quentin. And right after her affair with Dalton in the summer of 1909, he talks to his father about suicide. The wedding announcement finally comes to Quentin as his "death warrant." (Volpe iii) On the eve of the wedding he desperately begs Caddy not to marry Herbert but to run away with him and Benjy. Quentin is neurotically anxious more about the loss of Caddy herself than about the loss of Compson honour. When Caddy forces him to recognize, by her marriage, that she can never be what she was, he decides to commit suicide. It is significant that Quentin sees those aspects of Caddy as shadows, which he cannot accommodate into his ideal world.

Then what lies behind Quentin's fantasy of incest with Caddy? The creek scene has elicited divergent views. Jealous of her sexual attractiveness, her men, and her promiscuity, as some critics observe, Quentin attempts to win her away from the others. His thought of incest is a wish fulfilment of his unconsummated desire for Caddy. Others believe that the self-castrated Quentin, confronted with the fact of his impotence when Caddy tells him blatantly that a man of no sexual experience cannot understand her feeling for Dalton, tries to overcome his present torment by the power of words. But none of these views explains Quentin's real predicament. In keeping with the general tone of his monologue, it may be said that Quentin's sole desire is to keep his insulated world intact by denying the reality of Caddy's act and also of his own sexual maturity. He invents the plot of incest, paradoxically enough, to regain their common paradise:

> It was to isolate her out of the loud world so that it would have to flee us of necessity and then the sound of it would be as though it had never been . . . if I tell you we did it would have been so and then the others wouldn't be so and then the world would roar away. (112)

The false declaration of incest, which would isolate the brother and the sister from the "loud world," is the only way for the reflective Quentin to escape the ravages of time. In the "clean flames" of "eternal punishment," he and Caddy would be eternally together in the simplicity of their childhood relationship. Actual incest with Caddy "wouldn't have done any good" because it would equally alter his order. Hence the hell into which Quentin wants to escape with Caddy is not an actual hell reserved for actual sinners but an imaginary one that would bar them both from sex as a reality. When time betrays him, Quentin seeks the timeless in fiction.

Quentin's suicide is his final attempt to stop time which, as he now apprehends, might wear away even the kind of defense that he has built up against the intrusion of reality. On the last day of his life he desperately tries to evade the symbols of time. He tries to avoid his own "walking shadow." He breaks his watch. But he cannot escape from time itself as long as he remains alive. As long as he will remain alive, his paradise will keep slipping back. Only a sleep that knows no end can arrest time at a moment of imagined perfection. Quentin has "restored" his order by interpretation. And he cannot afford to lose it through time once again. He drowns himself before he comes "to believe that even she [Caddy] was not worth despair," that his ideals are all meaningless. (113)

With Jason's monologue we enter a world quite different from Benjy's or Quentin's, yet related to theirs through Caddy. Like his brothers, Jason also suffers from a deep sense of loss that can be directly attributed to Caddy's acts. But differences far outweigh resemblances. While Benjy loses the basic security of his life and

Quentin his emotional and moral anchorage, Jason loses nothing but a bank job. When Caddy's marriage fails, he loses the opportunity Herbert once promised him. Jason protests at his loss, and his protest takes the form of revenge. The Jason section offers "a third possible way of reacting to experience," as clumsy "yet as 'true' as the former two." (Vickery 286)

Jason is "sane," Faulkner says in the Appendix to his novel. But the statement is ironic. Jason, indeed, is the only one of the Compson brothers, who achieves "functioning adulthood." (Volpe 119) But he achieves it at the cost of all traditional, humanistic values. He criticizes his promiscuous niece simply because her actions will ultimately affect his self-contained world. He judges everyone by his commodity value. Even revenge is measured by money—the amount he extorts from Caddy. He is absorbed in the present, with no connections with the past unless the past yields "profit" to the present. We cannot rely on the views offered by such a man because they are bound to be perversely personal.

The reason why Jason's "truth" cannot be accepted lies more precisely in his "calculating approach to experience." He reacts logically rather than emotionally. Yet "logic, presumably the basis of human communication and hence of society, isolates Jason" as much as Quentin's emotional or moral obsessions and Benjy's complete dependence on sensations. (Vickery 286) His use of logic as a means to selfish ends leaves him most alienated among the Compsons. He is proud that he suffers from no self-delusions. But his overinsistence on facing facts and aspects, ironically, distorts his views of Caddy, his family and the whole human race. He cannot imagine the existence of facts other than the ones that directly concern him. As a result, Jason "sees certain things so clearly that all others escape him." (Vickery 286) He is not bothered for Caddy or Miss Quentin except when they become part of his pattern of loss, recompense and finally loss again. He never involved himself in the Compson affairs at the cost of his self-interest, but the sequence of natural events proves the futility of his careful logic. Miss Quentin runs away with his thievings, which destroys his work of years. Jason's thought-pattern is logical, a reason for which the reader may tend to accept his account as true; but it is the product of his (Jason's) own obsessions. If there is some method in Quentin's madness, there is madness in Jason's method. So Jason is no objective reporter, as some critics have claimed; *logic* replaces *truth* in his telling of the Compson story.

Jason may also be described as psychotic, "a man who honestly believes that two plus two equals five." (Kartiganer 336) He has adopted a practical code of living but his conduct has its nonpractical aspects. His organization of things is so confused and contradictory that he seems to lack the sense of conscious control which we identify with the analytic mind. He lacks the objective awareness that is required "to utilize reality." He never realizes that his own unwise act of withdrawing money to buy a car is what has actually reduced his position from partner to clerk in Earl's business. Again, when he should be following the fluctuating market closely, he follows his niece. Jason thinks that everything he does is purposeful, while all his actions turn out to be futile. His thinking is "a continuing process of rationalization," a justification of his illogical desires and acts. (Volpe 119) To accept his views is to go farthest from the truth. Jason is an average modern whose existence is "a chaos of confused motion, utter disorder within the mind." (Kartiganer 338)

Demonstrating the impossibility of arriving at the whole truth through the stream of private consciousness, Faulkner now tests the efficacy of the traditional narrative method. The telling of the Compson story from within passes to the telling from without. In the novel's last section, we have a detached narrator describing the characters and the events and interpreting them for us. Yet the question remains, can we accept the external view as final? To judge the Compsons by Dilsey's standards is to discover the cause of their tragedy as well as of their inability to see the truth. Conversely, to view Dilsey against the Compson background is to perceive the ultimate value and meaning of life in the face of all fragmentation and confusion. But are we sure that the perspective from which we are finally to view reality has no ironic implications?

Various contrasts between Dilsey and the Compsons are delineated with striking clarity. The Negro woman has a solidity of character that speaks of permanent human possibilities. She has served the Compsons through generations, through a succession of ups and downs. She is the still point of the turning household. Dilsey has assumed the maternal responsibilities shirked by the self-conceited Caroline. She has catered to all needs of the idiot child; she has ever tried to protect the impulsive Caddy; she has defended the vulnerable Miss Quentin from Jason's anger. Dilsey's simplicity and dedication are in sharp contrast to "the sterile and doomed philosophizing of Mr. Compson and Quentin, and to the meaningless logic of Jason." (Volpe 125) What sums up her character is her humanity. In the heart, not the mind, she finds the salvation of mankind. And it is from this humanity that the Compsons have deviated. Each of them seems to deny his involvement in "the sequence of natural events and their causes." (113) Each has created own world to justify himself. But Dilsey accepts whatever time brings and lives through it. By working with circumstance she creates order out of disorder. She is more preoccupied with the present because she knows that this is the only sensible way of living with time. The past is important to her insofar as it influences the present. She never seeks to perpetuate it as Quentin does, or to circumvent it as Jason attempts to do. Thus she discovers permanence in change. Dilsey is a living record of all that has happened to the Compsons, made significant by her compassion and endurance and courage.

Dilsey's participation in the Easter service reveals the full significance of her role and takes us beyond the closed world of the Compsons. The polarities of existence are brought out most emphatically in juxtaposition of her mystical experience at Church and Jason's mad chase of Miss Quentin. For the Compsons "the moral light rays emanating from Jesus" have dimmed through time, as Volpe observes, while for Dilsey "the rays burn brightly." In the "sterile waste land of the modern world," she is the symbol of resurrection and life. (125-26) Out of her actions and spiritual experience arise what Faulkner calls "the old universal truths" lacking which "any story is ephemeral and doomed—love and honor . . . and compassion and sacrifice." (qtd. Vickery 289) Dilsey's triumph, which comes of her clear understanding of human virtues seems to lend significance not only to her own life but to the book as a whole.

But is Dilsey ultimately relevant to the Compsons, or to "those assumptions of the nature of reality basic to the novel"? (Kartiganer 341) Unlike the alienated Compsons, Dilsey has a mythic view of the world that organized human life into an intelligible history. By endowing her with a vision of Christian order Faulkner sought to return to the traditional fictional method for creating meaning before his story ends. But the truth propagated through the character of Dilsey is remote from the complexity of existence by which the novel lives. Dilsey has what Kermode calls "a sense of an ending." The collapse of the Compson family symbolizes for her the demise of all chaos, bringing nearer the moment towards which history moves: "I've seed de first en de last. . . . I seed the beginnin, en now sees de endin.'" (185) She appears to have complete knowledge of the direction of every action and of the significance of every living moment. But the novel as a whole fails to confirm her truth, "in terms of either the resolution of action into meaning or the reconciliation of fragments into a controlling system." Dilsey's special understanding is unavailable not only to any of the major characters but also to the reader unless "he ignores three-fourths of the novel." (Kartiganer 341-42)

More important, Dilsey's vision does not correspond with the realities of her own life as evident in the last pages of the novel. In her routine round of resumed duties, she just lives her own "diminished present." Caught up in this "mundane, repetitive existence," she is no more than an indomitable "skeleton." (Kinney 316) Dilsey's faith has surely sustained her throughout, but she could never render the order of things. If she is still hopeful, her hope springs from a wilful ignorance of her present despair. Dilsey is so different from the Compsons; yet, like them, she "sees" what she was always prepared to see. Her faith is self-generated and kept alive by her irrational expectations which for her contain the truth. Faith by nature does not accommodate reason, but *communion* cannot replace *communication* in the world of the novel.

The ultimate meaning of *The Sound and the Fury*, therefore, lies in Faulkner's discovery of the poverty of created meaning. There are the grotesque orderings of Quentin and Jason, one seeking to construct a "reality" by stopping time, the other inventing "logic" to justify his wild thoughts and actions. Their monologues call into doubt the validity of any attempt to perceive the meaning of experience. This, in turn, also questions the efficacy of our constitutive consciousness to formulate the truth. Benjy's timeless perspective, though free of the distortions of Quentin and Jason, actually turns into "a frozen imitation of experience." (Kartiganer 342) And there is, finally, the detached narrator who strives for meaning by *imposing* order on things otherwise disorganized. But this amounts to a total disregard for what occurs in the first three sections. The novel thus appears to be an anthology of fictional forms, each one of which Faulkner tests in telling the Compson tale and finds wanting. However, this failure becomes itself "the form, and therefore the meaning," of *The Sound and the Fury*. (Kartiganer 340) Art cannot illuminate the real when there is no touchstone of veracity in life.

Works Cited

Faulkner, William. *The Sound and the Fury*. Ed. Minter. 1-200.

Kartiganer, Donald M. "The Meaning of Form in *The Sound and the Fury*," *The Fragile Thread: The Meaning of Form in Faulkner's Novels*. Amherst: Univ. of Massachusetts Press, 1979. 3-22. Rpt. Minter, 324-43.

Kinney, Arthur F. *Critical Essays on William Faulkner: The Compson Family*. Boston: G.K. Hall, 1982.

Millgate, Michael. "*The Sound and the Fury:* Story and Novel," *The Achievement of William Faulkner*. New York: Random House, 1966. 94-111. Rpt. Minter, 297-310.

Minter, David, ed. *The Sound and the Fury* (An Authoritative Text with Backgrounds and Criticism). By William Faulkner. New York: Norton, 1994.

Vickery, Olga W. "*The Sound and the Fury*: A Study in Perspective," *The Novels of William Faulkner: A Critical Interpretation*. Baton Rouge: Louisiana State Univ. Press, 1964. Rpt. Minter, 278-89.

Volpe, Edmond L. *A Reader's Guide to William Faulkner*. New York: Farrar, Strauss and Giroux, 1964.

Counterpointing the "Mammy" and the "Da": A Case Study of Dilsey in *The Sound and the Fury* and Christophine in *Wide Sargasso Sea*

RAMA KUNDU

The present paper proposes comparison of the treatment of the black woman servant figure in the American and the Caribbean contexts respectively with particular focus on the character of Dilsey in Faulkner's *The Sound and the Fury* (1929)[1] and of Christophine in Jean Rhys's *Wide Sargasso Sea* (1966).[2] Undeniably the two belong to two different chronotopes (as also do their writers); they are divided by the 'wide Sargasso Sea'—the great geo-political cultural divide. And although originally ancestors of both had been shipped over from Africa as slaves, in course of time they had imbibed newer and divergent ethno-cultural ways and life-patterns owing to their different continuum. However, certain points of comparison persist.

Faulkner had described *The Sound and the Fury* as the tragedy of two lost women, Caddy and Quentin, the mother and the daughter.[3] In this turbulent tragedy of passion and rebellion, confusion and chaos, Dilsey provides the only point of stability. She also proves a succour to the mother and later to the lonely helpless daughter. *Wide Sargasso Sea* is a sad tale of a creole girl of the Carib islands who had been married by a metropolitan British, robbed of her money and then systematically broken and finally deported to England to the attic of the country mansion of Rochester. It is actually Charlotte Bronte's *Jany Eyre* rewritten from the angle of Rochester's mad wife from Jamaica, who gets a voice here, a past, and an identity. As a child Antoinette had seen her mother turn mad at the shock of her little brother's death in estate-fire, then left by her second husband in the hands of paid people who sexually exploited the helpless woman. This terrible knowledge had undermined Antoinette psychically, so that later her calculating husband found it so easy to "break" her. It is a story of violence and dislocation, of racism-imperialism-androcentrism working hand in hand to perpetrate the tragedy of two lost women. And both the mother and the daughter, in their brief sad transit through this life get consistent affection, understanding and support from only one person; she is Christophine, Antoinette's 'Da' (nurse).

Both Christophine and Dilsey hail from ex-slave communities which had once been forcibly uprooted from their native place to serve alien white masters in alien lands; and though slaves no more in the continuum of the two novels, they remain servants nevertheless, and women servants, who had known the double ignominy of racism and sexism. As women of a marginalized group in their respective societies, these black servants were necessarily subjected to the double burden of bearing-rearing-homemaking for her own family as well as looking after the master's children and household. The life they had to encounter was, at its best, to say the least, difficult. What is interesting is to see how they negotiated with this life, and emerged as women of strength and dignity who could offer a counterpoint/solution to the problems of identity/selfhood—not only to the black but also to the white women of their respective milieu. Both anticipate, though in different ways, the New Woman of a later era.

Dilsey represents the Southern black woman of America—an emergent generation of blacks, still smothered by memories of slavery and yet in full possession of the self-esteem that helps to hold one's head high. In spite of the abolition of slavery, they are still little more than slaves, riddled by poverty and ignorance. But Dilsey stages a triumph above her narrowing circumstances through sheer strength of character and no external assistance.

In contrast to Dilsey, Christophine had herself been a slave once; she had gone through the s/exploitation of the slave-market as a commodity/labourer; then given away as wedding gift by her last master to his newly-wed second wife. But even after the abolition of slavery in the island she stayed on with the ex-master's family, by then quickly getting pauperised as the master died, the former servants refused to work, and the young beautiful wife, helplessly tethered to the place with two children, faced starvation. When thus deserted by all, it was only Christophine who came to the succour and helped them to survive through these hard times by means of her own personal influence among the blacks of the locality. Moreover, she had been a mother-surrogate to Antoinette (the name given to Rochester's first wife in Jean Rhys's novel) in her lonely childhood, a most sympathetic and understanding nurse or 'da.' She had remained loyal to the child through ups and downs, when the estate was burnt down, the mother Annette turned mad, the parents died; later when she grew up and got married, Christophine again came to serve the couple in the honeymoon house at Granbois. Soon afterwards, Antoinette started breaking down as her British husband began to show his hatred of the creole wife, and had servant girls in bed with a thin partition wall keeping her off. In her anguish she could turn only to Christophine—who was blacker than anyone and smelt of all the black women of her childhood—for comfort and support. Again, it was Christophine alone who stood up in defence of her '*doudou*,' though ineffectively but courageously. She had also given Antoinette a piece of practical advice—to pack up and go away from her husband since women must have "spunks" in order to survive in this hard world; she gave her own example: she had three sons, each by a different father, but she allowed "no thief husband to steal" her money. Antoinette had failed to act according to the advice and suffered miserably in consequence. But when finally she set fire to Rochester's house/her prison, she cried out only to Christophine for help. Though Christophine was miles away by that time, if at all alive, she helped her as it were by raising a wall of fire.

Perhaps because this is a novel written by a woman from essentially a woman's standpoint, the relationship between Antoinette and Christophine attains a most satisfying and enriching level of emotion and understanding. At the end Antoinette realizes that as a creole girl she does not belong to the colonist's milieu, but rather her true identity lies with the oppressed women of her own island, for whom Christophine stands as a symbol of assurance and confidence. As Laura Niesen de Abruna observes: "She demonstrates that bonding is possible for white Creole women and African-Caribbean women if the women can bracket the sexism, racism, and imperialism that are thrust upon them."[4]

This kind of awareness may not be found in *The Sound and the Fury* which is written by a male writer and in a different social context. But even here Dilsey emerges as a remarkable figure carrying significances beyond the immediate continuum of the text as counterpoint to a number of racist paradigms.

The portrait of Dilsey in Faulkner's most well-known novel has drawn the readers' attention. Though apparently Dilsey is no major character, nor is she involved in 'the sound and the fury' that occupies the main personae, yet she leaves a lasting impression on the reader. This was intended by the author as is evident from his apportioning the last section of the novel to Dilsey. Thus Cleanth Brooks, even while dismissing Irving Howe's claim about Faulkner's continuous moral growth in his depiction of the Negro,[5] yet concedes that Dilsey is "one of Faulkner's most sympathetic Negro characters, surely 'conceived in warmth' and 'developed in depth.'" (385) Of course this encomium does not suffice for the black feminist critics of our times. Barbara Christian's is a typical instance of this rejection of the 'mammy' myth, one of the stereotypes of black women as perceived by the white writers. She includes Dilsey too as part of this conventional pattern which epitomises the ambiguity of the white male's response to the black woman: "the way the guilty and the powerful always delight in looking obliquely at their guilt."[6] Christian is no less ironical in her summing up of the 'mammy' myth—the black female figure in Southern white literature,—the fat, nurturing, religious, kind, strong, enduring woman who is unable to do harm, and is of an all-giving nature. Thus she would angrily point her finger at the limitedness of white perception in this respect: "Who is a Southern black woman? To a white man, those words might connote a mammy, a good-looking wench, or Dilsey, as it did to Faulkner." (33)

It is but expected that as a model of Christian resignation and endurance, Dilsey may cease to appeal to the present-day reader, who has been taught to dismiss such values as the 'poor's opium'; or the exploiter's shrewd devices to keep the mill going. But Dilsey may still be considered in historical terms if not as a moral archetype or model. Christian's exasperation with the 'mammy' myth is understandable. But is Dilsey that simple, or to be that summarily dismissed? Does Dilsey epitomize abject surrender to the prevailing system or rather the beginning of an assertion of the New Woman—self-sufficient, self-conscious—who should be from the most underprivileged and exploited section of the society; a self-assurance that would get increasingly pronounced in the subsequent decades of

American history as well as global history.

It is rather unlikely of course that Faulkner intended to present a case either for the women or the Negro through Dilsey. Faulkner was never known for any pronounced feminist sympathies, and he had other types of Negroes to offer; even within this book Luster provides an example. It is more likely that Dilsey was imagined by Faulkner as an individual rather than as a stereotype. And what kind of individual is she? Apparently she is just any/every 'mammy,'—the kind, harmless, humble, serving creature. But that Faulkner intended her to be more than that is evident from the very patterning of the book. Dilsey is foregrounded in the last and only omnisciently narrated section (generally denominated by critics as 'Dilsey's section') that follows and sets in perspective the preceding disjointed fragments of separate interior monologues. It is also in this section that Dilsey, the poor old black woman, a real 'have not,' emerges as the most impressive 'counterpoint' to all the other 'points' represented by various members of the Compson family—old and young, decadent and confused alike.

Faulkner's critical attitude to all the other characters, irrespective of their colour or position, is obvious. But for Dilsey he reserves an unreserved respect. She is not once treated with disapproval or ridicule. No posture of kind condescension of a superior may be traced in Faulkner's treatment of the character.

Dilsey is one of Faulkner's noble Negroes. She is noble not because she is Negro but because of her very nature. She has been made to function in a difficult situation which is also typical of the mammy's world. She has held up her head in a world that would have rather knocked her down. She has to find a way of coping with a very hard life. She achieves this simply by being herself/what she is. Brooks finely sums up this way of her with reference to her relationship with Jason—the most difficult, mean and demeaning person in the text: "She forces Jason Compson to fear and respect her though she is armed with little more than a dedication so evident that Jason, in spite of himself, is overawed."[7] She is so sure of herself that she is not afraid of Jason who does not fear God or the laws, and shows the courage to protest against Jason's treatment of Quentin.

Not that Dilsey gets a recognition or appreciation of what she does for others. It is she alone who responds most adequately and affectionately to Benjy's helpless dependence, while Benjy's own mother almost grudges this attention. Apparently what Dilsey does for Benjy is out of pure self-motivation and not in obedience to any stricture from the employer. Even the small girl Quentin, whom Dilsey tries to mother is callous and harsh to her. Anyway, Quentin has been made cruel by a loveless home, and she despises both her uncles. But when the occasion arises, it is to Dilsey alone that she appeals for protection against the cruelty of the adults.

Mrs. Compson, who suggests a parody of the Southern white lady image—incompetent, ill-tempered, unable to cope with the small and big problems of life—provides a surface to reflect Dilsey's positive attributes by contrast. Dilsey is what Mr. Compson is not. Barbara Christian defines the Southern lady image—"the respectable lady, the desired concept of woman in the society" as "not only sexist and racist, [but] . . . also classist." (2) Faulkner, however, upholds the other woman of the lower "class" instead in comparison with the "lady." True, Dilsey is not analyzed in the Toni Morrison way, that is, in terms of the relationship between class, race, gender. Nevertheless, she emerges as the focus. Thus, not only the other characters but even the "lady" too would instinctively turn to Dilsey for physical and mental comfort. As she needs Dilsey's help to allay her physical chilliness, so she needs her in the moment of mental unease and spiritual confusion following Quentin's disappearance. Dilsey hands over the Bible to her which she does not open. This detail has been usually considered by critics as an ironical touch. But this may also be seen in another way. Dilsey's very act of handing over the Bible may be emblematic of an extension of confidence, a gesture of some deeper assurance, which may soothe even the ever-fretful Mrs. Compson in her spiritual chaos.

Again, Dilsey provides the counterpoint at a climactic moment in the novel; when Jason goes along on his frustrating search for Quentin and her money, Dilsey goes to the church and has her ecstatic vision of fulfilment. Unlike the fury of Jason, the dullness of Benjy, the confusion of Quentin (male) and Caddy, the chaos of Quentin (female) and Mrs. Compson, Dilsey proves to be a point, and the only one, of stability. It has not been an easy attainment. She had to bleed and sweat all the way, one may assume, to reach this position; the careful description of her physical appearance at the opening of the last section shows how a woman has been scarred, scathed and furrowed by life, eaten away/exhausted by the many claims of life. The "collapsed face" bears the expression at once "fatalistic" and that of a child's "astonished disappointment." Yet she carries on painfully, slowly but steadily with her head held high.

Not that Faulkner casts Dilsey on the typical soft-sweet model of the conventional 'mammy.' She has an element of toughness which makes her disregard unjust demands from her employer, or leaves her indifferent to the shallow snobbery of "trash white folks" on the way to church. Neither does she indulge in any illusions regarding the black. She knows that her own son Luster, the "nigger boy" has "got jes as much Compson devilment" in him. This rare insight and clarity is the gift of her toughness which has carried her through a long ordeal in which she had no capital but her physical energy to invest, and that was used abused s/exploited by the white employer as well as the black male at home.

Dilsey's much-emphasized and sometimes derided religiosity may also be seen in this light. Most conventional readers and critics are impressed by Dilsey's simple faith in contrast to Mrs. Compson's lack of belief.[8] The angry young women since the 60s might find Dilsey disagreeably (and conveniently for the system) addicted to the 'poor's opium.' However, it may not be far-fetched to see her religiosity from another perspective. The ecstatic vision at the church has been grabbed by critics as unmistakable evidence of her humble Christianity, her surrender to the values of suffering and endurance; but this may also be seen in relation to her own life with its crosses and nails and thorns, its lashes and disappointments; life-long suffering has given her a philosophical poise, so that she can identify with the suffering god. Religion only helps her to make sense of her painful long ordeal in her own way. Her own life has been crucifixed onto exacting daily duties over the years; there has been no respite, consideration, concession. Yet she has attained the release of resurrection/transcendence through sheer strength and self-discipline; having conducted her own life with dignity and poise, with fatalistic stoicism in spite of so many disappointments she is at last at peace with herself and the world. Caddy and Quentin had also suffered in their own way: they too had been subjected to the humiliation and cruelty of an insensitive male-dominated society. They too had bled, but unlike Dilsey, failed to find transcendence. "I've seed de first en de last" reads like the choric wisdom of an old matriarch who has made sense of events through suffering.

It is because of this hard-earned wisdom that Dilsey can stand as an epitome of order amidst pervasive chaos and confusion, by uniting work, order, tradition, nature, god. This order is further reflected in her sense of time. Perrin Lowrey notes the brothers' defective sense of time.[9] Indeed each of them fails to make sense of time, i.e. Benjy is not conscious of it at all; Quentin is puzzled and afraid; Jason is mechanically obsessed. Only Dilsey can derive the right time from the incorrect clock and work out her schedule accordingly. This adds an extra dimension to her perception of the 'beginning and the ending,' i.e., eternity as perceived in terms of human consciousness. Thus it is Dilsey who appears as the only "integrated" person;[10] and in spite of her being just a servant by status can unify, and sustain at least to some extent, the Compson household.

Critics like Isadore Traschen have preferred to perceive Dilsey in the light of "instinctive motherliness"—a myth revived by the negritude movement: "She is the Great Mother who feeds, warms, and cares for everyone. As such, she is natural, not sentimental . . . grounded in her faith and her self as the Mother she is sustained by a kind of well-being that finds miraculous expression in the fact that she sings. . . . Certainly nothing more clearly indicates her power of transcendence." (465)

However, Dilsey's worksong is no mindless cheerfulness. It springs from profundity, from a stoic mastery over personal sadness and trouble, and may fall in line with the typical rhythm of work-songs by black women[11]—just as her appearance—though neat and trim—still bears traces of fatigue, long-suffering, the sadness of a wasted life, and the ruins ravaged by time and experience. That this has not embittered her only underscores her extraordinary strength and vitality.

Indeed, by relating the woman's power of transcendence to her 'motherliness' negritude also attempts to impose a role and gender expectation on the black woman by creating the idealized image/assumption about the African woman as Mother Earth. Faulkner, however, does not appear to have intended Dilsey to be a role model, either as the 'great mother' or as the submissive, soft-sweet 'mammy.' Rather she emerges just as a remarkable individual—an old woman who has lost physical strength and charm, who has no material property, power, or social status, and who has still solved her own identity-problem, and has emerged as a self-assured, self-contained, self-sufficient individual who may be considered by 'the second sex' all over the world with admiration, as an early anticipation of the emerging 'New Woman' of our times who can stand on her own—alone—in the face of the heaviest odds.

Dilsey and Christophine thus represent the marginalized and oppressed victims of racism/sexism/imperialism in two countries, who prove—by means of their dignity, poise and courage—what a woman and an underdog with no power/status/possession could still achieve, and thus emerge as model and inspiration for oppressed women anywhere in the world, who would be in search of an identity.

NOTES

1. William Faulkner, *The Sound and the Fury* (1929; rpt. New Delhi: O.U.P., 1981).
2. Jeans Rhys, *Wide Sargasso Sea* (London: Oliver and Boyd, 1961), p. 33.
3. Michael Millgate, *Faulkner* (London: Oliver and Boyd, 1961), p. 33
4. L.N. de Abruna, "Twentieth-Century Women Writers from the English-speaking Caribbean," *Modern Fiction Studies*, 34:1 (1986).
5. Irving Howe, *William Faulkner* (N.Y.: Vantage Books, 1962).
6. B. Christian, *Black Feminist Criticism* (N.Y.: Pergamon Press, 1985), p. 3.
7. C. Brooks, *William Faulkner* (1963; U.S.A.: Yale University Press, 1976), p. 357.
8. *Ibid.*, p. 7.
9. P. Lowrey, "Concepts of Time in *The Sound and the Fury*," R.S. Downes, ed., *English Institute Essays* (N.Y.: Columbia University Press, 1952).
10. I. Traschen, "The Tragic Form of *The Sound and the Fury,*" *Recent Studies of American Literature*, ed. P.C. Kar and D. Ramkrishna (Hyderabad: ASRC, 1985), p. 464.
11. "Almost always the substances of the worksongs about or by women are sifted through the cry of hard times . . . (these) shape the songs and give even the gayest song an undertone of plaintiveness." Christian, p. 7.

Barthes, Bakhtin and the Faulknerian Counter-Mythology of *Light in August*

MANISHA MUKHOPADHAY

The creation of Yoknapatawpha County implies a dualism central to the works of William Faulkner. Yoknapatawpha, Faulkner's fictional reconstruction of the American South and the land of his birth, expresses his dramatization of what he understood as reality. This involved an awareness of the distinction of a modern society, reified in its history and institutions from an older order of myth and tradition. The creation of Yoknapatawpha was "a way of controlling, of ordering, of giving a shape and a significance to the immense panorama of futility and anarchy which is contemporary history." (Eliot 201)

This dualism of order and disorder, art and reality creates the dual perspective of Faulkner's fiction which views experience as at once meaningless and significant. This dichotomy helps to define the basic premises of Faulkner's fictional world by identifying the conflict between the autonomy of the artist and his immersion in history; his power to create an imaginary world free from the constraints of reality and the spatial and temporal coordinates that bind him to that reality. *Light in August* may be viewed as a significant attempt on Faulkner's part, at finding a way that could explore and dramatize the polyvalent significance of self, history and art in a modern world denied a fixed referential centre. The result is, what Mikhail Bakhtin has called, a truly polyphonic novel that views reality as essentially multiple in nature.

Light in August asserts the realitive nature of the Faulknerian vision. Its multiple discourses construct different versions of reality viewed from different perspectives which complement as well as counterpoint each other. The interaction of these versions of reality viewed from different perspectives constitutes the inner dynamics of the novel. The history of the real South and the Faulknerian meta-history of the mythic Yoknapatawpha are in a creative tension that envelopes the novel. The image of a bipolar society, that is fissured from within, hangs like a spectre over the novel. In *Light in August* Faulkner does not digress into an analysis of Southern history as he does in *Go Down, Moses* or in *Absalom, Absalom!* Instead he focuses on the dialetic produced by the subjective and objective dimensions of history. Thus Christmas' identity crises or Hightower's imprisonment in his self-created myth of his grandfather's heroism parallels the analogous history of the Old South but those are also potent novelistic images of that reality—individuals functioning in a bipolar society preoccupied with honour and shame, victory and defeat, white and black. In this novel the history of the land is internalized in the self-history, is realized and enacted in the biographical mode of existence. *Light in August* focuses on characters who are trying to define, or are in the process of re-defining or are in confusion about, their own identities. They are impelled to assimilate the burden of history—of the individual self and of the land—with the reality of the present moment. In the process they constitute their own mythologies. This mythified history of the self and that of the land are continuums which interact with and interanimate each other. Faulkner rewrites narrative using polyvocal and polymodal narration, fusing different perspectives and novelistic images to arrive at a reality that can accommodate the binary stories of Joe Christmas and Lena Grove, Percy Grimm and Gavin Stevens, the reality of Hightower and that of Byron Bunch and finds a figurative validation in what Roland Wesley has called "the triptych conclusion of the novel." (675)

II

Light in August raises some fundamental questions about the status of the 'real' in Faulkner's fiction. The creation of Yoknapatawpha emphasizes the power of the human mind to rearrange reality through the creative use of language. Yoknapatawpha is a word-oriented world that confronts the 'myth' of reality by mythifying it in turn to produce an 'artificial myth.' (Barthes 147) As Barthes has noted, this reconstituted myth is, in fact, a mythology, a counter-myth that subverts reality by re-creating it. It is the artist's way of countering the dominant myths of a culture that turns reality into an empty signifier and imposes upon it a signification convenient to its own needs. The history of Yoknapatawpha is created and shaped by the imagination of the artist. To Faulkner fictional structure was simply an attempt "to reconcile imagination and pattern." (Gwynn and Blotner, 52)

In *Light in August* this process corresponds to the subversion of the determinants of the novel as a genre—plot, linear narrative and character development. In *Light in August* Faulkner emerges as a modern writer whose subversion of the mimetic tradition led him to rewrite narrative not univocally but contrapuntally, using episodic representation and multiple perspectives, shifting among different plots and characters. Faulknerian discourse cannot be reduced to a fictional rendering of objective reality, it tries to establish a dialogical contact between the subjective and the objective that questions the very notion of the unity of a work of art.

In *Light in August* the scripting of different and various voices are punctuated by theatrical tropes. These different voice-zones are located at different distances from each other and arranged as dialogic counterpoints, they share an essentially ambivalent relationship with the discourse in which they are embedded—the novel as a whole. In *Problems of Dostoevsky's Poetics*, Bakhtin finds it fallacious to reduce Dostoevsky's protagonists 'to finalizing definitions, to find without fail a specific monological authorial idea.' (1984: 229) On the other hand, Bakhtin emphasizes the novel's dependence on the 'living mix of varied and opposing voices, developing and renewing itself,' (1981: 49) as the pre-dominant verbal mode of the novel. These "multiform elements in style and the variform dimensions in speech and voice" are stressed by Bakhtin, insists Patrick Samway, S.J., "since he considers the opposing centripetal and centrifugal natures of language not as a system of grammatical categories but as partaking and expressing a world view." (Honninghausen, 256) The multiple narratives of *Light in August* represent a reality that is fluid. Thus the two main character-zones of the novel, Christmas's and Lena's remain separate and antithetical, each qualifying the other and in the process acquiring an ironic over tone. If the novel insists anything it is that life transcends and resists definition, that incomprehensibility is a part of life's complexity. The novel is full of speculation, confusion and negation. The narrative voices do not necessarily locate the casual chain of human action and motivation. This narrative uncertainty is a part of the novel's reflexive design. Faulkner believed in the plasticity of experience and this is why in his art too, he consciously strove to break down rigidity and boundary, in the process, widening the generic scope of the novel.

III

In dramatizing the duality of the self and the world, Faulkner transforms it from a static opposition into a dialectic that symbolizes the antinomies of experience: life and death, order and chaos, action and inaction, illusion and reality, communication and its failure. Lena Grove travels the road 'with the untroubled unhaste of a change of season' (1967: 47) carrying the seed of life; Joe travels the road running away from himself and others toward death; Joe's rape of Joanna and his self- destructively violent nature are powerfully qualified by the fanatical violence of Percy Grimm; Hightower, conversely, opts for a life of non-action, living and reliving the myth of his grandfather's heroism; Joanna's imprisonment in the puritan-ethic of a patriarchal society is related to Doc Hines' obsession with sex and sin. The juxtaposition of the contraries of experience projects a binary universe that continually divides and fragments, that mythifies reality according to its own needs and forces it on the individual, frustrating his attempt to evolve a counter-mythology of his own.

In this context the reality of Joe Christmas is the most complex novelistic image of *Light in August*. It has an ambivalent relationship with the discourse in which it is embedded. The history of Joe Christmas, intrinsically related to that of the land of his birth, constitute an image of alienation both communal and personal—the isolation of a casteist society and that of a trapped individual. Joe is primarily a man without identity, his fabled negro blood renders him an outcast in both the black and the white world. As Byron observes, "there was something definitely rootless . . . as though no town, no city was his, no street, no walls, no square of earth his home." (27) Christmas is reduced to an empty signifier, literally as well as figuratively. Others mythify him and try to absorb him into their own fiction making process. Doc Hines fulminates about his being the seed of evil; it is he who precipitates the myth about Christmas' being a negro at the orphanage. The dietitian eagerly consumes the myth because it makes it easier to project upon Joe her own guilt-laden personal fictions, as is done by Joanna Burden at a later stage of Joe's life. His foster parent, McEachern thrust upon the child Joe a dehumanized calvinistic ethic of sin, damnation and punishment. As Warwick Wadlington says in *Reading Faulknerian Tragedy,* "All their fictions are informed by the underlying logic of actions-by-proxy epitomized in the Christian drama by original sin and vicarious purifying sacrifice. Joe's social status as an illegitimate orphan . . . who is putatively black corresponds to their Calvinistic versions of original sin, or the curse of predestined damnation." (155) Joe's very existence becomes tantamount to a cultural anomaly, by being neither black nor white he defies his culture's absolute 'either-or' categories and consequently fails to fit into the dominant culture's master-pattern. Because Joe accepts the governing myths of his culture that denies the individual his right to 'be,' he can interpret his situation only according to its dictates. The myth of his culture relentlessly transforms history into nature, forcing the individual to accept its mythical fabrications as the natural order of things, turning appearance into reality. As Barthes says, "myth has the task of giving an historical intention a natural justification, and making contingency appear eternal." Myth, continues Barthes, "remove(s) from things their human meaning so as to make them signify a human insignificance. The function of myth is to empty reality." (155)

Joe encounters the passivity of his situation by assuming responsibility for it: "thirty years that I have lived to make me what I chose to be." (251) He thinks that he has "chosen" the 'savage and lonely street' (243) of his perpetual flight of his own volition. His violence is part of this denial of passivity. Hence Joe is both the actor and the victim in the drama of Joanna Burden's rape and murder. The internal and external antagonism between Joe and Joanna is part of the binary orientation of Faulkner's novelistic discourse: the dichotomous arrangement of male and female, white and black, mind and body. Joe fears women and sexuality; "On all sides, even within him, the bodiless fecund: mellow voices of negro women murmured. It was as though he and all the manshaped life about him had been returned to the lightless hot wet primogenitive Female. He began to run." (107) Joe shuns the female world symbolized by the black women, yet seeks sexual gratification with Joanna, all the while resisting Joanna's sexual domination and his own submission to that dominance. Joanna, too, exercises her sexual choice with an ingrained feeling of guilt. Her subconscious craving for sexual expression is counter-pointed by her conscious condemnation of it. The patriarchal puritanical mindset conditions Joanna to suppress her natural physical expression and prevents her to attain a psychosexual wholeness. Thus instead of nurturing Joe in a meaningful way she fragments him further. Joanna, unable to come to terms with her sexuality, hovers between the two extremes of celibacy and nymphomania. And after her menopausal crisis when she reverts to spinsterhood she refuses to free Joe. Her insistence on prayer as a deliverance from sin echoes that of McEachern's.

Joe consistently rejects the larger religious drama that envelopes him, he accepts McEachern's corporal punishment but rejects the religious intonations; he refuses to be a mere player in Joanna's drama of sin and repentance. To Joanna, like her abolitionist grandfather, the word 'negro' is an abstraction; her cry "Negro! Negro!" (245) reduces Joe to the level of an abstraction—a subhuman entity, when she 'forces Joe to live her own myth' of a black lawyer, Joe refuses the role as given. Joe's beheading of Joanna is an illusory attempt on Joe's part to free himself from the dominance of women, codified religion and sex embodied by Joanna.

The discourse of Joe Christmas is not merely one of the need for recognition, which Carla Kaplan identifies as one of the most important tropes of modern fiction but—as Charles Taylor has written in *Multiculturalism and "The Politics of Recognition"* "of the condition in which the attempt to be recognized can fall." (qtd. Kaplan 153) The reality of a public world that encloses the subjective world of Joe and sets up a counterpoint to it continually thwarts his need for self-definition. Christmas' own attempt to analyse his situation brings out this dichotomy: "I have been farther in these seven days [following the murder of Joanna] than in all the thirty years, he thinks. But I have never got outside that circle. I have never broken out of the ring of what I have already done and cannot undo." (321) And then the quasi-omniscient narrator focuses on "the black shoes, smelling of a Negro: that mark on his ankles, the gauge definite and ineradicable of the black tide creeping up his legs, moving from his feet upward as death moves." (321) Likewise, Joe's realization that all he wanted was peace when juxtaposed against the agitated run that has been his life, results in a startling sense of dislocation: "'That was all I wanted', he thinks, in a quiet and slow amazement, "That was all, for thirty years. That didn't seem to be a whole lot to ask in thirty years.'" (313) It is characteristic of the Faulknerian counter-myth to insist that Joe's attainment of peace can only coincide with the irony of his death.

Christmas solicits death, his actions in Mottstown imply a ritualistic self-sacrifice: he visits a barber, buys himself a new outfit. Even at the moment of his death he does not resist it: "He crouched behind that overturned table and let them shoot him to death, with that loaded and unfired pistol in hand." (425) At the moment of his death, Joe figuratively becomes the black cross whose shadowy burden humanity continues to bear, Joe Christmas at the moment of his death is transformed from a passive signifier of social myths to a potent countermyth. His death at the hands of Percy Grimm demythifies the dominant structures of his culture, for the culture and its history precipitate the murder. To the members of the community who witness his death, he becomes a reality that cannot be denied: "For a long moment he looked up at them with peaceful and unfathomable and unbearable eyes. Then his face, body all seemed to collapse, to fall in upon itself, and from out the slashed garments about his hips and loins the pent black blood seemed to rush like a released breath. It seemed to rush out of his pale body like the rush of sparks from a rising rocket; upon that black blast the man seemed to rise soaring into their memories forever and ever. They are not to lose it, in whatever peaceful valleys, beside whatever placid and reassuring streams of old age, in the mirroring faces of whatever children they will contemplate old disasters and newer hopes. It will be there, musing, quiet, steadfast, not fading and not particularly threatful, but of itself alone serene, of itself alone triumphant." (439-40) Yet by making Joe's death a self-contained reality and not an instrument of significant change, Faulkner stresses the fact that the community remain mere spectators, they are unable to become religious witnesses, unlike Reverend Shegog's congregration in *The Sound and the Fury* where the community becomes an active participant in the Christian drama of redemption through sacrifice. This is part of Faulkner's inversion of the myth of Christianity: Christ redefined human identity while Christmas is a man without identity; Christ stressed the equality of men, Christmas has to function in an inequal and bipolar society. It is stressed by the visual picture of Joe who appears to be white in the negro church where he is perceived to be the very image of Satan. This inverted cultural drama is substantiated by the dichotomous arrangement of the true religion of man symbolized by the figure of crucified Christ and the negative dimension religion has acquired by getting codified into inflexible, dehumanized patterns symbolized by Hines, McEachern and the Burdens. It has become death-oriented: "not love, not life, forbidding it to others." (347)

IV

The role of witness, that the community fails to assume, falls upon Hightower. Hightower is the novel's witness. Hightower embodies the action-observation dichotomy symbolized by the word 'witness' who is both the agent and the patient, Hightower is a compulsive fiction-maker. Hightower's subjective fiction-making parallels Faulkner's. By using the church pulpit to propagate his private myth of his grandfather's glorious death instead of the shared narrative of Christianity, Hightower invites the community to participate in his myth. Though Faulkner sees the limitations of Hightower's personal fiction, he nevertheless acknowledges the reality of it as a potent novelistic image. As Bakhtin says, "The image of another's language and outlook on the world simultaneously represented and representing is . . . typical of the novel; the greatest novelistic images (for example, the figure of Don Quixote) belong precisely to this type." (1981: 45) Hightower anticipates the failure of his mythology and his consequent banishment from community, yet, in that very failure he locates a kind of triumph and overriding of conventions. His grandfather's death while stealing chickens is for him a triumph of non-conformism, a kind of mockery of death. Moreover, Hightower's vision of his grandfather is not a mere re-living glory: "I have been a single instant of darkness in which a horse galloped and a gun crashed." (465) He is both the writer and the player in this perpetual drama of death and a negation of death. Instead of renewing the communal narrative of Christianity, Hightower makes a travesty of it. Hightower's attempt to defy death by transforming the moment of his grandfather's death into a kind of eternal present that can be perpetually re-created, renders him a prisoner in life. He becomes an image of alienation. However, there is a movement towards rehabilitation. Through Byron's mediation, Hightower gets to participate both directly and vicariously in the lives of others.

The event of the birth of Lena's son rejuvenates him, "Life

comes to the old man yet," (383) he says of himself. He reads Shakespeare's *Henry IV* instead of the self-obsessed verse of Tennyson, which was his staple reading. And his re-orientation towards life seems complete when he perceives in Lena's baby a link with posterity. For the first time his belief in immortality finds a concrete human embodiment. He also feels oneness with nature, "feeling the intermittent sun, the heat; smelling the savage fecund odour of the earth, the wood, the loud silence." (384) But Hightower's most significant attempt to come out of his self-enclosed myth is his acknowledgement of responsibility in his wife's death. He sees for the first time that he has been the "author and instrument of her shame and death." (462) This leads to self-knowledge by destroying his illusion of being a self-contained entity: "If I am the instrument of her despair and death, then I am in turn instrument of someone outside myself." (465)

Yet it remains doubtful whether Hightower's re-orientation toward life can be termed a spiritual renewal. Hightower's visionary wheel in which the past and the present merge with the faces of the major characters of the novel and space and time coalesce can only be called a partial epiphany. In his epiphany, the reality of human suffering is qualified by the fantasy about his grandfather.

V

In stark contrast to the tragic reality of Christmas and Hightower is the pastoral idyll of Lena Grove and Byron Bunch. Lena's story provides a framework to the narratives of Joe and Hightower, creating a moral ambience that generates irony and affirms the multidimensional element of Faulkner's narrative art. Lena walks the tragic world of Christmas as an embodiment of contentment. Lena's subjective perception of her own situation contrasts sharply to the objective reality of her situation—she is an unmarried woman in an advanced state of pregnancy, travelling alone. She is so enamoured in her own fiction of finding out the father of her child that she effectively neutralizes the potential antagonism of a patriarchal society. The linearity of Lena's journey and her absolute certainty of achieving her goal are immune to disruption. Yet Lena's contentment resides on a tendency to refuse to acknowledge a reality that is not agreeable to her—Lucas's betrayal of Lena and his refusal to accept the responsibility of Lena and her child. In fact, the world of

Lena and Byron cannot escape the implications of the complex human realities that define the stories of Joe Christmas and Hightower.

It is to be noted that *Light in August* ends as a continuing discourse between the reader and the furniture dealer who narrates the journey of Lena and Byron. The furniture dealer is a compulsive fiction-maker and his anecdote about Byron and Lena is an instance of his own subjective fiction-making, replete with his own worldview about love and life in general. His prophecy about Lena and Byron's future together, remains just that, a prophecy. The tensions that characterize the relationship of Joe and Joanna and immobilize Hightower are transformed by the furniture dealer to mere human follies that do not prevent "the good stock peopling . . . the good earth." (384)

The sexual tension between Joe and Joanna finds an echo in the deferred physical union of Byron and Lena. Moreover, Byron's Quixotic assumption of the role of self-proclaimed protector of Lena that frees him from his reclusive stance and engages him in worldly action, is ironic. Lena's baby objectifies to Byron her lost virginity. Though he stays with Lena—"I'd be a dog if I quit now" (479)—the child is forever there to undermine his utopia. Further, Lena's baby links the novel's narratives of alienation. Mrs. Hines perceives him as an incarnation of Joe; he further parallels Joe in his status as a potential Christ-figure—with Byron as surrogate father, his family is an image of the holy family of Christ. Hightower, too, views him as his link with posterity. He is a receptacle for the legacy of the past and the promise of the future, renewal and destruction. Lena and Byron's linear journey is permanently disrupted by the tonal complexity of the narratives of Christmas and Hightower.

VI

In arguing the dialogic relationship of myth, history and narrative which produces the Faulknerian countermyth, it is important to stress the process by which Faulkner reverses conventional signification. The triad of word, meaning and reality is stretched to its limit. The word 'nigger' is one of the most enduring myths of Yoknapatawpha. The novel subjects the word to a relentless scrutiny until it reveals the dehumanizing societal pattern that has created it. The fact that Christmas 'appears' to be white enhances the irony of the whole situation and turns the word into an abstraction: "He don't look anymore a nigger than I do." (330) By blurring the distinction between appearance and reality, Faulkner makes the word tantamount to the guilt-consciousness of the human race. Likewise, by superimposing their gender archetypes of Lilith and Eve on Joanna and Lena, Faulkner stresses both the historical continuity of the cultural stereotyping of women and the ongoing cultural drama of suppression of the female voice. By an ironic reversal, the symbol of the cross, the image of crucified Christ have been appropriated by codified religion which uses it to perpetuate the status quo. Faulkner de-mythifies the dominant myths and reveals the historical reality that forms the bases of such cultural constructs.

The range of voices that compose the novel varies from the chameleon-like voice of the quasi-ominiscient narrator who dons different guises in the different character-zones of the novel to the cryptic voice of Joe marked by the suppressed confusions, tensions and antagonisms that torment him; from the self-obsessed rhetoric of Hightower's fantasy to the simple, earthy and colloquial dimension of Lena's speech; from the mechanized voice of McEachern to Doc Hines' monomaniac ranting; from the sonorous church music to the voices of the townspeople of Jefferson. All these voices are in dialogic contact with each other and shape Faulkner's doubly-oriented discourse—simultaneously representing and being represented.

Multiple voices coincide with multiple perspectives and a fragmented time-scheme. Our first image of Lena construed by the omniscient narrator is qualified by Armstid's impression of her, which foreshadows that of Byron Bunch. We first encounter Joe through Byron and then are given the chronotopic recapitulation of Joe's existence, as Bakhtin says, "The image of man is always intrinsically chronotopic." (1981: 85) We have Gavin Stevens' subjective rationalization of Joe's situation as black-white dichotomy that undermines the complex human reality of Joe's being. The end of the novel is narrated by a surrogate-narrator. These voices and perspectives break down the definitiveness of authorial omniscience and assert the fluidity of experiential reality that is refractive and multiple. As Faulkner says, "the aim of every artist is to arrest motion which is life and hold it fixed so that 100 years later, when a stranger looks at it, it moves again since it is life." (1968: 253) This dialectic of dynamism and inertia is the governing artistic principle of the novel, embodied by the central image of the novel: that of the road with which the novel begins and ends: the road that Christmas travels in circles and the road that stretches out before Lena in an uncomplicated lineality; the road through which Percy Grimm pursues Christmas. As Bakhtin notes in *The Dialogic Imagination*:

> On the road the spatial and temporal series defining human fates and lives combine with one another in distinctive ways, even as they become more complex and more concrete by the collapse of social distances. The chronotope of the road is both a point of new departures and a place for events to find their denouement. Time, as it were, fuses together with space and flows in it (forming the road); this is the source of the rich metaphorical expansion on the image of the road as a course: 'the course of life', . . . 'the course of history' and so on, varied and multileveled are the ways in which road is turned into a metaphor. (244)

VII

The Faulknerian counter-myth of *Light in August* corresponds to a de-mythification of history. Faulkner views history not as a narrative of past events but as a continuum that envelops the past and the present and affects what men do or suffer. For beyond the question of the documentation of history, is the question of the cultural interpretation of history, that process of cultural osmosis through which precipitations of history enter the experiential reality of the individual: the fragmentation wrought by history along racial lines destroys Joe Christmas internally and externally; the heroic code of ante-bellum south penetrates Hightower's fantasy and alienates him from society and meaningful human action; the Calvinistic dogma robs Doc Hines and McEachern of their essential humanity and reduces them to the level of automatons; the cultural script with its deterministic assignment of role-models destroys Mrs. Hightower and Joanna Burden. This ironic interplay between the subjective and objective dimensions of history transforms the Faulknerian meta-history of Yoknapatawpha into an 'artificial mythology' (Barthes 155) that is counter-mythical in intent. Faulknerian meta-history functions as a repository of the experiential reality of a race, that reflects, scrutinizes and explores the people's self-image. In Faulkner's fiction the history of the land and that of the people are never to be separated. Within this moral and aesthetic ambience the characters of *Light in August* become the living metaphors of the reality that surrounds and shapes them. These overlapping histories create the different strata of reality the novel encompasses and articulates. Thus, the separate plot paradigms of Christmas, Hightower and Lena are arranged as counterpoints in a dialogic relationship with one another.

Light in August scrutinizes the precepts of individualism and genealogy that are the basic components of human history; which Cheryl Lester considers to be conservative constructions: identity, autonomy, race, tradition, lineage, breeding, exchange of value, class, gender, isolation and difference. Just as Lacan's concept of the gaze seeks to explode the myth of a unified, unfragmented subject by stressing the conceptual double-image that the individual sees in the mirror that provokes simultaneous attraction and repulsion, Faulkner, too, destroys the notions of unity and symmetry of fiction by creating a reality that is fragmented and multiple, in a continual dialectical contention with itself. And this is what makes *Light in August* a cultural testimonial.

By focussing upon the attempts of the characters to come to terms with the flux that is life, the novel delineates the transaction between the human mind and the objective world. This in turn mirrors the creative process. The artist, too, is caught up in the dialectic of the self and the world: the work of art offers the artist's personal vision for public scrutiny. The artist's counter-myth is to interact with the personal myths of the readers and society. This process is what makes writing a cultural act. In *Light in August*, Faulkner relates the artist's transcreation of reality to man's attempt to extract a meaning from and impose a pattern upon human life which is also an attempt at self-definition. Faulkner reveals the essential futility of such an endeavour. Yet he never denies the fact that the attempt itself is significant and is a fundamental human need. In this paradox Faulkner locates the irony of history and that of the human situation.

Works Cited

Bakhtin, M.M. *The Dialogic Imagination: Four Essays by M.M. Bakhtin.* Ed. Michael Holquist. Trans. Caryrl Emerson and Michael Holquist. Austin: Univ. of Texas Press, 1981.

_____. *Problems of Dostoevsky's Poetics.* Ed. and trans. Caryl Emerson. Minneapolis: U of Minnesota Press, 1984.

Barthes, Ronald. *Mythologies.* Trans. Anette Lavers. New York: Hill and Wang, 1973.

Eliot, T.S. "*Ulysses*, Order and Myth" in *James Joyce: Two Decades of Criticism*, ed. Seon Givens. New York: Vanguard Press, 1948. First published in *The Dial*, 75, November 1923, 480-83.

Faulkner, William. *Absalom, Absalom!* New York Modern Library, 1966.

_____. *Faulkner in the University: Class Conferences at the University of Virginia 1957-58.* Ed. Frederick L. Gwynn and Joseph Blotner. Charlottesville: Univ. Press. of Virginia.

_____. *Light in August.* Modern Library, New York, 1967.

_____. *Lion in the Garden: Interviews with William Faulkner, 1926-62.* Ed. James B. Meriwether and Michael Millgate. New York: Random House, 1968.

_____. *The Sound and the Fury.* Penguin Modern Classics, 1964.

Kaplan, Carla. "Undesirable Desire: Citizenship and Romance in Modern American Fiction." *Modern Fiction Studies*, 43.1, Spring 1997. 144-69.

Lester, Cheryl "From Place to Place in *The Sound and the Fury*: The Syntax of Interrogation." *Modern Fiction Studies* 34.2, Summer 1988. 141-55.

Samway, Patrick S.J. "Narration and Naming in *The Reivers*" in *Faulkner's Discourse: An International Symposium.* Ed. Lothar Honnighausen. Max Niyemeyer Verlag Tubingen, 1989. 254-62.

Taylor, Charles. *Multiculturalism and 'The Politics of Recognition.'* Princeton, N. J.: Princeton Univ. Press, 1992.

Waddlington, Warwick. *Reading Faulknerian Tragedy.* Ithaca: Cornell Univ. Press, 1989.

Wesley, Ronald. "Ends and Loose-Ends: The Triptych Conclusion of *Light in August.*" *Modern Fiction Studies*, 31.4, Winter 1984. 675-88.

Rosa and the Sutpen Reality: A Reading of *Absalom, Absalom!*

NEERJA JAYAL CHAND

> I have the horrid suspicion that if enough people were to say "Boo," the entire structure of *Absalom, Absalom!* would disappear in smoke.
>
> Clifton Fadiman

Published first in 1936, William Faulkner's novel *Absalom, Absalom!* continues to arouse a lot of critical attention because of its complicated structure and the ultimate creation of an enigmatic sense of void and vacuum, embedded at the core of the Supten reality. In this, Rosa Coldfield or simply "Miss Rosa" has a unique and interesting role to play, both as a narrator and as an active participant in the unfolding of the Sutpen story and its eventual tragic conclusion. Critics[1] have emphasized the "highly romanticized" or even "Gothic" nature of Miss Rosa's version of the Sutpen story while referring to the narrative distortions that occur within each of the four principal points of view—of Miss Rosa, Mr. Compson, Shreve McCannon and Quentin Compson. However, for a more balanced critical evaluation, one must look again and explore further the role of Miss Rosa, especially in terms of the positive truth-revealing contribution it makes to the reader's awareness of the Sutpen material and of Faulkner's novel as a whole.

Since Rosa is one of the four narrators in the novel and the only actual participant in a personal drama (other three being one or two generations away) a study of Miss Rosa becomes both an analysis of the character and an examination of the structure of the novel itself. Commenting on the technique of multiple-narrators in his novel, William Faulkner acknowledged the aptness of the blackbird metaphor for understanding the 'truth' of the novel:

> It was, as you say, thirteen ways of looking at a blackbird. But the truth, I would like to think, comes out, when the reader has read all these thirteen different ways of looking at the blackbird, the reader has his own fourteenth image of that blackbird which I would like to think is the truth.[2]

In a sense, this 'fourteenth way,' the reader's, functions in the novel as a central vacuum: the Sutpen drama as reality is a void which no amount of verbal reiteration can communicate. Each narration can only be partial truth, and the revelation of each works in both directions, toward communicating a sense of the drama, but also a sense of the narrator. Thus, the structure of *Absalom, Absalom!* appears almost centrifugal: the power of each narration heightening the intensity of the reader's curiosity and sense of tragedy, yet making him aware, at each re-telling, of his distance from the center, from the 'truth' of Sutpen, as the narrator too continually realizes a sense of hollowness in what he says, of "absence" from the central truth. Miss Rosa demonstrates this structural principle of the novel, not only by her own sense of inability to penetrate the Sutpen family reality, but also in her apprehension of the fleeting quality of this reality itself.

While much critical discussion has centered on the boy-symbol which is an integral part of Sutpen's design, there is another child-figure in the novel, Miss Rosa Coldfield. The child metaphor becomes an identifying motif for Miss Rosa from the opening page of the novel:

> Miss Coldfield . . . sitting so bolt upright in the straight hard chair that was so tall for her that her legs hung straight and rigid . . . clear of the floor with that air of impotent and static rage like children's feet . . .[3]

Rosa identifies herself as a child when asked by her dying sister to care for the Sutpen children, when in actual age she is younger than they: "I, a child, a child, mind you," "I saw Ellen die with only me a child to turn to and ask to protect her remaining child." (15,18) Indeed, in Ellen's eyes her sister is a child, and Rosa's offer to prepare Judith for married life receives but mocking response. (71) And, in point of fact, Rosa Coldfield retains her child-status by affirming her role of a daughter *vis-a-vis* Goodhue Coldfield until his death and far into her own middle years.

So it is that in her opening narration (Chapter I), Rosa Coldfield perceives herself in the role of a child, unwilling or unable to cope with adult realities. Yet, it is through Quentin and Mr. Compson that the reader learns how little of childhood, of its carefree and joyful nature, that Rosa actually must have known. Quentin sees in her, not the child with adult responsibility conferred by an older sister, but

> the figure of a little girl, in the *prim* skirts and pantalettes, the smooth *prim* decorous braids, of the *dead* time. She seemed to stand, to *lurk*, being the neat picket fence of a small, *grimly* middleclass yard or lawn, looking out upon the whatever *ogre world* of that quiet village street with that air of children *born too late* into their parents' lives and *doomed* to contemplate all human behavior through the complex and needless follies of adults. (21-22, emphasis added)

The descriptive vocabulary chosen here by Faulkner (cf. the emphasis) prepares the denial of childhood that Rosa was subjected to by her maiden aunt.

The account of Rosa's early life (Chapter III) in the "closed masonry of females" (59) that was her home indicates that the child's preparation for girlhood was instead a distortion of her femininity:

> In a grim mausoleum air of Puritan righteousness and outraged female vindictiveness Miss Rosa's childhood was passed . . . while she waited for the infancy and childhood with which nature had confounded and betrayed her to overtake the disapprobation regarding any and every thing which could penetrate the walls of that house through the agency of any man. (60)

And, by comparison to Sutpen's Judith and Henry, this "face which never spoke . . . this small body . . . with its air of curious and paradoxical awkwardness"(65): indeed, this young sister of Ellen's could not have even been 'seen' by Thomas Sutpen, for she is a type of invisible figure, neither properly a child, nor quite a normal young maiden. Rosa is, rather, a 'maidenservant,' and it is with this skilful double view of her childhood that Faulkner prepares the reader for Miss Rosa's narrative (Chapter V) which will be for her both revelation of Henry's fateful act as well as communication of her private world of childhood.

In Rosa's narrative, two identifying motifs come together, that of childhood and a woman-motif that will be seen to function of presenting the main 'problem' of the novel, the truth-seeking about the Sutpen story. The image which links the two, child and woman, is that of wistaria: "Once there was (they cannot have told you this either) a summer of wistaria," (143) an image that is both private and personal, as chosen by Rosa, and in Faulkner's usage, a linking of the opening scene of Chapter I ("the dim coffin-smelling gloom sweet and over-sweet with the twice-bloomed wistaria," (8) to the continuation of that afternoon's session in Chapter V. As the 'substance of remembering,' the scent of wistaria summons up in Rosa's memory, in almost Proustian fashion, the childhood that was not.

> It was a vintage year of wistaria: vintage year being sweet conjunction of root bloom and urge. . . . But root and urge I do insist and claim, for had I not heired too from all the unsistered Eves since the Snake? (144)

To have been a child, Rosa would have to have become a woman; and in her unfulfilled, virginal state, she has been denied that metamorphosis, "warped chrysalis of that blind perfect seed." (144) Ellen the sister had been transformed ("swamp-hatched butterfly," 69), and her daughter Judith seemed to become the example for Rosa of the crossing of the threshold toward womanhood: "fourteen, four years younger than Judith, four years later than Judith's moment which only virgins know: when the entire spirit's bent is one anonymous climaxless epicene and unravished nuptial." (145) Through Judith, then, through focusing on her 'moment,' Rosa imagines leaving her childhood and following Judith into her relationship with Charles Bon:

> There must have been some seed he left, to cause a child's vacant fairy-tale to come alive in that garden. Because I was not spying when I would follow her. I was not spying, though you will say I was. And even if it was spying, it was not jealousy, because I did not love him. (146)

'Him,' 'the shape without even a face' (146): this is the image of Charles Bon, the photograph-lover whom Rosa can only contemplate by stealth, (147) as if capturing her womanhood in a dream-existence, each view of the image being a 'rehearsal,' a reiteration of that one step, not to be taken, toward womanhood.

Thus, while Rosa's experience of Charles Bon is that of the 'might-have-been,' (149) it is no less real: "that first year . . . during which Ellen talked to me of trousseau (and it my trousseau), of all the dreamy panoply of surrender which was my surrender," (149) for Rosa, this is a virtual existence, a love without hope, yet an absence that becomes more real than presence or possession, "'Don't talk to me of love but let me tell you, who know already more of love than you will ever know or need.'" (148)

The experience of potential womanhood is repeated for Rosa with Thomas Sutpen. The non-proposal of marriage is, for him, an 'interval of sanity' in an existence of madness, while for Rosa, a childhood of *cannot* is annulled in 'one red instant's fierce obliteration.' (163) This relationship, so brief, so tenuous ("no place, no niche, no interval for reply," (164) becomes no more than the love of Rosa for Charles, an absence that imposes as presence: "I was that sun, who believed that he . . . was not oblivious of me but only unconscious and receptive like the swamp-freed pilgrim feeling earth and tasting sun and light again and aware of neither but only of darkness' and morass' lack." (167-68) And, after the momentary illumination of possibility, Rosa's 'man'—'lose him, weep him'—becomes once again a 'walking shadow,' (171) dead to her before actually killed, and with him, the potential womanhood of Rosa, dead also.

The motif of childhood, then, serves not only to identify the figure of Rosa Coldfield but also to represent the particularity of her relationship to the Sutpen history. Moreover, the repetition of this motif in the closing chapter of the novel, where Quentin is narrator and Rosa participant in the drama, serves to link the various features of the characterization of Miss Rosa to the total story of Sutpen. In this final episode, Rosa becomes both childlike by her whimpering, yet impelled to seek the truth that the Sutpen house contains. She is described as both panting and whimpering—"It seemed to him [Quentin] that he could still hear her whimpering panting . . . she whispered whimpered . . . but he could hear her hurried breathing" (365) and one recalls the ending of previous narrated episode, the conversation (reconstructed by Quentin and Shreve) in which Bon reveals his Negro blood to Henry: "Suddenly Henry grasps the pistol, jerks it free of Bon's hand stands so, the pistol in his hand, panting and panting"; "Henry whirls; in the same motion he hurls the pistol from him and stoops again, gripping Bon by both shoulders, panting." (358) Thus, this image links Henry and Rosa in a facing-up to a truth; and for Rosa herself, the child and the almost-woman unite to confront the reality of Henry.

In this final episode, two child figures emerge, linked once again, as in the triumvirate of the Sutpen house: Clytie too is described here as 'doll-like' (368) while Rosa becomes also a 'mechanical doll' returning home to a 'doll-sized house.' (371) The two women are drawn together further by a repetition of the gesture with which Clytie stopped Rosa on another visit to the Sutpen house, the day of Bon's death: "the two of us joined by that hand and arm which held us, like a fierce rigid umbilical cord, twin sistered to the fell darkness which had produced her." (140) And in the final episode, the hand is 'struck away,' the 'sister' is toppled, and as Quentin picks her up, Clytie seems "no more than a handful of sticks concealed in a rag bundle." (370) Rosa ("almost as light as Clytie") acts here in iron determination, no longer entirely a child, the iron metaphor having carried through from the first description of Rosa to the iron-cold of Quentin's room (360) and finally to the 'dead rigid hard grip' of Rosa's fingers, a 'small mass of wire.' (365) In fact, it was Clytie who first saw beyond the child-facade of Rosa to this determination to know and experience: "she did me more grace and respect than anyone else I knew; I knew that from the instant I had entered the door, to her of who knew me I was no child. 'Rosa?' I cried. 'To me? To my face?'" (139) Thus, the child-figure has traversed the novel in both time and understanding, marking the stages of Rosa's awareness of the truth of herself and of Sutpen.

While the motif of child-woman structures Rosa Coldfield's participation in the Sutpen story, the theme of womanhood, on a more general level, carries the figure of Rosa beyond a personal drama and links her narrative to other forms of witness to the Sutpen tale. There is, in Rosa's telling of her own story, a concept of womanhood beyond the level of individual personality, and one which unites Clytie, Judith and Rosa in an existence of waiting for Sutpen, of waiting to be needed by him in the rebuilding of the

Hundred. "So we waited for him. We led the busy eventless lives of three nuns in a barren and poverty-stricken convent . . . three creatures . . . in whom sex was some forgotten atrophy like the rudimentary gills we call the tonsils." (155) This image of cloister and celibacy appears elsewhere, in Bon's description, to Henry, of the life of the octoroons: "creatures taken at childhood, culled and chosen and raised more carefully than any white girl, any nun." (117) Moreover, the octoroon who "reigns, wise supine and all powerful" recalls the child-Rosa, who was not a child but a watcher, a listener, an instrument of communication of adult-world disaster:

> that rapport with the fluid cradle of events (time) which she had acquired or cultivated by listening beyond closed doors not to what she heard there, but by becoming supine and receptive . . . listening to the prefever's temperature of disaster. (66)

The link between Rosa's child-life and the octoroon's way of life begins, moreover, on the first page of the novel, where into the wistaria vine outside Rosa's window come sparrows "in random gusts, making a dry vivid dusty sound before going away." (7) In Bon's conversation with Henry, the octoroons are compared to unique sparrows who do not come under God's universal Providence, but are subject to the limited providence of the white man. (115) Thus, the child-woman Rosa, the hun-women of Sutpen's house, the octoroon: all merge in a picture of womanhood that is denied its fulfillment, its full definition.[4]

While the themes of child and of womanhood are used to define the character of Rosa Coldfield and to integrate her point of view into the total Sutpen narrative, they operate also on an even deeper level, as a paradigmatic structure of truth-seeking in the novel. What Rosa Coldfield's child quality implies is, most importantly, the failure to attain full womanhood: it is a lack, an "absence" from womanness that forms the child in Rosa. Moreover, the same absence of fulfillment characterizes other major women figures of the novel: 'half'-sister, 'unwived widow,' while Ellen Coldfield and her spinster aunt escape into respective worlds of unreality.

Most significantly, Rosa participates directly in the drama surrounding Charles Bon's death, and it is this experience of truth-seeking which demonstrates for her, and for the reader, the impossibility of giving reality's weight to the event. On the day of

Bon's death, Rosa hurries toward Sutpen's Hundred, toward the act itself, yet her motion is stopped by Clytie, 'Cerberus,' 'sphinx face':

> and I running out of the bright afternoon into the thunderous silence of that brooding house where I could see nothing at first: then gradually the face, the Sutpen face not approaching, not swimming up out of the gloom, but already there, rock-like and firm and antedating time and house and doom and all. (136)

> The face stopping me dead (not my body: it still advanced, ran on: but I, myself, that deep existence which we lead. (137)

Clytie, the embodiment of the impenetrability of truth, stops Rosa here, and at the same time arouses in her a realization of herself as 'self-mesmered fool,' (140) as acting in a dream-state, as having always acted in a dream. The "might-have-been which is more true than truth" (143) appears here as not only the avoidance of recognizing the fact of death (Rosa has a momentary vision of routine reality, (140-41) but as avoidance of the might-have-been woman in Miss Rosa herself. As it is, Rosa is stopped short by Clytie, not by 'the Negro, the woman' but by 'it,' (140) that is, the Sutpen reality; and by the figure of Judith, embodying most particularly the personal might-have-been, the dream-love.

> and I stopped in running's midstride again though my body, blind unsentient barrow of deluded clay and breath, still advanced: And how I saw that what she held in that lax and negligent hand was the photograph, the picture of herself in his metal case which she had given him, held casual and forgotten against her flank as any interrupted pastime book. (142)[5]

Rosa thus awakens into a reality that brings regret—"why did I wake since waking I shall never sleep again?" (143) while even this 'reality' becomes its own dream-state, becomes negation of the act of murder, for Rosa, Clytie and Judith:

> No, there had been no shot. That sound was merely the sharp and final clap—of a door between us and all that was, all that might have been—a retroactive severance of the stream of

> event: a forever crystallized instant in imponderable time accomplished by three weak yet indomitable women which, preceding the accomplished fact which we declined, refused, robbed the brother of the prey, reft the murderer of a victim for his very bullet. (158)

The receding contours of the very act of Sutpen murdering Sutpen image the elusiveness of the truth of this family.

Stasis and movement, act and dream, reality and shadow—these are metaphors which express the dichotomy of narration, so many words that truth may still elude. Bon and Sutpen 'elude' Miss Rosa: she reiterates 'I never saw him,' the phrase referring to the once ogre-figure of Sutpen as well as to Bon about whom, alive and dead, Rosa could only conjecture. Thomas Sutpen of the post-war period appears elsewhere to Rosa a 'sentient though nerveless shell,' (159) living in a 'dream-cloudy shell' (163) on what had become 'Sutpen's One.' (168) And as the reality seems to evacuate from this once demon-like figure, so too the novel ends with the return of 'ghosts,' of Henry and Clytie, of Jim Bond, the idiot shadow of his ancestors, 'wraith-like and insubstantial.' (375) And the house itself, echoing in 'hollow profundity' (366) becomes nothing more than a 'monstrous tinder-dry rotten shell,' (375) ready to be burned.

The images link with one another, as do the various narrators, about the central reality of Sutpen. Yet, like "might-have-been" of Miss Rosa, the novel forms around a void which, by its perpetual "absence," imposes a presence more solid and meaningful than each of the narrators' versions. In a sense, the novel is the vacuum of which Shreve speaks, (361) filled with 'wraithlike and indomitable anger and pride,' and also with unfulfilled dreams and ghosts more real than the persons who try to exorcise them.

NOTES

1. Irving Howe, *William Faulkner: A Critical Study*; Frederic Hoffman, *William Faulkner*; Richard Adams, *Faulkner: Myth and Motion* and others.
2. Frederic J. Hoffman and Olga Vickery, ed., *Faulkner in the University: Class Conference at the University of Virginia, 1957-1958*

(Charlottesville: The University of Virginia Press, 1959).

3. William Faulkner, *Absalom, Absalom!* (Modern Library Edition, New York, 1964).

4. And even Milly Jones may be admitted to this group, for she too is a child-figure (363) whom Sutpen both sees and does not see, who supplants Rosa in her sister Ellen's bed, (134) and yet does not attain status in what Sutpen refers to as his stable.

5. In point of fact, the picture in the metal case is of the octoroon wife of Charles Bon. But of importance here is that Rosa Coldfield sees, in Judith's apparent indifference to the picture's meaningfulness, an indictment of her relationship to Charles in the light of Rosa's dream of such a relationship.

Thomas Sutpen: Ahab of the South

AMINA AMIN

Like all his major novels, Faulkner's *Absalom, Absalom!* is rooted in 'social reality' and 'historical perspective.' But to insist only on this feature of the novel is to limit both its range and profundity. At one level, Thomas Sutpen the central protagonist is the product of Faulkner's response to the ethos of his native South. But as Michael Millgate rightly observes, "the story of Sutpen has a range of reverberation extending far beyond the limitations of its Southern setting." (159) This argument is also supported by Cleanth Brooks, who insists that the character of Thomas Sutpen cannot be taken as an 'example' or 'emblematic' of the typical Southern Planter. (283)

The diverse features of Faulkner's style in *Absalom, Absalom!* have led critics to locate influences of both American and European writers on the work. Claims have been made of Faulkner being the 'inheritor' and 'a major twentieth century representative' of the American romance. This is not surprising in view of Faulkner himself acknowledging Hawthorne, Melville, Twain and James as "predecessors" and "masters from whom we learned our craft."

Referring to the Gothic characteristics of *Absalom, Absalom!* Millgate points out the close resemblance between *Absalom, Absalom!* and Hawthorne's *The House of the Seven Gables* and that between *Absalom, Absalom!* and Charlotte Bronte's *Jane Eyre*. And yet he also observes how the 'Gothic' in both *The House of the Seven Gables* and *Jane Eyre* is different from that of *Absalom, Absalom!* marked as the latter is by a kind of "uninhibited masculine violence." (163) Among nineteenth-century writers, according to him, only Melville's *Moby Dick* stands in this particular line. However it is his remark, 'There may indeed be traces of Captain Ahab in Faulkner's presentation of Sutpen,' that I find pertinent for the purpose of showing how closely Faulkner's portrayal of Sutpen resembles that of Melville's Ahab, in his monomaniac pursuit of his design.

One grants Brooks' contention that there is a 'spiritual kinship' between Sutpen and Ahab. But he also maintains that "the white whale that Sutpen pursued" is symbolically at least "the same creature that Ahab pursued: Being, itself, in its mysterious and finally incorrigible otherness." (296) However, it is difficult for one to grant that the "white whale" that Sutpen pursues is symbolically like Ahab's—'Being, itself.' For Sutpen, obsessed though he is with establishing his identity with reference to the social structure of the Southern Planter class, is never bothered by the question of 'Being' in the existential sense.

Looked at from a direct narrative sense, *Absalom, Absalom!* is Sutpen's story. It is he who dominates the action of the novel although he is projected in various shapes from the point of view of different minds. Thus Faulkner employs Rosa Coldfield to give her version of Sutpen's character. She employs a kind of verbal violence reminiscent of the language of Jacobean drama to "demonize" Sutpen. In her childhood Sutpen had appeared as the "demon-shape" who had married her sister Ellen to father "two half-ogre children." (13) What the reader gathers from her narrative on Sutpen is that for her he is 'the essence of all evil.' She is incapable of separating Sutpen the phantom, which is what she makes him out to be, from Sutpen the man. On the other hand Compson's account of Sutpen is that of a detached observer, impersonal and rational, denuded of the emotional vitality and violence of Rosa Coldfield. Compson examines Sutpen in relation to his society and time. He levels his focus both on the follies of Sutpen and the pettiness of the society of the Old South. For him, Sutpen is a character in a classical drama. Accordingly, the members of the Sutpen family are transformed by him into characters in a heroic drama. Their conflict is placed against the backdrop of 'Fate, destiny, retribution, irony.' If Compson's view is accepted then Sutpen has to struggle against two adversaries—reminiscent of classical tragedy—against the formidable adversary 'fate and destiny' and against his own 'inevitable doom.' However, it is given to young Quentin and his Harvard friend Shreve to recreate imaginatively Sutpen's tragedy. His is the task of an artist who has to create imaginative truth out of the differing and conflicting interpretations of Sutpen's story as told by Rosa and Compson. The first part of Sutpen's story Quentin already knows 'hearing his father talk about the man, Sutpen.' In fact that was part of the heritage of Jefferson's eighty years' heritage of how Sutpen "first rode into town out of no discernible past and acquired his land no one knew how and built his house, his mansion, apparently out of nothing." (11) While recreating this story, Quentin has also to satisfy the two facets of his own self—one bred in "the deep South dead since 1865 and peopled with garrulous outraged baffled ghosts" and the Quentin Compson "still too young to deserve yet to be a ghost," (9) preparing to go to Harvard. Try as he does to free himself from these almost irreconcilable interpretations of Sutpen's story, the latter remains "essentially unknowable" and teasingly elusive.

Much the same is Melville's approach to the representation of Ahab's character in *Moby Dick*. Unlike Faulkner he does not employ the multiple points of view as a technique of characterization. But Melville too creates a similar sense of mystery and an air of portentousness about Ahab, whether one considers him as a character or a symbol. The reader is told very little, beyond the essentials about Ahab's whereabouts. And even this comes obliquely, through ambiguous, half-hinting, half-revealing words dropped by various characters—from the vague hints that old Peleg, one of the principal owners of the *Pequod* drops about Ahab, from the mysterious remarks that Elijah drops even before Ishmael boards the *Pequod* and from the Old Manxman whom the crew of *Pequod* have invested with preternatural powers of discernment. The hints that Ahab's first mates and harpooners drop about 'moody, stricken Ahab' further intensify the sense of the mysterious and elusive about him. And the speculative and meditative tone that Melville at times adopts with regard to Ahab's character and his futile struggle against the white whale, further instils a sense of mystery which cannot be reasonably unravelled.

Another aspect of Sutpen's characterization that has a close resemblance to Melville's, is the way in which Faulkner describes the emergence of his protagonist in Jefferson. It is Compson who describes Sutpen's appearance to Quentin as he remembers Sutpen's arrival in the town:

> he looked like a man who had been sick. Not like a man who had been peacefully ill in bed and had recovered to move with a

> sort of different and tentative amazement in a world which he had believed himself on the point of surrendering but like a man who has been through some solitary furnace experience which was more than just fever . . . not so much physical as mental alone and unaided. . . . A man with a big frame but gaunt now almost to emaciation . . . his pale eyes had a quality at once visionary and alert, ruthless and reposed in a face whose flesh had the appearance of pottery, of having been coloured by that oven's fever either of soul or environment, deeper than the sun alone beneath a dead impervious surface as of glazed clay. (32-33)

This rather lengthy paragraph is quoted to show how there is a direct echo of a similar passage in *Moby Dick* where Melville describes Ahab as he makes his first appearance on the quarter-deck of *Pequod.* Awe-struck Ishmael says:

> There seemed no sign of common bodily illness about him, nor of recovery from any. He looked like a man cut away from the stake, when the fire has overrunningly wasted all the limbs without consuming them, or taking away one particle from their compacted aged robustness. His whole high, broad form seemed made of solid bronze and shaped in an unalterable mould; like Cellini's cast Perseus. . . . There was an infinity of firmest fortitude, a determinate, unsurrenderable wilfulness in the fixed and fearless, forward dedication of that glance. (120)

The resemblance between the two passages is so remarkable that it would not be merely a conjecture to suggest that Faulkner may have had Ahab in mind while describing Sutpen. Obviously, Faulkner's aim is to magnetize the reader to the heroic qualities of his protagonist which he gradually unfolds through the narratives of the three major characters in the novel. Both Ahab and Sutpen are specially moulded—one like Cellini's Persius, the other has the appearance of pottery with an impervious surface as of glazed clay. Both suffer from a malady which is more than just fever. Ahab looks like a man cut away from the stake when the first has overrunningly wasted all the limbs. Sutpen too looks as if he has undergone some solitary furnace experience for he is gaunt almost to emaciation. Ahab's glance shows his wilfulness, his fixed and fearless purpose. Sutpen's pale eyes have the quality of ruthlessness and repose which prompts Compson to say that 'it was in his face' that his power lay, "anyone could look at him say, given the occasion and the need, this man can and will do anything." (46) Both Ahab and Sutpen come from an ordinary stock of men. Ahab is a Nantucket Quaker; Sutpen belongs to a mountain settlement in Virginia. It is greatly to the credit of the writers that they have raised these ordinary men to the stature of heroes.

The ruthlessness with which Sutpen pursues his goal evokes mixed feelings of admiration and revulsion much in the same way Ahab does. Ahab's pursuit of the white whale is both 'admirable' and 'monstrous' and as such Ahab figures in the novel both as a 'hero' and a 'demon.' All the important spokespersons through whom the Sutpen story is unfolded are overawed by his mad pursuit of his 'design.' It is not Rosa Coldfield alone, distorted though her picture of Sutpen is, who 'demonized' him, although it is she whom the reader first hears calling him a 'demon.' Shreve too refers to him several times as 'the demon.' As he listens to Quentin trying to piece together Sutpen's story, the latter emerges as a 'Faustus,' a 'demon,' a 'Beelzebub.' Other epithets used by the characters in the novel are a 'fiend,' an 'ogre,' a 'djinn,' a 'blackguard,' a 'devil.' This is natural insofar as Sutpen's pursuit is terrifying in its monstrosity and destructiveness. But as the story develops and takes shape in Quentin's mind, Sutpen emerges as 'hero' too. The persistence and single-mindedness with which he sets out with his Hundred to build his design which he considers essential for power and respectability and the terrible way in which this design crumbles under the weight of his demonism gives him a certain awe-inspiring stature. Specially his heroic participation in the Civil War gains him the admiration of his people and offsets his monstrosity to a certain extent. Even Rosa Coldfield cannot ignore this 'villain dyed' man's 'valor' for which he receives a citation from his defeated Commander-in-Chief. Difficult though it is for her to accommodate this aspect of Sutpen's personality, she grants him the 'stature and shape of a hero.' However one misses in Faulkner's portrayal of Sutpen the 'humanities' which Peleg tells Ishmael Ahab possesses, and which Melville takes great care to portray throughout *Moby Dick*. There is no trace of the remorse Ahab expresses for the wrong he has done to his wife and children in the chapter entitled "The Symphony" in *Moby Dick*. Perhaps Faulkner intended to stretch Sutpen's monomania to its furthest limit to exclude any possibility of remorse for the injustice he has perpetrated on his family and everyone around him.

General Compson terms Sutpen's naive and confident belief in his ability to found a dynasty by which families in the South set such high value, his 'innocence.' Sutpen's 'innocence,' according to General Compson springs from a belief that "the ingredients of morality were like the ingredients of pie or cake and once you had measured them and balanced them and mixed them and put them into the oven, it was all finished and nothing but pie or cake could come out." (263) It is probably because of this 'innocence' that he drives himself to acquire 'money, a house, plantation slaves, a family and incidentally of course a wife.' At thirteen, he has faced the humiliation of being turned out from the front door of a plantation house by a negro slave. Sutpen considers this as a personal affront much in the same way Ahab considers the shearing off of his leg by the white whale as a personal affront. Ahab's 'innocence'—if one wants to apply the term to him—springs from his naive confidence that he will be able to destroy Moby Dick with the help of his crew. Sutpen's immediate reaction against his humiliation is to shoot the nigger. But it was not merely 'a question of rifles' for him. As Quentin learns from his grandfather, Sutpen's adversary was not the negro slave but a complex, baffling social system which allows a person 'to have what the plantation owner had that made him do what the man did.' Sutpen does not understand why his place should differ from the one he enjoyed in his mountain settlement. Since the incident at the front door, he cherishes a maniacal desire to dominate the world by assuming the role of his insulter, little realizing that he will become a victim of the very social forces which he has vowed to fight against. The fatal mistake Sutpen makes is that he divorces the evils of the plantation system and fights against them in isolation. Ever since that fatal encounter with the white whale, Ahab too cherishes thoughts of vengeance against it and identifies with it not only all his bodily woes but all his intellectual and spiritual exasperation. Ahab's monomania springs not merely from his injury but from his attributing that injury to an agent or principal whom he considers to be an embodiment of Evil. He dichotomizes Good and Evil in the Manichaean way and directs his energy to the eradication of Evil which confronts him in the form of the whale.

The monomania and single-minded ruthlessness with which Sutpen crushes every obstacle in his pursuit makes him demon. Every move he makes is calculated to contribute to his 'design' from which he has 'ejected the human content,' rejected his own human commitment, 'left humanity out of his plans.' He refuses to regard even his own family as other than instruments of his abstract design. He repudiates his first wife because she was not 'adjunctive or incremental to his design.' After establishing his Hundred on the land brought from the Indians, he marries Ellen Coldfield only to win respectability. He refuses to recognize his son Charles Bon only because he is the son of a mother who has 'negro' blood in her. He proposes to Rosa Coldfield but promises to marry her only if she begets a son whom he needs to perpetuate his lineage. He seduces Milly, Wash Jones' grand-daughter but rejects her because she has failed to bear him a son. In short in his monomania for his design, he violates all norms of humanity and morality. But nowhere does he appear more callous than when, in spite of all his pleas, he refuses to recognize Charles Bon as his son.

This shift from the centre of human commitment and the elevation of the self at the expense of familial and communal ties has been the pre-occupation of major American writers both in the nineteenth and twentieth centuries. American literature is replete with characters obsessed with a private dream which takes them away from reality at the expense of their humanity. This obsessive belief that there is no claim that cannot be satisfied nor any event which cannot be manoeuvred to conform to their dream world is to use Cleanth Brooks' phrase "an American aberration" or "American neurosis." (299) Hence Faulkner's exploration of this trait of the American character in *Absalom, Absalom!* with regard to Sutpen need not be taken as a direct echo of a similar preoccupation in Melville. However, it is interesting to find two eminent critics attributing the same kind of preoccupation on the part of the two great novelists. For in Thomas Sutpen, Eliot saw the same kind of a heretical sensibility on the loose as Matthiessen saw in Captain Ahab. Speaking of the over-indulgent and self-centred individualism that overtakes Sutpen, Eliot says: "When morals cease to be a matter of tradition and orthodoxy . . . and when each man is to elaborate his own then personality becomes a thing of alarming importance." (54) Matthiessen expresses a similar sentiment when he says: "Melville created in Ahab's tragedy a fearful symbol of the self-enclosed individualism, that carried to its furthest extreme, brings disaster both upon itself and upon the group of which it is a part." (459) Yet, Faulkner shows that though Sutpen falls through his own error—a fatal belief in the unassailability of the Self—that error is socially derived. For the South was paying the price through its Sutpens "for having erected its economic edifice not on the rock of storm morality but on the shifting sands of opportunity and moral brigandage." (260) It was one of the paradoxes of freedom in American society that in the hands of 'self-enclosed' individuals, it ended in the will to conquer and dominate. Ahab is a victim of just such a paradox. Like him Sutpen is a 'failed hero,' because he fails to gain any moral or social truth from his 'reverse of fortune.' Sutpen does not become aware, even at the last moment when he is shot dead, of the fatal flaw in his design. As Cleanth Brooks says: "Sutpen never really, acquires wisdom, for he never loses his 'innocence.' He will never learn." (308) His moral blindness and his egotism do not allow him to tear the veil of pride and look into himself. Ahab also meets his nemesis without the 'wisdom' or 'selfless resignation' that one associates with a tragic hero. Like him Sutpen decides to achieve a goal and he pursues it as if by compulsion. Like him too Sutpen justifies his action by an appeal to a force over which he has no control.

"This whole act's immutably decreed," cries out Ahab to Starbuck, when the latter beseeches him to avoid the impiety of wreaking vengeance on a dumb brute. "I am the Fates' lieutenant. I act under orders." (552) Sutpen justifies his fatal compulsion in a similar manner when he tells Quentin's grandfather that all of a sudden he discovered not what he wanted to do but what he just had to do, had to do it whether he wanted to or not". (220) Thus both Ahab and Sutpen do not accept any moral responsibility for their actions. No purgation transforms them. In their death 'fatal pride' meets its rightful end. They evoke terror in the reader but not unmixed pity. Both die as 'failed' heroes.

Works Cited

Brooks, Cleanth. *William Faulkner: Toward Yoknapatawpha and Beyond.* Baton Rouge: Louisiana State University Press, 1990.

______. *William Faulkner: The Yoknapatawpha Country*. Baton Rouge: Louisiana State University Press, 1990.

Eliot, T.S. *After Strange Gods*. London, 1934.

Faulkner, William. *Absalom, Absalom!* New York: The Modern Library, 1964.

Hoffman, Fredrick. *William Faulkner*. Twayne's United States Authors Series. Bombay: Popular Prakashan, 1967.

Matthiessen, F.O. *American Renaissance*. Delhi: Oxford University Press, 1973.

Melville, Herman. *Moby Dick*. San Francisco: Rinehart Press, 1957.

Millgate, Michael. *The Achievement of William Faulkner*. New York: Random House, 1966.

Vickery, Olga. *The Novels of William Faulkner*. Baton Rouge: Louisiana State University Press, 1959.

The Unvanquished: Faulkner's Nietzschean Skirmish with the Civil War

JOHN LOWE

> Yes we shall not die unregarded by the gods.
> A third shall come to raise our cause, a son resolved honouring
> his father's blood
> A great oath, sealed in sight of gods, binds him to exact
> Full penance for his father's corpse stretched dead in dust.
>
> Aeschylus, *Agamemnon*

> A good war makes sacred almost any cause.
>
> Nietzsche

When readers who only know Faulkner's "master works" think of his treatment of the Civil War, the Sutpen saga of *Absalom, Absalom!* (1936) inevitably comes to mind, or perhaps Gail Hightower's pathetic stirring vision of his Confederate grandfather in *Light in August* (1932). Faulkner's interest in these narratives, however, hardly centers on the war itself: even in *Absalom*, set before, during, and after the war, virtually nothing is seen of combat, the ravaged countryside, or, except as their physical decline reflect the psychological distress of his central characters, the impoverished condition of civilians. One becomes more aware of the actual face of the war in one of Faulkner's more neglected works, *The Unvanquished* (1938), which assembles a varied set of characters (all ages, all classes, both sexes, both races) and subjects them to the twin catastrophes of war and history.

With some rather notable exceptions, however (Cleanth Brooks leads the dissenters), most critics have found it a minor work, and virtually all of them view its treatment of the Civil War as a cop-out, a lapse on Faulkner's part into an easy defense of the Old Order, popularized in an earlier time by romantic and racist Plantation School writers like Thomas Nelson Page.[1] Page and his school, however, were more than romantic; in refighting the moral issues of the war in popular fiction, they sought "justice" for the South, a justice the region failed to achieve in battle.[2]

Nostalgic writing and cycles of revenge have something in common: they both grow out of death and remembrance. Stark Young's romantic best-seller about the Civil War and Reconstruction, *So Red the Rose* (1934), suggests this fact immediately; the first lines of its epigraph, taken from Edward Fitzgerald's *Rubáiyát of Omar Khayyám*, read: "I sometimes think that never blows so red/The rose as where some buried Caesar bled."[3] Whether or not they had "unjustly slain" relatives to think of as "buried Caesars"—and both Faulkner and Young did—white Southerners everywhere, it seemed, had a story to tell about their experiences during the war. Indeed, Mark Twain remarked in *Life on the Mississippi* that in 1883, Northerners rarely discussed the Civil War; in the South, however, "every man you meet was in the war . . . every lady you meet saw the war," and for both sexes it is "the chief topic of conversation, forming what A.D. is elsewhere; they date from it . . . all day long you hear things 'placed' as having happened since the waw; or du'in the waw; or be'fo' the waw; or right aftah the waw; or about two yeahs or five years befo' the waw or aftah the waw."[4] Amid Twain's humorous remarks, we find an awareness of the Southern habit of imaginatively interbraiding the war, tale-telling, self and history. But Twain also understood the stultifying influence of the war, which extended the sway of pretentious, romantic narrative and language over Southern letters, a tendency that had begun decades earlier with the vogue for Scott's novels: "Sir Walter had so large a hand in making Southern character . . . that he is in great measure responsible for the war . . . the North had thrown out that old inflated style, whereas the Southern writer still clings to it . . . the authors write for the past, not the present; they use obsolete forms and a dead language. But when a Southerner of genius writes modern English, his book goes upon crutches no longer, but upon wings." (501-2)

But even those who eschewed flowery language in favour of vigorous modernism continued to write about the war. As Lewis Simpson has observed, the obligation of the Southern writer "to serve as a witness, not to the actual historical event, but to the remembrance of it, was a force in shaping the vocation of the writer in the South from Thomas Nelson Page to Ellen Glasgow to Faulkner, Allen Tate, Katherine Anne Porter, Robert Penn Warren, and Eudora Welty.[5]

Indeed, some of the best writing about the war occurred much later, when grandchildren of combatants looked back to the most stirring event in their family's history. This was certainly true for Stark Young, whose novel quickly transforms its lighthearted opening motif of veranda banter into a more serious formulation. A character remarks, "I haven't forgotten what your father said to me when my husband died. That a sacred memory is the most valuable thing one may have, to live by through the years," (76) a line that reverberates with the credo of the Lost Cause.[6] This cult of remembrance intruded repeatedly in everyday conversation, but was carried on more formally by many civic and religious organizations, and found its most permanent expression in the arts, particularly in literature, perversely illustrating Nietzsche's observation that we have art in order not to die of the truth.[7]

The opportunities and problems attendant upon such a cultural inheritance for a writer are best examined in the work of the South's greatest writer, Stark Young's good friend and fellow Mississippian, William Faulkner, who no doubt read *So Red the Rose* with great interest, both because it treated his own state and culture, and because its popular success pointed to an opportunity for Faulkner to mine his own family's Civil War lore. The book Faulkner then wrote, however, *The Unvanquished*, stands apart from the nostalgic tradition epitomised by *So Red the Rose*, which though beautifully written, was replete with all the clichés of the genre. Faulkner, even while using and exploiting that tradition by incorporating elements not only of Young's novel, but also earlier ones such as Thomas Nelson Page's *Red Rock* (1899), transcended it. This authorial traffic operates both ways, however; Young, a frequent visitor to Oxford, borrowed from Faulkner family myths to augment those of his own family; he had already based some of the characters in his 1928 novel, *The Torches Flare*, on Faulkner and his family, and had noted Faulkner's transformation of the Falkner family legends into fiction in the opening pages of *Sartoris* (1929). There, Bayard I is an aide-de-camp of Jeb Stuart, just as Young's character Duncan Bedford is in *So Red the Rose*.

Despite these cross-currents, the attitudes of the two authors toward their material could hardly be more different. Over two hundred pages pass by in Young's novel before the war actually intrudes, in the form of young Edward McGehee's coffin, which is brought home to Montrose after Shiloh. Before this rupture, Young leisurely demonstrates, through a careful amassing of quotidian detail, the textures of Southern plantation life. His domestic mode of narration quite resembles the exquisite embroidery of Eudora Welty in *Delta Wedding*, but also that of Michael Cimino in the first half of his film *The Deerhunter*, where an immigrant-American community is observed close-up at a wedding for almost an hour before the young men involved in the scene are transported to the hell of combat and captivity in Vietnam. Similarly, after Edward's death, *So Red the Rose* erupts with violence, death, and transformation. In each work, the author-director seems intent on employing a narrative strategy that best emphasizes what war displaces.

Faulkner, however, front-loads his narrative with gently mocking humor, as he presents Granny and the boys coping with the Yankee invasion of Mississippi, which opens the book. Gradually, however, the mood and tone of the novel darken as Granny and Ringo sink ever deeper into a cycle of deception and thievery, culminating in Granny's murder. The rest of the novel doubles this narrative line with the story of John Sartoris's corruption, fall, and death during Reconstruction, thereby intensifying the focus for Faulkner's real subjects, two intertwined questions: how does one view and interpret great historical events, particularly when one is involved in them, and secondly, what is justice? Both issues receive analysis through Faulkner's focus on the cycles of revenge.

As this suggests, *The Unvanquished* is a far more disturbing book than many readers realize. Far from being a costumed romp, it moves from comedy to tragedy in a probing examination of issues that also troubled Nietzsche: the will to power, the excesses of virtue, the relationship of justice and revenge, and the dangers involved in distorted perceptions of history. It was written at a central moment in Faulkner's career, as he worked simultaneously on his masterwork, *Absalom, Absalom!* Writing the former helped him work out problems he had encountered in the first drafts of the latter book; it also began his exploration of the New South and what he would later present as advanced Snopesism on the one hand, and the corrosive racial and historical concerns of *Go Down, Moses* on the other. *The Unvanquished* was retrospective as well, in that it reached back into Faulkner's actual and fictional pasts to examine the origins of the lovingly embellished, nostalgic forms of antiquarian storytelling that are exemplified by an older Aunt Jenny and jovial Old Man Falls in *Flags in the Dust*, two characters who replicate relatives and friends of the Falkner family. Finally, the novel provides the necessary ground, albeit retrospectively, for the World War I edition of Bayard Sartoris, and moves Faulkner even closer to his equally haunted doubles, Quentin Compson, Gail Hightower, Isaac McCaslin, and us. Significantly, this backing and filling in of his "postage stamp of soil" contributed to Faulkner's growing effort to try to explain the present by understanding its past—particularly its racial past, which is less emphasized than one might expect in *The Unvanquished* only because he was simultaneously foregrounding it in *Absalom*.[8] He was aware that this hermeneutic task had implications for the future too, and was correct; for the Civil War and the legacy of slavery haunt us yet.

To accomplish these ambitious aims, *The Unvanquished* integrates the physical realities of the war with ambiguous abstractions of historicity. The central focus of the book is the participant observer, Bayard Sartoris, whose changing moral attitudes toward the war, history, and tradition develop through three modes of historical consciousness, outlined by Nietzsche in *The Use and Abuse of History* (1873-1876). The first phase, the monumental, a preoccupation with the classical and the rare, is necessary for the person of action and power, who requires examples from the past for inspiration and instruction, examples unavailable among contemporaries. Monumentalism suggests continuity among heroic ages, but as Nietzsche points out, it "lives by false analogy," and like the other two modes, can be dangerous when taken to extremes.[9] A second mode, antiquarianism, functions well for the reverent conservator of the past. It endorses tradition and sanctions a "way of life." Unfortunately, it tends to be indiscriminate in equating the past and value, takes a narrow outlook, discourages innovation, and can eventually mummify life, rather than preserve it.

The third mode, the critical way, helps one to break up the past and utilize those elements worth saving in a new construct, while discarding others. But this method, too, has dangers; one can become too cynical or pessimistic to effect heroic action. All three modes can become insufferable, either through "abuse," to use

Nietzsche's term, or by being taken too far. Abuse I understand as involving actual corruption, i.e. using the principle to pursue immoral acts. Obsessive extension of the program might not involve conscious malevolent intent, but could have equally dangerous results, including unconscious corruption. Ab Snopes and Grumby would be obvious "abusers" in this reading, while Granny, John, and Drusilla might be judged as taking concepts too far. Faulkner, however, makes his readers uncomfortable by making it increasingly difficult to make a distinction such as this among the book's various transgressors.

As Bayard Sartoris moves through these modes of historical consciousness, we find that other characters share these three stances, illustrating on the one hand that such attitudes toward history play useful functions in human affairs, but that each stance in turn, if abused, can wreak havoc. The stances also dictate certain paths for narrative technique; in dramatizing Nietzsche's tri-partite description of historical stances, Faulkner reveals his awareness of what Hayden White has demonstrated, namely, that these three modes in turn lead to specific forms of respective literary representation: the metonymic, the synecdochic, and the ironic. (351)

Faulkner may or may not have read Nietzsche, but he had certainly read writers who were strongly influenced by Nietzsche's thought, such as Swinburne, Mencken, H.G. Wells, Ludwig Lewisohn, and especially Willard Huntington Wright, author of *The Creative Will* (1916). Nietzsche, like Faulkner, always understood the man of letters as the custodian of history, and clearly recognized the prophetic potential in such a function: "Thus history is to be written by the man of experience and character. He who has not lived through something greater and nobler than others will not be able to explain anything great and noble in the past. The language of the past is always oracular: you will only understand it as builders of the future who know the present. We can explain the extraordinarily wide influence of Delphi only by the fact that the Delphic priests had an exact knowledge of the past; and, similarly only he who is building up the future has a right to judge the past." (41)

Similarly, Faulkner discounted the benefits "research" could have for a writer, instead emphasizing experience, observation, and imagination.[10] Finally, *The Use and Abuse of History* was written during the 1870s, when Germany was under the sway of Hegel's rationalist formulations of historicism. Nietzsche believed that

Hegelianism was in danger of stifling any creative construction of a new future. Faulkner was dealing with a similar moment in Southern and American cultural development as he wrote *The Unvanquished* and *Absalom*, as a Depression-weary America sought surcease in a romantic construction of the past, especially the Southern past, which had now become a national metaphor for America's fall from the pastoral, prosperous golden age into the Dis of urban, economic and industrial chaos.

Monumentalism

Born too late for the Civil War, too early for World War II, and cheated out of a combat assignment during World War I, Faulkner had to find something great and noble in the tasks he set himself as a writer. Thus, despite his claim for "experience" and "observation," "imagination" had to provide most of the impetus for *The Unvanquished*, and this was fuelled by the stories he heard over and over from "these old undefeated spinster aunts."[11]

Initially,. *The Unvanquished* concentrates on Bayard and Ringo's adolescent, monumental view of the war and their metonym for the South, Colonel Sartoris. Their perspective in many ways matches the naive faith Southerners had in their soldiers early in the war. In "Ambuscade," the boys create a miniature map of Vicksburg out of mud and chips, dreaming of victory and glory as they imagine the absent Colonel participating in such actions. Narrating above the scene, an older Bayard muses: "He was not big; it was . . . the things he did . . . in Virginia and Tennessee, that made him seem big to us." Astride his huge horse, Jupiter, equipped with his sabre, Sartoris looms up like an equestrian monument. His very smell intoxicates Bayard: "that odor in his clothes and beard and flesh too which I believed was the smell of power and glory, the elected victorious."[12] Later, Bayard realizes that this masked something else, "the will to endure, a sardonic and even humorous declining of self-delusion, a quality John loses years later, when his will to power, already bloated by the excesses he committed during the War, intersects with the corroding currents of Reconstruction.

Heroic metonymy came naturally to a populace addicted to romantic fiction. Bayard notes the presence of novels by Cooper, Scott, and Dumas in the Colonel's library; John has lost one of these romances while in retreat, signifying the diminishment of these sustaining images in a war that increasingly differs from those described in books. Other volumes concern law, history, and codes of moral behavior: Coke, Littleton, Josephus, the Koran, Mississippi reports; *Napoleon's Maxims*, books of astrology, and works by Jeremy Taylor. Why did Faulkner include this list? Certainly, it suggests the novel's preoccupation with history, the possibility of heroic action, and the need for fighting against seemingly fixed fate ("the stars"), while staying true to established principles and traditions in the face of changing circumstances. Taylor, the author of both *Holy Living* and *Holy Dying*, served as chaplain to King Charles I during the British Civil War, but emerged from the war "unvanquished." John Sartoris has much in common, in his short stature and in his biography, with Napoleon. Like him, he survives initial defeat to wage new campaigns, but ultimately suffers a final defeat. Both begin their careers dedicated to equality and noble ideals, but become increasingly despotic and non-democratic. The monumentalist glorification of Napoleon after his death parallels the mythology of the Lost Cause.[13]

Bayard and Ringo, bearing before them the heroic monumental model, avenge Granny's death during John Sartoris's absence. Her murder offers the most shocking moment in the book, partly because she too receives an ingeniously diminishing monumental presentation. Her "mules and silver" business begins as a comedy, and with the best of motives; after the Yankee commander's orderly mistakenly issues her 110 mules and ten chests of silver instead of the two mules Old Hundred and Tenney and the single chest of silver, she becomes a Robin Hood in Crinoline, stealing mules via forged orders, and reselling them to the Yankees, in order to help the poor country-people near Sartoris. Surely one of the most moving scenes in the book is the Sunday service where she and Brother Fortinbride distribute the illegal bounty to the gaunt, poorly clad hillfolk. Her obsession with endurance and charity, however, leads to the corruption of greed and power, to dealings with the sleazy Ab Snopes and diabolical Grumby, and ultimately to her death. Granny ironically dies because she wants to believe Grumby's claims that he fought on the Southern side during the war, which would make him a gentleman and thus worthy of a business deal. The irony doubles when one remembers she "believes" this on the basis of his tattered raiding commission from General Forrest. As Bayard tells us, "you couldn't tell if the original name [on the commission] was

Grumby or not," (171) so she likely places faith in a bogus document, just as her own victims in the Union Army have. The boys, however, are blind to this. To them, she is their beloved matriarch, represents the monumental image of the Southern lady, and must be avenged. Taking blood for blood, Bayard and Ringo nail Grumby's hide to the compress door and wire his severed hand to Granny's grave marker, causing Uncle Buck to attribute their success to their model: "Ain't I told you he is John Sartoris' boy?" (213)

And yet, as Bayard's troubled conscience ultimately teaches him, monumental history lessons, and especially those written by war, are misleading, for each catastrophe one must deal with is different: certainly, the brutal, cold, lonely and terrifying blood hunt and capture of Grumby proves a far cry from Bayard's image of his father's wartime heroics. The guilt it causes is unexpected, and is compounded by his growing understanding of Granny's corruption.

Nevertheless, the nobility of the boys and Uncle Buck's suffering during the pursuit, rather than the actual killing, move us, and parallel the endurance of the gaunt folk who crowd the church for Granny's handouts. Faulkner constantly compares these heroes of the quotidian with the "monumental" equestrian warriors of Confederate myth, both here and in *Absalom*; his interest in "the structures of everyday life"—especially evident in the scenes that focus on Judith, Clytie, and Rosa during the war in *Absalom*—also privileges women and radically undercuts the monumental history then being taught in the schools. In cutting across racial and class lines as well, he expands the synecdoche that Young's characters would use only within their own class, and thus opens the parameters of antiquarian representation. As Nietzsche, Faulkner, and even Young knew, purely monumental history, of the type immortalized in Bancroft's *History of the United States* (1856-74), ultimately lies, since it strives for an impossible and deceptive synthesis by using false analogy.

We would do well to remember, however, that Faulkner learned more directly about the dangers of monumental concepts of history by studying and frequently honoring the myths and realities surrounding the history of his great-grandfather, Colonel William Falkner, whose fabled exploits as a Confederate warrior and later a frontier capitalist and duelist placed him squarely within Nietzsche's formulation of the hero. Moreover, many of Faulkner's casual remarks betray a predilection for monumental history. He once claimed "From '70 on to 1912-13, nothing happened to Americans to speak of." Thus John Sartoris II, Bayard's son and father of the twentieth-century twins, John and Bayard, is denied the possibilities of heroism: he lived "in that time when there was nothing that brought thc issue to him to be brave and strong or dramatic—well, call it dramatic, not brave, but dramatic, nothing happened to him. But he had to be there for the simple continuity of the family."[14] Interestingly, this description fits Faulkner's father, Murry, even better, as he never served in a war.

Finally, we remember at this point how passionately Faulkner wanted to participate in World War I, the depth of his disappointment that he failed to do so, and the extent of his posturing, replete with an unauthorized uniform, after the war, as a wounded combat veteran, the man who has passed the hero's "test." His early works frequently glorified and romanticized war and soldiers, as in *Soldiers' Pay* (1926), *Sartoris* (1920), and the several short stories set during the Great War he never experienced; in all these military vignettes that preceded *The Unvanquished*, he frequently further heightened and empowered martial narrative through an overlay of sacral numina. This tendency would wind like a thread through Faulkner's entire life, as a letter to his stepson, regarding the latter's possible induction during World War II, indicates:

> But it is the biggest thing that will happen in your lifetime. All your contemporaries will be in it before it is over, and if you are not one of them, you will always regret it. That's something in the meat and bone and blood from the old cave-time, right enough. But it's there, and it's a strange thing how a man, no matter how intelligent, will cling to the public proof of his masculinity: his courage and endurance, his willingness to sacrifice himself for the land which shaped his ancestors. I dont want to go either. No sane man likes war. But when I can, I am going too, maybe only to prove to myself that I can do (within my physical limitation of age, of course) as much anyone else can to make secure the manner of living I prefer and that suits my kin and kind.

He concludes by hoping his generation isn't going to be regarded as "another batch of decrepit old men looking stubbornly backward at a point 25 or 50 years in the past."[15] Amazingly, Faulkner sent a good luck piece to his nephew James, about to go into battle in 1943, adding, "I would have liked for you to have had my dog-tag. R.A.F., but I lost it in Europe, in Germany. I think the Gestapo has it; I am very likely on their records right now as a dead British flying officer-spy."[16]

These episodes and pronouncements, when set beside his fiction, form a pattern of ambivalence toward warfare, which on the one hand, he sees as glorious, part of a masculine tradition with particular relevance for his family, and the ground for heroic action. On the other hand, throughout his work, and especially in *A Fable*, Faulkner deplores violence in every form, and understands how dangerous notions of romantic chivalry can be, when harnessed to the will to power. In many ways, this ambivalent attitude toward war and heroism squares with that of Nietzsche, who in *The Use and Abuse of History*, asks us to consider a man swayed and driven by strong passion, whether for a woman or a theory. "His world is quite altered. He is blind to everything . . . though his perception were never so intimately felt in all their color, light and music. . . . All his judgments to value are changed for the worse . . . and yet this condition, unhistorical and antihistorical throughout, is the cradle not only of unjust action, but of every just and justifiable action in the world." (9) Late in *The Unvanquished*, Drusilla, speaking for herself and John, echoes this concept of origins in virtue: "Sometimes I think the finest thing that can happen to a man is to love something, a woman preferably, well, hard hard hard, then to die young because he believed what he could not help but believe and was what he could not (could not? would not) help but be." (261) Unlike Nietzsche, however, Drusilla fails to see the trap inherent in such a position, and thus embraces what kills Granny, John, and by extension, the Old South. The pattern on corruption exemplified in Granny and John receives grandiloquent codification and justification in Drusilla.[17] She declares John's dream greater than Sutpen's, "which is just Sutpen"—John's, she insists, is for this "whole country which he is trying to raise by its bootstraps" and yet he carelessly kills a poor man who once served in his troops, betrays his business associates, flaunts the community's laws, and neglects his family. As Goethe once remarked, we cannot help developing our faults at the same time as our virtues,[18] and this is the case with Granny, John, and Drusilla as well. They personify how the South, writing its martial and sacral narrative first in deeds and then words, exaggerated its valor, endurance, and courage, but with a mindset that came at the cost of rationality, tolerance, and a sense of true historicity.

The Antiquarian Mode

Just as stultifying, if taken too far, or abused, is the antiquarian sense of history. *Flags in the Dust*, set in post-World War I Yoknapatawpha, gives us an older Aunt Jenny and her male counterpart, Old Man Falls, as antiquarian priests of the past. Their lovingly embellished retellings of Sartoris Civil War exploits seem useful to *them*, in that the stories preserve family legend and tradition and promote narration. This pair represents Faulkner's fond memories of his own aunts who similarly tended the shrine of the fallen. Jenny retells the old legends, layering yet another coat of patina on them, demonstrating how language creates and sometimes misleads the process of historical Reconstruction: "as she grew older the tale itself [the story of the first Bayard Sartoris's death prior to the second battle of Manassas] grew richer and richer, taking on a mellow splendor like wine; until what had been a hare-brained prank of two heedless and reckless boys wild with their own youth, was become a gallant and finely tragical focal-point to which the history of the race had been raised from out the old miasmic swamps of spiritual sloth by two angels valiantly and glamorously fallen and strayed, altering the course of human events and purging the souls of men."[19] And in fact, the South actually grew proud of its inebriation from such heady brew; in *So Red the Rose*, a New Jersey professor visiting the South claims. "The fact is it never existed, but Southerners are already busy creating a romantic Old South." Young's mouthpiece, Hugh McGehee, responds. "But the point does not turn on whether some old fool of a colonel—or some scatter-brained old lady—is what we think he is—or she is. No, no. The point turns on what we believe in and desire, and want to find embodied somewhere, even in them." (384)

For Jenny's great-nephews Bayard and his twin, John, however, such tales offer a seductive but false image of the Great War they are drawn to, and after John's death in combat and Bayard's return to South, the same tales provide a condemnatory measure of his failure either to find glory in the war, like John (in deeds and then death) or to bring his brother safely home. As Nietzsche noted, the antiquarian mode is useful only when it is necessary to preserve values: in better times, it only serves to undervalue present growth, (20) as it valorizes the past as a golden age, blindly democratizing random elements of that past in a general embrace of synecdoche—for example, venerating each and every antique object or action simply because of age, rather than practicing a scale of value among antiquities. Such uncritical veneration found communal expression in the various commemorative organizations like the Sons and Daughters of the Confederacy, and the many genteel authors of the moonlight-and-magnolia school. It has its own trivial form today when antique collectors hang an old butter churn on their wall beside a Rembrandt Peale. More seriously, in Faulkner's time and ours, traditional practices of racial segregation have been venerated to forestall integration. Like *Flags, The Unvanquished* takes this form quite seriously as a potentially fatal force.

In *So Red the Rose*, too, antiquarianism has good and bad aspects. As Young lovingly recreates the multiple rituals of everyday life on the plantation, from the conventions of veranda conversation to the matter of table settings, the antebellum plantation clearly emerges as a pinnacle of civilization; all possible exceptions are dealt with through negative stereotyping or comic diminishment, or they are simply ignored. This proves particularly true with the black characters and the overall problem of slavery. The synecdochic approach of the novel is signalled early on when Agnes McGehee declares to a guest, "you may not get everybody straight . . . but it's no matter, you can take it all as just one company. I always say to strangers in Natchez they would make a mistake trying to remember each separate person. Yes, I say, they must take it all as one." (10) Accordingly, the war only brings out the best in the characters. The women, already virtuous and robust, become stoic priestesses, first of the homefront, then of the Lost Cause. The gentlemen, already valiant, prove their battlefield bravery, and then, during Reconstruction, their nobility and dignity, by refusing to consort with "trash" carpetbaggers, poor whites, and freed slaves.

Here, Faulkner's contrast with Young again proves instructive. Like many other antiquarian authors, Young falsified history in the service or a racist ideology: Mrs. McGehee's "all" refers only to well-born whites. The omniscient narrator exclaims, midway through the novel, "It was during the siege of Vicksburg that the first negroes were enlisted in the Federal Army. The agents did not spread the information that General Sherman had done this against his will and had declared that as soldiers the negroes were a joke." (229) In the most sensational scene in the book, drunken and cursing black soldiers break into Montrose plantation, invade the pregnant daughter Belle's bedroom, beat her mother, Agnes, torch the library, and deliberately destroy an oil portrait of Henry Clay. Plantation slaves join the looting while the house burns.[20] By contrast, although *The Unvanquished* deals with race only tangentially, for the most part, it treats Africans-Americans sympathetically, and shows them as diverse and fully human.

As this discussion suggests, however, both Young and Faulkner seem to agree with Lukács that "What matters therefore in the historical novel is not the re-telling of great historical events, but the poetic awakening of the people who figured in those events. . . . [I]n order to bring out these social and human motives of behaviour, the outwardly insignificant events, the smaller . . . relationships are better suited than the great monumental drama of world history."[21] The difference, of course, lies in the respective author's definition of "poetic," which enjoys a much fuller spectrum of representation and moral value in Faulkner, who has no interest in *mere* "Lost Cause" nostalgia, domestic detail, sacralization, and historical editing. We know he was intent on avoiding this from his comments in 1934 as he worked on *Absalom*, which would be tied together by Quentin Compson of *The Sound and the Fury*; having Quentin tell the tale made all the difference, for as Faulkner explained, the boy's "bitterness," which was projected on the South, "in the form of hatred of it and its people" would be useful in getting "more out of the story itself than a historical novel would. To keep the hoop skirts and plug hats out, you might say."[22]

Where did these hoop skirts and plug hats go? Obviously, many critics see them reappearing in *The Unvanquished*. Oscar Cargill, speaking for many, summed it up: "As he smooths the substance of *The Unvanquished* between his tongue and his palate, the average reader is little likely, so it would seem, to detect any sand in the chocolate cream. The romantic Faulkner has scored a touchdown on the realistic Faulkner."[23] Granny and Drusilla do wear hoop skirts, as do most of the women in the novel, for that is what women of this class wore then. Faulkner uses that skirt, however, to hide Bayard and Ringo after they shoot a Yankee's horse out from under him, thereby providing some rich humor.[24] But the real point of the scene is the unexpected humanity of the Yankee officer, who sees the bulge and says nothing, because, as he says, "I have three boys myself, you see. And I have not even had time to become a grandparent." (38) Colonel Sartoris's plug hat appears, but on his servant Louvinia's head, illustrating the dislocation of a world turned upside down. Faulkner wickedly signifies here and elsewhere on the Plantation writers, whose literary progression into the twentieth century had already produced Young's work, and would culminate in the "hoop skirt/plug hats" synecdoche of *Gone with the Wind.*

Still, Faulkner and Nietzsche agree that one cannot totally dismiss collectively perceived history. Nietzsche observed the danger we risk by rejecting the stereotypes of antiquarians: "though we condemn the errors and think we have escaped them. We cannot escape the fact that we spring from them." (21) The problem for the artist, who must transform history—and in Faulkner's case, family history—into art, is to preserve the figurative ground, while simultaneously stripping away its illusions. Let me put this another way: Ralph Ellison has stated that "Faulkner, perhaps more than any other white writer, started with the stereotype of the Negro minority, accepted it as containing some truth, and then sought out the human truth which it hides."[25] Ellison thus suggests that Faulkner is engaged in an artistic husking of stereotypes, and indeed this becomes his response, not only to racial history but to antiquarian narratives of war and history in general. In all his treatments of the Civil War, he endeavors to recast and reinterpret history, even as he attempts to preserve the still-sustaining elements of historical myth.

As a way of keeping the "hoop skirts and plug hats" from intruding in *The Unvanquished*, Faulkner employs what I shall call the rhetoric of absence. In the broadest sense, he simply refuses to provide readers with some of the staples of the antiquarian genre, such as long, loving descriptions of idyllic gardens and landscapes, decor, women's ethereal beauty of person and dress, or detailed enactments of Southern rituals such as meals, holidays, and the like. But there are always "traces" of all this, as in Granny's reading of the cookbook, Drusilla's yellow ballgown, or the description of the law professor's study. More importantly, Bayard suggests what has been lost or what part of the Southern dream has failed to materialize by citing its absence; he brings it up and immediately annuls it, thereby providing what resembles a palimpsest, a tablet on which previously erased texts are faintly visible—or, to use a more contemporary term, he thereby creates the "trace" of a presence. For Gayatri Spivak, Derrida's concept of trace is the "mark of the absence of a presence, an always already absent present." As she points out, in this system of reference, language itself is a trace-structure, effacing itself even as it presents its legibility.[26] Faulkner practices this kind of erasure and deconstruction throughout *The Unvanquished.* A key metaphor for this process appears early in the novel, as Bayard and Ringo create their children's version of Vicksburg out of water, chips, and mud. Faulkner intends their childish fantasies to emblematize the romantic embroidering of the "Lost Cause" that began even before the war started with the South's grandiose claim for its extraordinary culture, its divinely sanctioned slavery, the beauty and refinement of its ladies and the gallantry of its cavaliers. Faulkner's own relatives were major practitioners of Southern mythology and devotees of the "Lost Cause," and his contemporaries carried the tradition on into Faulkner's mature years. Repeatedly, as author he too builds up a house of romantic words, only to demolish it time after time, with modernist irony and skepticism. Like Loosh, the soon-to-be-freed slave who sweeps the chiptown down, saying "There's your Vickburg!" (5) Faulkner deconstructs reader's romantic notions about Southern history saying, "There's your Lost Cause!" Again, this links Faulkner with Nietzsche. The philosopher thought that tragedy worked in a similar manner: "It shares with the Apollonian the strong delight in illusion and contemplation, and yet it denies that delight, finding an even higher satisfaction in the annihilation of concrete semblances."[27]

Another remarkable aspect of *The Unvanquished*, its gradual stylistic shift from comedy to tragedy, has contributed to general critical revaluation of the novel. In 1930, Faulkner had dazzled the critics with his intermingling of grotesque humor and profound tragedy in *As I Lay Dying,* a self-described "tour-de-force." Paradoxically, Faulkner's switch to a *traversal*, rather than a scrambling of the generic spectrum in *The Unvanquished* has led some critics to dismiss the book. But we may appreciate more his method of gradually moving from jovial comedy to brooding tragedy if we consider Bakhtin's discussion of how epic, tragic, lyric and philosophical works have inevitably become subjects of parodic mimicry. "It is as if such mimicry rips the words away from its object, disunifies the two, shows that a given straightforward generic word—epic or tragic—is one-sided, bounded, incapable of exhausting the object;

the process of parodying forces us to experience those sides of the object that are not otherwise included in a given genre or a given style." However, he warns, "It was not, after all, the heroes who were parodied, nor the Trojan War and its participants; what was parodied was only its epic heroization; not Hercules and his exploits but their tragic heroization."[28] The South, frequently compared to Troy in its fall, had been churning out sentimental, elegiac narratives and poems about the war for decades when Faulkner began his Civil War novels. Miss Rosa's poetry (which Faulkner pointedly never quotes in *Absalom*) offers an example. By "ripping away" pious platitudes early on in *The Unvanquished* through gentle parody, Faulkner sets himself free to reset the pseudo-tragic genre as genuine tragedy.

But always remember the trace. Faulkner has no interest in what Nietzsche calls the practice of "Historical justice," or what we might call today "presentist" criticism. Nietzsche sees this as a "dreadful virtue" because if it has "no constructive impulse behind the historical one" and if one turns all into a matter of historical knowledge, one can destroy even a religion, for "a thing can live only through a pious illusion. For man is creative only through love and in the shadow of love's illusions, only through the unconditional belief in perfection and righteousness." (42) Thus Faulkner's practice of erasure, rather than effacement, punctures false consciousness, but allows transcendent aura and true mythic presence to survive. For both Nietzsche and Faulkner desperately seek the reintroduction of what the former calls "astonishment" into our frame of reference.

Bayard Sartoris employs a language born of history out of romance, but erases it by negation. In a typical passage, the narrator, musing on the reflections of those left on the home front while the war wages, himself reflects:

> So we knew a war existed; we had to believe that. . . . Yet we had no proof of it. In fact, we had even less than no proof; we had had thrust into our faces the very shabby and unavoidable obverse of proof, who had seen Father (and the other men too) return home, afoot like tramps or on crowbait horses, in faded and patched (and at times obviously stolen) clothing, preceded by no flags nor drums and followed not even by two men to keep step with one another, in coats bearing no glitter of golden

> braid and with scabbards in which no sword reposed, actually almost sneaking home to spend two or three or seven days performing actions not only without glory [plowing, etc.]. . . . Father's whole presence seemed . . . to emanate a kind of humility and apology, as if he were saying. "Believe me, boys; take my word for it: there's more to it than this, no matter what it looks like. I can't prove it, so you'll just have to believe me." (107-8)

This type of erasure, which provides our imaginations glimpses of the traditional props of martial narrative but then promptly snatches them away, thus leaves the trace but also serves to underscore the hard truths of war, hidden beneath the glittering stereotypes.[29] Moreover, John's "believe me" summons up the concept of sheer faith, and the aura such faith always casts over its articles.

Bayard similarly retells the definitive action of the war, at least for his boyish imagination, the great locomotive chase that Drusilla narrates in "Raid." Although Faulkner never spells it out, this refers to the famous Confederate theft of a locomotive from Yankee-held Atlanta, and the pursuit Union troops made on a second train. "But they never caught it. . . . They tore the track up so we couldn't do it again." (112) This thrilling tale also spins out through the language of absence, as it must, for it has to substitute for the no-show of the original dream: "to have it happen, where we could have been there to see it, and were not: and this no poste and riposte of sweat-reeking cavalry which all war-telling is full of, no galloping thunder of guns to wheel up and unlimber and crash and crash into the lurid grim-glare of their own demon-served inferno which even children would recognise, no ragged lines of gaunt and shrill-yelling infantry beneath a tattered flag which is a very part of that child's make-believe." (108) What could be more revealing than the implications of these two passages? All the images of glory conjure up the romantic aspects of war, only to be defaced, erased, culminating in the emasculated image of the empty scabbard (erection/deflation) and the suggestion that it had all been child-like make-believe.

Similarly, Faulkner, by contrast, takes a modernist's pleasure in his brilliant display of war's disjunctions, blurring lines of gender, class, and race. All types of social boundaries topple as the characters struggle to adjust. A good example appears in "Riposte in Tertio," when Granny distributes the profits from her mule and silver operation to the poor hillfolk. Here a genteel Southern lady takes on a male role by leading a congregation of Methodists, Episcopalians, and others in a service of survival, accompanied by her "partner," a black slave. Every class of Southern society crowds into the church to share in illegal booty. Brother Fortinbride's homely eloquence underlines the empty rhetoric of the episcopal divine.

On other occasions, Faulkner's prose employs ingenious spatial trickery right out of *Alice in Wonderland* to suggest how topsy-turvy the world has become. Bayard has seen his father reduced in several dimensions—the proud Colonel astride Jupiter becomes a tattered yeoman, sweating like a hog in the swamp to build a pen for his stock. But Faulkner goes much further than mere reduction. He employs a distinctly surreal, modernist mode of psychic perspective that mirrors the dislocations of war. While the first story, "Ambuscade," begins with a monumental, vastly expanded image of John Sartoris, Bayard, while watching the road from the cedar copse for Yankees, falls asleep and seems to watch as the entire plantation vanishes, leaving a space as "empty as the sideboard" (which has had its usual silver service taken away for hiding). A "drove of little tiny figures" appears on it, including "Father and Granny and Joby and Louvinia and Loosh and Philadelphy and Ringo and me." The reduction at play now instead of magnification occurs because of fear—and Bayard wakes to see a Yankee on horseback, tellingly employed in looking at the house through a field glass. After Bayard thinks he has shot the Yankee, "the house didn't seem to get any nearer; it just hung there in front of us, floating and increasing slowly in size." (30) Other examples could be cited of this surreal mode, which Faulkner employs throughout the novel to suggest the dislocations in perspective forced by the ruptures of history.

Sometimes these disjunctures are terrifying, as when houses disappear; sometimes they entertain. The duelling locomotives, which have left their "trace" in the bizarrely twisted railroad tracks, are pressed into narrative service as warring knights, to make up for the loss of monumental flesh-and-blood heroes: it is "as if the gray generals themselves had sent the word, had told them, 'You have suffered for three years; now we will give to you and your children a glimpse of that for which you have suffered and been denied.'" (111)

This scene employs one of many stratagems Faulkner devised for conveying a sense of history and great events without attempting to describe in detail the actual historical events themselves. He recognized the impossibility of conveying the scale of the war and Reconstruction in a short novel, so he has only suggestions of the mass movements of troops, of civilian dislocation, of battles; he shows more interest in conveying economic, philosophical, moral, and metaphysical aspects of the war. These concepts fuse brilliantly in the masses of slaves marching towards "Jordan"—lacking an economic base, they seek salvation in spiritual goals. Here and in actual skirmishes with the Yankees, Faulkner, like Scott, Cooper, and Tolstoy before him, selected episodes that represent the historical moment. As Lukács stated, and Faulkner obviously knew, the historical novel does not replicate history but demonstrates through artistic means the meaning and effect of it. (43)

The Critical Way

Bayard's own monumentalist and antiquarian veneration of the martial past works, although with diminishing returns, until his father's death forces him to shoulder the task of revenge once again. Importantly, throughout the novel, Bayard has been relatively untouched by the corruption going on around him. He tells us that the mule-stealing operations of Granny and Ringo are largely outside his domain, and during his father's increasingly corrupt activities during Reconstruction. Bayard sequesters himself in a genteel law professor's home. His one sin, killing Grumby, has been a crime of honor justified by his society, but one that has nevertheless sullied his own self-image; he also expresses dismay to Drusilla over John's killing of the Burdens: "They were men. Human beings." (257) He is in danger, however, of being pulled into the vortex, for John tells him: "I have not needed you in my affairs so far, but from now on I shall . . . what will follow will be a matter of consolidation, of pettifogging and doubtless chicanery in which I would be a babe in arms but in which you, trained in the law, can hold your own—our own." (266) Furthermore, Bayard's comrade Ringo has likewise been corrupted, relishing the mule-scam operation and suggesting to Bayard that they bushwhack Redmond the way they did Grumby, failing to see the moral distinction between the two acts.

The final section of the book creates a philosophical skirmish for Bayard with Redmond, a man his father has goaded beyond endurance, an honorable man, and a lawyer—and Bayard is studying law himself. He is thus forced into yet another reassessment of his father's history. The solution Bayard works out (confronting Redmond unarmed) redefines the antiquarian impulse to honor the old code of the duel, itself a microcosm of the script of war. Bayard thus moves through and beyond the third mode of history, what Nietzsche called "the critical way": breaking up the past, salvaging its best traditions, and building a new future, which is what Bayard hopes to do, not only for himself, but for his society. The critical way has its own pitfalls, however; its form of literary expression, irony, can deepen into cynicism and pessimism, which can be just as paralyzing as monumentalism and antiquarianism. We find two good examples of this trap in Mr. Compson of *The Sound and the Fury* and *Absalom*, and John Sartoris just before his death. Here the thinker runs the risk of finding fault in everything, rejecting the ancestors (and therefore forfeiting the opportunity to learn from both their achievements and their failures), or trusting nothing, even oneself, thus in effect cancelling out the possibility of sustaining the better qualities of the modes of monumentalism and antiquarianism.

Nietzsche recognized this, and warned against an "excess of history" drawn from any or all three of the modes he listed. As an antidote, he championed "the man with the feeling and the strength for justice." (34) This helps us see that Bayard, in seeking justice from Redmond, actually moves beyond the critical mode as well, synthesizing the best of all three modes, in an effort to wrest a positive future from an imperfect but still valuable past. He performs the necessary critical act, yet unlike his father, avoids cynicism; rather, he synthesizes the best of the past, the needs of the present, and a plan for the future, into his quest. As Nietzsche declared, "only he who is building up the future has a right to judge the past." (41)

One must be struck here by the parallels of Nietzsche's philosophical project and that of literary modernism after World War I. A tireless literary experimenter and disciple of modernist masters such as Eliot and Joyce, Faulkner obviously saw the connection of these modes of historical perception and the formal techniques of modernism, especially as practiced in *The Waste Land*. Remarkably, his own breakup and reconstitution of premodern literary conventions so marked in earlier books such as *The Sound and the Fury* and *As I Lay Dying* have no equivalent forms here. Corollaries abound, however; Faulkner sets up and then violates generic expectations repeatedly, deconstructing genteel plantation narrative, the idea of the Southern hero and heroine, black/white modes of racial representation, and social hierarchy and tradition.[30] Faulkner's aesthetic objective thus echoes the moral one of his hero—to retrieve amid the ruins that which is best, and rebuild for the future, thereby following Aristotle's paradoxical dictum that all things must change over time if they are to remain the same.

Nietzsche recognized the problem revenge poses for humanity. His alter ego Zarathustra asserts that "man's deliverance from revenge is the bridge to the highest hope . . . and a rainbow after long storms."[31] This may seem to contradict his better-known theories of the superman and the will to power, but what Nietzsche meant here was that revenge is driven by the feeling of being vanquished and injured—precisely the motivation of the South in Reconstruction. Revenge, however, is the curse of the South, for its endless repetitions have led to physical devastation, personal corruption, racial catastrophe, and breakdown of the law. Paradoxically, the superman can emerge only when he assigns primacy to life and creativity over violent methods of revenge.

In Nietzschean terms, then, Bayard moves into the critical mode of history and creates a new meaning for past traditions, while simultaneously re-instating the law; he does this by drawing a limited horizon around himself to ascertain his own deepest needs and those of his culture. This involves a *forgetting* of blindly followed formulas: not an erasure of the past but rather, again to use Nietzsche terminology, an extraction of *poison* from the past, thereby achieving, finally, the super-historical.

How is all this dramatized? Part of the reason for *The Unvanquished*'s lack of prominence in Faulkner criticism stems from Bayard's failure to articulate the intricate thought processes that must accompany his actions. We have no analysis of the way Bayard feels as he goes to meet Redmond; instead, we see what he sees—the men watching him on the porch of the Holston House, the scuff marks countrymen have made over the years climbing up Redmond's stairs, the small, neat sign announcing Redmond's profession. All of these may be semiotically interpreted, but represent meager fare compared to the banquet of commentary provided in Faulkner's other narratives by Quentin Compson, Darl Bundren, Shreve McCannon, Ike McCaslin, the garrulous Ratliff, or the ultimate gasbag, Gavin Stevens.

Bayard's *moral* achievement, however, overshadows theirs, and Faulkner does allow him to note in the concluding chapter, "I realized then the immitigable chasm between all life and all print—that those who can, do, those who cannot and suffer enough because they can't, write about it." (262) We perhaps valorize the narrators of *Absalom* over Bayard partly because it is precisely their tell-all, extravagant rhetoric we desire, rather than his type of restraint. But his narrative techniques are perfectly in keeping with his character; as Gerard Genette has suggested, "Between the information of the hero and the omniscience of the novelist is the information of the narrator, who disposes of it according to his own lights and holds it back only when he sees a precise reason for doing so."[32] Perhaps Bayard, as narrator, believes that only silence can "erase" the extravagances of the monumental and antiquarian modes of history, which lead, as demonstrated, to an excess of metonymy and synecdoche that chokes out vitality.

And in fact, stoic silence and heroic suffering operate throughout *The Unvanquished* to say what language never can. The woman Grumby's men rape merely moves her bloody mouth to cry, "Kill them"; Granny, Bayard and Ringo, watching their mansion burn, can only endlessly repeat, "The Bastuds." *The Unvanquished* has been accused of being indulgent and romantic but, in fact, at least in its rhetoric, seems relatively spare, restrained, somewhat Doric, when compared to the Corinthian extravagance of *Absalom*, which was being written contemporaneously.

Bayard also keeps silent for another reason: his actions, not his words, must speak to the communal representatives, assembled in the square outside, watching. As custodian of community mores, the heir of the outstanding community figure and elected leader in time of martial law, and, after John's death, its acknowledged leader when law as they know it collapses, Bayard knows his role. But he also understands that his father's integrity collapsed under these pressures; in a liminal time, Bayard must set the standard for the intermediate codes. He sees the need to build on the principles of the past, but also knows that the old standards led to the war and ultimately, on a more personal level, to the corruption and death of John and Granny, his actual father and surrogate mother—and these old standards were always crystallized through floods of rhetoric.

Ursula Brumm has suggested that for Faulkner history is a preoccupation, a responsibility, and a burden on the mind, so much so that it required the development of a new technique of narrative structure, a central intelligence, "a character with a highly refined consciousness and conscience, whose main preoccupation was the scrutiny and evaluation of history in its meaning for the present." She also suggests that *The Unvanquished* is inferior to *Absalom* because the latter is constructed as the "learning process of a historical consciousness," while the former book is a "historical tale in the straight traditional way . . . but experience and recollection . . . are not internalized."[33] Brumm's description is quite accurate as to *Absalom*, but surely Faulkner's route there doesn't invalidate the alternative posed in *The Unvanquished;* spareness is not inherently inferior to excessive rhetoric, but many critics have shared Brumm's view that *The Unvanquished* must be given relatively low marks in assessing Faulkner's canon because it can't compare to the rhetorical magnificence of *Absalom*. Perhaps an awareness of the narrative techniques Faulkner employed for Bayard, which I have sketched above, can help us avoid this impasse in the future.

We can better see how Faulkner works these issues to a final synthesis by attending to the specifics of the final chapter, "An Odor of Verbena." Bayard has been studying law over the past three years, during a time when his father is becoming more remote, despotic, and preoccupied. One of the books previously ensconced in John's library among the romances was Coke on Littleton, and it is precisely this book—a commentary on law—that Bayard is reading as we regreet him, now a man of twenty-four, living in the home of his law professor, Wilkins, who, Faulkner tells us, will later become a judge. This man has gradually become a kind of surrogate father for Bayard, and thus supplements the surrogate mother role played by Aunt Jenny. Faulkner underlines this when Wilkins atypically and violently flings open the door to announce John's death: "Bayard, Bayard, my son, my dear son." Later that evening, at Sartoris, Aunt Jenny will say, "Goodnight, son." (277) These "parents" replace John and Granny, and their modes of vengeance; they are primarily concerned about Bayard, rather than John's sacred memory, but the community expects exact loyalty to blood. George Wyatt, representing the men of the town, bridles when suspecting Bayard's cowardice: "Who are you? Is your name Sartoris? By God, if you don't kill him, I'm going to." After Bayard reassures him ("I'm tending to this. You stay out of it. I don't need any help"), Wyatt too says, "You'll have to excuse me, son." (284)

Such authorial maneuvers help Faulkner set Bayard up not only as THE Sartoris, but THE son, who, in an ironic and intended inversion of the Scriptures, may not be allowed to let this brimming cup of vengeance pass from his lips.

Such Christian thematics emphasize Bayard's attempt to replace the Chthonian values of the community with the only others he knows—those of Christianity and civil law. What were Faulkner's concerns here? One had to be the Chthonian nature of vigilante justice (an oxymoron if there ever was one). Faulkner was obviously thinking of the racist and illegal operations of the Klan when he wrote this book, but he prefers to problematize the issue by confining it to situations where the perpetrators have a just complaint, but no public means of redress. Their code of conduct, however, is literally "an eye for an eye," so he and Bayard tread a thin line here, for like the other men in their families and the people of the South after the war, Faulkner and Bayard are supremely conscious of the need for redeeming honor and dignity—something that at first seems out of reach for a Christian humanist, who might be expected to turn the other cheek.

And indeed, Aunt Jenny has formulated a variant of this formula for Bayard: she tells him not to be influenced by the hysterical Drusilla, his dead father, or the revenge-bent soldiers of his father's old troop; Jenny knows he isn't afraid, and says that she will still think well of him, "Even if you spend the day hidden in the stable loft." (280) The identification of the hiding place with the infancy of Christ surely clinches the act of nonviolence with an extremely passive concept of Christianity, the type exemplified by Harriet Beecher Stowe's Uncle Tom, who is beaten to death and sainthood without offering any resistance. The problem Bayard faces—and it is the problem of the South as a whole during Reconstruction—is the problem of all Christians/humanists in a secular world. Melville, dealing with similar issues in *Moby Dick*, compares images of God the Father and Christ that have appeared in Italian painting: "When Angelo paints even God the Father in human form, mark what robustness is there. And whatever they may reveal of the divine love in the Son, the soft, curled, hermaphroditical Italian pictures, in which his idea has been most successfully embodied; these pictures so destitute as they are of all brawniness, hint nothing of any power, but the mere negative, feminine one of submission and endurance, which on all hands it is conceded, form the peculiar practical virtues of his teachings."[34] Bayard does indeed replace the primitive concept of Justice with a Christian model, but the image of Christ here is muscular Christianity, a code of strength and courage, whose image would be that brawny, confident Christ of the same Michelangelo's *Last Judgment*. We must also note, however, that Bayard nevertheless has discarded values he once held, values that led him not only to murder but to mutilation and dismemberment of a dead body. Further, his approach works only because Redmond is a moral man. Otherwise, Bayard would be duplicating Granny's error in meeting Grumby.

Bayard is unarmed, with no weapon either to initiate an attack or respond to one; Redmond has a gun, but realizing immediately Bayard's shift to a new code, is unable to use it except in a parody of its purpose: he deliberately misses the target. This silent exchange between Bayard and Redmond takes place above the gunfire and offers a dialogic for healing and restoration of the law. This is appropriate, for in typological terms, Bayard's mission is to restore the covenant of the higher law, a law that had been disrupted by the Yankee's cruel new concept of taking the war—total war—to the population as well as to the opposing army. Once loosed, this daemon took other forms after the conflict in the terrors inflicted by marauders such as Grumby and his son. Consequently, Bayard and the South must learn to come to grips with history and the endless cycles of revenge by rejecting the past embrace of *memento mori* in favor of *memento vivere*. Bayard before Redmond revises the early, hopeful spirit of John Sartoris, the man who created, not the destroyer, and takes it into the realm of "higher law" John never practiced.

In terms of narrative, the creation of a non-duel operates along the lines of presence-by-absence and erasure that we discussed earlier. But the scene also pulls all the strands of the pre-existing levels of the narrative together in a powerful climax, and thus represents a classic pattern in the novel, the testing of the hero. We might add that Bayard is testing himself here as well. The scene thus offers a form of repetition, in that it repeats the testing of the hero that occurred in the search for and killing of Grumby. But Bayard in thinking through that action and its consequences, now seeks a higher level of conduct, and thus a more difficult test, what Kierkegaard calls a true repetition rather than a mere recollection.

For Nietzsche, revenge forms an insuperable barrier to becoming whole, yet the antidote is a muscular form of Christianity, which Nietzsche professed to hate; but such an approach of course also recreates what Nietzsche described in a more secular manner: "you will find the virtuous man will always rise against the blind force of facts, the tyranny of the actual, and submit himself to laws that are not the fickle laws of history. He ever swims against the waves of history, either by fighting his passions, as the nearest brute facts of his existence, or by training himself to honesty amid the glittering nets spun round him by falsehood . . . history also keeps alive for us the memory of the great 'fighters against history.'" (54) Bayard becomes just such a figure in "An Odor of Verbena," as he challenges the desiccated codes of behavior that have until now been central to his family, the Mississippi frontier, and Southern and American culture in general.

Lukács has claimed that the successful historical novel must depend "upon a rich and graded interaction between different levels of response to any major disturbance of life. It must disclose artistically the *connection* between the spontaneous reaction of the masses and the historical consciousness of the leading personalities." (44) When one passes Faulkner's text through the filter of Nietzsche's historical prism, it becomes clear that *The Unvanquished* passes Lukács' test in triumphant fashion. In his courageous deconstruction of pious histories and narratives, Faulkner locates the pitfalls and possibilities of historical memory and narrative, providing both blueprint and instruction for using the past to rebuild the social and cultural realm we all inhabit.

NOTES

1. For representative favorable and unfavorable readings of the novel, consult Cleanth Brooks, *William Faulkner: The Yoknapatawpha County* (New Haven: Yale University Press, 1963), pp. 75-79, and Michael Millgate, *The Achievement of William Faulkner* (1963; rpt. University of Nebraska Press), pp. 165-70, respectively. The general dismissal of the novel began when the book appeared, largely because the proletariat-based critics of the thirties and forties were understandably impatient with works that seemed to deal with romantic formulas and vanished economic elites. Curiously, while contemporary critics will challenge their literary elders quite readily on a "big

book" like *Absalom* or *Go Down, Moses*, they tend to accept prior negative readings of agreed-upon "minor" works of major authors. This is regrettable, since *The Unvanquished* could be a central text for some interesting Faulkner critics, such as Carolyn Porter and Eric Sundquist. Porter's *Seeing and Being: The Plight of the Particular Observer in Emerson, James, Adams, and Faulkner* (Middleton, Connecticut: Wesleyan University Press, 1981), examines participant observers in the Yoknapatawpha sagas, but ignores Bayard Sartoris. Sundquist's *Faulkner: The House Divided* (Baltimore: Johns Hopkins University Press, 1983) discusses Faulkner and the Civil War but doesn't discuss *The Unvanquished*. Sundquist relegates much of Faulkner's fiction, in terms that would include *The Unvanquished*, to a shelf of books that are of interest "only because he wrote [them]." (xi)

2. The role of popular fiction in shaping the memory of the war and binding up the nation's psychic wounds has recently been traced by Kathleen Diffley's *Where My Heart is Turning Ever* (Athens: University of Georgia Press, 1992).
3. Stark Young, *So Red the Rose* (New York: Scribner's, 1934), n.p.
4. Mark Twain, *Life on the Mississippi* (1883; rpt. Mark Twain, *Mississippi Writing* [New York: Library of America, 1982], p. 491).
5. Lewis Simpson, "On William Faulkner's *Absalom, Absalom!*" *Classics of Civil War Fiction*, ed. David Madden and Peggy Bach (Jackson: University Press of Mississippi, 1991), p. 152.
6. For two very thorough but contrasting views of the Lost Cause and its partisans, consult Charles Reagan Wilson's *Baptized in Blood; The Religion of the Lost Cause, 1865-1920* (Athens: University of Georgia Press, 1990), and Gaines Foster's *Ghosts of the Confederacy: Defeat, the Lost Cause, and the Emergence of the New South* (New York: Oxford University Press, 1987).
7. Cited in Hayden White, *Metahistory: The Historical Imagination of Nineteenth-Century Europe* (Baltimore: Johns Hopkins University Press, 1973), p. 339.
8. John Sartoris's corruption becomes complete only in the final story, "An Odor of Verbena," which was written some time after the first six stories for the final rounding out of the novel. Faulkner's stories "Ambuscade," "Retreat," and "Raid" appeared in the *Saturday Evening Post* on September 29, October 31, and November 3, 1934. A hiatus ensued while Faulkner worked in Hollywood. "Skirmish at Sartoris," which would be the sixth chapter in the novel, was published in *Scribner's Magazine* in April 1935. After holding "Riposte in Tertio" and "Vendée," the fourth and fifth stories for two years, the *Post* published them in November and December, respectively, 1936. In 1937 Bennett Cerf decided to publish the series if Faulkner

would provide a concluding story and more continuity. Accordingly, Faulkner rewrote the already published stories and added "An Odor of Verbena." Details may be found in John Pilkington, "Strange Times in Yoknapatawpha," in *Fifty Years of Yoknapatawpha*, ed. Doreen Fowler and Ann J. Abadie (Jackson: University Press of Mississippi, 1986), pp. 71-89. There are indications that Faulkner also intended Colonel John to be revealed as less than admirable. In his short story "There Was a Queen" (1932) an omniscient narrator reveals that Elnora, a mulatto servant, is Bayard's half sister. Faulkner seems to have barred himself from dramatic use of this information in *The Unvanquished* by adding that it was likely that neither she nor Bayard knew this. This information suggests that Faulkner might have toyed with the idea of making Bayard and Ringo brothers, but instead worked out that concept in *Absalom*, for Elnora is Ringo's sister. His parents are Euphony and Simon, the latter being John Sartoris's body servant and companion during the war. John's betrayal of Simon further suggests the sexual triangle of Zack Edmonds and Molly and Lucas Beauchamp in *Go Down, Moses*. For a detailed chart of Sartoris genealogy, white and black, consult Edmond L. Volpe, *A Reader's Guide to William Faulkner* (New York: Noonday Press, 1964), p. 67.

9. Friedrich Nietzsche, *The Use and Abuse of History*, trans. Adrian Collins (Indianapolis: Bobbs-Merrill, 1949), p. 41.
10. Frederick L. Gwynn and Joseph L. Blotner, ed., *Faulkner in the University: Class Conferences at the University of Virginia, 1957-1958* (New York: Vintage, 1965), p. 251.
11. *Ibid.*, p. 249.
12. William Faulkner, *The Unvanquished* (1938; rpt. New York: Vintage, 1966), pp. 10-11. Perhaps to bolster heroic images such as this, Faulkner made a number of changes in the Sartoris story published in 1929. John Sartoris's two daughters are nowhere to be found in *The Unvanquished*; indeed, one could multiply these sorts of omissions rather easily—where, for example, is the dashing Bayard I, brother of Colonel John? *Sartoris* tells us of his glorious but foolish death while raiding General Pope's camp in search of anchovies. He is missing here, possibly because Faulkner streamlined his Sartoris material for short-story settings, and then decided not to restore them when he combined the stories into *The Unvanquished*. Twinning John would have undercut his tragic, dashing presence, especially since Bayard I's death operates in the sentimental, comic mode. Much of the overdone, sometimes silly comedy Faulkner had woven about the original Sartoris stories published in magazines is deliberately pared away too; although the comic central story of Granny and the mules is retained, it changes in character as it unfolds and ends in tragedy.

13. Bayard equates himself, Ringo, Joby and Loosh with Napoleon's troops in their admiration of the similarly small hero. John Sartoris, (p. 14) and, in fact, a string of references to Napoleon appears throughout the novel, demonstrating that Bayard's sense of monumental history doesn't come solely from romantic novels; the little general's *Maxims* are in the Sartoris library, and his monumental history has obviously been appreciated, for Ringo's full name is Marengo. This Italian town was the site of Napoleon's miraculous victory in 1800 over the Austrians under Melas. Desaix arrived with fresh troops to save the French, but was killed during the battle. Napoleon's ability to "rise again" obviously would make him a figure of added resonance after the war, but he in any case offers a stirring example of monumental history.
14. Gwynn and Blotner, p. 251.This statement about the non-heroic John Sartoris II would seem to be one of those instances where Faulkner forgot the details of his prior characterizations. In *Sartoris* we are told that Old Bayard's son John succumbs in 1901 to yellow fever and "an old Spanish bullet-wound," (90) so he must have participated in the Spanish-American war.
15. Joseph Blotner, *Selected Letters of William Faulkner* (New York: Random House, 1977), p. 166.
16. *Ibid.*, p. 170.
17. Drusilla seems to be modelled on the heroines of the Old Colonel's works about the Mexican War, *The Spanish Heroine*, a novel *The Siege of Monterrey*, a poem; both poems feature a heroine who dons a man's uniform and fights on the battlefield. *Siege*'s frontispiece featured a woodcut of Isabel, a Joan of Arc in the field. She begs her lover not to go into battle, offers her body as a bribe, and scoffs at honor (for a full discussion of the Old Colonel and his works, see Donald DuClos, "Son of Sorrow: The Life, Works, and Influence of Colonel Williams C. Faulkner, 1825-1889," Diss., University of Michigan, 1962). Drusilla, by contrast, inverts all three of these goals but offers the same kind of physical bribe to Bayard. But Drusilla becomes transformed by the war and hardened. She becomes a kind of avenging Fury long before John Sartoris dies, helping steal the ballot boxes on her wedding day, then egging her husband on in his ruthless campaign against first the carpetbaggers, which culminates in the murder of the Burdens, and then in his campaign for personal and capitalist power which in turn culminates in his murdering one of his former soldiers. Finally, when John himself is killed, Drusilla, bordering on madness, becomes a kind of Lady Macbeth, offering Bayard not a dagger, but pistols; to him she is "the Greek amphora priestess of a succinct and formal violence." (p. 252) She is a monumentalist historian with a vengeance.

18. Cited in Nietzsche, *The Use and Abuse of History*, p. 4.
19. William Faulkner, *Flags in the Dust* (New York: Random House, 1973), p. 12.
20. In these scenes, the rampant blacks, rather than the Yankees, are the epitome of evil; in the ashes, later, the family finds one "chocolate cup of Dresden, the roses on it still fresh," (p. 345) a talisman of "white culture" unvanquished by the blacks; it is also an eerie prefiguration of Kurt Vonnegut's metaphor in *Slaughterhouse Five* (1969), when an American prisoner finds a perfect figurine in the ashes of devastated Dresden.
21. George Lukács, *The Historical Novel*, trans. Hannah and Stanley Mitchell (1963; rpt. Lincoln: University of Nebraska Press, 1983), p. 42.
22. *Letters*, pp. 78-79.
23. Oscar Cargill, *Intellectual America: Ideas on the March* (New York: Macmillan, 1959), p. 382.
24. Faulkner likely drew his inspiration for this scene from Young's *So Red the Rose*; there, Miss Mary Cherry, an incorrigible spinster of sixty who visits both plantation homes in the novel, turns out to be adept at smuggling goods in and out of the Yankee lines, putting boots, shoes, and quinine under her skirts. There, the device is played mainly for laughs; Mrs. Bedford tells her ailing husband the stories to cheer him up: "the pickets let her pass," to which he replies, "Now that shows one of two things; either their lack of courage or her lack of fascination." (p. 235)
25. Ralph Ellison, *Shadow and Act* (New York: Vintage, 1964), p. 43.
26. Gayatri Spivak, "Translator's Preface," Jacques Derrida, *Of Grammatology*, trans. Gayatri Spivak (Baltimore: Johns Hopkins University Press, 1974), p. xvii.
27. Friedrich Nietzsche, *The Birth of Tragedy and the Case of Wagner*, trans. Walter Kaufmann (New York: Vintage, 1967), p. 142.
28. Mikhail Bakhtin, *The Dialogic Imagination: Four Essays*, ed. Michael Holquist, trans. Caryl Emerson and Michael Holquist (Austin: University of Texas Press, 1981), p. 55.
29. I spoke earlier of Faulkner's erasures; one reason, perhaps, he was successful in keeping the "plug hats" and "hoop skirts" out of the book was that Edward Shenton's pictures put them back in. The seven illustrations Shenton did for the book (a frontispiece depicting John Sartoris holding a Confederate flag in one hand and a drawn sabre in another, plus illustrations for each of the seven chapters), with one exception, all include weapons. The other is the portrait of Granny, clad in hoop-skirt and bonnet and holding a parasol (her weapon), walking bravely into the woods to meet Grumby at the start of "Riposte in Tertio."

30. Along these lines, Susan Donaldson, in "Dismantling the *Saturday Evening Post* Reader: *The Unvanquished* and Changing 'Horizons of Expectations,'" in *Faulkner and Popular Culture*, ed. Doreen Fowler and Ann J. Abadie (Jackson: University Press of Mississippi, 1990), pp. 179-95, has offered an ingenious reading of the way Faulkner sets up and then explodes conventional readers' expectations, particularly in the final form the novel took after he revised the original *Saturday Evening Post* stories.
31. Friedrich Nietzsche, *Thus Spake Zarathustra*, trans. Thomas Common (New York: Modern Library, 1917), p. 107.
32. Gerard Genette, *Narrative Discourse*: *An Essay in Method*, trans. Jane E. Lewin (Ithaca, New York: Cornell University Press, 1980), p. 206.
33. Ursula Von Brumm, "Forms and Functions of History in the Novels of William Faulkner," *Archiv*, 209 (1971-72), pp. 53-54.
34. Herman Melville, *Moby-Dick, or, The Whale* (1851; rpt. New York: Houghton Mifflin, 1956), p. 293.

This article was published in *The Mississippi Quarterly*, Vol. XLVI, No. 3, Summer 1993. Reprinted with permission.

"Old Man": A Critique

P.G. RAMA RAO

William Faulkner's "Old Man" is one of the two stories which originally appeared in 1939 under the title *The Wild Palms*. The two stories, which were to be published separately later as "Old Man" and "The Wild Palm," were curiously mixed up in this book by the author who alternated their chapters in an obviously planned way. But, some years later, when asked about it, he replied that he alternated the chapters as it was found that each story was too brief for book publication separately.[1] This gives us the impression that Faulkner had originally conceived the two stories as separate novels though he found a thematic link between them later. But, later on, at the Nagano Seminar, we find him answering the question "what kind of effect did you intend in that story [*The Wild Palms*]?" as follows: "To tell the story I wanted to tell, which was the one of the intern and the woman who gave up her family and husband to run off with him. To tell it like that, somehow or another I had to discover a counterpoint for it, so I invented the other story, its complete antithesis, to use as counterpoint. And I did not write those two stories and then cut one into another."[2] This answer baffles us completely. Faulkner's contradictory statements on this subject in two different interviews should caution us against taking seriously a writer's utterances about his own work in an interview. Most of Faulkner criticism has regarded "Old Man" as a thematic contrast to "The Wild Palms," and not as an individual work, obviously because of the original form in which the author offered it and his subsequent comments.

When read as an individual work, complete in itself, "Old Man" reveals itself as a typical example of some of Faulkner's thematic pre-occupations and fictional techniques, and of his metaphysics of time. The subject of the story is the great Mississippi flood of 1927 in which the struggles of a convict, who paddles a boat in order to rescue two people, are dramatized. The convict succeeds in rescuing only one of them, a pregnant woman, suffers and struggles helplessly but with indomitable courage and endurance on the waters, does not think even for a moment of escaping even though he has many opportunities, and finally returns to the penitentiary with the boat and the rescued woman, thus setting a shining example in honesty and duty to most people outside the prison. The "Old Man" of the story is the Mississippi river, the "father of waters." Whatever happens to the young convict happens to him because of the "Old Man" and the young man passes through the most memorable experience of his life as he struggles against the "Old Man," endures and survives, only to report honestly at the penitentiary at the end.

Describing the Mississippi flood of 1927, Lyle Saxon says:

> The levees fell to pieces faster than the wires could twang the news to the papers. Men saw marvels of modern engineering topple like tooth pick fortresses, and they realized again, what they had been about to forget, that the river was no less than it had been in pre-levee days, but remained in spite of human efforts the same muddy miracle it was when de Soto found it. They did not wonder that the Indians prayed to the Mississippi. They knew why the Nile and the Tiber had been gods. *There is something terrible and yet maliciously gleeful about the river when it breaks its man-made manacles*, something human with a kind of Frankenstein-humanness.[3] (Italics mine)

This passage throws light on the in-built pattern of contrast between the mighty river breaking its manacles, working havoc, and the convict keeping his courage against heavy odds. The emphasis seems to be placed on the importance of keeping one's manacles. The breaking of restraints in favour of absolute freedom in "The Wild Palms" to which "Old Man" is said to be an antithesis, is thus represented by the flood in the framework of "Old Man" itself.

The flood, apart from being an important theme in the story, virtually determines the mechanics of narration which serve to unfold the meaning of the story:

> Here they both saw and heard movement—the slow profound

> eastward and upstream ("It's running backward," one convict said quietly) set of the still rigid surface from beneath which came a deep faint subaquean rumble. . . . It was as if the water itself were in three strata, separate and distinct, the bland and unhurried surface bearing a frothy scum and a miniature flotsam of twigs and screening as though by vicious calculation the rush and fury of the flood itself, and beneath this in turn the original stream, trickle, murmuring along in the opposite direction, following undisturbed and unaware its appointed course and serving its Lilliputian end, like a thread of ants between the rails on which an express train passes, they [the ants] as unaware of the power and fury as if it were a cyclone crossing Saturn.[4]

The three strata of the Mississippi flood reflect the three levels of narration in the story. The first of these three levels is the omniscient narration done by a God-like narrator who is above the events described in the story, above even the great flood which he can vividly describe across the levels and the Indian mounds, and for whom time is not a matter of progression but a continuum. He sees the whole of it, and so if the interest is to be focused on any single event or experience, the narration has to be in retrospect, through the consciousness of one of the characters. This flash-back narration is at the secondary level in the story.

The omniscient narration is demanded by the great flood which represents the fury of nature and brings into focus the suffering of people and the sins committed with impunity by those in authority. This narration corresponds to "the bland and unhurried surface" of the flood which is perfectly motionless and flat. "It looked as if you could walk on it. It looked so still that they did not realize it possessed motion until they came to the first bridge." (85) Such is the nature of narration at this level, as the omniscient narrator provides us with a sort of aerial view of the flood and the broad framework of the story. Something happens to the flux of time here also, and we do not realize that it possesses motion until we come to the first bridge with the convicts and see the second stratum of the water which is "the rush and fury of the flood itself" screened by the first stratum.[5]

The second stratum of the water, which has a backward motion, ("It's running backward," one convict said quietly) and against which the tall convict contends, is related to the flash-back narration of his experiences by the tall convict. At this level of narration we have a narrator (the tall convict) and a listener (the plump convict), though the general method is still the third-person narration and we keep on hearing the voice of the omniscient narrator from time to time. The narration here involves the convict's struggle against the fury of the flood on which the interest is apparently focused. But it is not his struggle that is important here but the meaning of this struggle which is unfolded by the third level of narration. The third stratum of the water, which is the original stream "following undisturbed and unaware its appointed course and serving its Lilliputian end, like a thread of ants between the rails on which an express train passes," corresponds to the third level of narration involving the convict's action in following his appointed course undisturbed by the horrible experiences he passes through, and serving his "Lilliputian" end—"Lilliputian" in relation to the vast convulsions of the Mississippi and his own horrible experiences on it, and also because his honesty and sense of duty go unnoticed by the authorities. This "original stream" or the Mississippi proper is the "Old Man" and Faulkner seems to emphasize the third stratum of the narrative, which lies screened by the two strata above it and calls for a closer critical attention.

"Old Man" is primarily the tall convict's story. But the omniscient narrator describes the second convict who does not play an active role in the story in greater detail in the opening section of the story. The fact that this convict is sentenced to a hundred and ninety-nine years at the penitentiary for a crime committed by some body else who escaped (81) is a significant comment on the kind of justice dispensed in the country and on the value of time, which stands suspended for some of the convicts as it is for the omniscient narrator operating at the first level of narration. The plump convict serves as a device of disclosure in the story for he listens to the tall convict's story, making comments and asking questions now and then, and throwing some light on the situation, apart from giving us a sense of suspension of time by his absurdly long sentence, which somehow makes everybody look a prisoner in the world, as everybody seems to be in the eyes of Faulkner's omniscient narrator.[6]

The tall convict's flash-back narration takes place seven weeks after he sets out on his rescue operation. He is given up for lost by the plump convict who rescues himself with the help of a tree as the boat turns turtle. But the tall convict holds on to the paddle and the boat and succeeds in rescuing the woman in the tree. He is acutely conscious of his responsibilities. He has to pick up the man on the cotton house and his fellow convict who vanished upward into a tree "like in a translation out of Isaiah," and do something about the pregnant woman in the boat. As he paddles on and on, struggling against a hostile current which hurls him repeatedly on to the bottom of the skiff, the omniscient narrator tells us: "It merely seemed to him that he had accidentally been caught in a situation in which time and environment, not himself, was mesmerized; he was being toyed with by a current of water going nowhere, beneath a day which would wane toward no evening; when it was done with him it would spew him back into the comparatively safe world he had been snatched violently out of and in the meantime it did not much matter just what he did or did not do." (104) He is to learn later that he is being toyed with by something more than a current of water which is a symbol of that greater and more malignant force, the power of which is effectively brought out by the static picture of the time and environment being "mesmerized." This traumatic experience on the raging water makes him think of the penitentiary as a "comparatively safe world," while the passage quoted above makes us think of the closed world in which we live, not knowing that it is a huge prison where we are toyed with by mysterious forces.

As it becomes clear to him that there is no question of rowing the boat as he likes, his only worry is to do something about the pregnant woman and get rid of her. But he wants to do it the *right way* "not for himself, but for her." It is not difficult to get rid of her. Her could put her back into another tree any time. This moral stance in the convict, his insistence on doing the right thing, is what primarily engages our attention at the third level of the narrative. He does not even bother to examine her when he rescues her "since that first startled glance had been ample to reveal to him all the generations of her life and background, who could have been his sister if he had a sister, his wife if he had not entered the penitentiary at an age scarcely out of adolescence." (105) He does not, even for a moment, entertain the idea of escaping. He only wants to find somebody to whom he could surrender her and then return to the prison. But he comes up against difficulty after difficulty. Fate is so cross with him that he is not even allowed to surrender at Baton Rouge where the soldiers fire on him as he walks towards them to surrender.

During his nine-day idyll on the Cajan country, where he subjugated the alligators in single combat while the Cajan and his friends watched in open-mouthed admiration, he finds the joy of working for his livelihood which he was denied at the penitentiary where "he had been permitted to toil but not to work." (159) But even this pleasure is taken away from him by the "cosmic joker" when he, the Cajan, and others are evacuated as the levee is to be dynamited.

When the "Old Man" had recovered from his debauch, back on banks again, "the tall convict, in a faded but recently washed and quite clean suit of penitentiary clothing," reports to the deputy sheriff saying: "yonder's your boat, and here's the woman. But I never did find that bastard on the cotton house." (172) That the convict values his character above everything else is evident from the way he reacts to the suggestion of the man on the shanty-boat that he should burn his penitentiary clothing. He tells the man the circumstances under which he and his partner were given the boat and what happened subsequently and "now all in the world he wanted was something flat to leave the woman on until he could find an officer, a sheriff." (120) Then he thinks of home, friends and familiar places and the Sunday games and the picture shows—a very tempting prospect indeed. But his moral conscience and sense of responsibility assert themselves and put down the temptation, as he thinks of his own character:

> But most of all, his own character (Two years ago they had offered to make a trusty of him. He would no longer need to plow or feed stock, he would only follow those who did with a loaded gun, but he declined. "I reckon I'll stick to plowing," he said, absolutely without humor. "I done already tried to use a gun one time too many"), his good name, *his responsibility not only toward those who were responsible toward him but to himself, his own honor in the doing of what was asked of him, his pride in being able to do it, no matter what it was.* (120-21, Italics mine)

The convict's character, his essential morality, seems central to the story. He is a human being and so subject to temptations as when he is tempted by visions of his house and friends and, for a moment, by the woman he has rescued. "But they were just seconds because in the next instant his whole being would seem to flee the very idea in a kind of savage and horrified revulsion." (180) This revulsion might be due to the fact that his sense of responsibility towards her is outraged by his momentary temptation. He is certainly not a saint for we find him succumbing to the demands of the flesh twice in the story; but the text of the story reveals him as a man of character and strong moral convictions.

In the convict's last flash-back account we are told about his one time fiancee who dropped him after his incarceration and married another. He divulged his plan about the projected train robbery to her and "possibly if it had not been for her he would not actually have attempted it." (183) This experience makes him dislike women bitterly and the story ends with his unprintable expletive concerning women. This explains his strange attitude to the rescued woman whom he regards as his responsibility and nothing more.

At the first level of narration, which is resumed by the omniscient narrator after the flash-back ends with the convict's return to the Parchman prison, we find the Governor's emissary and the warden wondering what to do with the convict who has returned after having been reported dead to the higher authorities. They are outraged by his honesty. The Governor's emissary is against holding an investigation and they are not prepared to find fault with the Deputy Warden who is politically influential. So they sentence the convict to ten years more at the penitentiary for attempting to escape, a crime which was never even dimly contemplated by him. This is the "cosmic joker's" last joke on the convict. But the convict takes it calmly. He does not even ask why: "'All right,' the convict said. 'If that's the rule.'" (177) He has done whatever he was asked to do in the right way to the best of his satisfaction against impossible odds. The convict's honesty and sense of honour and his dignified bearing under severe stress make the cosmic joker's joke fall flat. It takes away the sting from the sentence and the reader's reaction at the end is a mixture of contempt for administrative corruption and injustice on the one hand and admiration for the innocent victim whose conduct puts the administrators to shame on the other, and not one of pity for the convict.

Faulkner seems to uphold the honesty and sense of responsibility of man in a hostile universe. A man may be rendered impotent and helpless by superior forces but if he sticks to the values he prizes, he not merely endures, but prevails, and his will be a moral triumph.

This puts us in mind of Faulkner's Nobel Award Acceptance Speech in the course of which he says:

> He [the writer] must teach himself that the basest of all things is to be afraid; and, teaching himself that, forget it forever, leaving no room in his workshop for anything but the old verities and truths of the heart, the old universal truths lacking which any story is ephemeral and doomed—love and honor and pity and pride and compassion and sacrifice.[7]

If we look at the story from the mythical point of view, the convict strikes us as a hero who ventures forth from the world of commonday, like the mythical hero, into a region of supernatural wonder and, after encountering fabulous forces there (which are represented by the great flood, the alligators and other hazards in the story), returns. He brings back more than a woman and a boat. He brings a lesson in honesty, courage, endurance and duty.[8]

The three-tier narrative technique adopted by Faulkner seems determined by the theme and purport of the story. The omniscient narration at the primary level presents a panoramic picture of the Mississippi flood as well as of a corrupt social and administrative set-up; the flash-back narration at the secondary level focuses attention on the protagonist's travails on the waters; and the meaning of the story which involves the convict's single minded (but almost instinctive and unaware) pursuit of his moral responsibility corresponding to the Mississippi ("Old Man") following "undisturbed and unaware its appointed course" lies at the tertiary level. The two upper layers of the story, gradually become transparent revealing the whole meaning and the moral force of the convict's conduct against the background of a hostile river (which is made clear at the secondary level) and an immoral administrative set up (which is treated at the primary level.)[9]

NOTES

1. Lavon Rascoe, "An Interview with William Faulkner," *Western Review*, 15 (Summer 1951), pp. 300-4, quoted by William Van O'Connor, *The Tangled Fire of William Faulkner* (Minneapolis, 1954), p. 105. Malcolm Cowley, in *The Portable Faulkner*, published "Old Man" separately, and the two stories are published separately in paperback editions.

2. *Faulkner at Nagano*, ed. Robert A. Jelliffe (Tokyo: 1966), pp. 79-80. Irving Howe, in his *William Faulkner: A Critical Study* (New York: 1952), pp. 172-79, points out many thematic connections between the two stories.
3. *Father Mississippi* (New York: 1927), pp. 298-99. Michael Millgate, *The Achievement of William Faulkner* (London, 1966), p. 325, tells us that Faulkner owned a copy of this book at the time of his death and observes that "it seems likely that he had earlier drawn upon it for some details of the 'Old Man' material."
4. William Faulkner, "Old Man," *Three Famous Short Novels* (New York, 1942), p. 85. Subsequent references are to this edition.
5. Jean-Paul Sartre's view that there is no progression and that there is only past, no future, in Faulkner's work is significant: "Faulkner's vision of the world can be compared to that of a man sitting in an open car and looking backwards." ("On *The Sound and the Fury*: Time in the Work of Faulkner," *Literary and Philosophical Essays*, trans. Annette Michelson, New York: Collier Books, 1962), p. 87.
6. The omniscient narrator in Faulkner's *Light in August* makes the following remark about Joe Christmas who decides to run away from McEachern's house: "He felt like an eagle: hard, sufficient, potent, remorseless, strong. But that passed, though he did not then know that, like the eagle, his own flesh as well as all space was still a cage." (New York, 1950), p. 140.
7. *American Literature 1890-1965: An Anthology*, ed. Egbert S. Oliver (New Delhi, 1967), p. 83.
8. Joseph Campbell, *The Hero with a Thousand Faces* (Princeton, 1968), p. 30.
9. This is the farthest we can reasonably go in mythical or symbolistic interpretation here. For example of what look like exercises in critical gimmicry, see Richard J. Stonesifer's treatment of the convict as Don Quixote reversed, "a cruelly ironic modern counterpart of the idealistic knight" in "Faulkner's *Old Man* in the Class Room," *College English*, 27 (February 1956), pp. 254-57, and John Feaster's treatment of the convict's journey as severance from the mother-surrogate, viz., prison, effected by the father-surrogate, viz., the Mississippi or the "Old Man," and of the whole story as one of inter-uterine regression in his "Faulkner's *Old Man*: A Psycho-analytic Approach," *Modern Fiction Studies*, 13 (Spring 1967), pp. 89-93.

This article was originally published in *Indian Journal of American Studies*, vol. 1, No. 4, November 1971. Reprinted with the kind permission of the author.

Compulsive and Revisionary Repetition in "Barn Burning"

RICHARD C. MORELAND

While reading the typescript of *The Mansion,* Faulkner's Random House editor, Albert Erskine kept finding "discrepancies and contradictions" between the earlier, already published novels of Faulkner's *Snopes Trilogy* and this typescript of the last, in which Faulkner retold some of the same stories about some of the same events and characters, but retold them differently. As Erskine reported these discrepancies and contradictions, Faulkner became somewhat impatient with his editor's worrying so much about what Faulkner thought would pose problems only for readers he tended to call "academical gumshoes." He agreed to correct some such discrepancies, but eventually decided to let many more stand uncorrected, and decided to steal our gumshoe thunder by writing a prefatory note to the novel asserting his awareness of many of these discrepancies and explaining his reasons for letting them show. Erskine had already offered what would have been a New Critical line of defense in suggesting that these three novels might not be a trilogy after all (Blotner 1720-35), implying that Faulkner could fall back safely on the idea that each of his novels was an autonomous new creation by a peculiarly literary genius, who would therefore speak the language of poetry and religion, identified at the time as a language of oracular paradox.[1] But this was not the explanation Faulkner gave. Instead, perhaps more candidly, he says in his prefatory note that over his life's work of writing he has continued to *learn* more than he knew before about the human heart and about his characters. If readers notice differences, then, in Faulkner's repetitions or rewritings of previous work, perhaps we should not gloat so thunderously that

Homer nods, but neither should we pass over such discrepancies silently, apologetically, or sentimentally as part of this Mississippi native's woodsy wildness, something only a "better craftsman" like Pound or Hemingway would have bothered to prune and tame. These repetitions and especially the differences they emphasize might represent, instead, importantly critical, published revisions of Faulkner's ongoing thinking and writing, revisions not just of minor details but of whole plots and structures of thought, revisions, even, of (modernist and structuralist) assumptions about how thought is structured and how it changes. In the course of Faulkner's career, he constantly recycled and refit plots, episodes, characters, and phrases from poems to stories to filmscripts to novels to other stories and other novels: not only were such repetitions and differences unusually prolific and undisguised, they amounted to an ongoing critical project, as he repeated certain dominant structures of thought in the post-Civil War American South and the post-World War I United States and Europe, first to explore and understand their motivations and consequences, then critically to revise certain structural contradictions and impasses that were shared by both these postwar cultures, and that were elaborated in Faulkner's own and others' literary modernism.

Faulkner's revisions of his modernism involved an important shift in the function of repetition, both in his own work and also in its historical and literary contexts as he understood them. In order to understand this shift, the notion of repetition with a significant, critical difference, which I will call *revisionary repetition*, should be distinguished from repetition of another kind which I call, after Freud, *compulsive repetition*. Revisionary repetition repeats some structured event, in order somehow to alter that structure and its continuing power, especially by opening a critical space for what the subject might *learn* about that structure in the different context of a changing present or a more distant or different past. As Sartre says, "a life develops in spirals; it passes again and again by the same points but at different levels of integration and complexity." (106) This is the kind of repetition I have attributed to Faulkner's revisions of his modernism. But in compulsive repetition, it is precisely this unpredictable possibility of critically altering a familiar structure in the light of changing or different circumstances which repetition attempts to avoid. It attempts to expunge or ward off all such changes and variations as insignificant departures from an abstractly unchanged, unaffected original. Even the most unpleasant, restrictively habitual repetitions may seem in this way preferable to the unpredictability and impurity of change and difference. Inasmuch as every repetition, then, involves both an identity of the same content or structure and also a difference and change at least in time and context, compulsive repetition attempts to exclude that difference and change; revisionary repetition attempts to alter the structures of identity. This is of course a functional—not an absolute—distinction. Even compulsive repetition is never static, try as it may. Given a linguistic, social or psychological structure of such continuing power that it cannot be simply ignored, forgotten, or denied, but must be more or less acknowledged as a repetition, either compulsively or in a spirit of critical revision, revisionary repetition works to inscribe marks of change, specificity, and difference within and around that structure. Whereas compulsive repetition tends to repeat the familiar and familial, revisionary repetition places these familiarities (with critical effect) in the midst of irrepressibly ambivalent, fearful, but strong desires for other voices.

The issue of these two kinds of repetition arises in Faulkner's work in two ways, as method and then as topic—topic for a critique that led in turn to a shift in method. In his novels before *Absalom, Absalom!* Faulkner's method shared a tendency with that of other modernists (as described especially by Michael O'Brien 138-45) toward repeated juxtapositions of various "unified sensibilities" from the past—Eliot's Elizabethans, Joyce's Greeks, Yeats's Byzantines and Celts, the Southern Agrarians' Agrarian South—and the supposedly meaningless disarray and banality of everyday modern life, typically represented from an ironic distance as a "heap of broken images."[2] As Faulkner extended his treatment of such broken images in *Light in August* and especially *Absalom, Absalom!* from the realm of the personal and familial toward the racial and historical,[3] and from metaphysical themes of destruction and loss toward social, historical themes of change and difference, he explored and analyzed certain compulsive habits of memory, narration, and (in)action on the parts of his characters—in their protomodernist vacillation between a more or less explicit nostalgia for a diseased social structure and the ironic contemplation of scenes of its inevitable and total collapse—that were in many ways similar to modernist methods of his own. After interrupting his work on *Absalom* for a parodic treatment of cosmopolitan literary modernism in *Pylon*,

Faulkner continued to examine in these characters of the postwar South the social and historical motivations and consequences of their now more culturally dominant vacillation between forced nostalgia and bitter irony. In *Absalom* Faulkner traces the motivations of such a vacillation not to the deeper metaphysical nature of time and loss[4] but to the social and historical climate of disillusionment, defeat, and depression that was already decades old, somewhat threadbare, and all too familiar in the South in 1909-10 as his characters remembered it—and that was even more familiar by the time Faulkner was writing this novel in the 1930s, when World War I and the Great Depression had pulled the rest of the United States and Europe into a similar but much wider cultural climate of disillusionment.[5] Turning his own relatively longer and more intense regional, historical, and personal familiarity with such a climate to critical advantage, Faulkner began to discover and demonstrate in *Absalom* how this repetitive vacillation between nostalgia and irony in reaction to such disillusionment works—by attempting retroactively to ward off and soften the impact of a once unexpected blow, forestalling the implications of historical change and difference by insisting on the unchanging drama of fated destruction and loss. While Faulkner thus comes to understand the motivations of such a vacillation between nostalgia and irony, he also comes to understand its consequences when it becomes a compulsive impasse attempting indefinitely to exclude change and difference, often with an increasingly frustrated violence. Faulkner's critical explorations of this repetitive impasse as a historical topic in *Absalom* led him to seek a way out in "Barn Burning" and *The Hamlet*, by revising a scene that in *Absalom* is said to have started a series of compulsive repetitions (from which neither Sutpen nor his various biological and cultural descendants could escape). In finding a way out of those repetitions for Ab Snopes, Faulkner also discovered his own way out of certain widespread, compulsive modernist methods, finding in this new process of revisionary repetition both a strikingly different fictional method and also openings for several new, formerly marginalized topics, notably the makeshift economy and precarious humor of the Old Southwest; mourning as a way of working through the relentless and hollow repetitions of melancholia; and blacks' and women's critically different voices.

In this essay I will point to certain promising openings for such new topics, focusing instead on "Barn Burning" as a pivotal moment in Faulkner's career, poised between one method of repetition and the other, turning from the compulsive toward the revisionary for a change in method that made such changes in topics possible. The crises in one mode of repetition (in *Absalom*) that led Faulkner toward the other mode, or the different projects and results of Faulkner's ongoing revisionary repetitions in *The Hamlet, Go Down, Moses,* and *Requiem for a Nun* is left out of the purview of this essay.

An exemplary site for Faulkner's discovery of his way out of his native culture's and his artistic peers' compulsive repetitions is a series of repetitions and revisions of one particular structured social event in *Absalom, Absalom!* It is the scene where the ragged young Thomas Sutpen comes with a message from his tenant-farming father to the majestic front door of the planter for whom his father works. The liveried black slave who opens and bars the door tells Sutpen "even before he had time to say what he came for, never to come to that front door again but to go around to the back." Stunned and shattered here by his own social silencing and exclusion, Sutpen idealizes and internalizes the image of a planter perfectly purified, invulnerable, and invisible somewhere inside the house. Years later Sutpen represents this scene to General Compson as the determining incident—a primal scene, as it were—at the very origin of his life's design to found his own family dynasty inside the same unviolated, unbroken Southern plantation tradition. He represents it as a primal scene, that is, in the sense of his being henceforth powerlessly compelled only to re-present and to repeat what he thinks he has learned here once for all about the structure of his society and even of life in general. The rest of *Absalom* traces Sutpen's and his adopted culture's variously relentless, compulsive repetitions of this same structured social event, this apparently inescapable primal scene of purifying exclusion.

In "Barn Burning," published three years later, in 1939, Faulkner returns to this scene again, not compulsively, however, but in order to make significant revisions, and to open a critical space for reconceiving this oppressive primal scene. Again a poor-white boy inclined to idealize the planter's house sees his own way into the front door of that house barred by a liveried and insulting black servant; however, this time the boy, Sarty Snopes, is accompanied by his less impressionable father, Ab Snopes, who is not awestruck by the insult but has clearly expected and provoked it, and who responds by pushing his way inside to deliver his message anyway by smearing horse manure on the blond rug inside the door. After some ambivalence about his father's peculiar writing style (what Kristeva might call a minor revolution in poetic language), Sarty eventually repeats his society's tendency to refuse to read such gestures at writing difference, and repeats its violent condemnation and exclusion of Ab's social difference as only so much social filth. At least from Sarty's frightened and therefore humorless perspective, Ab's potentially critical difference seems here a failed and fatal alternative.

However, Faulkner himself would enlarge prolifically on this same critical and creative potential for revising the plantation society's primal scene, as he rewrites it once again as an opening episode of *The Hamlet*, published another year later in 1940.[6] He now replaces Sarty's frightened, humorless perspective on Ab's "bad attitude" at the planter's door with V.K. Ratliff's humorous appreciation of Ab's singular history and his singularly unsettling provocations. Whereas in "Barn Burning" Sarty thinks Ab's attitude at the planter's door leads toward his inevitable, tragic (actually uncertain) death at the end of the story, in *The Hamlet*'s version Ratliff enjoys telling of Ab's repeated escape from that expected tragedy and of his surviving to outrage the planter's categories again and move on to Frenchman's Bend. By placing the scene at the opening of volume I of *The Snopes Trilogy*, the longest, most sustained work of his career, Faulkner makes this episode a primal scene now of a different kind. It is the occasion not for compulsive repetition but for humorous appreciation and elaboration as an exemplary scene of critical escape from reductive and oppressive social categories and oppositions, a scene that points a way out for others without pretending to point the one new way.

I have mentioned humor, mourning, and different voices as three openings for critical escape from *Absalom*'s compulsive primal scene, openings which Faulkner discovered in his revisionary repetition of that scene in "Barn Burning" and which he explored farther in his continuing revisions of that scene in *The Hamlet.* But in order to explain better Faulkner's discovery in his fiction of these openings for critical and revisionary escape, I should first explain briefly here the nature of those compulsive categories and oppositions in *Absalom* which Faulkner felt an increasing need to revise as he examined their social and historical implications. For in *Absalom*, while he does not yet open a way out of those compulsions,

Faulkner does already discover and demonstrate the profoundly ambivalent motivations and extremely violent consequences of both the "innocent" and the "ironic" forms they tend to take in *Absalom*, as in much other modernist literature.

Thomas Sutpen's so-called innocence consists in his imitating and repeating, apparently without self-consciousness, apology, or extenuation, his society's essential gesture of self-purifying exclusion, that gesture he thinks he learned once and for all in his primal scene. In his internalization of his society's idealized image of the planter, Sutpen has erased from his own late memory the ambivalence of having been once, himself along with his closest family and friends, on the outside of that planter's door, wanting to get inside but all too closely tied emotionally and socially to those people and memories he would leave outside. It is this suddenly frightened and confusing ambivalence which motivates the violent imposition of the culturally dominant, idealized image of the planter on his consciousness. The emotional violence of this reductive, willful solution to his ambivalence has the social consequence that Sutpen (like others before him) repeatedly defends that same compulsively purified image of the planter and himself by violent social exclusions throughout his life. On the model of this first class exclusion, he later excludes his first wife, Eulalia, and his first son, Charles Bon, because of their race, and his second daughter (by Millicent Jones) because of her gender.

Faulkner makes both the emotional violence and the social violence of these repeated exclusions clear already in *his* representation of Sutpen's primal scene. It was "like an explosion," (192) Sutpen said. His sudden internalization of the planter's monumental image with no remainder of "ashes" or "refuse" from his formerly groping ambivalence takes the form in the novel of a primal scene—not in the early Freudian sense of an original, determining encounter with an unalterable knowledge, but in the later Freudian sense of a "theoretical fiction" of such an origin, a fictional origin that is always already a simplifying, focusing repetition of more confusing earlier and later memories.[7] In Faulkner's novel Sutpen's primal scene imposes itself at the origin of his life's design as a violently reductive, purifying solution to his emotional confusion about two previous repetitions of this same socially structured event. In those two previous scenes, however, there had seemed to be more room for Sutpen's awareness of his own and others' ambivalence with regard to the violence of the event, whereas in the third that potentially critical awareness of ambivalence and violence is silently excluded from what has become a socially structured, ideologically naturalized event. Faulkner thus analyzes both Sutpen's emotional readiness as an outsider to adopt a neatly reductive, already culturally dominant ideology, and also Sutpen's representative Southern and American attraction to this particular ideology, as he will also analyze others' attractions to other particular ideologies and positions.

In the first of these three scenes, Sutpen is traveling with his father from the frontier society of the West Virginia mountains into the plantation society of Tidewater Virginia. While they are still on the margin of that plantation society Sutpen sees his first slave in the act of carrying and throwing Sutpen's drunken father out the door of a doggery; the slave's mouth is "loud with laughing and full of teeth like tombstones" (182): by comparison with Sutpen's later primal scene, here both the emotional ambivalence and the violence of this temporary, tenuous social exclusion are unmistakable. These become less clear, however, in the second scene, set farther into plantation country, as Sutpen watches his father being "not even allowed to come in by the front door" of taverns and then being ejected, but with "no laughter and jeers to the ejecting now, even if the laughter and jeers had been harsh and without much gentleness in them." (183) Sutpen still misses here the harsh laughter of the doggeries' frontier humor for what it did acknowledge of his and others' ambivalence toward, and mutual vulnerability to, such acts of physical and social violence. Sutpen can still notice here the absence of such laughter as a sign of this society's ideological naturalization of this still palpably unnatural event. In the scene I have called Sutpen's primal scene, however, this potentially critical but confusing perspective is eliminated from his henceforth compulsive repetitions of the scene, as if from the very start: Sutpen accepts and teaches himself once and for all (though the lesson must be learned and taught with repeated, increasing violence) this naturalization of a social act as a simple, even an unobjectionable fact, a fact or presence which other re-presentations can only repeat, without significantly reinscribing or altering what they re-present.

These compulsive repetitions tend to take one other main form in their vacillations in *Absalom* and in Faulkner's earlier modernist work. Quentin Compson, in his self-conscious irony toward Sutpen's innocence, seems aware, as Sutpen was not, of what is repressed and excluded in these compulsive, repetitive acts of purificatory exclusion. However, Quentin's postwar Southern, postwar modernist irony offers only a mirror image of those same compulsions, an attempt to resolve at a higher level—but in the same terms—those oppositions made uncomfortably clear by Sutpen's innocent imitations of this society's defining structure. Irony here represents what has been repressed and excluded in innocence, but represents it only as the still repressed and excluded, without giving any articulate voices of their own to those repressed emotions or those excluded other subjects. That is, irony here preemptively, cautiously represents what innocence has repressed and excluded, but represents it only in the safely generalized, still repressive terms of the same opposition, in some version of what Conrad and Eliot called "the horror" and what Joyce called the "nightmare" of history. It is what Faulkner in *Absalom* represents as the repeatedly repressed and excluded voice of human suffering, desire, and grief heard only in the safely inarticulate, undifferentiated sound of the black idiot Jim Bond's howl.

The particular version of his society's compulsively repeated primal scene on which Quentin himself gets stuck is the scene when Thomas Sutpen's son Henry bursts into his sister's room to announce he has just murdered her fiance, Charles Bon, at the front gate of the Sutpen plantation. Having been ambivalently attached to Bon as a friend, Henry has just repeated his father's act of purifying exclusion at the plantation gate in a gesture of protecting his sister's and his family's honor from the "spot" of black blood which he has discovered in Bon. Having thereby secured his own place, as it were, in the *father*'s place on the inside of the plantation threshold, he enters now into his sister's room as if "into his own," as if to claim now the father's oedipal prize. But he discovers he is now again on the outside bursting in, coming face to face in his sister's room with Judith half naked and sewing her wedding dress: he is coming face to face, that is, with his own incestuous erotic desire and the violence he has done to Judith by seeing her as an oedipal prize rather than as another subject, capable of speaking from her *own* erotic desire, if he could have listened. Quentin's ironic fixation on this scene does represent some such discovery, on Henry's part, of the violent repression of his ambivalence toward both Bon and Judith, as well as the violent exclusion of Judith's and Bon's own (i.e., different, specific) subjectivities, in his compulsive repetition of his father's primal scene. Presumably Quentin also recognizes in this scene his own ambivalence toward his own sister Caddy and the violence his fixation on her virginity does to her as another subject, capable of her own erotic future. But if Quentin and Henry here do somehow confront ironically that other subjectivity which in their innocence they have previously repressed, it is not now to let that other subject speak in a different voice, but only to fixate on the scene of their own ironic discovery of the exclusion, represented here as a discovery not of particular other subjects but of their own mirror image in the form of the inescapable Other—the Other escapable only in Henry's death as in Quentin's impending suicide. As long as that other is only *the* Other, one can only be inside or outside the door, either father or son, either in possession or not in possession of the contested object of desire. Only when the contested object speaks as another recognizable subject, speaking thus outside the terms of this opposition—only then can the compulsive repetition of this opposition be broken. Here that other voice might have been that of the liveried slave whom Sutpen meets on the threshold of the plantation. Or it might have been the voice of the sister whom Henry finds in two places at once, both inside the plantation ideal, purified and protected from Bon but also outside that same ideal, excluded and silenced as subject with Bon. Such voices are almost everywhere silent in *Absalom*, even though Faulkner's irony like Quentin's almost everywhere here represents their silence and the doors that repeatedly close them out.

In "Barn Burning" the critically different voice at the threshold of the plantation, though hard to read, is that of the poor-white Ab Snopes. Standing alongside Ab on that precarious margin, Ab's son Sarty is tempted in his ambivalence and fright, as Thomas and Henry Sutpen were, to accept his society's compulsive resolutions of that fearful ambivalence. For the sake of such resolutions, Sarty is prepared to accept certain implicit oppositional terms for what he feels in his ambivalence, even though (or perhaps because) those oppositional terms violently bar the door to his father Ab and translate Sarty himself inside the house, in another compulsive insistence on self-purifying exclusion. Ab, however, here at the door and throughout the story, repeatedly provokes, frustrates, and escapes all such attempts by his society to account for him in terms of its usual mediations and resolutions: Ab provokes those resolutions to the point of exposing the violence of those oppositions they usually disguise in order to preserve and repeat them compulsively. Ab also speaks and writes here and intermittently throughout the story in his own critically different voice and style, effectively setting these dominant oppositions *and* their dialectical resolutions off to one side of what they cannot account for—not by oversight but by design—what those oppositions and resolutions are constructed in order to leave out of account. Thus Sarty cannot or will not listen to the singular impertinence of Ab's own history and potential humor, a voice the narrator here urges readers to read better than Sarty does. It is an impertinence which Faulkner himself would return to read much more elaborately and appreciatively in his next rewrite of this scene one year later in *The Hamlet.*

In the version of the scene at the planter's door in "Barn Burning," set thirty years after the war, Sarty attempts two different currently available cultural means to resolve the ambivalence he feels. His first, more innocent attempt is in terms of a plantation myth which has become in many ways stronger after the war than before. It is the now nostalgically idealized myth of the plantation as trickle-down source of moral and even economic blessings to all its humble dependents. Sarty has felt with disturbing ambivalence the stark contrast between the apparently invulnerable "peace and dignity" of the planter's house, and his own father's world of frightening social and economic violence and indignity. Sarty seeks a sentimental resolution to that ambivalence in the hope for a moral change in his father's character under the influence of "the spell of the house": "*Maybe he will feel it too. Maybe it will even change him now from what maybe he couldn't help but be.*" But instead of this baptism and redemption of Ab in the planter's image, Faulkner's revision here of the scene at the planter's door represents Ab's muddying of the water. Instead of dissolving Ab's difference into its mythically purifying solution, the spell of the house is broken by Ab's indelible signature on the blond rug placed just inside the door. Ab tests this false welcome by wiping the horse manure on his boot on the expensive, imported rug, provoking another of his perennial exclusions in terms of those same compulsive social and economic oppositions which are only disguised and not revised by such mythic attempts to resolve the social division. Thus even Ab himself repeats the myth of the magical plantation house to Sarty, but in order to suggest a revision of what he knows is Sarty's awestruck view of that mythic house: "'Pretty and white, ain't it?' he said. 'That's sweat. Nigger sweat. Maybe it ain't white enough yet to suit him. Maybe he wants to mix some white sweat with it.'" (12) As in his markings on the rug, Ab revises by smudging here Sarty's and their society's mythic image of the plantation as radiant and redeeming source of beauty, deadliness, and moral improvement, to stress instead its relation to its dependents (and labor pool) in the underlying, oppositional terms of exploitation and purificatory exclusion. Its cleanliness functions not to redeem blacks and poor whites "from what maybe they couldn't help but be"; its cleanliness rather functions and exists at the direct expense of those blacks' and poor whites' excluded and degraded toil. Thus too when the planter brings the rug for Ab to wash the tracks out, Ab has his daughters wash the rug (and ruin it) with their own "harsh homemade lye" and a handy fragment of field stone: Ab here again rejects this ritual gesture at settling and resolving his differences with the planter, by instead exaggerating the compulsive violence of this compelled erasure of his signature, the planter's attempt to erase Ab's singular, ineradicable mark of his difference on the rug.

Let me point out, however, that Ab's apparent irony here, in his smudging of Sarty's innocence, and in associating himself with manure, with slavery, and with blackness, is in fact not irony but a potential humor, not a compulsive self-exclusion but a revisionary repetition of such exclusions. It represents a potential for speaking and writing humorously aside from those same compulsive oppositions. Quentin's irony in *Absalom* only represents and confronts, even if within himself, a blackness that he still finds, for all his irony, no less horrifying than Thomas or Henry Sutpen did. Quentin's irony is a cold comfort in private surrender and disillusionment—ultimately a suicidal disillusionment enforcing the same horror upon himself. Ab's potential humor similarly repeats those violent oppositions usually smoothed over but still compulsively repeated in his society's dominant gestures at resolution (including the gesture of irony). But Ab's potential humor is a much more active strategy than Quentin's irony, repeating and provoking those same inadequate oppositions, but only in order then to escape them, setting them critically to one side of what they cannot account for in his own singular history and peculiarly critical, potentially humorous stance and agency. Even Sarty recognizes that Ab's character is captured and framed adequately by neither the spell of the plantation house nor their tenant house's squalor, where "His father appeared at the door, framed against that shabbiness, as he had been against that other bland perfection, impervious to either." (13) In other such overtly inadequate descriptions of Ab in terms of ready oppositions—as, for example, "at once formal and burlesque" in his dress or as "shabby and ceremonial" in his actions (20)—we can perhaps understand better now the function of Faulkner's often-noted stylistic tendency (I would say the subtly changing tendency) to oxymorons. These "uncorrected" stylistic discrepancies and contradictions are not a sign of Faulkner's bad habit of thinking in obscurantist paradoxes, as Walter Slatoff and others have charged, nor are they a sign of his achieving resolutions of such paradoxes in his art, as some have no doubt defended him on New Critical grounds. They are rather instances in miniature of his increasingly revisionary repetitions of such inadequate ready oppositions, and of his rejection of those stylistic resolutions that would often only disguise those same inadequate oppositions.

Sarty's other attempt at a peaceable resolution of his emotional and social ambivalence is in terms of the law, another attempt at resolution which Ab sets aside as one more compulsive repetition only raised to a higher ground. When Sarty first sees the apparently magical plantation, he thinks "*Hit's big as a courthouse*," (10) and this immediate association with the law suggests the force of this other main cultural alternative for resolution of social differences when the old plantation magic fails. Thirty years after the war, the planter's feudal privilege over his tenants still largely exists, but it is subject to question on supposedly higher moral and legal grounds, as even Sarty knows. Like irony in *Absalom*, here the law will recognize Ab's existence, but in implicitly repressive terms.

The background for the court trial is that Ab's ruining the rug again in washing it has provoked the planter to an angry, indiscreet assertion of absolute legal sovereignty over his tenant as he declares he will write into Ab's contract unilaterally a charge of twenty bushes of corn. He says this figure is meant not to cover the damages to the rug, but to "teach" Ab to wipe his feet before he enters the planter's wife's house. The planter insists, that is, not on his own economic or legal rights, but on requiring from Ab a gesture of feudal obeisance to the lady of the manor. (16) At these signs of an oppositional, arrogantly despotic relationship between planter and tenant, Sarty all too eagerly restores his allegiance to his father on now higher moral and legal grounds that offer him new hope for his father's moral and legal recognition and redemption, as well as his own emotional resolution: "'You done the best you could!' he cried. 'If he wanted hit done different why didn't he wait and tell you how?'" (16) This rather desperate moral claim for Ab's good intentions, however, completely misses the point—or avoids the point—of Ab's violent way of washing the rug. In pretending that Ab would have washed the rug in the way the planter wanted, if only the planter had made his instructions clear, Sarty is hoping again that his father did want to settle his differences with the planter, and wanted to settle them in the planter's way. Ab, however, harshly rejects any such moral whitewash of his contrary behavior, knowing that any such moral resolutions in this society will implicitly favor the planter, by leaving the deeper structural oppositions in place. He does not want to erase and be forgiven for his mark on the planter's rug; he wants a more adequate reading of that mark.

Ab's legal claim in his suit is only superficially the same as Sarty's moral claim. Ab, too, repeats the planter's instructions and claims he followed the letter if not the spirit of what the planter told him to do. However, the motivations and consequences of Sarty's and Ab's two repetitions of these instructions are altogether different (in ways that you may have guessed). Each one's kind of repetition reflects a radically different conception of law and language. Sarty hopes, compulsively, that in repeating and following only the letter of those instructions, their spirit should somehow follow. Their letter should have been an embodying *symbol* of the planter's intention, which Ab would have done his innocent best to read. The consequence of this conception of law and language when a difference exists in interpretation, as in Ab's suit, is that one meaning is judged more reasonable than another, one as the spirit or tenor and one as merely the letter or vehicle of the disputed language or symbol. Thus Ab loses his suit, for the social hierarchy in the trial matches this hierarchy of representation, with meaning conceived of as an interior presence at the privileged center of all its different but always secondary re-presentations in language, representations that are either faithful to that true meaning or only literal-minded, poor imitations. On the other hand, Ab's own repetition of the planter's instructions in the trial is revisionary, repeating the letter of those instructions not as symbol but as *sign* or *trace*, not as an embodiment of only the planter's intention, but as a negotiable social *contract* or temporary, local *pact*[8] between them both, open to certain legitimate social differences of interpretation. Ab insists on his own contrary interpretation of the planter's instructions by refusing the vast, unspoken social axiomatic of reasonableness and "mere" respect for the expectations of people like the planter and the planter's wife. When the justice rephrases and reinterprets the planter's instructions in line with this socially reasonable interpretation, Ab's long silence emphasizes the legal partisanship and privilege of the justice's decision against Ab, exposing it in its function as not an impartial resolution but another forcible exclusion of Ab's meaning in favor of the planter's that makes of Ab not another speaker of this society's language, but one of its socially illiterate victims. Likewise Ab's suit focuses critical attention on the supposed fairness of the justice's "settlement" when that settlement has to be imposed in a context of such extreme social and economic inequality that the planter's ninety-five-dollar cash loss on the rug has to be figured as equal with Ab's five-dollar loss in uncertain future earnings.

This same extreme inequality is one reason barn burning was such a favorite form of violent protest for Ab as for many others in the postwar South, as Albert C. Smith has recently documented.[9] Those blacks and poor whites who owned virtually no property had in that lack of property both a simmering motivation for arson and also a strong protection against a like revenge, either by the property owner or by the law, since their own property had always already been taken from them, and since their labor was often a source of profit to their landlords. Ab can repeatedly set planters' barns on fire and move to the side as the planter appears to battle his own shadow in a rage. In battling the fire and then in trying to prosecute the arsonist, the planter here rather more clearly than usual is battling not against Ab himself but against a consequence of the planter's own over-extended monopoly on property and wealth. The planter's repeated exclusion of the poor white from his property reaches here its economic crisis, in an enraged attempt to repeat the exclusion even when there is no one left there to exclude.

Ab thus dangerously brings to a head his society's dominant oppositions by provoking the planter to repeated fits of rage. Sarty, in his mounting fright and confusion, is unable to read Ab's critical, potentially humorous way out of those oppositions, and Sarty's own emotional ambivalence with regard to those oppositions reaches a crisis as well. Sarty finally cannot appreciate Ab's unaccountable difference from his society's dominant dialectics of master and slave, planter and tenant, white and black, clean and filthy, legal and criminal; unable to read Ab's difference as a potential criticism of the exclusive terms of those dialectics, Sarty reads it more simply as a condemnation of Ab and perhaps of Sarty himself. Sarty feels forced to choose, and, in the terms most ready to hand, his choices are always already made, there merely for him to repeat. Earlier, Ab tried to describe their family "blood" to Sarty in terms of a shared kinship and loyalty. But when Sarty realizes that Ab is preparing to burn another barn, he violently recoils from that blood—recoils as Thomas and Henry Sutpen did in similar moments of nauseated horror—from a "blood" that seems now hereditarily, almost inescapably tainted and cursed. Sarty therefore bursts out of his family's tenant house and bursts in through the front door of the planter's house. He thinks he can force an apparently final, apocalyptic resolution to all these frightening oppositions by enabling the planter to catch Ab in the act, Sarty effectively calling down on Ab both the planter's mythic power and the legitimating force of the law When he later hears the planter's shots from the direction of the fire, Sarty turns away from the scene to light out for the territories, but the narrator comments that his terror seems resolved now, once and for all. His sudden grief when he thinks his father is dead threatens momentarily to upset this resolution again as Sarty calls out, "Pap! Pap!" but he is unprepared at this point for the more attentively specific work of mourning, resorting for now to what Freud describes as the compulsive, stalled idealizations and repetitions of melancholia, idealizing the more personal, more ambivalent term "Pap! Pap!" into "Father! Father!" and introjecting his father's memory in his society's crudest terms of heroic idealization: "He was brave! . . . He was! He was in the war! He was in Colonel Sartoris' cav'ry!" As the narrator intercedes to object, this idealization of Ab completely ignores and excludes Ab's own singular history as not a soldier of either army but a professional horse trader throughout the war. Sarty excludes that singular history to translate (and traduce) Ab's memory instead to the inside of his society's most unambivalently nostalgic, heroic myth. Ab's violence is redeemed by his supposed service to the one Cause, a cause that was defeated but that was supposedly without internal division, a cause whose despotism has supposedly been focused only on another race and its violence focused supposedly only on an "alien" army. Ab has provoked here that myth's determined ignorance of his situation before, during, and after the war as also in his apparent murder now.[10]

Ab does suggest (to Faulkner, as it were) an alternative to this apparently final, compulsive repetition of this society's self-purifying exclusion of its own bad blood and the history of that bloodline. If we return to the afternoon in town between the trial and the barn burning, we find Ab talking and listening at a horse-lot fence and in the blacksmith shop, where Sarty hears his father tell "a long and unhurried story out of the time . . . when he had been a professional horse trader." (19-20) This is as much as we hear in "Barn Burning" of such long and unhurried horse-trading stories, but this is stuff of the same tradition of Old Southwestern and frontier humor on which Faulkner would draw for a different fictional method and different fictional topics from those of his earlier, more modernist writing.[11] Instead of representing his society's compulsively repeated exclusions of what it repeatedly cannot exclude, and instead of repeating the intensities and the inescapable ironies of this apparently unalterable socially structured or metaphysical event, Faulkner would begin increasingly himself to tell such long and unhurried stories. He would continue to repeat such powerful, restrictive oppositions and resolutions, but he would also rewrite them; he would critically and humorously reshape and reconceive those dominant oppositions in the presence of other unaccountably different voices. Thus his novels would take the form of proliferating series of sketches, or collections of short stories that repeatedly overflow their traditional generic boundaries as stories of revealing, essential single events.

Not only as method but also as topic, the Old Southwestern and frontier tradition of horse-trading stories would become in Faulkner's work what Walter Benjamin discusses as an endangered and dangerous memory (253-64)—a precapitalist or marginally capitalist social and economic tradition on which Faulkner would draw in *The Hamlet* and steadily thereafter for his own critical alternative to both the property-based capitalism of the Old South and the money-based capitalism of the New. In stories of trading in *The Hamlet*, for example, when unexpected differences arise about a verbal or written agreement, there is no appeal to what the more powerful or respectable or wealthy party really meant, as in the case of the planter's instructions for cleaning the rug. The accepted challenge and the intersubjective appeal of trading for both parties is to read each other carefully and probingly for signs of differences, to try to account for or to accept the risk of those always unpredictable differences, and then to accept that a deal is a deal. To trade with Ab would mean to know you are risking trading at least partly on Ab's singular terms. In Ratliff's retelling of the "Barn Burning" story in *The Hamlet*, he stresses and appreciates both the potential humor and the potential for economic criticism and change in Ab's acute understanding of his own social and economic relationships with the planter. After ruining the planter's rug, bringing him to court, and burning his barn, Ab enters the planter's house on his way out of town the next morning to say, "It looks like me and you aint going to get along together, . . . so I reckon we better quit trying before we have a misunderstanding over something." (I7) Of course they *have* had a misunderstanding, but the misunderstanding has been the planter's, who has consistently refused to read the signs of Ab's singular difference from the usual categories of planters and their humble tenants. The planter has been particularly unprepared for the unsettling possibility that Ab would repeatedly find more effective ways to take advantage of his lack of social dignity and property, particularly in daring to burn the barn. It is precisely this possibility that Ab's next landlord learns about in hearing Ratliff retell this story in *The Hamlet*, and this possibility becomes, for Ab's son Flem, a silent bargaining partner used to get himself some property.[12]

To conclude this essay, this humorous possibility of an unexpected economic leverage is by no means the only topical opening out of "Barn Burning" and into *The Hamlet* and Faulkner's later work. In *The Hamlet* Ratliff will expand on the "Barn Burning" story to remember Ab from a time before he was "soured," a time when his humor and love for his wife enabled him to escape not only the terms of the Old South's plantation myth and economy, but also the terms of the New South's money-based economy, those differently restrictive terms in which his son Flem would get so skillfully entangled. Ratliff's own ambivalent and affectionate memories of Ab's singular history and character will also provide an example of that same long and unhurried work of mourning which will become a more central topic in *Go Down, Moses*. In Faulkner's ongoing revisions of the primal scene I have discussed, as well as of other such socially structured events, he will listen more closely and specifically not only for the singular voices of white trash males such as Ab and Flem, but also for other critically different voices that have been similarly concealed, such as those of blacks and women (as in *Go Down, Moses* and *Requiem for a Nun*). These voices will suggest new topics; they will also throw into relief the fact that modernism's supposedly universal consciousness was a consciousness predominantly middle class, white, and male. This was a fact about modernism as about the postwar South's dominant culture which becomes most clear in Faulkner's most demanding elaboration and test of that modernism in the social and historical context of the postwar South, as he examined modernist attitudes and habits first as cultural symptoms and habits, then as willful, often violent social exclusions.

Perhaps I should add a note on one peculiarity of my method here. While I often criticize New Critical readings of Faulkner, I have honored the same New Criticism's injunction to close reading of Faulkner's texts. Paul de Man has recognized the particular "insight" such close reading has provided in tracing informing oppositions down to minute details and nuances of literary expression, even if such insight has usually come only at the expense of a certain "blindness" to historical and social circumstances deemed to be outside the text. (20-35) Faulkner has had more than his share of such New Critical close readings, notably by Cleanth Brooks. With the benefit of more recent structuralist, Marxist, and deconstructive readings like those of Wesley Morris, Carolyn Porter, John Irwin, and John T. Matthews, I hope to push this method of proof in close reading somewhat farther to show that the oppositions isolated by Faulkner's New Critical readers may in this phase of Faulkner's work be charged with a blindness not only to the history and society "outside" the text, but also to odd details, nuances, discrepancies, and contradictions "within" the text, if that text is reread closely enough—as Faulkner was himself rereading it in his own ongoing revisions of previous work. My own close readings show, I hope, how those informing literary and historical oppositions repeatedly (and productively) fail to exclude, or to contain, certain other competing voices both outside and inside the text.

To put this another way, I want to acknowledge the methodological debt that American deconstructive criticism owes to the New Criticism's tradition of close reading, but at the same time I also want to insist on the possibility that deconstructive and other poststructuralist criticism might acknowledge the ethical and political implications of the questions posed in literary and other social texts more candidly than the New Criticism has, and more candidly than structuralism and even poststructuralism itself always has. Faulkner's modernism does not just self-destruct, caving in on a vacuum within itself. It sees ghosts and hears voices, both within its own "Dark House" and without, ghosts that begin to materialize and voices that grow haltingly but increasingly articulate and specific.[13] Whereas Hemingway buries such ghosts and voices in ominous allusions to the bulk of the iceberg hidden beneath the controlling surface, even the surface of Faulkner's writing is everywhere disturbed by and drawn toward other voices in the (always social) text.

NOTES

1. Michael Millgate, for example, whose focus is the discrete, finished artifact and the original "conception" it completes in a "wholly organic structure," (186) is surprised that Faulkner could ever have considered including a version of Wash Jones's story near the beginning of *The Hamlet*, taking Faulkner's hindsighted word for it that the story had no place in the book at all: "It seems remarkable that Faulkner should ever have thought that 'Wash,' much of which he had already incorporated into *Absalom, Absalom!*, might find a place in the 'Snopes Saga.'" (184-85) I will suggest instead that much of Ab's story as Faulkner used it near the beginning of *The Hamlet* had already been told as Sutpen's (and Wash's) story in *Absalom*, and that this is a typical and even crucial kind of connection between works that are rarely such distinct performances as Millgate often assumes, but repetitions and revisions of previous works, repetitions to be considered not as unoriginality but sometimes as critique. See Millgate, *The Achievement of William Faulkner* (New York: Random, 1966).
2. My somewhat reductive characterization here of modernism addresses a set of oppositions actually quite important in modernist literature and society, but they are also a select group of oppositions that have

been actively promoted and canonized by modernist writers themselves, notably Eliot, and by Southern Agrarians later turned founding fathers of the New Criticism, such as Tate and Warren. Less critical of these oppositions than Faulkner was, the New Criticism has largely obscured the social and historical context of modernist strategies of irony, ambiguity, and unresolved tension in juxtaposition, for example, by making them into general criteria for aesthetic merit. The most influential Faulkner critic in this tradition is of course Cleanth Brooks, who tends to measure change and difference in Faulkner's work against a vast backdrop of "true community" (found in the agrarian societies and in the pastoral tradition of literature), a backdrop against which Flem Snopes, for example, takes his measure as a "sinister deformation of universal human nature and a terrifying vision of appetitive man, modern style." See *William Faulkner: The Yoknapatawpha Country* (New Haven: Yale University Press, 1963, p. 368. Also, *William Faulkner: Toward Yoknapatawpha and Beyond* (New Haven: Yale University Press, 1978), p. xii.

3. Richard H. Brodhead (among many others) also sees the source of Faulkner's achievement in these two novels in his exploration of larger social and historical contexts. I disagree, however, that Faulkner reaches a "final knowledge" about certain "essential realities," especially "a past lost to memory but still so potent that it dooms the present to repeat it." (9) This is precisely the kind of ironic repetition Faulkner subjects in *Light in August* and especially *Absalom* to social, historical, and critical scrutiny. The historical context provides not just variants of an essential myth (though characters try to think so), but challenges to that myth by other myths and by other excluded voices. The "logic of remaking" so well described by Brodhead in Faulkner's career up to *Absalom* also continues beyond *Absalom*, not merely in efforts at consolidation and completion (Brodhead, Stonum), but in a radical revision of his earlier work, looking progressively farther back into increasingly difficult issues, first of class (in *The Hamlet*, 1940, looking back at *Absalom*, 1936), then race (in *Go Down, Moses*, 1942, looking back at *Light in August*, 1932), then gender and sexuality (in *Requiem for a Nun*, 1951, and *The Reivers*, 1962, both looking back at *Sanctuary*, 1931). See Brodhead, ed., *Faulkner: New Perspectives* (Englewood Cliffs: Prentice-Hall, 1983). Also Gary Lee Stonum, "Faulkner's Last Phase," *Faulkner's Career: An Internal Literary History* (Ithaca: Cornell Univ. Press, 1979), pp. 153-94.

4. This is one significant difference between my reading of *Absalom* and that of John T. Irwin, with its emphasis on an inexorable process of repetition and revenge in the artist's and the son's futile struggles with the immutable structures of time, originality, and secondariness

as such. I would agree more, though, with his reading of *The Sound and the Fury* were he to differentiate more between the two novels.

5. David Minter has suggested to me that this familiarity with defeat and poverty may account for some of Faulkner's influence in Europe and in other, "always already poverty-stricken parts of the world."
6. "Barn Burning" at first began Faulkner's manuscript of *The Hamlet*, then during the writing of the novel he detached this version (soon publishing it as a short story), and replaced it in chapter I of the novel with Ratliff's substantially rewritten version of the story as told to Jody Varner. See Millgate 185.
7. On this alternation in Freud's treatments of the primal scene, see Ned Lukacher, *Primal Scenes: Literature, Philosophy, Psychoanalysis* (Baltimore: Johns Hopkins Univ. Press, 1986) pp. 136-67.
8. The "trace" and the temporary, local "pact" would represent further stages (than "sign" or "contract") in Ab's effective deconstruction of his society's assumptions about language and law. Gregory S. Jay usefully differentiates and historicizes Saussure's stress on the (diachronically) "arbitrary" but still (synchronically) systemic qualities of the *sign*, and then Derrida's stress (in his reading of Saussure in *Of Grammatology*) on the asystemic, historical, political qualities of the sign, as represented by the terms "trace" or "gramma" (Jay 187). In terms of the law, Derrida does appreciate, however, Saussure's greater suspicion of such systemic qualities in his demystification of a "social contract" theory of language, with the result that he presumes "that a law accepted by a community is a thing that is tolerated and not a rule to which all freely consent" (Saussure 71, qtd. Jay 162). On the notion of consent to social "pacts" see also Jean-Francois Lyotard, *The Postmodern Condition: A Report on Knowledge*, trans. Geoff Bennington and Brian Massumi (Minneapolis: Univ. of Minnesota Press, 1985), p. 66.
9. This intriguing history of barn burning was brought to my attention by Wallace Warren.
10. Mitchell Breitwieser suggests that Freud's and more recently Abraham and Torok's and Derrida's accounts of the stalling effect of melancholia ignore "the pre-emptive intrusion of ideology into the course of mourning": "In his introduction to the work of Nicolas Abraham and Maria Torok, Derrida claims that for Freud mourning accomplishes an *introjection* whereas melancholia is stalled by having *incorporated* the dead: introjection brings the image of the dead into full assimilation with the self, but incorporation assimilates the dead as an alien presence, a *crypt* in the midst of the self with which the self does not communicate. This distinction is useful, but does not seem to me complete: in the case of the sort of prolonged and intimate contact that exists between family members, the dead does not

need to be introjected into the self because that self is in large measure already determined by the history of the relation—the task is not to bring the dead in, but to convert the dead from being an element of life *taken for granted* to being an object of representation, to being an inner image with which the self can communicate to the limit of all the messages that memory proposes." ("Early American Antigone," *Theorizing American Literature: Hegel, the Sign, and History,* ed. Bainard Cowan and Joseph R. Kronick (Baton Rouge: Louisiana State Univ. Press), p. 8.

11. On the critical potential of humor in the history of American literature, and for useful distinctions between irony and humor, see especially Neil Schmitz, *Of Huck and Alice: Humorous Writing in American Literature* (Minneapolis: Univ. of Minnesota Press, 1983).
12. Again, I am reading Ab's signature and his escape as one way out of one particular set of confining (mostly class-related) cultural alternatives, and not as the one new way out of all such cultural oppositions (assuming any such perfect escape from culture were either possible or desirable). His method of reinscription and escape serves here as a model for other, more difficult escapes from other, more stubbornly naturalized oppositions, to be examined more critically later in Faulkner's career. Ab's violence toward blacks, toward women, and toward his son Sarty is obvious throughout the story. It is not in defense of this violence but in an effort to understand it—the "savage blows . . . but without heat" (6)—that I might add that Ab seems here to be passing on, in a more explicitly despotic, violent form, the naturalized, axiomatic social and economic violence he feels directed against himself. That is, Ab savagely, bitterly exaggerates, while still repeating, the racism and patriarchal sexism of his society and class, a repetition that is in these cases unrevisionary and uncritical unless perhaps in the otherwise unaccountable, unarticulated *force* of his smoldering rage.
13. "Dark House" was Faulkner's working title for the manuscript of the novel eventually titled *Absalom, Absalom!*

This article, in a slightly altered form, was previously published as the introductory chapter of *Faulkner and Modernism: Re-reading and Rewriting* (Univ. of Wisconsin Press, 1990). Reprinted with kind permission.

Sir Gavin and the "Slain Wolf": *Sir Gawain and the Green Knight* as Guidebook to Faulkner's "Go Down, Moses"

JUDY HEN

Gavin Stevens, white gentleman lawyer from Jefferson, Mississippi, is "the designated paladin of justice and truth and right" in William Faulkner's short story, "Go Down, Moses" (the final story in the collection by the same title).[1] If Stevens is "designated paladin"—appointed to the office of champion—the reader must pause to contemplate Faulkner's diction and motives. Why in the midst of a starkly raw narrative does Faulkner choose to use archaic language? If we follow Faulkner's apparent logic, we must seek the cause Stevens pursues. It is not that of a lady fair, but of "a Negro murderer," Butch Beauchamp, local boy on the eve of his execution in Chicago, for murdering a policeman. (287) Stevens' 'Grail' is the "catafalque [of] the slain wolf," which "must come home." (287; 283) The given name—Gavin—appears to be a derivative of Gawain, and "the slain wolf" is the crux of his quest. Faulkner seems to have an added dimension in the undercurrent of his little-examined story, "Go Down, Moses"; *Sir Gawain and the Green Knight* acts as a guidebook for the interpretation of "Go Down, Moses."

In both texts there are sharp contrasts between the protagonist and the antagonist, which make the conciliatory endings all the more decisive. In *Sir Gawain and the Green Knight*, the protagonist, Sir Gawain, is "tested [so] that he may reveal his true self in his behaviour."[2] In "Go Down, Moses," the trial which Gavin Stevens must undergo is to discard his inborn prejudice against 'Negroes'[3] and to perform a humanitarian deed. If the task had been more attractive, the story might sink into sentimentality. However, Faulkner means to emphasize the subtle changes that Stevens experiences as he rejects the feudal past of the American South, and emerges emotionally strengthened, though surprised at himself.

In both *Sir Gawain and the Green Knight* and "Go Down, Moses," the antagonists are presented in far greater detail than the protagonists; the effect is one of studied exaggeration, and subseqeunt deflation. In *Sir Gawain and the Green Knight*, the Green Knight taunts the members of King Arthur's court, calling them "beardless boys"—he goads King Arthur to action, but it is Sir Gawain who will undertake the challenge of his life. (line 298)

The Green Knight is "an awesome fellow / Who in height outstipped all earthly men," nevertheless, he is

> The handsomest of horsemen, though huge, at that;
> For though at back and at breast his body was broad,
> His hips and haunches were elegant and small.
> (ll. 136-37, 142-44)

As befitting medieval literature, the anonymous author's agenda is apparent to the reader, though not without subtlety. The narrative aims to impress with its layering effect, and to strengthen the way of life of the court of King Arthur. The Green Knight's axe is "huge and monstrous,/A hideaous helmet-smasher"—thus when Sir Gawain volunteers to champion his liege, the act gains greater proportions. (ll. 208-9) By emphasizing the relative differences in size, the Green Knight is made to be a more formidable opponent, and Sir Gawain's status grows in importance.

As fitting the codes of chivalry, Sir Gawain is suitably modest:

> I am the weakest, the most wanting in wisdom, I know,
> And my life, if lost, would be least missed, truly (ll. 354-55)

Although the outcome seems clear from the beginning of *Sir Gawain and the Green Knight*, still the reader wishes to be regaled with rich detail to support his innate desire for the protagonist to overcome the antagonist.

Faulkner opens "Go Down, Moses" with a synechdochic portrait of the antagonist, from "face" to "hair" to "head." (277) Initially, the reader meets only the isolated physical attributes, although they are presented with an insider's knowledge: "The face was black, smooth, impenetrable; the eyes had seen too much." (277) The reader is drawn to this inscrutable African mask—"the head resembled a bronze head, imperishable and enduring." (277) The irony in the use of eternalizing qualities—"imperishable" and "enduring"—is still lost on the unsuspecting reader. Just as *Sir Gawain and the Green Knight* is typically medieval, so "Go Down, Moses" is modernist in the "unease" that it calls forth in the reader.[4] The narrator always seems to be one sinister step ahead of the reader.

Continuing the representation of the antagonists, the Green Knight's hair "[w]as shorn below the shoulder, sheared right round," (ll. 183-84) while Butch Beauchamp's "negroid hair had been treated so that it covered the skull like a cap, in a single neat-ridged sweep, with the appearance of having been lacquered, the part trimmed out with a razor." (277) Each man's aspect is so concise, it is indeed monstrous to oppose such mathematical precision with the havoc each has or will carry out.

Whereas in *Sir Gawain and the Green Knight* we must wait until close to the end to discover Sir Gawain's fate, Butch's is revealed almost at the beginning of "Go Down, Moses." In *Sir Gawain and the Green Knight* tensions build, while in "Go Down, Moses" they are deflated, which supports the opposing aspects of medieval and modernist styles.

There are precise dimensions to the clothing: the Green Knight has

> A two-third length tunic, tight at the waist,
> A comely cloak on top, accomplished with lining.
> Of the finest fur to be found. (Fit 1, 151-53)

Butch is similarly dandified: "He wore one of those sports costumes called ensembles in the men's shop advertisements, shirt and trousers matching and cut from the same fawn-coloured flannel." (277) As details accumulate, the reader develops a stance toward the antagonist of each text, before she discovers the protagonist. Interestingly, neither Sir Gawain nor Gavin Stevens is sketched in even the barest outlines of physical attributes or of dress. As protagonists, they rise (or fall) on their inner strengths alone.

Ambiguity pushes the texts forward. The Green Knight promises to reveal his identity after the conditions of his "game" have been fulfilled by Sir Gawain. Conversely, in the first part of "Go Down, Moses" there is a "young white man sitting with a broad census-taker's portfolio"; his innocuous questions provide the reader with the identity of the possessor of "a voice which was anything under the sun but a southern voice or even a negro voice." (277) It is as if Faulkner identifies with the reader who is reluctant to include Butch in the fellowship of classic Southern culture. Like the Green Knight, the interviewee has disguised himself (even down to his accent), in order to confound and confuse. When he asserts his true name, Samuel Worsham Beauchamp, the deception is revealed: "'Wait.' The census-taker wrote rapidly. 'That's not the name you were sen—lived under in Chicago.'" (277)

In a subtle way, Samuel Worsham Beauchamp (aka Butch) must want his identity made known, in spite of his protestations otherwise. When the census-taker asks him "'If they dont [sic] know who you are here, how will they know—how do you expect to get home?,'" Butch displays understandable indifference—"'What will that matter to me?'" (278) Nevertheless, the concealment and subsequent revelation of Butch's identity is what forces Gavin Stevens into the role of savior. "And that's who I am to find, save" he wryly comments, upon realizing that he has been mysteriously chosen to fulfill a portion of the white-man's burden, by sponsoring Butch's 'homecoming' for burial by his grandmother. (280)

Our last view of the young murderer occurs when "they came and slit the expensive trousers and shaved the expensive coiffure and led him out of the cell" on the way to his execution. (278) Faulkner makes it clear that outward appearances cannot save anyone. The executed murderer's body hovers over the whole narrative; in fact, Butch-in-death has far greater influence than Butch-in-life.

So too, the spectre of the blow that Sir Gawain must receive from the Green Knight to fulfill his part of the "game" hovers over *Sir Gawain and the Green Knight*:

> But though the end be heavy, have no wonder,
> For if men are spritely in spirit after strong drink,
> Soon the year slides past, never the same twice;
> There is no foretelling its fulfilment from the start. (ll. 496-99)

The reader awaits with dread "the Michaelmas moon, / With winter threatening there" just as Sir Gawain does, so that the inescapable will arrive. (ll. 532-33)

When the scene abruptly switches in the second part of "Go Down, Moses," we are startled to find that we are still "[o]n that same hot, bright July morning," but Faulkner has switched the venue to the office of "the county-attorney [with] . . . a thin, intelligent, unstable face"—Gavin Stevens. (278) The connection between the occupant of "the steel cot in the steel cubicle" and the owner of the "rumpled linen suit from whose lapel a Phi Beta Kappa key dangled" is now sealed. (277, 278) The savior of the criminal is an erudite, "whose office was his hobby . . . and whose serious vocation was a twenty-two-year-old unfinished translation of the Old Testament back into classic Greek." (278)

A more incongruent pair cannot be found as Butch Beauchamp and Gavin Stevens. The catalyst who will bring them together is "a little old negro woman with a shrunken, incredibly old face beneath a white headcloth and a black straw hat which would have fitted a child." (278) Her counterpart in *Sir Gawain and the Green Knight* is "[m]ost beautiful of body and bright of complexion." (ll. 943) Faulkner persists in inverting the fairy-tale quality of the medieval poem, as part of the modernist tendency to undermine our expectations.

The two women, separated by eons of time and experience, propel Sir Gawain and 'Sir' Gavin to fulfil their respective destinies. The lovely lady of the castle "[w]ith laughing lips, and air / Of love" offers: "My young body is yours,/Do with it what you will." (ll. 1206-7, 1237-38) Sir Gawain is tricked by flattery into accepting kisses from the lady, which he willingly surrenders to the lord of the castle each evening, in exchange for the spoils of the hunt—deer, boar, and fox. However, he conceals the life-saving gift of the green belt.

Gavin is 'courted' and persuaded by an unlikely handmaiden to the old negress—Miss Worsham—a white woman who is "quite old . . . thin, erect, with . . . a faded hat of thirty years ago, in rusty black, with a frayed umbrella faded now until it was green instead of black." (281) It is Miss Worsham who is responsible for Gavin's inevitable decision to bring Butch's body "home," and she shall, with her indominatable will, let Gavin know that a plain "box" is not fitting for a man with her "father's name—Samuel Worsham." (282, 283) This reminder of the interracial basis of many old Southern families, and of the responsibility that whites have toward 'their' Negroes, cast the deciding vote. The condescending, middle-aged "paladin" galvinizes himself into action, and organizes most of the town of Jefferson into contributing toward the expenses of shipping Butch's body in an elegant coffin covered with flowers, though he himself and the newspaper editor have to pay the largest part: "Stevens passed from store to store and office to office about the square . . . with his set and rapid speech: 'It's to bring a dead nigger home. It's for Miss Worsham.'" (284) Miss Worsham is also the one who escorts Gavin Stevens into the incongruous house of mourning, where he comes to pay his last respects to a dying way of life, wherein "the four of them—himself, Miss Worsham, the old Negress and her brother—made a circle about the brick hearth on which the ancient symbol of human coherence and solidarity smouldered." (285)

The tie that binds these people is not just the executed murderer; it is the interconnectedness forged by Southern prejudice. While Gavin Stevens does Mollie Beauchamp's and Miss Worsham's bidding, he still refers to Butch as a "nigger." (284) The "few ashes [which] smouldered faintly" in that hearth connect to the ash from Butch's last cigarette, and to his grandmother, Mollie Beauchamp, who is described as having "no more of weight and solidity than the intact ash of a scrap of burned paper," bringing home to Gavin Stevens the burden that the white man bears for having created such a predicament. (285, 278)

Sir Gawain also emerges from the trial of his integrity a wiser man. He had purjured himself by denying the gift of:

> this belt of green,
> As long as he laps it closely about him,
> No hero under heaven can hack him to pieces,
> For he cannot be killed by any cunning on earth. (ll. 1851-54)

Sir Gawain, though embarrassed to have his duplicity revealed, nevertheless emerges triumphant from the test, and "truthfully told them of his tribulations" at the court of King Arthur when he returned. (ll. 2495) He submitted to the axe of the Green Knight, in return for his (Sir Gawain) having decapitated the Green Knight. As a reminder, he shall carry "the scar of the snick on his neck/Where bold man's blow had hit, his bad faith to/Proclaim." (ll. 2498-2500)

What Gavin Stevens is left with is a debt of more than one hundred dollars and a desk piled with two days' work. Faulkner knows "that beautiful was damned" and thus he sees "the need for redemptive style, in the new decadent fashion."[5]

Sir Gawain has admitted his faults, and receives even more accolades for that; he is scrupulously human. Medieval culture tends to view the world in terms of black and white, with no between shades; there is either good or evil, triumph or defeat. In Faulkner's world, the situation is far more complex. Butch's grandmother has received what she perceives as due her and her grandchild, regardless of his criminality. Gavin Stevens submits to the moral blackmail, knowing that the feudal mentality of the South fosters both mutual animosity and interdependency. The 'hold' that Mollie Beauchamp and Miss Worsham produce to goad Gavin Stevens to action is the very essence of culture in the post Civil War South. Gavin Stevens understands that once he has fulfilled his end of the 'bargain' by setting in motion the means to carry out the 'good deed,' he has completed his function, as far as Mollie Beauchamp and Miss Worsham are concerned. He has reached both inner knowledge, and some insight into the feelings that he shares with Mollie Beauchamp: "*It doesn't matter to her now. Since it had to be and she couldn't stop it, and now that it's all over and done and finished, she doesn't care how he died. She just wanted him home, but she wanted him to come home right.*" (288) By acknowledging Mollie Beauchamp's "right" to bury her grandson the murderer, Gavin Stevens allows himself to be just as human as Sir Gawain has been proven. Although Butch Beauchamp may be a "slain wolf," 'Sir' Gavin did not flinch from the blows to his white pride, and deigned to collect money "to bring a dead nigger home." (284)

There is no way we can prove (or dispute) that William Faulkner sat with a copy of *Sir Gawain and the Green Knight* while he composed "Go Down, Moses." Nevertheless, a connection has been noted. The differences between the two texts, other than the obvious gap of five hundred years between composing them, is the cultural milieu in which each was created.

The medieval *Sir Gawain and the Green Knight* subscribes to the bravery and modesty necessary for the role of "paladin" in King Arthur's court. Faulkner reveals the split personality of the white community in the South, by presenting an unexpected aspect of that supposed white patriarchy. The 'happy' ending of *Sir Gawain and the Green Knight* draws from an optimistic tradition which believes in the ultimate triumph of virtue. Faulkner's quizzical ending of "Go Down, Moses" is typical of modernism. The moment of meeting lies with the protagonists's self-knowledge. Such similarities between *Sir Gawain and the Green Knight* and "Go Down, Moses" are striking, and noting them adds to our appreciation of the depth of Faulkner's skill.

NOTES

1. William Faulkner, *Go Down, Moses* (Harmondsworth: Penguin, 1942), p. 287.
2. "Introduction," *Sir Gawain and the Green Knight*, 2nd ed., trans. and intro. Brian Stone (Harmondsworth: Penguin, 1959, 1976), p. 19.
3. The term, "Negro," has been privileged over the term "Black" or "African-American" because it is the word used by Faulkner in the text of "Go Down, Moses."
4. Malcolm Bradbury, *The Modern American Novel* (Oxford: Oxford Univ. Press, 1983), p. 62.
5. *Ibid.*, p. 87.

The Poiesis of Description: Imagery in *Intruder in the Dust*

PRAMOD K. NAYAR

Literature evokes images before the mind's eye. Descriptions "bring alive" places, objects, people and events. They are staged for the eye to register and the mind to interpret. Imagifying is therefore a poiesis, a making-up.

Any analysis of the poiesis of description straddles (uncomfortably) the realms of reception aesthetics and cognitive psychology. This is so because an analysis of the process of imagifying must take into account the effect of the process on the eye. This paper hopes to unravel the strategies of description, and hence of perception, in Faulkner's *Intruder in the Dust* (1948).[1] Obviously a discussion of the novel's thematic preoccupations is left out in order to concentrate upon its imagery. Likewise, the symbolic values of the images are also not emphasised.

Faulkner adopts three main strategies of image-making: saccades and parataxis, gestural and translocal imagifying and visual deficiency. The three methods are meant for certain types of images, as we shall see. More often, imagifying in the novel consists of at least two of these strategies working in tandem.

Faulkner first "fixes" our vision. For this purpose he adopts both a contextual and a grammatical tactic. Faulkner's novel seldom allows the eye to rest on one object. There is no "zooming in" but rather a *series* of vision fixations. The contextual method is employed when the reader's attention has to be drawn to a large object, or one which is quite near. The object is given to the reader in a *single* focusing movement. For example: "the last of the sun coming through the mulberry tree the window behind him onto the table." (29-30) Here a solitary image is provided (the sun coming in), fixing our gaze on *one* movement alone. However it is not enough to focus our gaze on the sun. Specific details are to be given for contrast. To this end Faulkner focuses our attention, *next*, onto progressively *smaller* objects. Our serial eye movement is then controlled by the contrasts thus located: sun vs table, sun vs window and so on.

The contrasts and less pleasing images are summoned up by the grammatical mode of vision fixing. To complete the above quoted description: "The last of the sun coming through the mullberry tree through the window behind him onto the table the stacked untidy papers the inkwell the tray of paperclips and fouled rusted penpoints . . . stained unwashed coffeecup and saucer." (29-30) Grammatically the singular—the sun—has modulated into the plural—the papers, paperclips, penpoints and so on. The singularity of the sun is emphasised visually *and* grammatically. Amongst the welter of small and ugly objects the last of the sun seems bright. The reader's attention is thus fixed, even in retrospect (i.e., when his gaze has shifted onto smaller things) on the sun. A progressive movement *down* the order is then made. From larger objects to smaller ones, from well defined (spatially, geometrically) ones to blurred ones. "Stacked papers" and the "tray" are preludes to viewing "rusted penpoints" and a stained coffeecup (the stain being rarely clear), all being definitely smaller images. Examples of this type of progressively diminishing vision fixing can be multiplied from the text. Another good illustration, for example, is Faulkner's description of the town Square. (178)

Once the reader's vision is fixated on the objects, a convergence or divergence of vision is created. In the above example we have noted how Faulkner transfers our gaze onto progressively smaller items. This is a convergence of vision which is reserved for near objects. Divergence occurs when the eye tries to take in distant ones. I believe that Faulkner imposes both types of vision in the novel. This mixing has been termed "vergence."[2] Vergence is a mixture of convergence and divergence. For instance, we are first directed to well-defined and nearer objects. We note the very second paragraph of the novel: "He was . . . *standing* . . . *under the shed* in *front of* the closed blacksmith's shop *across* the street from the jail." (5, emphasis mine) We take cognizance of the man's posture and his exact spatial location. Our vision is made to converge on these details. The details are also limited syntactically, by their presence in a *single* sentence. Thus a linguistic convergence is also attained, reminiscent of the grammatical aspect of vision fixing noted earlier. However Faulkner also includes corner-of-the-eye vision when he describes the larger locale: the shop, its position vis-a-vis the street and the jail. This is a divergent vision where the peripheral details are also registered by the eye.

Faulkner's combination of the convergent and divergent vision in the space of one solitary sentence is the vergence of his poiesis. The aim is to induce the reader to record disparate elements of the scene *simultaneously*.

Another example of Faulkner's superb strategy of vergence is available in the penultimate paragraph of the novel. The black man Lucas Beauchamp has "unknotted the sack" and "dumped the pennies" on the "desk." He then begins to count them "moving *each one* with his *forefinger* into the first *small mass* of dimes and nickels." Faulkner then goes on: Lucas "snapped the purse shut . . . put it back inside his coat and with the other hand shoved the *whole mass* of coins . . . across the table." He then takes a "bandana handkerchief from the *side* pocket of his coat." (238, emphasis mine)

The paragraph juxtaposes syntactically and hence visually the small and the large: solitary coins and the forefinger, sack and purse, purse and coat, a "whole mass" and "*the* [i.e., solitary] crumpled bill," a large handkerchief and a side pocket. Our ocular focus is thus a vergence: due to the alternation between elements.

In Faulkner's novel the vergence is sometimes jerky and on occasions smooth. Jerky, violent and discontinuous eye movements are saccades.[3] In Faulkner saccades occur frequently where the reader's eye is made to undergo rapid shifts of focus. I will illustrate this saccadic movement with Faulkner's description of black houses:

> The paintless Negro cabins where on Monday mornings in the dust of the grassless treeless yards halfnaked children should have been crawling . . . broken cultivator wheels and wornout automobile tyres and empty snuffbottles and tincans . . . smoke blackened iron pots should have been bubbling over woodfires . . . sagging fences of vegetable patches and chickenruns . . . drying overall and aprons and towels and union suits. (142)

The cataloguing of things goes on for some length. From the syntax it is clear that Faulkner is not providing the textual equivalent of a cinematic slow panning. It is quick, jerky and saccadic. We register houses, playing children and an assortment of scattered objects. Our vision jumps rapidly over a wide site littered with these objects.

To increase the complexity of his saccadic narrative Faulkner at times provides an olfactory image. As in this description: "Then his Uncle opened the door and at once they smelled the coffee and the frying hogmeat . . . walking across a linoleum-floored dinning room." (105) The complexity occurs because Faulkner refuses primacy to the ocular image. To emphasise the locale of the *dining room*, Faulkner provides a quick "view" (smell) of the food. The two events—opening the door and the smell correspond to the beginning (a) of the paragraph and (b) of the description. Yet again the contextual and grammatical methods are employed. However the shift of the type of image (olfactory to ocular) is itself saccadic. Before we can "inhale" (to steep ourselves in the olfactory image!) the impressive description Faulkner shifts us onto the sherriff, his clothes and immediate geographical position. This is a meta-saccade where disruptive imagifying is achieved through a rapid shift of the type of image.

Since the vision fixing is saccadic, Faulkner's syntax is naturally rapid and discontinuous. In other words, the narrative is paratactic where coequal terms are arranged minus the conjunctions. In Faulkner, parataxis is the norm for all descriptions. To re-emphasise and recall a point made earlier, there does not appear to be any sequential or semantic relation between the elements described. Any of the examples quoted above (except perhaps of Lucas counting his money, where there is a definite chronological sequence) suffices to illustrate Faulkner's use of parataxis. I believe that the use of saccades and parataxis in narration inspires and makes inevitable a more alert reading.

The work of Wolfgang Iser has emphasised the text's indeterminacies and gaps.[4] Iser has argued that a reader constructs "bridges" across these gaps. This means we hypothesise to fill up the paratactic arrangement. Faulkner refuses this crucial role of the reader. Since the images rarely have a cause-effect or chronological sequentiality, we are not required to fill the "places of indeterminacy," to borrow a serviceable phrase from Roman Ingarden. Thus parataxis seems to leave redundant the reader's role in making the description "complete." Apparently.

Parataxis helps to register the parts-within-the whole of a visual array.[5] The reader makes the integration (or hypotaxis, to use the opposing term to parataxis) in her/his perception while retaining the awareness of the individual elements. Hence we take in incongruous elements, constitute the entire scene, but are left feeling the separateness of objects.

There is, I suggest, following Barbara Herrnstein Smith's formulation, a "retrospective patterning."[6] (119) We perceive a hypotactic ıntegration in retrospect, usually after an event following the description. For instance, we can reuse the second paragraph of the novel. We have noted how the corner-of-the-eye vision includes a jail and the boy's elusive location ("where his uncle would be less likely to see him." [5]) In retrospect we understand the inclusion of the jail in the description and the emphasis laid on Charles's not very visible vantage point. The jail houses a murderer Lucas whom Charles knows. A murder and the prison are not associated, generally, with boys. Hence the boy's desire to stay hidden and our attention drawn to his location and the jail. This retrospective hypotactic patterning provides an aesthetic satisfaction. In Faulkner this hypothesising occurs around the parataxes (since we "fill in" the reason for description and not the description itself in any sequentiality).

Parataxis also helps set off elements. We have noted the way the reader's eye is drawn to the sun in one of the descriptions. In Faulkner there is a "co-locational order"[7] where one referent is placed in relation to another. There is a primary object—the boy, the sherriff, the sun, black cabins or Lucas in the examples mentioned above. The traditional method of "setting" is here achieved with heightened effect. For the background we have the mundane items catalogued by Faulkner. Yet in this ordinary atmosphere, extremely significant events occur. On these occasions the shock of the events registers immediately since they stand in sharp contradistinction to the atmosphere. We can illustrate this use of parataxis and saccadic movement for atmosphere creation by looking at the jail scene. Faulkner describes the jail, its inmates and the rather taciturn jailer—Faulkner has provided a usual prison setting. (54-56) Then suddenly, our vision confronts Lucas the murderer. We read on to discover how Lucas is quietly dignified in his imprisonment. Then he hires a white lawyer to defend him against the charges of murdering a white man. (54-72) The parataxis thus bursts Lucas onto the reader. This is a heightening of the tension in the novel since the events that follow are crucial to the story. Faulkner's asyndetic syntax provides better aesthetic "thrills" (since the novel *is* a thriller) than a cause-effect format of narrative. The parataxis helps the atmosphere and our retrospective patterning.

Faulkner's novel combines saccadic descriptions with more sedately narrated ones. These slower descriptions are particularly reserved for mobile imagery. Moving images in *Intruder in the Dust* are gestural or translocal. Gestural images are those where parts of a stationary object are in motion. For example, Miss Habersham sitting in a chair is immobile. But Charles could see "the steady motion of her hand and elbow." Here Faulkner arrests the gestural image with a typical saccade: our focus is simultaneously drawn to the "flash and flick of the needle in her hand" and Charles's uncle. The description of Miss Habersham's knitting continues as gestural imagery interspersed with such disruptive references: Charles's uncle's location and a car. (134)

Or Faulkner focuses the reader's gaze on the movement itself, a translocal (since the immediate location changes) image. The objects move relative to the environment. A beautiful description of the night expedition to the graveyard is illustrative. Charles is on a horse and urges it into a "shambling halfrun halfwalk." The imagery now becomes translocal: "The road lay pale and empty before and behind him too; the lightless houses and cabins squatted or loomed beside it . . . the heady scent of flowering orchards lying across the road for him to ride through. . . . One weak flash and glare revealing for a second the empty road's the dark and empty land's irrevocable immitigable negation." (91-93) In this Hardyesque image the other objects squat by the wayside, i.e., stay still while the horse moves. This vivid description is a typical translocal image in combination with a saccade. The saccade here is the description of a vision, a "would-be" scene: a crowded road full of "mud-stained cars, the empty trucks . . . and the saddled horses and mules." (92)

Hence saccadic and paratactic descriptions of imagery coexist with extremely powerful mobile images of either the gestural or the translocal kind. Each type, I believe reinforces the other.

A third consistent feature of *Intruder in the Dust* is crucial phases of "vision deficiency." At these phases the imagery is deliberately of the indistinct. Adapting Collins's theory, (156) two types of visual deficiency are distinguishable in the text. There may be visual deprivation due to absence of photic stimulation. This arises due to extensive use of darkness and shadows. The graveyard scene is a good example. Faulkner places the "heart" of the novel in a dark atmosphere where things lie "invisible in the dark" (98) or have to make do with small doses of radiance from the solitary flashlight. (90-91) This visual deficiency has literary and figurative significance. The grave is itself dark, and especially so at night. The expedition is an attempt to solve a dark mystery (a murder). There is also some symbolic significance since murder is a black deed. The reader is thus, in retrospect again, satisfied at the use of visual deprivation, since the solution of the mystery at the end of the novel, requires the darkness at the beginning.

Visual deficiency in the novel's imagery is also due to homogenised visual fields. There is a featureless landscape—the route to the graveyard—where distinguishing features are unavailable. (91-94) Another example of this strategy is found in Faulkner's description of the "Faces": "Myriad yet curiously identical in their lack of individual identity, their complete relinquishment of individual identity into one." (133) Visual deprivation thus creates an intense atmosphere, where events are waiting to happen.

Faulkner's imagery is then highly powerful. The saccades, images of movement and visual deficiency help the reader's alertness. It is this brilliant use of the visual aspect of reading that makes Faulkner's novel enjoyable.

NOTES

1. William Faulkner, *Intruder in the Dust* (Harmondsworth: Penguin, 1972).
2. Christopher Collins, *The Poetics of the Mind's Eye: Literature and the Psychology of Imagination* (Philadelphia: Univ. of Pennsylvania Press, 1991), p. 103.
3. *Ibid.*, p. 99.
4. Wolfgang Iser, *The Act of Reading: A Theory of Aesthetic Response* (Baltimore: Johns Hopkins Univ. Press, 1978).
5. Collins, p. 102.
6. Barbara Herrnstein Smith, *Poetic Closure: A Study of How Poems End* (Chicage: Univ. of Chicago Press, 1969). Though Smith's study is mainly of poetry, her formulations have been applied to understand novels too.
7. The term comes from Leonard Talmy's essay "How Language Structures Space" (1983), qtd. Collins, p. 114.

The Initiation of Chick Mallison

ISAAC SEQUEIRA

The term "initiation" was probably used for the first time by anthropologists to denote the rites of passage from childhood or adolescence to maturity, that were practised by many primitive cultures and early civilizations. The rites consisted of trials by ordeal, feats of strength and courage to test the candidate's endurance and loyalty to the tribe or community. In some cases, initiation was simply a ceremony performed to facilitate the candidate's change in status upon the onset of puberty, or formal entry into a clan or society. Joseph Campbell, who has made a thorough study of the hero-initiate of myth, religion and history, states:

> The so-called rites of passage, which occupy such a prominent place in the life of a primitive society (ceremonials of birth, naming, puberty, marriage, burial, etc.), are distinguished by formal, and usually very severe, exercises of severance, whereby the mind is radically cut away from the attitudes, attachments, and life patterns of the stage being left behind, then follows an interval of more or less extended retirement, during which are enacted rituals designed to introduce the life adventure to the forms and proper feelings of his new estate, so that when, at last, the time has ripened for the return to the normal world, the initiate will be as good as reborn.[1]

In a whole chapter devoted to initiation, Campbell goes on to say that "The traditional idea of initiation combines an introduction of the candidate into the techniques, duties and prerogatives of his vocation with a radical readjustment of his emotional relationship to the parental images. The mystagogue (father or father-substitute) is to entrust the symbol of office only to a son who has been effectually purged of all inappropriate infantile cathexes. . . . [The invested] one is the twice born."[2] The ritual of confirmation in Christianity, the thread ceremony (second birth of the twice-born) in Hinduism, and the Jewish *Bar mitzvah* are similar to these initiation rites. Today, fraternities, sororities and secret societies have elaborate initiation ceremonies, which mark the entry of a candidate into their exclusive circles.

The "initiation" of fiction, however, bears only a peripheral or tangential relationship to this kind of initiation. Only in some cases, as in Faulkner's *The Bear*, is the initiation of the fictional heroes accompanied by ritual. Almost in no case is it a group or social activity since the protagonists achieve initiation on their own, after an intense and personal experience.

Ordinarily, the word initiation is used in connection with the process of maturation of adolescents. However, adolescence is not an easy term to define or limit. One can talk of physical, intellectual, social, emotional and moral adolescence, of which only physical adolescence, because of the obvious symptoms of puberty, can be dealt with some certitude. For instance, except for physical adolescence, it is difficult to discuss the other kinds of adolescence in terms of age. The age span for physical adolescence can be set between ten and twenty-four years of age. On the other hand, characters in fiction like people in real life have different age periods for the other kinds of adolescence. That means they achieve intellectual, social and moral maturity at different ages, sometimes well beyond the age of twenty-four. For instance, Francis Macomber of Hemingway's "The Short Happy Life of Francis Macomber" achieves moral manhood in his thirties; Professor Moses Herzog of Saul Bellow's *Herzog* achieves emotional maturity when he is middle-aged.

However, with the advent of Freud and Jung, and the study of the human psyche, a new emphasis was placed on the awareness of sub-conscious motives, on the conflicts between reality and pleasure principles, especially in the adolescent. Freudian psychology taught that the conflicts the child felt would invariably be heightened during adolescence. It made the novelists aware of the importance of the process of initiation, ,and provide them with scientific or near-scientific material to work with. The Jungians helped to clarify the use of myths and archetypes in literature. They offered the theory that archetypes recur to writers and readers because they embody ancient and primordial experience of the race which survive in the collective unconscious. The important archetypes that the fiction of adolescence uses are: the descent of the protagonist into Hades or Hell, the "Night Journey," the search for a father or father-figure, the quest, the cycle of death and rebirth, the process of initiation. One of Jung's significant contributions to the literature of initiation is his theory of the "individuation process." "Individuation" is a psychological "growing up," the process of discovering those aspects of one's self that make one an individual apart from others. It is a process of recognition, of self-awareness, the understanding of one's weaknesses and strengths, that takes place as one matures. "The meaning and purpose of the process is the realization, in all its aspects, of the personality originally hidden away in the embryonic germplasm; the production and unfolding of the original potential wholeness."[3]

Definition of Initiation

After considering the various definitions of initiation set forth by prominent critics like Leslie Fiedler,[4] Ihab Hassan,[5] Cleanth Brooks and Penn Warren,[6] Mordecai Marcus[7] and others, I have formulated the following definition: Initiation is an existential encounter or a series of essential encounters in life, almost always painful, with experience, during which the adolescent protagonist gains valuable knowledge about himself, the nature of evil, and the world. The knowledge is accompanied, by a sense of the loss of innocence and a sense of isolation, and if it is to have any permanent effect at all, must result in a change in character and behavior; for if knowledge does not change an individual's thinking and behavior, no learning—no acquisition of knowledge *per se*— has taken place. The change, in almost every case, leads towards an adjustable integration into the adult world.

Initiation is classified into three kinds: (1) Decisive, (2) Uncompleted, and (3) Tentative. The first is the highest order of initiation. The decisive initiate goes through the whole painful process successfully—gains valuable knowledge about himself, his identity, the nature of evil, and the world. He experiences an initiatory loss of innocence and a sense of isolation, and finally accepts adult society in spite of his disillusionment with it. The second category defines initiates who cross the threshold of initiation but are still confused as to the direction in which they should proceed. The third deals with initiates who go through the process of initiation up to a point. They experience pain and disillusionment and come to the threshold of initiation but are not able to cross it. The three categories are discussed in relation to the three kinds of modern fictional heroes, (1) the *pharmakos* (scape-goat or victim), (2) the *eiron* (ironic protagonist), and (3) the *alazon* (braggart rebel).

II

In his famous Nobel Prize acceptance speech in 1950 William Faulkner said that, for the writer of today, only the problems of the human heart in conflict with itself were 'worth writing about, worth the agony and the sweat.' Two years earlier he had embodied this idea in what has turned out to be one of his most popular novels, *Intruder in the Dust* (1948). Though the book has been called 'William Faulkner's Reply to the Civil Rights Program,'[8] I think it is primarily an account of the heart of Chick Mallison, the young protagonist, in conflict with itself, and in conflict with his society. And this conflict, an important part of his painful maturation process, results in Chick's decisive initiation.

The conflict for Chick revolves around one of Faulkner's important themes, race relations in the South. Chick comes up against the dual standards of the South in its attitude toward race. There is one code of justice for the Whites and another for the Blacks. Though he is only twelve years old when he begins to think about these things, Chick at first responds like a typical Southern white adult—the Negroes must be taught their place in society, and, what is more important, taught to keep to it. (*We got to make him [Lucas] be a nigger first. He's got to admit he's a nigger. Then maybe we will accept him as he seems to intend to be accepted.*) It is only when he realizes the essential humanity and individual dignity of a man like Lucas Beauchamp, the Negro in the novel, that he begins to feel that something is rotten in the state of the South. Like Huck Finn's conflict in relation to Nigger Jim, Chick's conflict resolves into the struggle between the 'deformed conscience' and the 'sound heart,' what he has been brought up to believe about the Negro and what his own humane judgement tells him about the Negro. It is a measure of his initiation that, like Huck again, he listens to his 'sound heart' and decides to go to the Faulknerian version of hell rather than leave Lucas Beauchamp to the tender mercies of the lynch mob.

That Chick, the 'tyro,' is decisively initiated into manhood and adult society is not a little due to his two 'tutors,' men who couldn't have been more different from each other, Lucas Beauchamp, the intractable, arrogant, solitary mulatto descendant of Carothers McCaslin, and Gavin Stevens, the urbane, cosmopolitan, yet dyed-in-the-wool Southerner uncle of Chick. The former, though directly responsible for making Chick feel anger, frustration, guilt, and finally a sense of identification, is instrumental in Chick's *rite de passage* to manhood. While Gavin Stevens, intellectually a cosmopolite and a believer in the rights of the Negro but emotionally still tied to the typical attitude of the South, is instrumental in leading Chick back into Southern society which at one time he had thought of repudiating. Chick meets his first 'tutor' at the age of twelve. While on a rabbit shoot on Edmonds' farm, and walking across a footlog over a stream, he slips and falls into the icy waters of the stream. His Negro companion, Aleck Sander, tries to get a pole to him so that he can pull himself out of the creek. At that moment he hears the voice of a man, who turns out to be Lucas, telling Aleck to get the pole out of Chick's way so that he can get out. Here, straightaway is the first lesson the 'tyro' learns from the 'tutor,' stand on your own feet, 'pay your own way.'

In spite of Chick's protestations about going home, Lucas takes him to his house, asks him to strip off his soggy clothes, and gives him a quilt to wrap around. The quilt has the unmistakable odour of Negroes, and envelopes Chick like a 'cocon,' a word that is specially significant in the context of initiation. In a significant passage Faulkner foreshadows, at this time, the future experiences of the new initiate:

> The smell meant nothing now or yet; it was still an hour yet before the thing would happen and it would be four years more before he would realize the extent of its ramifications and what it had done to him and he would be a man grown before he would realize, admit that he had accepted.[9]

The 'thing' reported as about to happen in an hour is Chick's foolish attempt to pay Lucas for the meal he had eaten there after getting himself dry. Chick's action is prompted by the code of behaviour he has learned from the white society he is a part of, the 'deformed conscience' which tells him that one must never be indebted to the Negro. The proud old Lucas refuses to accept the money and Chick experiences a strange combination of rage and shame. The rage is felt by his 'deformed conscience' at being rejected by a mere Negro; the shame is felt by his 'sound heart' because he has violated the hospitality of a fellow man. These two emotions play an important part in all of Chick's actions, lead him towards his initiation, and help him to realize the ramifications of his actions four years later, when Lucas is accused of killing a white man and is in need of help.

Chick's stripping off of his clothes in Lucas's house has a great deal of symbolic meaning. If he is to embark on decisive initiation he has to cast off, as he has his sodden clothes, all his Southern prejudices and accept the Negro as a fellow man and an individual in his own right. He has to come to terms with the Negro smell (a very effective crystallizing detail in Faulkner's poetic description) and the negritude of his neighbours—Faulkner considers the stripping off of the clothes symbolically important enough to repeat it near the end of the novel. While talking to his uncle, Gavin Stevens, his second 'tutor,' Chick undresses in preparation for bed. Stevens, his social 'tutor' is trying to reconcile Chick to his Southern tradition. He tells Chick that instead of running away from Southern society he should stay on and try to change it, without any aid from the North. And while Chick stands almost completely naked before his uncle, he is told:

> Some things you must always be unable to bear. Some things you must never stop refusing to bear. Injustice and outrage and dishonor and shame. No matter how young you are or how old you have got. Not for kudos and not for cash: your picture in the paper nor money in the bank either. Just refuse to bear them. (206)

Having stripped himself of the clothes of prejudice, of childhood, at the age of twelve in Lucas's house, he now dons the *toga virilis* of initiation and understanding, at the age of sixteen in his own house, after he has helped to exonerate Lucas from an unjust accusation, and saved him from the murderous intentions of a lynch mob. The boy has now become a man, and has paid his debt to Lucas. The tenderfoot scout has graduated to the rank of an eagle scout.

The four years between these two strippings-off have, however, been very painful and slow for Chick. The conflict in his heart has raged and the process of maturation during the period has been slow and tortured. After returning from Lucas's house he finds that his debt of obligation to Lucas weighs heavily on him. He is at a loss as to how to deal with the proud intractable Negro who goes about dressed like his white progenitor, Carothers McCaslin, even to the detail of the swaggering rake of the hat, the watch chain, and the gold toothpick, who says 'ma'am' and 'sir' to white folks without meaning them to be servile or even respectful terms.

At the prompting of the 'deformed conscience' Chick tries to repay his obligation by sending a fairly expensive flowered imitation silk dress to Molly, Lucas's wife. But Lucas sends him a gallon bucket of fresh home-made sorghum molasses through a white farm-boy. All his attempts to gain a 're-equalization, reaffirmation of his masculinity and his white blood' fail until a few months later he sees Lucas in town. Lucas, without the tooth-pick in his mouth for the first time, looks straight ahead and passes him by without any acknowledgement or greeting. Chick is happy that at last the debt is forgotten and that he himself is forgotten. However, he learns a year later that Molly had died on that day and the old man was mourning the loss of his wife. Chick thinks to himself: 'She had just died then. That was why he didn't have the tooth pick . . . . *He was grieving. You don't have to not be a nigger in order to grieve.*' (25) This is a very important insight into the humanity of the Negro that helps to make Chick's initiation a decisive one. This is also the insight that helps him to realize much later, when he is helping the sheriff to dig the grave of Vinson Gowrie, that a 'violent foulmouthed godless old man [Vinson's father] who had happened to lose one of the six lazy idle violent sons' could also grieve.

This insight bears comparison with the one Huck Finn has when he realizes that Nigger Jim is grieving for his children, and that Jim is capable of the tender care and anxiety of a father for Huck also. The essential humanity of the Negro is once again borne in upon the mind of the young Southern initiate. Like Huck's, Chick's sympathies are enlarged and broadened to encompass the

Negro and the outlaw. He realizes that the Negroes and the white trash are just as susceptible to the noble human sentiments as any self-righteous Southern White is.

Another important indication that Chick's initiation is well under way and that the 'sound heart' is gaining over the 'deformed conscience' is Chick's almost uncanny responsiveness to Lucas's mute appeal in the jail. Chick and his uncle visit Lucas who is in jail because he is suspected of having shot and killed Vinson Gowrie. Lucas asks Stevens to defend him in the court, for a fee. Stevens, in spite of his Harvard and Heidelberg training and his cosmopolitan outlook, is too much of a Southern White even to entertain the idea that Lucas could be innocent. He agrees to be defence counsel but he has already made up his mind that Lucas is guilty, and that his only hope is in pleading for clemency on the basis of his age. Lucas, sensing this attitude, stiffens up and refuses to give further information about the killing. He says, 'I ain't got friends. . . . I pay my own way.' (64) Nevertheless, he senses the sympathy and understanding in Chick's eyes and silently he looks at Chick with 'that mute patient urgency' till it is time for his visitors to leave the cell.

On the pretext of taking some tobacco to Lucas, Chick goes back to the jail alone and talks to him. Lucas tells him that he has not killed Vinson. His gun is a Colt forty-one and Vinson was killed by some other calibre pistol. He makes the fantastic demand that Chick go out to the Gowrie graveyard at Caledonia Chapel and take a look at the body. Chick's first reaction is outraged disbelief:

> *Me? Me?* It was like something you have dreaded and feared and dodged for years until it seemed like all your life, then despite everything is happened to you and all it was just pain, all it did was hurt and so it was all over, all finished, all right. (68)

The very idea is horrifying and painful. Nevertheless, Chick realizes that it is the only way he can repay Lucas, and that he alone can save Lucas from the lynch mob that is soon to mobilize under the vengeful clan of the Gowries from Beat Four. This is the terrible existential choice Chick is faced with: to go out and dig up the body of Vinson, alone, because he could expect no one to believe Lucas's tale and hence expect no help, or have the death by lynching of an innocent man on his conscience for the rest of his life. He is first tempted to run away from the problem, to saddle his horse, Highboy, and leave Jefferson far behind, but later he decides to undertake the almost impossible job so that he can get rid of the festering debt to Lucas, and more importantly because he would never be able to live with himself for having belonged to a white community that had lynched a black man who might have been innocent.

He asks Aleck Sander to help him go out and dig up the grave, but Aleck refuses to be involved. Even he is convinced that Lucas is guilty and believes that 'it's the ones like Lucas makes trouble for everybody.' (85) When Chick tells his uncle what Lucas told him his uncle rejects the story as a lie that a man desperately trying to save his life would tell. Fortunately for Chick, Miss Habersham, an elderly spinster, scion of one of the oldest and most respected families in the area, is present while he is talking to his uncle. A sense of loyalty to Molly, who had grown up with her, prompts her to help Chick. Between the two of them they convince Aleck to go along. After a great deal of trouble, and under the constant threat of being caught by the fearsome Gowries, the grave is opened only to discover not the body of Vinson Gowrie but that of Jake Montgomery. This is enough evidence to prove that the real murderer of Vinson is trying to prevent further investigation. Chick goes back and this time has no difficulty in convincing his uncle and the sheriff, Hampton, of Lucas's innocence.

Meanwhile the citizens of Jefferson are getting ready to lynch the arrogant old Negro who had all his life been a thorn in the flesh of the Whites. The lynching can be prevented only if the body of Vinson is found and the evidence against the real murderer established. Because of the efforts of Stevens and Hampton the evidence against the real murderer, Crawford Gowrie, Vinson's own brother, is established and the lynch mob vanishes like chaff before the wind.

Chick goes through a profound existential crisis at this point. He has shown up Southern justice for what it really is. It is interested not in justice for its own sake, but in keeping the 'nigger' in his place. It knows how to deal with 'nigger' murderers but when faced with the murder of White by White, brother against brother, the first crime of Cain, it turns tail and flees. Chick is overwhelmed with shame at being a part of a community that has this code of justice: 'he now recognized the enormity of what he had blindly meddled with and . . . his first instinctive impulse—to run home and fling saddle and bridle on the horse and ride as the crow flies into the last stagger of exhaustion . . .' (137) Like Ike McCaslin of "Go Down, Moses," he is tempted to repudiate and give up Southern society. Both he and Ike have had Negro 'tutors,' Lucas Beauchamp and Sam Fathers; both have been initiated into the knowledge of evil and an understanding of the human values of courage, dignity, loyalty, and humility. But, whereas Ike, not having a social 'tutor' to help integrate him into society, achieves only a partial uncompleted initiation into society, Chick is fortunate in having a second 'tutor,' his uncle, who, in spite of his tedious moralizing and theorizing about the South, convinces him to accept Southern society with all its flaws and shortcomings.

Chick, being an *eiron* character, realizes that an individual can have only a limited degree of freedom to exercise his moral choices. He learns that his moral choice must be made within the social framework, that he has a share in the shame and dishonour of the South, that his 'deformed conscience' is a part of it, and finally that he can't run away from it. He begins by making an uneasy truce with necessity and gradually learns to identify with his community.

His uncle tells him of the great need for maintaining the homogeneity of the South against the inroads of the North, the need to change their society from the inside, the need to fight for 'the postulate that Sambo is a human being living in a free country and hence must be free,' the need to set Sambo free themselves because nobody else can. Stevens inculcates in him a sense of his duty not only as an individual but as a responsible member of his society.

It is a measure of Chick's decisive initiation that he accepts these ideas despite the anger and shame that Southern society had aroused in him earlier. He even finds it in his heart to identify with the world at large, to immerse 'the proud vainglorious minuscule which he called his memory and his self and his I-Am into that vast teeming anonymous solidarity of the world.' (207) The final seal to Chick's decisive initiation is set when he realizes that he has been self-righteous and supercilious towards his people. A strong sense of identification with them grows in him and he feels

> that fierce desire that they should be perfect because they were his and he was theirs, that furious intolerance of any one single jot or little less than absolute perfection—that furious almost instinctive leap and spring to defend them from anyone so that

he might excoriate them himself without mercy since they were his own and he wanted no more save to stand with them unalterable and impregnable: one shame if shame must be, but one expiation since expiation must surely be, but above all one unalterable durable impregnable one: one people one heart one land. (209-10)

NOTES

1. Joseph Campbell, *The Hero with a Thousand Faces* (New York: Pantheon Books, 1949), p. 10.
2. *Ibid*, p. 136.
3. C.G. Jung "The Archetypes of the Collective Unconscious," *The Collected Works of C.G. Jung*, ed. Herbert Read et al. (New York: Pantheon Books, 1966), Vol. VII, p. 110.
4. Leslie Fiedler, "From Redemption to Initiation," *New Leader*, XII (May 26, 1958), p. 22.
5. Ihab Hassan, *Radical Innocence: Studies in the Contemporary American Novel* (New York: Harper and Row, 1961), p. 41.
6. Cleanth Brooks and Robert Penn Warren, *Understanding Fiction* (New York: F.S. Crofts, 1943), p. 344.
7. Mordecai Marcus, "What is an Initiation Story?" *The Journal of Aesthetics and Art Criticism*, XIV, No. 2 (Winter, 1960), pp. 221-28.
8. Edmund Wilson, 'William Faulkner's Reply to the Civil-Rights Program,' *Faulkner: A Collection of Critical Essays* (Englewood Cliffs, New Jersey: Prentice-Hall, Spectrum Books, 1966)
9. William Faulkner, *Intruder in the Dust* (New York: Random House, Modern Library College Edition, 1948), p. 11. All further references are to this edition and will be indicated by page number in parentheses.

"Belonging to the Business of Mankind": The Achievement of *Big Woods*

DAVID PAUL RAGAN

Despite the fact that it has been largely ignored by students of his work,[1] Faulkner's *Big Woods* extended the author's life-long habit of not repeating himself and of providing new challenges for his readers. Following his practice in novels such as *The Unvanquished, The Hamlet,* and *Go Down, Moses,* which incorporated previously published short stories, Faulkner drew together materials which had appeared as early as 1930 for this collection of hunting stories. And though he departed from that earlier practice as well—typically in *Big Woods* he limited the implications of the material, shortened and condensed, rather than enlarging and expanding, as he had usually done for earlier works—Faulkner obviously considered the volume a serious artistic project, one in which he advanced some of the most important and moving themes he dealt with in the final decade of his career.

When the collection appeared in October 1955, most reviewers criticized it as a lesser effort, one which lacked the power and range of earlier Faulkner works from which parts of it were drawn. As Malcolm Cowley put it, its strengths had "been achieved too much at the cost of other books from which the material was taken by right of eminent domain."[2] Other reviewers labelled the volume a mismatched group of previously published selections designed only to make money. Even so perceptive a critic as Warren Beck suggested that "a fragmented and even denatured Faulkner is being peddled."[3] Such comments fail to consider the author's craftsmanship, signalled in the fact that much of the material, such as the prose introductions to several of the stories, was almost completely rewritten. And even when a piece was incorporated essentially unchanged, its context within the new volume forces the reader to interpret it differently, for he finds his expectations significantly altered by the surrounding material. The collection consists of four hunting stories: "The Bear," "The Old People," "A Bear Hunt," and "Race at Morning," all previously published.[4] A narrative selection serves as a prelude to the entire book, and another one serves as a sort of postlude, or epilogue; other passages provide transitional links or interludes between the stories. Each of these pieces was drawn from work already published,[5] but each has been carefully adapted for its thematic and structural purpose within the collection.

That Faulkner took the project seriously is indicated by the changes he made in the material. With the exception of "The Old People," each of the four stories comprising the volume has been revised: "The Bear," as Faulkner explained at the University of Virginia, appears in its story version without section 4[6]; changes in "A Bear Hunt" and "Race at Morning" help to bring them into greater conformity with other stories in the collection by altering characters, chronology, and emphasis. Even the function of "The Old People" is very much different since it follows "The Bear" in *Big Woods*, instead of preceding it as in *Go Down, Moses.*[7]

The author's concern with the artistic integrity of the book is even more evident in the careful orchestration of the prologue, the interludes between the stories, and the epilogue. In an interview with Harvey Breit before the publication of *Big Woods*, Faulkner referred to these "remarks" which he had written for the stories as "interrupted catalysts."[8] Though this term is quite possibly only the result of Faulkner's disagreement when Breit inquired if they were "commentaries" on the stories, his statements emphasize the extent to which he conceived of these sections as independent of their sources. The reader already acquainted with Faulkner's fiction will quickly recognize that they have been extensively revised from their original forms. Within the context of *Big Woods*, such alterations are completely justified, and criticism that the extractions violate the original versions fails to comprehend their function within the collection. They provide transitions between the stories, set the tone for each individual piece, underline themes of the collection as a whole, and create a sense of progression in both space and time. These special purposes are indicated by the fact that all the passages are printed in italics on unnumbered pages; the fact that their right margins are not justified gives them, as Glen Johnson has suggested, the appearance of blank verse.

The great interest Faulkner took in the preparation of *Big Woods* is also clearly demonstrated in his concern over the "decoration," pen-and-ink drawings by Edward Shenton, who had provided the illustrations for *The Unvanquished.* In an unsigned letter to his editor, Saxe Commins, in February 1955, Faulkner made careful suggestions about the dummy prepared by Shenton. The letter implies detailed prior discussions with the artist about the nature of the illustrations. Although Faulkner requested certain alterations, the letter reveals that he was generally delighted with Shenton's work. The importance of the drawing to the total design of the book is expressed in Faulkner's comments about the sketch of Isaac and Sam saluting the buck, intended to precede "The Old People":

> The drawing is splendid. To Mr. Shenton: would you risk suggesting Sam Fathers is an Indian to this extent? He is bareheaded, his hair a little long, a narrow band of cloth bound or twisted around his head? or maybe definitely long hair showing below a battered hat? Since you are not illustrating, but illuminating (in the old sense) you could have any liberty you like.[10]

In a closing addition to the letter, possibly written the following day, Faulkner reconsidered some of his suggestions and decided that "Mr Shenton is doing so well, I am extremely timid about getting in the way." (377) The final drawings conform closely to Faulkner's suggestions and play an important role in the book's celebration of the wilderness and the hunt.

Clearly, then, Faulkner approached the task of assembling *Big Woods* with a dedicated craftsmanship similar to that he had employed throughout his career. By examining each section individually, we can appreciate both the extent of his imaginative commitment and the measure of his success.

The prologue introduces the reader both to the entire collection and to the first story, "The Bear." The typescript setting copy[11] reveals that Faulkner used tearsheets from 101-5 of the prose narrative prefacing Act Two of *Requiem for a Nun*, to which he added only one word at the beginning: "Mississippi." This name is an important clue to the nature of the section, which sets the actions of the book within a continuum of human activity played off against the background of the rich wilderness. Specifically, the prologue details the various groups of men who displace one another, beginning with the Indians and concluding with "*the Anglo-Saxon, the pioneer, the tall man, roaring with Protestant scripture and boiled whisky.*"[12] With the introduction of the Anglo-Saxon, Faulkner also begins the development of one of the book's major themes: man's exploitation of the wilderness and closely related to it, his eventual loss of the values he learns there in the hunt. Faulkner goes on to describe how the Anglo-Saxon becomes "obsolete," following the pattern established earlier by the Indians, Spanish, and French; the final image of man in the section is of the murderer, who is driven to crouch in a deep thicket awaiting those who will carry him to this execution. (The image will be repeated in the interlude between "The Bear" and "The Old People.") The piece concludes by contrasting the modern emphasis upon acquisition with the natural fertility described in the beginning. The fertility gives rise to exploitation; the result is uncontrolled avarice and rapacity: "*all men's mouths were round with the sound of money; one unanimous golden affirmation ululated the nation's boundless immeasurable forenoon: profit plus regimen equals security.*" (7) As the tone of the piece makes clear, however, this security is purchased only at the price of man's loss of the wilderness. Thus, the first section telescopes the major themes of the book and previews the destruction of the Big Woods which will be depicted in "The Bear" and later in the collection. Structurally, of course, it anticipates Isaac's celebrated comments about the revenge of the wilderness in the epilogue.

A central concern in *Big Woods* is man's ability to cope with the losses occasioned by this destruction. The theme is at the heart of "The Bear," the text of which is virtually unchanged from *Go Down, Moses* except for the deletion of section 4. However, its position as the first story points out its importance to Faulkner's purposes. The opening paragraphs provide a sharp contrast to the ending of the preceding section. In them, Faulkner defines the qualities men cultivate through the hunt in terms of the hunters themselves: "It was of the men . . . hunters, with the will and hardihood to endure and the humility and skill to survive." (11) These are the virtues cultivated through hunting. Appropriately, the first story is the most detailed presentation of these qualities in action: "The Bear" presents Isaac's apprenticeship in the wilderness, and the reader learns how patience and humility and endurance function there. But the story does not stop with Isaac's acquisition of these characteristics; the deaths of the bear and Sam Fathers and the passing of the wilderness introduce the theme of change and man's ability to deal with it. The destruction of the woods in the final part parallels the exploitation described in the prologue; the changes in both sections stress another important lesson to be learned in the woods—adaptability. Isaac develops this quality in his confrontation with Old Ben at the end of part 1. In order to deserve a vision of the bear, he must approach it on its own terms. However, to complete his maturation, Isaac must apply the principle of adaptability to the larger context of human society outside the wilderness. On the surface, Isaac appears to be more successful in this respect in *Big Woods* than in *Go Down, Moses*, since the section of the novel which describes his repudiation of his inheritance and its responsibilities is not part of the story. He is not intimidated by the trip to Memphis, as Boon is, and at the end of "The Bear" he is better able than Boon to cope with the loss of the woods. Boon becomes completely disoriented by the change. He loses all feelings of comradeship with his fellow hunter in his selfish, pathetic attempt to put his gun together and kill the squirrels in the gum tree. His inability to use the gun symbolizes his inability to cope with the encroachment of civilization.

Although Isaac is better equipped to accept the loss of the Big Woods than Boon, he too has difficulty adapting. Though he had thought himself prepared, he is shocked by the extent of the devastation when he returns. As a defense, he creates a romanticized vision of the hunt as he remembers it, immortally played off against a wilderness which now exists only in his imagination. He refuses to accept the change and begins to insulate himself from the present world; the epilogue details the final result of that tragic process. "The Bear" then, presents the book's most complete statement of the virtues to be acquired in the wilderness; but at the same time it shows that these virtues are meaningful only if applied in situations outside the Big Woods as well as in the hunt itself, an idea which will be underlined in "Race at Morning."

The interlude which follows "The Bear" was adapted from the short story "Red Leaves," and it serves to link "The Bear" and "The Old People" through contrasting points of view and related imagery. David Burggraf correctly points out that the majority of changes in the creation of this section involve alterations in point of view, shifting the perspective from the Indians to the slave whom they pursue. (28-32) Thus, it presents the hunt from the vantage point of the hunted rather than the hunter. Still, the qualities which motivate the chase are much the same. Hunter and hunted respect one another; when the Indians capture the Negro, Basket says, "'*You ran well. Do not be ashamed.*'" (105) Other revisions relate more directly to the themes established earlier in the book; still others are designed to contribute to its over-all unity. For instance, to the list of game Issetibbeha and the slave had pursued in "Red Leaves," Faulkner adds "*sometimes even a bear come up from the Big Bottom along the river.*" (99) Certain additions associate the slave with the wilderness, as Old Ben had been associated in "The Bear." New material presents the Negro's memories of his life before his original capture, thus linking him with the natural forces embodied in the Big Woods. (105.1-13) As an extension of these symbolic connotations, Faulkner adds passages emphasizing the slave's fate, which is roughly the same as that of the wilderness: "*for the first time he realised his true situation, how desperate, how irrevocable, how doomed.*" (103) Thus the slave becomes the personification of the wilderness; the final four pages of the section, which closely follow part VI of "Red Leaves," dramatize the inexorable end of the slave's attempt to save his life. His attempt, like the future of the woods he represents, is doomed.

The emphasis upon the Indians and their relationship to the wilderness makes this interlude an effective transition between "The Bear" and "The Old People," for Sam Fathers is a central presence in both stories. The position of "The Old People"—following "The Bear"—underlines the training Isaac receives under Sam's tutelage. Many of the images in "The Bear" recur, and the expansion of these images, particularly those associated with Isaac's killing his first deer, accent the virtues man acquires through the hunt. Burggraf points out that one thing gained by the position of "The Old People" is "to give much more significance . . . to the vision of the ghost deer, which . . . is the central formulating vision upon which Isaac builds his life's strategy." (32) But we should not lose sight of the fact that in placing "The Old People" after "The Bear," Faulkner is also challenging his reader in a way reminiscent of some of his most experimental fiction.[13] He invites the reader to consider these works and their characters independently, apart from their roles in *Go Down, Moses*. Obscure references in "The Bear" are now clarified: the reader discovers more about the relationship between Sam and Isaac as well as that between Isaac and Cass; Jobaker, who is only referred to in "The Bear," is introduced more fully; the circumstances of Sam's ritual death are made clearer by the hints of Sam's participation in Jobaker's death. On the other hand, certain events in "The Old People" which the reader may not notice as significant in *Go Down, Moses* must be reconsidered when that story follows "The Bear": the reference to "Boon Hogganbeck's old gun with which he never killed anything larger than a squirrel and that sitting" (127) adds further irony to the ending of "The Bear," as does his boast that he could have killed the buck with his pocket knife if he had known of its presence. The persistent futility of Isaac's imaginative vision of the eternal wilderness as he rides the wagon with the trophies out of the Big Woods is emphasized by the last section of "The Bear" as well. But perhaps the chief aspect of the story which the reader must reconsider is the salute, "Oleh, Chief . . . Grandfather," (135) with which Sam addresses the totem buck. In *Big Woods,* Sam's salute is preceded both by Isaac's saluting the rattlesnake at the end of "The Bear" and the slave's addressing the water moccasin in the prologue to the story. The mystical associations of Sam's actions are thus seriously undercut in *Big Woods* by his use of a phrase linked earlier in both cases with destruction, sickness, and death.

The potency of the salute is not completely diminished, however, since Sam addresses the buck as embodying the life force which he finds in the woods, in all living things. The vision of the buck is central to Isaac's experience, and his conversation with Cass about it at the end of the story becomes a means of evaluating man's approach to the lessons learned in the wilderness. Cass's comments emphasize the value of experience:

> And even suffering and grieving is better than nothing; there is only one thing worse than not being alive, and that's shame. But you can't be alive forever, and you always wear out life long before you have exhausted the possibilities of living. (137)

This speech stresses the importance of respect for all life; Man's experience of the Big Woods must be placed in the context of his total world. As the epilogue shows, it is this part of the lesson which Isaac fails to assimilate completely. But the value of life and the conservation of life-force the earth manifests have reverberations in *Big Woods* beyond Isaac's individual experience. The respect for life exhibited by nature itself stands as condemnation of the greed and rapacity which are dramatized in the prologue to the collection. The resources of the earth are to be used wisely by man, not ruthlessly destroyed.

The value of life in its various forms which Cass mentions becomes the theme of the next interlude, which Faulkner drew from his story "A Justice." The extensive alterations he made in the material, however, would perhaps make it more accurate to describe the piece as based upon an incident in "A Justice." The setting copy for this section shows that Faulkner changed his conception of the opening to highlight his themes more directly. The original beginning describes in comic terms how the steamboat died and how Doom's decision to bring it to the plantation arose from his genuine concern for the welfare of his people. The revised opening adds that the white men had "*removed the swimming machinery and carried it back to Vicksburg and now the steamboat belonged to anyone who wanted it, assuming anyone was that foolish.*" (139) Interpolated passages continue to show that Doom had already claimed the steamboat and intended to bring to the plantation, even though "*That sand-bar was twelve miles away and that steamboat was almost as large as the House.*" (140) The additions emphasize the senselessness of Doom's decision; he exploits his people much as men exhaust the wilderness. Indeed, his exploitation adds to the destruction of the woods since the trees have to be cut down for the twelve miles to make a path for the steamboat.

Faulkner made additional changes in the ending. The cancelled first version of the last page shows that he added two very significant passages. The first enlarges Doom's will to power and his ruthless control over the people, who could go about their business "*until, that is, the Man thought of something else arduous and unpleasant for them to do.*" (141) Thus he takes the same grim attitude toward his subjects that the men in the prologue take toward the resources of the wilderness. Untempered even by humor, much less by wisdom, his commands become oppressive and cruel. The second of the passages added to the revised conclusion stresses the effects of this cruelty. It depicts Herman Basket, who, remembering the arduous task of moving the steamboat, must go outside it to sleep. Faulkner adds that Basket had to "*find a thicket so dense and distant*" (142) that he could see neither the House nor the steamboat. Doom's cruelty drives Basket into hiding much as the exploitation in the first interlude had driven the murderer into his thicket.

The material drawn from "Red Leaves" serves as an appropriate transition, signalling an alteration in the mood of the book. It indicates a change in tone, shifting from the elegiac to the comic, though there is no corresponding change in theme or purpose: the comedy of "A Bear Hunt" is dark humor, a mere facade to mark men's avarice. But there are other changes as well; the movement of the steamboat and the conflict between the Indians and the slaves they own in the preceding two interludes reveal the changes, often destructive to the tribe, which result from contact with the white man, the "Anglo-Saxon" of the prologue. But the advance of time has also brought significant alterations in the hunt. A new generation of hunters now pursues the game; only Uncle Ike remains from the group in "The Bear." What is more, the world of the story is different. The Big Woods have receded farther and farther toward the delta, and the loss of the wilderness has precipitated a lessening of the positive qualities associated with the hunt in "The Bear" and "The Old People." Even the Indians have all but completely abandoned their traditions; they now support themselves by moonshining, as do many of their white neighbors, and they have become almost entirely dispossessed: "a remnant of a once powerful clan of the Chickasaw tribe. . . . They now had American names and they lived as the sparse white people who surrounded them in turn lived." (148) The central concern of "A Bear Hunt" is to dramatize the loss of traditional values common to both the Indians and the hunters.

The alterations Faulkner made in including "A Bear Hunt" in *Big Woods* link the story more closely with those which precede it and continue the thematic development of the interlude. The changes occur almost entirely in the first part and relate to the central characters. The setting copy, tearsheets of the text from *Collected Stories,* includes two typed insertions. The first changes Lucius Provine to Lucius Hogganbeck and sketches in his background. The second, briefer addition establishes that the title of the Major de Spain in this story is only honorary; the younger Major, significantly, is a banker. Apart from these additions, the first section, narrated apparently by Quentin Compson, makes clear that the world he knows growing up is vastly different from that of the young protagonist of the first two stories—Isaac McCaslin. (This fact hints that the world of "A Bear Hunt" is likewise different from that known by the final young hunter in the book—the narrator of "Race at Morning.")

The tale related by Ratliff presents even more serious changes in the character of the hunt and the nature of the hunters. Hogganbeck's problem is hiccups, and while on the surface the problem is merely a comic device, it enables Faulkner to develop more completely the book's serious themes of the effects of the vanishing woods upon the men who still hunt. Lucius has acquired his hiccups by overeating, a fact indicative of his lessened stature. But more significant is the reaction of the other men to this predicament. They offer him no aid, merely sending him from one place to another so he will not disturb their hunting or their rest. Ratliff makes Lucius the butt of a joke and evokes from him damning criticism of the attitudes of the hunters: "Hit ain't a man hyer has got any mercy on me, white or black. Hyer I done suffered and suffered more than twenty-four hours without food or sleep, and not a sonabitch of them has any mercy or pity on me!" (156) The selfishness of each character in the toy, even Uncle Ike, underlines what the loss of the wilderness, which has resulted from similarly selfish attitudes, really means: the earlier feeling of comradeship is almost completely missing. The differences, as Burggraf points out, are reinforced by the mechanical imagery, which projects the story into the modern world. (99) Lucius, for instance, is compared with a hay baler (152), a gasoline engine (153), loud-speakers (153) and a car. (155) These references point to the modern economic forces which contribute to the disappearance of the wilderness and the resulting dehumanization of man. Even Ash's explanation of why he had set up Lucius with the Indians is placed in economic terms.

The fourth interlude, drawn from Faulkner's essay "Mississippi," extends this emphasis upon economics. The section as it appears in *Big Woods* is substantially rewritten and is closely related to the themes of the prologue. It begins by discussing the effects of development upon the land, and continues with an interpolated passage depicting the destruction of the Big Woods and the passing of time as related specifically to Isaac:

> *when Old Isaac McCaslin was a boy he shot bear and deer and wild turkey after less than a day in mule-drawn wagon: even*

> *when he had got old enough for young men to begin to call him uncle Ike and the distance was fifty miles instead of twenty, it still took only a part of a day in the automobile, even though the roads were dirt ones. Now they had concrete: a hundred miles instead of fifty, then two hundred instead of one as the wilderness dwindled southward into the notch of the hills and the Old Man. (166)*

The reference to the Old Man provides transition to a section taken with only minor alteration from "Mississippi"—a description of a flood. The river, unlike the woods, remains invulnerable to man's attempts to control it. During the flood man finds himself dispossessed of the land. Ultimately, however, the flood is part of the cyclical processes of nature, and when the waters recede, the land is even richer. Ironically, it is the richness, the fecundity, which had instigated the process of exploitation and destruction.

The conclusion departs from "Mississippi" to focus once again upon Isaac McCaslin. Sam Fathers and Old Ben are evoked as the loss of the wilderness is rendered with elegiac nostalgia. Isaac envisions the last stand of the Big Woods, in which he would play a part. The strength of his defense would be "*life and memory*" (171) though, and the reader understands that such defenses would be almost useless against the economic forces described in the beginning. Still, Isaac's presentation here is clearly sympathetic; his effort at preservation is even endowed with a certain poetic heroism: "*Oh yes, he would think; me too. I've been too busy all my life trying not to waste any living, to have time left to die.*" (171).

This emphasis upon life looks forward to the themes of the final story in *Big Woods*, "Race at Morning." Like "A Bear Hunt," the story is set in modern times, but both the humor and the themes are of another order entirely. Unlike the preceding tale, "Race at Morning" describes a genuine hunt for game. Yet the chase is different from that depicted in the "The Bear" as well. A clue to this difference is provided in the interlude which intoduces it; the goal of the hunt is now "*not to slay the game but to pursue it, touch and let go, never satiety.*" (170) Although the chase itself is comic, it is heightened by powerful description of the beauty of the woods and the nobility of the deer, magnifying the tragedy inherent in their destruction for selfish economic gain.

Most of the additions Faulkner made to "Race at Morning"

serve one of three functions: they place the action on a more symbolic level; they add to the humor; they emphasize the beauty of the wilderness.[14] The longest addition (180.20-29) concerns the horse, Dan, which becomes a beast of almost mythical ability, linking him with both Lion and Old Ben. Another added passage describes the deer himself in supernatural terms, "like that old son of a gun actually was a hant, like Simon and the other field hands said he was," (181) reminding the reader of the tremendous buck at the end of "The Old People." The descriptions which Faulkner included as part of the narrator's perception are also reminiscent of Isaac's reverent attitude toward the Big Woods; the boy describes the sun as "bright and strong and level through the woods, shining and sparking like a rainbow on the frosted leaves." (181) Such additions place "Race at Morning," like the first two stories in the book, on the level of symbolic ritual.

Other parallels between "The Old People" and "Race at Morning" point toward the latter's purpose in the collection. Like the earlier story, "Race at Morning" concerns a boy's education in the wilderness; and once again the significance of his experience is verbalized by an older man, in this case Mister Ernest. Further, the lesson itself has close ties with Cass's speech concerning the value of life. The event under consideration is Mister Ernest's allowing the great buck to go free after he and the boy had chased it all day. When the narrator confronts him about it, Mister Ernest explains his reasons: "Which would you rather have? His bloody head and hide on the kitchen floor yonder and half his meat in a pickup truck on the way to Yoknapatawpha County, or him with his head and hide and meat still together over yonder in that brake, waiting for next November for us to run him again?" (197) The significance of the hunt has been altered in light of changes in the environment. A similar alteration is required on a larger scale, as Mister Ernest had stated earlier; when the boy declares that he would be a hunter and farmer too, Mister Ernest says:

> That ain't enough any more. Time was when all a man had to do was just farm eleven and a half months, and hunt the other half. But not now. Now just to belong to the farming business and the hunting business ain't enough. You got to belong to the business of mankind. (196)

This statement, appearing near the end of the final story in *Big Woods*, is central to understanding the themes of the book as a whole. It condemns those who destroy the land, the wilderness, for their own profit, but it also condemns those like Isaac McCaslin, who wish to keep the land intact for equally selfish reasons. Both ignore the "business of mankind" for more limited interests; both disregard responsibilities to the larger human community.

Isaac's tragedy is underlined by the epilogue to *Big Woods*, based upon "Delta Autumn," which serves as a coda to the entire collection. Though Isaac now speaks in first person, he is no longer even a participant in the hunt. He describes his final trip into the Big Woods with the men who are children or grand-children of the original hunters. Material added to the section related it more closely to other units in *Big Woods*. To the list of the original hunters given in "Delta Autumn," for instance Faulkner appends "*Boon Hogganbeck, the forty-year-old adolescent boy who killed the big old warp-footed bear with his bare hands and a pocket-knife.*" (204) As in "A Bear Hunt," names are changed; Isham becomes Young Ash, (206) and the young Negro is called Joseph. References to the "Big Bottom" become "Big Woods." (206) All these changes add to the essential unity of the book, as do Isaac's reminiscences of the hunt described in "The Bear." These memories increase the elegiac tone of the epilogue and provide a sharp contrast to Isaac's last comments.

The closing lines of the book arise from the old hunter's conversation with Legate over the dead deer. The material is substantially revised from the version in "Delta Autumn"; the setting copy shows that a cancelled draft of the conversation was altered to make it more direct and brutal. Isaac realizes that Roth kills does because he (Isaac) had failed to instill in him a genuine respect for the wilderness, an aspect of the boy's education which Mister Ernest does not neglect in "Race at Morning." After his altercation with Roth over the shotgun, Isaac thinks: "*But it is too late, too late not just now, this mining, not even yesterday, but already too late much longer ago than any of these.*" (211) It is too late because so much of the wilderness has been destroyed, but on a more personal level it is too late because Isaac has failed even in the simple contribution he could make to its preservation: the proper initiation of his kinsman. Isaac's final lament over the loss of the wilderness becomes heavily ironic, since he apparently fails to recognize his own responsibility.

The epilogue is important to an understanding of the book's unity, achieved through complex thematic interaction among the various sections. When Isaac remembers the first deer he killed, he expands the implication of the ritual which followed: "I slew you; my bearing must not shame your quitting life. My conduct forever afterward must become your death." (207) Echoing comments by both Cass and Mister Ernest, this statement reveals that the hunt should instill respect for life in man, respect for the possibilities of existence. But this respect is not an end in itself; it must be transferred from the hunt to the world beyond, the world of which the Big Woods are less and less a part. As the final section makes clear, Isaac has ultimately failed to comprehend the real significance of the hunt, even of the wilderness itself. He feels alive only during the two weeks he spends in the woods each November, and this attitude is a denial of Cass's emphasis upon the multiplicity of experience. His attitudes in the epilogue are life denying; they indicate that the destruction of his own spirit, of his sense of possibility, is even more complete than the loss of the woods he so mournfully laments.

But the themes of *Big Woods* reverberate beyond the individual situation of Isaac McCaslin. The heedless leveling of the wilderness results in a very real tragedy because with the passing of the woods passes much of the nobility and heroism man can achieve in them. This loss is a major part of the revenge Isaac mentions in the closing lines of the book: "*No wonder the ruined woods I used to know don't cry for retribution. The very people who destroyed them will accomplish their revenge.*" (212) In the total presentation of the wilderness theme, though, Isaac's despair must be contrasted with Mister Ernest's insistence upon possibility: "The best word in our language, the best of all. That's what mankind keeps going on: Maybe." (197) These two comments represent opposing attitudes toward the challenges of the modern world and toward the specific themes of the book. The destruction of the woods is terrible, but the inability of man to deal with the loss is even more so. Thus, the final purpose of *Big Woods* is much broader than "a celebration of the wilderness and a lament for its disappearance."[15] It is a complex study of man's struggle to function successfully in his world, to cope with the circumstances of his life and with the changing forces of his environment.

NOTES

1. *Big Woods* has certainly received less serious attention than it deserves, and little useful criticism exists. A couple of studies mention it briefly, usually comparing it adversely (and unfairly) with *Go Down, Moses*; Michael Millgate's comments in *The Achievement of William Faulkner* (New York: Vintage Books, 1971) are typical in this respect; he finds that "Faulkner did not intend it to be anything other than a celebration of the wilderness and a lament for its disappearance." (213) The only full-length study is David L. Burggraf's dissertation, "The Genesis and Unity of Faulkner's *Big Woods*" (Ohio University, 1975). Although Burggraf has a detailed chapter on the revision of material for *Big Woods*, his study is flawed by factual errors and by his tendency to evaluate the sections of the book in light of their original forms. A more useful approach is taken by Glen M. Johnson, whose "*Big Woods*: Faulkner's Elegy for Wilderness" (*Southern Humanities Review*, 14 [Summer 1980], pp. 249-58) is an examination of the theme of the vanishing wilderness in the book, which he rightly evaluates according to its own merits.
2. Malcolm Cowley, "Life of the Hunter," *New York Times Book Review*, 16 October 1955, p. 4.
3. Warren Beck, "The New Faulkner," *College English*, 17 (December 1955), p. 183.
4. Both "The Bear" and "The Old People" had been chapters of *Go Down, Moses* (New York: Random, 1942). "A Bear Hunt," which appeared first in *The Saturday Evening Post* (10 February 1934), had been included in *Collected Stories* (New York: Random, 1950). *Race at Morning*, which was also published in *Post* (5 March 1955), was first collected in *Big Woods*.
5. The prelude to "The Bear" was taken from *Requiem for a Nun* (New York: Random, 1951); the sections preceding "The Old People" and "A Bear Hunt" are extensively revised excerpts from "Red Leaves" and "A Justice" respectively, both of which had appeared in *Collected Stories*; a rewritten section of "Mississippi" (*Holiday*, 15 [April 1954]) serves to introduce "Race at Morning"; the epilogue is an extensively revised version of "Delta Autumn," chapter six of *Go Down, Moses*.
6. Referring to the removal of section 4 of "The Bear" when printing it apart from *Go Down, Moses*, Faulkner stated: "To have taken that story out to print it alone I have always removed that part, which I have done" (*Faulkner in the University*, ed. Frederick L. Gwynn and Joseph L. Blotner [New York: Random, 1959], p. 4.)

7. Evidence that the positioning of "The Bear" and "The Old People" had been carefully considered is provided by a letter from Faulkner to his editor, Saxe Commins, in late June 1995: "Was our original plan for 'The Bear' to precede 'The Old People'? If it was, the order is right. Though on seeing the galley, it struck me that 'The Old People' should come first, since it is first in the boy's experience. But if we originally set 'The Bear' first, then that first thought is the right one" (*Selected Letters of William Faulkner*, ed. Joseph Blotner [New York: Random, 1977], p. 382).
8. *Lion in the Garden: Interviews with William Faulkner, 1926-1962*, ed. James B. Meriwether and Michael Millgate (New York: Random House, 1968), p. 83. The interview first appeared in the *New York Times Book Review*, 30 January 1955.
9. Johnson, p. 249.
10. *Selected Letters of William Faulkner*, pp. 376-77. The special value Faulkner placed on Shenton's drawings is emphasized in their being referred to on the title page as "Decorations," rather that illustrations.
11. For a description of the setting copy, now on deposit in the Alderman Library at the University of Virginia, see James B. Meriwether, *The Literary Career of William Faulkner* (Columbia: University of South Carolina Press, 1971), pp. 79-80.
12. William Faulkner, *Big Woods* (New York: Random, 1955), p. 4.
13. The resulting juxtaposition of chronology recalls some of Faulkner's boldest structural experiments. He had, in fact, contemplated a similar juxtaposition in *Go Down, Moses*: the pagination of the typescript reveals that at one time Faulkner had positioned "Delta Autumn" so as to precede "The Bear," though he later decided upon a more direct chronological approach.
14. Apparently Faulkner made these alterations to the galley proofs of *Big Woods*. Setting copy for "Race at Mornimg" was galley proofs from the story's appearance in *The Saturday Evening Post*, and no substantive changes were indicated. James B. Meriwether has suggested to me the possibility that Faulkner had composed "Race at Morning" especially for inclusion in *Big Woods*, perhaps as a deliberate reversal of some of the hunting themes of "The Old People" and "The Bear."
15. Millgate, *The Achievement of William Faulkner*, p. 213.

This article originally appeared in *The Mississippi Quarterly*, Vol. XXXVI, Summer 1983, No. 3. Reprinted with permission.

The Snopes Trilogy

ANDREW HOOK

Let me begin with cards clearly on the table. I share the conventional view that the so-called Snopes trilogy—*The Hamlet* (1940), *The Town* (1957), *The Mansion* (1959)—is not one of Faulkner's very greatest achievements. Fine as they are in their different ways, these novels, unlike say *The Sound and the Fury, Light in August,* or *Absalom, Absalom!*, are not among the great novels of the twentieth century. Then, equally conventionally, I find *The Hamlet* easily the best of the trilogy novels. And lastly, I go along with those who find the story of Mink Snopes easily the finest thing in *The Mansion.* Given this degree of unexceptionality of critical judgment, what I propose to do in the first part of this essay is try to think around the various dimensions of the three novels so as to indicate how such judgments are ultimately arrived at.

More recent work has not succeeded in displacing Edmund Volpe's seminal assessment of the Snopes trilogy in *A Reader's Guide to William Faulkner*. Volpe's account is full of telling observations, but at this stage I want to draw attention only to one:

> Faulkner's masterpieces are great artistic creations because they create an overwhelming emotional current—despair, or pity, or outrage, or incredulity, or indignation, or horror—that tears the reader from his familiar moorings and sweeps him into a world created, shaped, and illuminated by Faulkner's personal vision of life.[1]

I am not wholly convinced that Faulkner's 'personal vision of life' has to be involved, but otherwise I find this passage profoundly true. It explains the particular quality of *intensity* that seems to me to be totally characteristic of Faulkner's writing at its best. And it is precisely its possession of this quality of intensity that marks *The Hamlet* off from *The Town* and most of *The Mansion*, and thus aligns the earlier book with the great works of Faulkner's first and most creative period. As well as intensity, however, *The Hamlet* creates a world of apparent stasis or permanence; Frenchman's Bend and the countryside surrounding it seem to be part of a permanent, unchanging, rural Southern world which Faulkner creates with a masterly vividness and immediacy:

> The team, the buckboard, went on in the thick dust of the spent summer. Now he could see the village proper—the store, the blacksmith shop, the metal roof of the gin with a thin rapid shimmer of exhaust above the stack. It was now the third week in September; the dry, dust-laden air vibrated steadily to the rapid beat of the engine, though so close were the steam and the air in temperature that no exhaust was visible but merely a thin feverish shimmer of mirage. The very hot, vivid air, which seemed to be filled with the slow laborious plaint of laden wagons, smelled of lint; wisps of it clung among the dust-stiffened roadside weeds and small gouts of cotton lay imprinted by hoof- and wheel-marks into the trodden dust. He could see the wagons too, the long motionless line of them behind the patient, droop-headed mules, waiting to advance a wagon-length at a time.[2]

The sensuous effectiveness of this appears almost casual, effortless: a relaxed, vivid presence, like that of the group of men in their faded denim shirts and jeans whittling on the verandah of the Varner store. The step from this static, permanent, almost timeless rural scene into the world of legend and myth is a short one; this is how Faulkner is able to allow some of his characters—Eula, Flem, Ike—and the events in which they are involved, to acquire something of the quality of archetypal myths. From the very beginning of his career, Faulkner seems to have taken on board Eliot's advice to his contemporaries to adopt Joyce's method of using myth as a way of giving significance to 'the immense panorama of futility and anarchy which is contemporary history.'[3] In *The Hamlet*, so firmly anchored in the vividly recreated landscapes and settings of the rural South, the method is still at work, enlarging and universalizing the meaning of the minute particulars of character and event. Flem Snopes appears first in the novel as a face at a window. Then this:

> One moment the road had been empty, the next moment the man stood there beside it, at the edge of a small copse—the same cloth cap, the same rhythmically chewing jaw materialized apparently out of nothing and almost abreast of the horse, with an air of the completely and purely accidental which Varner was to remember and speculate about only later. (20-21)

Flem seems, as it were, to materialize out of nowhere; he is simply a presence—and that is what he remains from the beginning of *The Hamlet* to the end of *The Mansion*.

Volpe speaks of the 'tonal and thematic contrasts' that shape and structure the meaning of *The Hamlet* given the fact that Flem remains an absent presence for most of the novel. (307) More basic still, perhaps, is the contrast between the slow, unhurried, almost static world of the novel and the amazing intensity of action and feeling in the stories it contains. The two elements play off against each other in a manner that heightens both, and contributes significantly to that 'unmooring' of the reader's familiar sense of reality to which Volpe refers. Ultimately, however, Faulkner's fictional reality is a creation of his language and style. In all of his best work language and style seem to set aside referential reality; the reader has to repossess, re-read the world. Rather than describing reality, Faulkner's rhetoric constantly creates or recreates it. It exists only in and through the words; rich and detailed, it is nonetheless independent, suspended, beyond time and space. Conventional grammar and syntax are often sacrificed to allow the emergence of this new world in which past and present, the immediate and the mythical, the static and the transient, flow in and out of each other. In the case of *The Hamlet*, style lends additional intensity to the given intensity of action, event and feeling:

> The moon was almost full then. When supper was over and they had gathered again along the veranda, the alteration was hardly one of visibility even. It was merely a translation from the lapidary-dimensional of day to the treacherous and silver receptivity in which the horses huddled in mazy camouflage, or singly or in pairs rushed, fluid, phantom, and unceasing, to huddle

> again in mirage-like clumps from which came high abrupt squeals and the vicious thudding of hooves. (247-48)

The ponies described here are extra-ordinary, preternatural, the moonlight simply reinforcing their larger-than-life, almost surreal existence. But the particular effects of such a descriptive passage in fact mirror the essential characteristics of the stories that *The Hamlet* tells: Flem Snopes's rapacious acquisitiveness; Eula's sexuality; Labove's passion; Mink Snopes's fury; Armstid's treasure lust; Ike's love for his cow; Lump Snopes's greed. All of these, as well as a whole series of inset life-stories, episodes, or incidents, are characterized by the same sense of a driving intensity of felt experience. The Snopes establish themselves in Yoknapatawpha County by actual and threatened barn-burning. But flames and fire are appropriate metaphors for the all-consuming passions that seem to possess and drive so many of the characters in *The Hamlet*, and are communicated to the reader by a constantly and cumulatively creative language and style.

It is the general absence of any comparable passionate intensity that explains the relative inferiority of *The Town* and *The Mansion*. For long stretches of both these novels a kind of relaxed, meditative rumination replaces intensity. Perhaps on occasion Gavin Stevens's mental agonizings attain a kind of intensity of their own, but it is still an inadequate substitute. Indeed, the use of Stevens as a narrator—along with Charles Mallison and V.K. Ratliff—is the obvious source of the problem. Stevens is both character and narrator in both novels, and his personality seems to set the tone of both works. Stevens may or may not be a Faulkner mouthpiece—the truth probably is that sometimes he is, sometimes he is not. But as Harvard graduate, Heidelberg Ph.D., lawyer, humanist and romantic idealist, he has little in common with the driven characters of *The Hamlet*. Of course he is caught up in the events he describes, and he has passions and feelings of his own, but there is simultaneously a quality of intellectual detachment about him; he is a tolerant, liberal observer of the complexities of life. Thus he—and his fellow narrators—work to distance the reader from the events they describe, keeping the imaginative pressure at a noticeably lower level. Faulkner himself was quite aware of the change: 'Doing a little work on the next Snopes book,' he wrote to Saxe Commins, 'have not taken fire in the old way yet, so it goes slow.'[4] About the same time he wrote to his young friend Jean Stein seeking reassurance over the Snopes material he had sent her:

> I still feel, as I did last year, that perhaps I have written myself out and all that remains now is the empty craftsmanship—no fire, force, passion anymore in the words and sentences. (391)

For me at least, this is more or less accurate. What one misses above all in *The Town*—and in much of *The Mansion* too—is just these particular qualities at the level of language and style, words and sentences. Faulkner was in no sense written out; but his stance towards his material had changed in the direction suggested by his readiness to employ Gavin Stevens as his principal narrator.

Seventeen years separate *The Hamlet* and *The Town*, and of course there is no reason why Faulkner should have attempted to re-achieve in the later novel what he had done in the earlier one. Cleanth Brooks reminds us that we do well to try to read *The Town* 'by its own light and to judge it by its own standards.'[5] (However Brooks goes on to take the somewhat extreme position of suggesting that readers of the trilogy might well be advised to omit reading *The Town* altogether and move straight from *The Hamlet* to *The Mansion*). Again, many elements of the Snopes trilogy had been gestating for much longer than seventeen years, and Faulkner himself drew attention to this point in the prefatory note he wrote for *The Mansion*. He said he knew that there were 'discrepancies and contradictions' between different elements in the stories written at widely different times: these were due to the fact that the author had learned 'more about the human heart and its dilemma than he knew thirty-four years ago.' Faulkner implies by this that there is no reason to expect the trilogy to contain any kind of uniformity or consistency in such areas as tone, attitude, or vision. The trilogy has changed as its author has changed. Some commentators on the trilogy have indeed tried to argue that Faulkner's comment has a substantially wider significance than a simple defence of local discrepancies and contradictions.[6] Faulkner does actually mean that he has learned more about the human heart: *The Town* and *The Mansion* are the work of an older and wiser man. Specifically, in the later novels, the characters who appear in *The Hamlet* as archetypes, larger than life embodiments of primitive human passions and drives, are now scaled down to more recognizable, complex, human beings. Perhaps so. But whatever the cause, the result is a lessening of impact upon the reader. Stevens, Mallison, and Ratliff, mediating to the reader the activities of the inhabitants of *The Town* and *The Mansion*, seem to some degree to defuse their impact. Faulkner himself seems sometimes to be aware of this: he tells us that Stevens talks too much. In *The Town* he allows Ratliff to observe of Stevens: 'You never listened to nobody because by that time you were already talking again.'[7] Not that Ratliff's judgment compares in severity with that of young Charles Mallison made, not in the trilogy, but in *Knight's Gambit*:

> What surprised him was his uncle: that glib and talkative man who talked so much and so glibly, particularly about things which had absolutely no concern with him, that his was indeed a split personality: the one, the lawyer, the county attorney who walked and breathed and displaced air; the other, the garrulous facile voice so garrulous and facile that it seemed to have no connection with reality at all and presently hearing it was like listening not even to fiction but to literature.[8]

But such acid comments by his fellow-narrators have little effect on that aspect of Faulkner which seems to coincide with Stevens's wordiness, and Stevens remains the dominating voice in both *The Town* and *The Mansion*. Of course not all commentators are quite so critical of Stevens. It is Warren Beck, in *Man in Motion*, who has written easily the most elaborate account of the Snopes trilogy. Throughout his book, Beck argues for the coherence, consistency and sustained imaginative achievement of all three novels; one can only agree with Cleanth Brooks that anyone seriously concerned with the trilogy must consult such a sensitive and intelligent book. Hence when Beck makes the following observation on those of us who see the Mink Snopes story in *The Mansion* as easily the most brilliant and compelling thing in the two later novels, one is bound to pay attention:

> those who praise the Mink Snopes portion as though it were self-sustained and extractable are perhaps only failing to sense how much their response draws on the rest of the trilogy, through a reader's marginal consciousness of the relevant, and particularly as to the tangential illumination projected across

the action by Stevens, Ratliff, and Charles.[9]

Beck may very well be right. But one cannot help noticing that none of these three narrators tell the story of Mink. Instead Faulkner reverts to the anonymous, authorial narrative voice which had appeared throughout most of *The Hamlet.* I would argue that it is only thus that Faulkner could have achieved the remarkable feat of bringing the reader over to Mink's murderous side.

Brooks is right to suggest that Faulkner does not make it easy for us to admire Mink Snopes. (220-21) In *The Town* Ratliff calls him 'the only out-and-out mean Snopes we ever experienced' (71); and the murder of Houston in *The Hamlet* is an outrageous act unredeemed even by its inevitability. The murder of Houston does not surprise us; it is at one with the urgent, unyielding intensity of Mink's savage stubbornness, perseverance, and driving desperation. If the gun had not exploded, he, we feel, would have done. Given this pitching of Mink beyond any normal pitch of intensity, inevitably there are suggestions of the transformation of the poor, downtrodden, struggling dirt-farmer, into someone epic, even heroic. Nonetheless, after the murderous ambush of Houston, another driven man, the reader's sympathy is more with Houston's indomitable and faithful hound, refusing, despite Mink's repeated assaults, to abandon its dead master, than with Mink himself. Yet in the subsequent episodes, despite this background, Faulkner reverses the situation. Denied help of any kind by Flem, Mink is sent to Parchman jail in 1908; manoeuvred by Flem into a futile attempt to escape, he is caught and resentenced in 1923; finally pardoned he leaves Parchman in 1946 having served thirty-eight years. His one surviving aim is to kill the kinsman who has betrayed him. In the course of the brilliant narrative account of how he does it, Mink re-emerges as a character of heroic and epic proportions. Just as Dickens achieves a powerful imaginative identity with the hunted Bill Sikes after the murder of Nancy, so Faulkner compels us into sharing Mink's unswerving conviction of the absolute necessity of his doing what he has set out to do. Mink's intensity is transferred hypnotically to the reader; his concerns—over the unfamiliar world he finds himself in after the long years in Parchman, over his tiny hoard of dollars, over the ancient pistol and cartridges he buys, over 'Old Moster's' sense of justice—echo increasingly as our own. Stevens and the other narrators become involved in Mink's story;

but the narrative itself remains independent of them, and perhaps that is its strength.

Late in *The Town*, Charles Mallison, the youngest of the three narrators, has an exchange with Ratliff about the use or non-use of Southern vernacular forms of speech. The point at issue is the use of 'drug' for standard English 'dragged.' Charles objects to Ratliff's use of the standard word, arguing that the vernacular form has a greater potency: '"drug" sounds a heap more dragged than just "dragged."' However Ratliff retorts that for ten years he has been trying 'to say words right'; he has had the same argument with Charles's uncle who ended up saying 'ain't I got as much right to use your *drug* for my *dragged* as you got to use my *dragged* for your *drug*?' (236) Without making too much of this minor, if somewhat odd, exchange, one might argue that it hints at some degree of ambivalence on Faulkner's own part over issues that include but go beyond the question of the kind of language in which *The Town* and *The Mansion* is written.[10]

The Hamlet is a wholly Yoknapatawpha County novel. *The Town* and *The Mansion* are Yoknapatawpha novels only to a limited degree. The link between Yoknapatawpha and the blossoming of Faulkner's creative genius is beyond dispute; from the point of view of imaginative creativity he himself insisted on the central value of his 'own little postage stamp of native soil' as a kind of inexhaustible 'gold mine' which he could go on exploiting.[11] Of course the Jefferson of *The Town* and *The Mansion* is part of Yoknapatawpha, but the felt experience for the reader is somehow very different. It is all more up-to-date. V.K. Ratliff's use of 'drug'—not to mention Stevens's—is in danger of seeming merely quaint, a touch of local colour. This seems to me to point to the larger problem. Faulkner's brooding genius seems to have required a sense of the South and Southern history for its fullest articulation. The minute particulars of Yoknapatawpha County, which lend such a tangible, sensuous reality to the scenes and settings and landscapes, the contexts and characters of Faulkner's major narratives, all seem to belong to an older, unchanging, Southern world. Conspicuously absent from this world is any sense of *contemporary* America. *The Town* and in particular *The Mansion* are very much a different matter. Gavin Stevens and Charles Mallison belong to a world in which 'dragged' has supplanted 'drug.' The action of *The Town* goes back to the period before World War I and goes on into the 1920s; *The*

Mansion covers the period of the 1930s and 1940s. More important is the way in which action and characters are caught up—at least to some degree—in the major, external historical events of these decades. Thus the novels contain comment on public events to a degree that is noticeably greater than is the case in the fiction of Faulkner's great period. Why this matters is that, in my view, Faulkner and his narrators rarely have especially compelling things to say about the contemporary modern world. Perhaps Volpe is correct when he suggests that the problem is 'Faulkner's emotional detachment from his material.' (330) Certainly there is a qualitative difference between Faulkner's references to, say, the Spanish Civil War, and the American Civil War. Faulkner knows about the former but is possessed by the latter: the result is writing of very different degrees of intensity.

Perhaps the underlying point is Faulkner's familiar conviction that there is no such thing as the past:

> There is no such thing really as was because the past is. It is a part of every man, every woman, and every moment. All of his and her ancestry, background, is all a part of himself and herself at any moment.[12]

Just this metaphysic of time is of course built in to all of Faulkner's fiction. Over and over again he insists on and dramatizes the notion that the past is never over; that both present and future are contained in the past; that the present is only the confirmation of what has already happened. Even his style, or at least one aspect of his style—the long, winding, ungrammatical sentences—appears to be a rhetorical articulation of such a metaphysic: within the single unfolding sentence past, present and future hang compacted and suspended.

When he was writing the Snopes trilogy Faulkner clearly felt about the nature of time just as he had always done. But in *The Town* and *The Mansion* the interweaving of past and present, the retelling of the past in the present, the present's confirmation of what was always going to happen—these phenomena have gained a somewhat mechanical air. And contemporary history itself is no more than that: a given backdrop against which present events are foregrounded. Faulkner's profounder sense of history, of the past's continuing presence, now operates to a major degree only within the history of his own creative life as a writer. What any analysis of the writing history of the Snopes trilogy reveals is the astonishing degree to which it represents a rewriting of Faulkner's own writing history. The origins of the Snopes as a potential subject for Faulkner lie back in the early 1920s at the very start of his writing career. In a very real sense he never stopped writing about the Snopes throughout his entire writing life.

Of course Faulkner's readiness to rework and re-deploy existing material is a constant factor in his writing practice. But nowhere is this readiness carried so far as in the case of the Snopes trilogy. *The Hamlet* involves the revising and retelling of five existing, published stories; *The Town* incorporates two more existing stories; and *The Mansion* two more again. Then *The Town* retells a great deal of what had occurred in *The Hamlet*, while *The Mansion* involves still further recapitulation: stories already told are told again. Faulkner always insisted that the four sections of *The Sound and the Fury* were four attempts to tell the same story, and that the Introduction he wrote for the Modern Library edition was a fifth attempt. The same principle is at work in the Snopes trilogy producing in some instances the well known discrepancies in the different accounts of the same events which so worried Faulkner's original editors. The author himself did not regard these lapses as very important. In a letter written while he was working on *The Mansion*, he insisted that his characters were for him 'quite real and quite constant'; he may sometimes forget what they did,

> but the character I don't forget, and when the book is finished, that character is not done, he still is going on at some new devilment that sooner or later I will find out about and write about.[13]

In other words, like the past, a character is never over. As John E. Basset puts it, in *The Mansion* the theme of the return to the past 'becomes Faulkner's method: conscious revision of earlier material in a process of both recapitulation and transformation.'[14] Hence at the end of the day there is no closure to Faulkner's fiction; here in the Snopes trilogy even his method of composition can be seen as another enactment of the view inherent in his employment of a variety of narrator figures each one commenting on the other and on the events and characters they describe. Finally there can be no single, true story: the same story can be told and retold by one voice or several. No one version is ever the final version.

That Faulkner's method as creator and narrator so resists closure should warn us not to look for the absolutes of moral judgments in the content of his fiction. Hence it is surprising to discover that some of the most hotly debated critical issues in the Snopes trilogy focus on questions of moral judgment. Most commentators agree that throughout the trilogy V.K. Ratliff is a sympathetic figure. A major opponent of Snopesism, in the course of the trilogy he wins some battles even if he loses others. As a narrator he seems to emerge from the American Western tall-tale tradition; one feels that Ratliff and Mark Twain would have got along pretty well. But of course Ratliff is an active participant in the affairs of Yoknapatawpha County, not just a sidelines narrator. Hence questions about his behaviour may well arise. Presumably most readers approve of Ratliff's manoeuvrings over Mink's sewing-machine and the goats which lead to Flem's at least partial defeat early in *The Hamlet*; equally, though a shade or two less persuasively, we accept that his falling for the salted mine trick later on in *The Hamlet* reveals his sharing in the weaknesses of ordinary humanity. It is his behaviour in another episode that has been seen as giving rise to a moral problem.

A central concern of 'The Long Summer' section of *The Hamlet* is Ike Snopes's love for a cow. For the idiot Ike the cow is a love-object with all the grandeur and beauty of the most legendary and fabulous females in world history. Given his cow by Houston, Ike and his beloved become a money-spinning peepshow for Lump Snopes. Ratliff puts an end to the affair. It is this intervention that has sparked critical argument. Some commentators rebuke Ratliff for allowing conventional notions of moral decorum to take precedence over human concern for the pitiful Ike: Ratliff's outrage, it is argued, is destructive of Ike's love.[15] Ike's love is pure and harmless; it is a positive in the bleak, self-seeking world of Frenchman's Bend. But Ratliff chooses to wipe it out.

Now it is true that Ratliff himself is less than certain that his actions and motives are beyond reproach:

> 'I aint never disputed I'm a pharisee,' he said. 'You don't need to tell me he aint got nothing else. I know that. Or that I can sholy leave him have at least this much. I know that too. Or that besides, it aint any of my business. I know that too, just as I know that the reason I aint going to leave him have what he does have is simply because I am strong enough to keep him

from it. I am stronger than him. Not righter. Not any better, maybe. But just stronger.'[16]

Nonetheless, I am not inclined to think that this is an issue on which Faulkner invites the reader to pass judgment—either for or against Ratliff. Quite fundamental to Faulkner's fiction is the absence of authorial intervention for moral or any other reasons. It is something of a cliché to suggest that great writers allow their characters independent life; in Faulkner's case the cliché contains a large measure of truth. His letter on the characters in *The Mansion*, quoted above, may strike some readers as either naive or precious; but his practice goes a long way towards authenticating the implied position. Faulkner's characters are exactly men—or women—in motion; they take possession of the stories in which they are involved; driven, doomed, or whatever, they seem simply to be themselves, doing whatever they are compelled to do. Ratliff being Ratliff intervenes as he does; the rightness or wrongness of the intervention, except insofar as he himself debates it, is not the issue. In conversation at the University of Virginia, Faulkner said: 'Maybe the writer has no concept of morality at all, only an integrity to hold always to what he believes to be the facts and truths of human behaviour.'[17] Not, I agree once again, that there is anything very exceptional about such a view; most modernist writers, at least, would subscribe to it. Certainly in Faulkner's case there is never any question of a rush to judgment; we may not admire what Flem Snopes does, but to condemn him as bad or evil hardly seems relevant. Certainly to arrive at such a judgment seems not to be Faulkner's reason for writing about him. One may choose to agree or disagree with Ratliff's actions over Ike and the cow, but no critical issue is in fact involved; condemnation or approval of Ratliff is not the point. 'There aren't any morals,' Stevens said. 'People just do the best they can.'[18] Warren Beck is probably right to argue that Stevens speaks here with his author's voice. (116)

As a final statement, an ultimate truth, such a conclusion may seem modest indeed. Nonetheless, it may be in part what Faulkner means when he insists in the note prefaced to *The Mansion* that he has learned more about the human heart and its dilemma than he knew thirty-four years before. Certainly the statement is part of the 'poor sons of bitches' motif which most commentators agree seems to sum up Faulkner's sense of the human condition at the end of the

Snopes trilogy. We may recall that 'the poor son-of-a-bitch' is Owl-eyes' epitaph upon Jay Gatsby at the end of Fitzgerald's novel; but Nick Carraway invites the reader to see some larger meaning in Gatsby's fate. The Snopes trilogy offers no such larger meaning. Only the splendid poetry of Gavin Stevens, near the end of *The Town*, looking down in 'the dying last of day' watching the fireflies 'myriad and frenetic, random and frantic, pulsing; not questing, not quiring, but choiring as if they were tiny incessant appeaseless voices, cries, words,' looking down upon the whole world of Yoknapatawpha County, creating in firefly words 'this miniature of man's passions and hopes and disasters—ambition and fear and lust and courage and abnegation and pity and honour and sin and pride.' (271) Or the equally blazing final paragraph of *The Mansion* recording Mink Snopes's absorption into the earth:

> the ground already full of the folks that had the trouble but were free now, so that it was just the ground and the dirt that had to bother and worry and anguish with the passions and hopes and skeers, the justice and the injustice and the griefs, leaving the folks themselves easy now, all mixed and jumbled up comfortable and easy so wouldn't nobody even know or even care who was which any more, himself among them, equal to any, good as any, brave as any, being inextricable from, anonymous with all of them: the beautiful, the splendid, the proud and the brave, right on up to the very top itself among the shining phantoms and dreams which are the milestones of the long human recording—Helen and the bishops, the kings and the unhomed angels, the scornful and graceless seraphim. (398)

No larger meaning perhaps; but life is permanently enriched by Faulkner's art.

NOTES

1. Edmund Volpe, *A Reader's Guide to William Faulkner* (London: Thames and Hudson, 1964), p. 330.
2. William Faulkner, *The Hamlet* (London: Chatto and Windus, 1957), p. 150. All subsequent page references are to this edition.
3. See T.S. Eliot, 'Ulysses, Order and Myth,' *The Dial* (November, 1923), pp. 480-83.

4. See Joseph Blotner, ed., *Selected Letters of William Faulkner* (London: Scolar Press, 1977), p. 390. Faulkner was writing in December 1955 or January 1956.
5. Cleanth Brooks, *William Faulkner: The Yoknapatawpha Country* (New Haven and London: Yale University Press, 1963), p. 193.
6. See, for example, Woodrow Stroble, 'Flem Snopes: A Crazed Mirror' in Glenn O. Carey and Woodrow Stroble, ed. *Faulkner: The Unappeased Imagination, A Collection of Critical Essays* (Troy, New York: Whitston, 1980), pp. 195-212.
7. William Faulkner, *The Town* (London: Chatto and Windus, 1958) p. 199. All subsequent references are to this edition.
8. William Faulkner, *Knight's Gambit* (London: Chatto and Windus, 1951), pp. 122-23.
9. Warren Beck, *Man in Motion: Faulkner's Trilogy* (Madison: University of Wisconsin Press, 1963), p. 130.
10. Earlier in the novel Charles Mallison tells us that while he was just City Attorney, Gavin Stevens talked 'Harvard and Heidelberg'; running for County Attorney he 'began to talk like the people . . . saying "drug" for "dragged."' See p. 147.
11. See Joseph Blotner, *Faulkner: A Biography* (London: Chatto and Windus, 1974), Vol. I, pp. 526-27.
12. Frederick L. Gwynn and Joseph L. Blotner, ed., *Faulkner in the University* (Charlottesville, Virginia: The University of Virginia Press, 1959), p. 84. Quoted by Beck, p. 192.
13. See Blotner, II, pp. 1657-58.
14. John E. Basset, 'Yoknapatawpha Revised: Demystifying Snopes,' *College Literature*, 15 (1988), p. 145.
15. Both Thomas Y. Greet in 'The Theme and Structure of Faulkner's *The Hamlet*' and Joseph Gold in 'The Normality of Snopesism' adopt this position. Their essays are reprinted in Linda W. Wagner, *William Faulkner: Four Decades of Criticism* (Michigan State Univ. Press 1973), pp. 302-18 and 318-27. Brooks, pp. 407-10—defends Ratliff.
16. It is impossible to provide a page reference for this passage from the Chatto and Windus edition as, extraordinarily, the relevant closing section of 'The Long Summer' chapter was cut out by the English publishers.
17. *Faulkner in the University*, p. 267. Quoted by Beck, p. 116.
18. William Faulkner, *The Mansion* (London: Chatto and Windus, 1961), 3, p. 392.

This essay was previously published in A. Robert Lee, ed., *The Yoknapatawpha Fiction* (London: Vision Press, New York: St. Martin's Press, 1990), pp. 165-79. Reprinted with kind permission of the author.

On *The Reivers*: From the Last Chapter to the First

AMITABHA SINHA

That this last novel of Faulkner is one with some sort of difference from the familiar ones by him has been widely acknowledged, of which, perhaps, James M. Millard's helpful article, "Faulkner's Golden Rook: *The Reivers* as Romantic Comedy"[1] is the best, typical instance. My point is that the novel is yet something further than that: it deviates from the *Faulkner canon as a whole*, for it is certainly not just another novel with a sense of decay, with no tortured, anguished mind within it, nor tortuous methods, which, justifiably, have hoisted him to the stature of a big novelist; not an overwhelmingly Faulkner-friendly man that I am, I can, do, sincerely appreciate those aspects. Yet, nevertheless, I *further appreciate* the fact of *The Reivers* reversing,[2] perfectly, obviously, all those appreciable tendencies, thereby, as the jargon goes now, opening a new "horizon of expectations," of, from, the Faulkner world.

II

For one thing, the novel is what I rather prefer to call a comic pastoral—remembering Millard's comedy as "romance"—that is favourably yet contrastively parallel to fellow-writer Hemingway's third last novel (obviously *The Old Man and the Sea*) which is a near-tragic pastoral (letting alone the fact that each has been called a novella or short fiction: *The Reivers* has been so described by James Fergusson).[3] What I feel is that this comic pastoral is one with a few remarkable things within it, going further than the certainly presented comedy-romance-fairytale overtones which Millard refers to throughout his article; it is a lusty narrative teeming with romping laughter, of sheer lark, about the three young and older men playing truant in a borrowed (?) car, then on horseback, which does not tally at all with familiar Faulkner-fiction; what further emphasize is an indisputable and tender human touch which gives full meaning, with the successful aplomb of a none-too-inhibited hilarity, to this novel.

III

Yet, this is certainly not just one simple comedy, pastoral, or whatever; it is imbued with a series of subtly winding intricacies, serious, artistic. To indicate them, I should like to begin from its conclusion (which I consider to be of first significance), the scene in which Lucius, young hero, and Everbe, obviously the foremost woman in the narrative, talk to one another about her new-born child:

> What are you going to call it?
> "Not it," she said, "Him. Can't you guess?" . . . "His name is Lucius Priest Hogganbeck," she said.

The fact is, she has christened the brat, fathered by her (now) husband, Boon Hogganbeck with Lucius's name and title, now, what is rather striking is the sexual overtone of what she says: obviously, this is the sort of talk that a woman will/may have with her husband or lover ("can't you guess?"); simultaneously, a tone of affection is implicit within the proud announcement to Lucius himself, so younger than she ("His name . . . Lucius . . ."), a motherly affection, nearly; simultaneously yet, the final name within the name is that of Boon, father of the child, the actual husband; implicitly, she wishes to be both mother and lover to Lucius—a comic inversion of the Oedipal world; nevertheless, within this amalgam, Lucius-Boon, signifier of a mother-lover relationship (intended by her), the tender, human touch is obviously present. If this juxtaposition of opposites fused together is not intricate, what is?

IV

Within the same last chapter, intricacy of a further sort is seen: for, while, palpably, the theme of maturation of Lucius's innocence seems its major keynote, the assortment of three, Lucius, Everbe and Boon, who are related with one another there, strikes a separate note, for *together, they become open* to two interpretations. On the one hand, Lucius, young boy, might implicitly be said to be much too precocious a boy, in the context of some of the things he does (going to Miss Reba's house of assignation, for instance), Everbe nothing further than sinning woman (which, indeed, she has been) who has finally fastened upon Boon, then Boon nothing further than a madman and a hooligan (he did want to shoot a negro at the beginning of the novel). Alternatively—and the novelist obviously prefers this interpretation by way of their names—they are something different altogether, that is, metaphorically and literally. While Lucius means *light*, which he does bring to the Memphis world from Jefferson, through his benevolent goodwill to the inhabitants, he is also *Priest*, the man who actually arbitrates, impersonally, with the benevolence, over that world; Everbe is the opposite of *Neverbe* (implicitly), symbolic of non-nihilism, faith; Boon is obviously *boon*, to Everbe, near the conclusion of the novel. Obviously, again, negatives have been inverted by the text by this namewise metaphorical craft.

V

Further, there is the grandfather towering above them all, contributing to the intricacies, in his suave monologue to Lucius in the same chapter, with "gentleman" as his text, fusing typical Southernism with a world of sheer humanity, irrespective of regions, territory. For, while "gentleman" is indicative of feudalism, which at least was, the hallmark of Southernism in an American context, in a context of say, the world at large, it may convey the sense of an ideal man with strength of a noble mind, its courage. This is achieved by the repetition of "gentleman," the tone of the repetition, with the way in which it is said by grandfather.[5] The word is repeated four times in 48/50 lines of grandfather's monologue: "gentleman always"; "gentleman can"; "gentleman accepts"; "gentleman washes his face." While *always* indicates consistency, *can* implies capability, *accepts* conveys the sense of stoic courage, while *washes . . . face* (after crying) humorously, affectionately, ironically implies that while a boy is *not a man*, he is, at least, potentially *a gentleman* (thus reminding Lucius of what he is capable of). (302-3, my italics) By substituting words, "perfect man" or "true man," in those lines, one sees, how "gentleman" becomes the emblem of an ideal man, something like a metaphor of the novel's theme.

VI

Yet, implicitly, there is another intriguing intricacy: who is the narrator? While Lucius is, inevitably, an ambivalent tone foxes one when the novel opens. Now, if the first line be considered the first paragraph, the narrator, within the second paragraph says, "We—your grandfather and I . . ." (7) Who is/are this "you"? Obviously an audience, naturally indicating the oralism implicit in the narrative, and, considering "*your grandfather*," perhaps Lucius's younger brother, who nevertheless is a minor character with scanty significance, or, plausibly, Lucius's grandchildren, as the following paragraph (mine) indicates, obviously.

VII

That issue consists in discerning the nature, persona, that is, of the "grandfather" in the self-contained one-line paragraph of the novel: "*GRANDFATHER SAID*" (7, italics mine)[6] which opens the narrative. Grandfather may perhaps be interpreted as Lucius's grandfather, a major character of the novel; the ambivalence is in what this grandfather says, and of Boon, of all people: "this is the kind of a man" (7, referring to Boon's subsequent shooting escapade). This comment or opinion better suits Lucius who introduces (and indeed *tells*) the narrative, rather than the grandfather-character who, further, is scarcely likely to be so concerned with Boon in the way Lucius is. If the argument is accepted (and why not?), Lucius is that *grandfather* who "SAID"; the colon following the "SAID" is graphologically important, which plausibly makes Lucius's grandchildren, the audience, referring to Lucius, themselves becoming, in a narrative frame-method, the narrator/s in those two words. For all this, Lucius is certainly the narrator of the corpus of the novel, whether a boy-narrator or grandfatherly narrator introduced by his grandchildren/grandchild, the narrator/s in the first line. Yet the ambivalence (small idea maybe) is a not-to-be missed, intriguing subtlety.

VIII

Who is the *major* narratee (another jargon), nevertheless? Lucius, obviously, re-discovering his lost innocent world (of Jefferson, token of the past—the story is set in 1905 or thereabouts) through his "reiving" maturation. Yet Lucius's focus is mainly on Boon, from among all the characters he keeps moving with; it should be remembered that, at the conclusion he is concerned with Boon (through the talk with Everbe), while, in the first incident of the novel, after it opens, he is similarly concerned with Boon maniacally jumping to his negro-shooting spree. In a sense, therefore, Boon is the novel's hero, too, who matures into a loving, affectionate man, totally separate from his previous semi-humanity (although he remains rowdy, loud all the time), and this aspect of Boon finds expression through the sensibility of Lucius *as narrator*. Therefore, Lucius and/or Boon are/is hero-narratee/(s): another ambivalence, indeed an ambiguity, which is not to be ignored.

IX

Surely, what I have called the intricacies are a few aesthetic, narrative jolts, non-Faulknerian. There is one further: true to its subtitle, *A Reminiscence*, the novel is one of the past, memory, indisputably Faulknerian; that reminiscence is, nevertheless, re-enacted, as though the narrative were of the present: the horse-race, the Hell Creek thrills, and so on, are obviously incidents with *present* appeal. Obviously, there goes a yet further two-fold nuance: past-present amalgam, the now-then interaction.

X

Now, to wind up. Obviously, these intricacies, assumably conscious on the novelist's part, are what writers called postmodern delight in. For instance, the Southernism so celebrated in Yoknapatawpha is present in full tact, although none of its features is foregrounded, prevented by the introduction of an overarching human world: to take an instance or two, the Southern grandfather, who is simultaneously acceptable to the world at large through his gentle humour and assertiveness; or Ned the negro, one of the reivers, who is made to say something Northern, on humanity:

"that's where people starts." (243) A similar sense is found in duofold womanhood: of Everbe with her lust co-existing with motherliness, and of the Everbe-Minnie contrast-parallelism (both "sinning" women, one going beyond that, and another contained within it). Then there is the permissive open world of sexuality—Lucius with all these women and Miss Reba, yet funnily handled, with no bite in it. These are things from which some new-modern writers (of America) might have taken a hint or two. Be that as it may, the text of *The Reivers* has indeed reived familiar Faulknerism, has de-Faulknerized Faulkner, so to say, has produced a non-Faulknerian Faulkner. This is what, according to poststructuralism, much in favour among many, is a new "horizon" (I hinted that at the beginning), periphery, play, or why not "subversion." (!/?) Nevertheless, one wishes this novelist had lived longer just to write a few such novels.

NOTES

1. In *Makers of the Twentieth-Century Novel*, ed. Harry Garvin (London: Associated University Press, 1977), pp. 211-27. See also Judith Bryant Wittenberg, *Faulkner/ The Transfiguration of Biography*, Ch. 12, "Nunc Dimmittis: *The Reivers*" (Lincoln: University of Nebraska Press, 1979), p. 236.
2. I find that the same precise pun appears in Wittenberg, p. 242. Surprising as that is, the *words here* are invented by me.
3. See James Ferguson, *Faulkner's Short Fiction* (Knoxville: University of Tennessee Press, 1991).
4. William Faulkner, *The Reivers/A Reminiscence* (New York: Random House), 1962, p. 305.
5. James N. Millard (p. 226) refers to this incident, although his interpretation, scanty as it is, does not tally with mine; Wittenberg (p. 245) does the same, with scanty and simplistic interpretation.
6. These two words are in capitals in the Random House edition, which have a certain graphological effect that supports my opinion; not so in the Penguin edition.

Case for Teaching Faulkner Overseas: Some Talking Points

HOWARD R. WOLF

I have been assigned the task framing the "big picture," so I want to say first that my remarks are addressed to teaching Faulkner to "overseas" students. I think that what we might call the "general" problems and value of teaching Faulkner at the undergraduate level would be similar in most parts of the world, perhaps even in France where Sartre had put Faulkner on the map as early as 1933 by writing a preface for *Sanctuary*[1] and where he had said that "Pour les jeunes en France, Faulkner c'est a dieu."[2] They would certainly be similar in what we might call "traditional" societies.

I think also that the problems and value of teaching Faulkner are related in general to the teaching of other "difficult" modern and post-modern Western writers in traditional societies where patterns of narration tend to be sequential (if circular), univocal, where the representation of the world tends to be stable, and where the coordinates of time and space (however culture-specific) tend to be standard for the culture and are not subject to radical reconfiguration by individual authors.

The value and usefulness of teaching Faulkner in many parts of the world today, is first, I suppose, that he is a major author who belongs to the world. He is precisely the kind of author whose achievement helps define world literature, so it is appropriate that his work should cross boundaries.

He is an author whose work represents the maturation of American culture; and if we wish to raise the ante and suggest that America may even be a civilization (I'm not sure about this), we would introduce Faulkner's work as evidence.

His work represents the use of American English in its most

complex form. For those interested in the English language (from a literary or linguistic perspective), Faulkner's work holds as much potential interest as Shakespeare or Joyce, writers who, of course, had a great influence upon him.

Faulkner's work reveals the legacy and burden of the past (the need for a myth and the need to redefine that myth within changing circumstances for the present). Because so many traditional societies are in a state of transition today—moving from colonial to post-colonial circumstances, moving from an agricultural epoch to a technological and informational era—Faulkner offers special opportunities to discuss cultural transition.

Needless to say, since many societies in transition (Hong Kong, India, Malaysia) find themselves using the language (English) of a previous "master" to come to terms with their own futures, Faulkner's charting of racial/ethnic and linguistic inter-relationships (written and oral traditions, for example) offers special opportunities for analysis and discussion.

Since Faulkner's work deals at many levels and in different ways with the relationship between victors and victims, oppressors and oppressed, "master" and "slave" (in actual or virtual terms), and "superior" and "inferior" peoples and races, students in most parts of the world would have little difficulty understanding his major themes.

Faulkner's "universals" are built up from and out of a thousand particulars, so that students in another culture have an opportunity to grasp the concrete formation and implication of these particulars in what we might even call an "anthropological" sense.

Difficulties of Teaching Faulkner Overseas

Most of the undergraduates whom one teaches overseas are trying heroically to learn basic English at the same time that they are studying some American literature. Faulkner's stylistic genius (like Shakespeare's or Joyce's or Henry James's) makes the acquisition of basic English difficult. Washington Irving, Mark Twain, Jack London, Pearl Buck and John Steinbeck serve the needs of the students more obviously than does Faulkner's richly textured, but often difficult, poetic prose.

The study of Faulkner makes most sense overseas within the context of a developed American Literature and/or American Studies Program; but few countries offer such programs at the present time, and where such programs exist, they face different kinds of budgetary (Fulbright) and historical problems (rise of Japanese Studies *contra* US, for instance, Hong Kong University).

Although Faulkner's "genealogical" interests are consistent with the family constellations of traditional cultures (the "joint" family in India, for example), the very complexity of his genealogy makes it difficult to teach any one story separate from others. This was a problem for the American audience itself, and it took Cowley's famous *Portable Faulkner* (Viking, 1946) to provide a context for the "saga of Yoknapatawpha County, 1820-1945." (Cowley, 69)

So what does one teach, and where does one begin?

Although Modernism and post-Modernism are much in fashion at the upper end, so to speak, of the profession at home and overseas, it is still the case, at least in places where I have taught and lectured (Turkey, Malaysia, Hong Kong, India, Korea, Thailand, Philippines, Taiwan, Japan, China), that students approach literature, for better and worse, with an essentially nineteenth century perspective. They expect literature to be a reflection of life; and they expect it to be reflected in a mirror that gives a realistic and naturalistic image; that is a "copy" of what it looks at. They do not expect or understand (at first, if at all) refractions, distortions, and multiple images (as in Welles's *Lady from Shanghai*).

Faulkner wrests his sense of life and literature, to be sure, from the earth and guts; he is deeply humanistic (as his Nobel statement makes clear: "I decline to accept the end of man,"[3] but his effort to put that experience "all in one sentence," (Cowley, 14) "not only the present but the whole past on which it depends and which keeps overtaking the present, second by second," (Cowley, 112) is often puzzling to overseas students who are unfamiliar with the Proustian claims of advanced Western literature.

I think of my own teaching of American literature overseas as part of an experiment in democracy. I like to think that my style of teaching—open, dialogic, sometimes spontaneous and improvisational—supports some of the thematic emphases of the material itself. I see myself as a standard bearer in international terms of the "spirit of '76." I feel that I am not fulfilling my mission when I control the use and distribution of all the words. I have found in teaching Faulkner (again, one of many difficult authors) that the students are less able to participate than they are when, say, discussing, Hawthorne or Hemingway where the formation of sentences is lucid and seemingly transparent.

NOTES

1. Robert Penn Warren, ed., *Faulkner: A Collection of Critical Essays*, p. 272.
2. *The Faulkner-Cowley File*, Malcolm Cowley, ed., *Letters and Memoirs, 1944-1962* (New York: Viking, 1966), p. 24.
3. Richard D. Heffner, *A Documentary History of the United States* (1985), pp. 303-4.

Hollywood, the Film Scripts and the Neglected Genre of Faulkner's Career

SOMDATTA MANDAL

It is a well documented fact that William Faulkner's relationship with Hollywood was something unique—something of a love-hate one. Unlike F. Scott Fitzgerald, who encompassed his entire literary world with the myth of Hollywood, Faulkner's ambivalent attitude towards Hollywood in general and the film industry in particular, becomes even more interesting because of the fact that in spite of spending so many years as a script-writer there, he produced only one short story "Golden Land" based entirely on his sojourns in the film colony. As subjects, Fitzgerald and Faulkner obviously have a lot in common. Both had several of their works committed to celluloid and both preferred writing fiction to composing screenplays, though both were willing to serve time in Hollywood in order to subsidize their careers as novelists. Referred to by Jack Warner as "schmucks with Underwoods," Faulkner took offence at the tawdriness of Hollywood and felt himself artistically compromised: "Movies and I don't agree chronologically. In Oxford there is one show at seven o'clock, and the town goes to bed at nine-thirty. It's not that I don't like the movies, but my life just isn't regulated that way."[1] In another interview in *The Paris Review* in 1956, when the interviewer asked him about how to get the best results in working for the movies, Faulkner unequivocally stated:

> The moving picture work of my own which seemed best to me was done by actors and the writer throwing the script away and inventing the scene in actual rehearsal just before the camera turned. If I didn't take, or felt I was capable of taking, motion picture work seriously, out of simple honesty to motion pictures

> and myself too, I would not have tried. But I know that I will never be a good motion picture writer; so that work will never have the urgency for me which my own medium has.[2]

In an earlier interview given in 1937 for *Memphis Commercial Appeal*, Faulkner told his interviewer that his "general impression of Hollywood . . . is that of a very wealthy, overgrown country town. In fact, it reminds me very much of a town that has sprung up as a result of an oil boom."[3]

There are innumerable stories that have been told about Faulkner in Hollywood: how he asked his employers if he could work at home, then drove down to Mississippi when they said yes; how he escaped a party by climbing out a second storey window and down a trellis; how he hired a male nurse to see that he arrived at work on time during his drinking bouts; how he hauled a pregnant horse to Mississippi because "no mare of mine is going to foal in California"; and how he asked Clark Gable, "And what do *you* do?" In the spring of 1932, when he arrived for his first day of work at Metro-Goldwyn-Mayer, Faulkner's head was cut and bleeding, displaying the obvious sign that the studio's newest screenwriter had been drinking. "We're going to put you on a Wallace Beery picture," a supervisor told Faulkner, who announced that he had been hit by a cab in New Orleans. "Who's he?" said the author about Beery, then a big star. "I've got an idea for Mickey Mouse."

The best example which shows that Hollywood ("the only place where you could be climbing up the ladder and still get stabbed in the back") was unassimilable to Faulkner's imagination of course remains "Golden Land."[4] The title ostensibly satirizes the utopian vision of Southern California; and clearly, the story does impugn that bland, rootless, sterile culture that so repelled Faulkner—"the land, the earth which spawned a thousand new faiths, nostrums and cures each year but no disease to even disprove them on—beneath the golden days unmarred by rain or weather, the changeless monotonous beautiful days without end countless out of the halycon past and endless into the halycon future." (725-26) Whenever Faulkner talked about Southern California in his own voice, he agreed with his narrator here. He spoke characteristically of Hollywood in 1944: "They worship death here. . . . They don't worship money, they worship death." (Blotner, *Faulkner II*, 1162)

Faulkner's abiding dislike of "Tinsel Town" has led some commentators on his life and work to surmise that he carried out his studio assignments rather hastily and carelessly, just to "take the money and run." Yet, there is a great deal of evidence that Faulkner did conscientiously try to give the studios that hired him an honest week's work in return for his weekly wages. In fact, the sheer number and variety of the forty-four scenarios to which he applied his creative energies over the years attest to the seriousness with which he viewed his obligations to his employers. Samuel Marx, chief of the story department at M-G-M while Faulkner worked there, vouched for that seriousness in more than one interview in later years. So when we find Faulkner confessing to Saxe Commins that "I have never learned how to write movies, nor even to take them seriously. . . . I don't think I need the money at present, and that is the only reason I would have to try the job, or any movie job,"[5] we feel that he is being too modest. In 1942, when he owed a big bill at the grocer's, Faulkner had written to Warner Brothers and said that he would work for whatever they gave him, if they paid his way to Hollywood. It is true that Jack Warner liked to boast how he'd got "America's best writer for $300 a week" but the screen credits Faulkner got for *The Big Sleep, To Have and Have Not*, do not confirm his declaration that he "doesn't really know the trade." It is also widely known how Faulkner would often forget where he was and would compose monologues that ran page after page, more suitable for *The Sound and the Fury* than for a Hollywood feature. "I'm supposed to say all that?," a confused Humphrey Bogart had asked on the set of *To Have and Have Not* after the novelist handed him a speech that lasted six pages. Howard Hawks, whose support for the author is also well-documented, is said to have saved the situation by saying, "Bill, that's fine," and he and Bogart then revised the speech themselves. Faulkner's jobs done for Howard Hawks, working with him on the set, inventing new scenes and writing new dialogue do seem somewhat contradictory to the letter which he wrote to Malcolm Cowley from Oxford on October 18th, 1945 stating that "it took [him] about a week to get Hollywood out of [his] lungs,"[6] and he was "just happy that the damned west coast place [had] not cheapened [his] soul." Nearly a year before his September 1945 departure from Warner Brothers, he expressed his belief that he could keep "Hollywood" and Yoknapatawpha separate, mutually exclusive: "I can work at Hollywood 6 months, stay home 6, am used to it now and have movie work locked off in another room."[7]

The paradox about Faulkner's relationship with Hollywood remains that it was his script writing assignments for various Hollywood studios and his sale in 1938 of the movie rights of *The Unvanquished* that had sustained him financially during the decade of his most impressive fiction writing. Meta Carpenter Wilde, with whom Faulkner had a long-term affair in Hollywood, aptly summarizes the novelist's dilemma: "When he was in Hollywood, the tug of Oxford kept Bill in a restive state. Now that he had let it draw him back, there was a counter pull to me in Hollywood, a retortion, and again peace of place was denied to him."[8]

II

Between 1932 and 1954, William Faulkner worked on more than forty-four film properties owned by five of America's major studios, M-G-M, Universal, Twentieth Century-Fox, RKO and Warner Brothers. From time to time in the '40s and '50s, he also developed more than a dozen other ideas for the cinema and television. Because only about sixty percent of the projects on which he worked were ever produced, and since Faulkner played an important but minor role as script consultant to Howard Hawks on many of those which did not reach the screen (he received film or television writing credits for only nine productions), according to George F. Hayhof,[9] the person who wishes to gain a thorough understanding of Faulkner's cinematic works must study many hundreds of pages of treatments and screenplays—some of which exist in a number of draft stages—as well as prints of films.

One major problem for critics has been the lack of easy accessibility to originals or copies of Faulkner's writings for Hollywood. While a number have been among his papers at the University of Virginia for almost twenty years, most were not retained by the author and have survived only in private hands or in the script vaults of the film studios. Sometime back, however, Faulkner's own collection of his film scripts has been supplemented by the deposit of material from six of his projects for M-G-M, and by a gift of another six from Twentieth Century-Fox. As a result, scripts from approximately half of Faulkner's projects for film and television have been gathered in one location and made accessible to scholars. The publication of various other screenplays edited by Louis Daniel

Brodsky and Robert W. Hamblin[10] gives us further insight into Faulkner's artistic oeuvre. Of the total four years that Faulkner spent in California, there is no evidence that the period spent in the studios had much influence on the technique of the novelist's later fiction. As Joseph Blotner has suggested, Faulkner's experience is rather unusual in that some of his literary preoccupations occasionally slip into his movie work, and not, as is frequently the case, the other way round. (Edward Murray even believes that the pre-Hollywood *The Sound and the Fury* and *Light in August* are more cinematic than *A Fable* (1950), which was originally intended as a scenario.[11]) Blotner believes that the two scenes in *The Southerner* (1945) which Faulkner worked on with director Jean Renoir, suggest parts of *Go Down, Moses* (1942) and that *Deep Valley* is similarly evocative for one familiar with the novelist's canon.

While in New York in late 1931, Faulkner had been approached about writing screenplays in Hollywood, and he spent much of 1932 there on contract to M-G-M. His first success with screen writing was his work on *Today We Live* (1933), for director Howard Hawks. In the course of their work together, Hawks discovered Faulkner's talent as "script doctor" and often used him to revise scenes in screenplays by other writers. Faulkner spent a few weeks doing script writing on location in New Orleans in April 1933, and in 1935 he went back to Hollywood where he spent five weeks working for Twentieth Century-Fox. The product of this visit was *The Road to Glory* (1936), for which he wrote the screenplay with Joel Sayre. He was in Hollywood for much of 1942-45, and wrote the screenplay with Jules Furthman for the 1945 film version of Ernest Hemingway's *To Have and Have Not* and with Furthman and Leigh Brackett, the screenplay for the 1946 production of Raymond Chandler's *The Big Sleep*. In 1953 and 1954 he worked on *Land of the Pharaohs* (1955) with Harry Kurnitz and Harold Jack Bloom. Apart from these memorable productions there are several other scripts over which Faulkner toiled but unfortunately they were never produced.

III

Before assessing some of the available film scripts, it would not be out of place to make a brief mention about some of the notable Faulkner adaptations, and especially the novelist's reaction to each of them. The first Faulkner novel to be made into a movie was his sensational potboiler, *Sanctuary* (1931), which Paramount released in 1933 under the title *The Story of Temple Drake*. In 1961, it was remade again but not with much success. M-G-M's adaptation of *Intruder in the Dust*, published in 1948 and released as a film the following year, remains the best Hollywood treatment so far of a Faulkner property. The novelist himself was quoted as saying at the premiere in his hometown of Oxford, Mississippi: "All in all I think it is a good movie." Several years later, *The Tarnished Angels* was freely adapted in 1958 from his 1935 novel *Pylon* and a screen version of *The Hamlet* appeared as *The Long Hot Summer* in 1958, though most people objected to the non-Faulknerian happy ending. When finally in 1969, *The Reivers* (1962) appeared on the screen, all the reviewers seemed happy. Edmond L. Volpe observed: "*The Reivers* . . . is a natural for Hollywood. Faulkner probably never turned out so tailor-made a script when he was actually writing for the movies. . . . [T]he novel could be transferred [easily] to the screen to provide sentimental comedy in the tradition of Clarence Day's *Life with Father*.[12] That the subject matter of *The Reivers* was made to order for Hollywood seems clear from the enthusiastic review of the film by Kathleen Carroll in the New York *Daily News* (December 26, 1969): "If all you wanted for Christmas was a nice movie about nice people, then *The Reivers* . . . is the perfect present. With its sugarspun characters and homespun charm, it is like watching the very best of Walt Disney. And what could be nicer than that?" Louis Daniel Brodsky was even eulogical about the novel itself: "Cinematic in its surface presentation, it would manifest an easy adaptability to the film medium: without stretching, *The Reivers* even might be considered Faulkner's most self-consciously constructed and successfully articulated 'screenplay'!"[13]

IV

Among the first three story outlines that Faulkner wrote for Warner Brothers Pictures in the early 1940s, "Country Lawyer" seems to be the most interesting and impressive to both general readers and Faulkner scholars. Attempts to develop a movie script based on Bellamy Partridge's book of reminiscences had earlier been initiated in 1941; and Faulkner, who was assigned to the project from March 20 to April 6, 1943, was the sixth writer to be asked to try his hand at producing a workable script. Unlike the previous scenarists, however, Faulkner showed little inclination to remain faithful to Partridge's text. On the contrary, he transferred the setting from Phelps, New York, to his own fictional domain of Jefferson, Mississippi, and drew heavily upon this imaginary realm in creating an original story line. Thus, "Country Lawyer" represents one of the few instances in which Faulkner sought to adapt and extend his Yoknapatawpha material to the purposes of Hollywood. "The Life and Death of a Bomber" belongs to the considerable body of patriotic writing that Faulkner produced in support of the Allied effort in World War II. Written in 1943 after a tour of an aircraft factory in San Diego, the story was initially planned to provide favourable publicity for Consolidated Aircraft the way an earlier Warner Bros. film, *Wings for the Eagle*, had done for Lockheed. By dramatizing how selfish interests contribute to a delay in the construction of a bomber and thus undermine national security, Faulkner's story makes a poignant argument for civilian support of the nation's servicemen. As Faulkner's letters from this period reveal, the opportunity to write wartime propaganda of this type provided an alternate means of serving his country after he had been judged too old for active duty as a pilot. "The Damned Don't Cry" is once again a revision work entrusted upon Faulkner to revise a previously-rejected screenplay based on Harry C. Hervey's novel, The Damned Don't Cry. As in the case of "Country Lawyer," Faulkner had taken great liberties with the original plot, particularly in the handling of the central character, Zelda O'Brien. According to Brodsky and Hamblin, these three works provide the 'insight' into "the working of Faulkner's creative genius." Faulkner observed on numerous occasions that a work of fiction derives from "observation, experience and imagination." In their amalgam of incidents and ideas drawn from first-hand observation, personal experience, reading, research, and imaginative invention, these stories present capsule versions of Faulkner's fictive design.

Falling in the same category of patriotic writing as "The Life and Death of a Bomber" are the two other important and fully-developed screenplays, "The De Gaulle Story" and "Battle Cry." It is not at all surprising that Faulkner was strongly attracted to the story of Charles De Gaulle and the Free French movement. From his earliest days he had been enamoured of romantic heroes who embodied courage and action. So his enthusiasm for his first assignment is quite understandable and he admitted in a letter (*Selected Letters* 157) that "it is a good idea" and he "will be proud to work with it and hope and trust [he] can do it justice." So, for much of 1942, deducting from the massive, exuberant outpouring of material he produced for "The De Gaulle Story," Faulkner actually found gratification from, as well received recompense for, his work as Hollywood scriptwriter. Faulkner started work on "Battle Cry" in April 1943. For "Battle Cry" too, he wrote a "First Extended Treatment" and retained it verbatim in his "Second Temporary Draft." Meant to celebrate the bravery and steadfast loyalty of the American, French, English, Chinese, Dutch and Russian forces to the causes of liberty and universal peace, this script was remarkable for its experimental form. In fact in its variegated shifting in and out of time sequences and montaging of disparate scenes and locations, it more closely approximated one of his own novels, *As I Lay Dying*, than it did movies of the period. A month later, Faulkner described the project in a letter to his daughter Jill, expecting it to be "a big picture" (*Selected Letters*, 173-74) and to his wife Estelle, that he "will stick at this picture until Hawks says it's finished, my part of it, I mean." (177) Faulkner's euphoria was of course short lived as abruptly and without any advance warning, the project was cancelled.

Edward Murray assumes that perhaps at the bottom Faulkner never wanted to make too much money in, or from, Hollywood. (He once tried to sell *Absalom, Absalom!* [1936] to the movie moguls, and asked for only fifty thousand for that magnificent novel.) Shortly before his death in 1962, the writer told a group of students at the University of Virginia:

> There's some people who are writers who believed they had talent, they believed in the dream of perfection, they get offers to go to Hollywood where they can make a lot of money, they begin to acquire junk swimming pools and imported cars, and they can't quit their jobs because they have got to continue to own that swimming pool and the imported cars. There are others with the same dream of perfection, the same belief that maybe they can match it, that go there and they resist the money. They don't own the swimming pools, the imported cars. They will do enough work to get what they need of the money without becoming a slave to it, and that, in that sense, it is as

> you say, it is going to be difficult to go completely against the grain or the current of a culture. But you can compromise without selling your individuality completely to it. You've got to compromise because it makes things easier.[15]

Faulkner never deceived himself about his screen-writing work. He said once: "I don't like scenario writing because I don't know enough about it."[16] At another time, referring to his fellow scenarist Harry Kurnit, the novelist explained: "He understands footages and that sort of thing. I just try to figure out what a character would be likely to do in a given situation."[17]

The question naturally arises as to whether this kind of collaborative work actually inhibited Faulkner as a script writer. He once informed an interviewer that "a moving picture is by its nature a collaboration, and any collaboration is compromise because that is what the word means—to give and to take."[18] Critics have offered conflicting evaluations of Faulkner's screenwriting abilities. Jerry Wald for example, remarks: "[Faulkner] had a particularly excellent sense of story construction, but his actual writing was rather indifferent."[19] On the other hand, Howard Hawks once reflected: "[Faulkner] has inventiveness, taste, and great ability to characterize and the visual imagination to translate those qualities into the medium of the screen. He is intelligent and obliging—a master of his work who does it without fuss."[20] Malcolm Cowley has argued that Faulkner's movie work merely called forth his "talent," or conscious craftsmanship, while his "genius" or unconscious inspiration, was involved in novel writing.[21] Edward Murray feels: "Had Faulkner been permitted to write and direct his own movies (the way Norman Mailer and Alain Robbe-Grillet are doing today) perhaps his 'genius' would have manifest itself on the screen, too."[22] Whether we agree with any particular point of view or not, one thing remains clear. However slight it might seem to certain serious Faulkner scholars, the novelist's jaunts into Hollywood, his attitude towards the moving picture industry, his experiments in writing film scripts—all contribute to our understanding of this serious, modernist, experimentalist novelist that William Faulkner essentially was. As Meta Carpenter Wilde and Orin Borsten aptly described his situation:

> In 1943, Faulkner needed, wanted, chose to be in Hollywood.

This was the romantic dream that only he, of the two of us, held to the promise of higher earnings, a screen credit at long last, perhaps a communication from the War Department: "We have reconsidered your request. . . ."

What he drew from Hollywood from 1942 through 1945—the love, the financial security, the unexpected friendships, the terrible frustrations, the bitterness—would fuel the great work yet to come upon his return to Oxford and Rowan Oak.[23]

NOTES

1. Quoted in Gene D. Phillips, *Fiction, Film and Faulkner: The Art of Adaptation* (Knoxville: Univ. of Tennessee Press, 1988), p. 7.
2. Quoted in *Lion in the Garden: Interviews with William Faulkner, 1926-62*, ed. J.B. Meriwether and Michael Millgate (New York: Random, 1968), p. 241.
3. *Ibid.*, p. 33.
4. William Faulkner, "Golden Land," *Collected Stories* (New York: Random, 1950), pp. 701-26.
5. Letter to Saxe Commins, March 16, 1955. *Faulkner: A Comprehensive Guide to the Brodsky Collection,* Brodsky and Hamblin (Jackson: University Press of Mississippi, 1984), vol. II, p. 178.
6. *Selected Letters*, p. 205.
7. *Ibid.*, p. 186.
8. Meta Carpenter Wilde & Orin Borsten, *A Loving Gentleman: The Love Story of William Faulkner and Meta Carpenter* (New York: Simon & Schuster, 1976), p. 101.
9. George F. Hayhof, "Faulkner in Hollywood: A Checklist of His Film Scripts at the University of Virginia," *Mississippi Quarterly,* 31, Sum '78: pp. 407-19.
10. Louis Daniel Brodsky, Y. Robert and W. Hamblin have edited several volumes of Faulkner's screenplays. Of them the most notable are *The De-Gaulle Story* (Jackson: Univ. Press of Mississippi, 1984) *"Country Lawyer" and Other Stories for the Screen*, 1987; *Battle Cry: A Screenplay,* 1984.
11. Edward Murray, *The Cinematic Imagination: The Writers and the Motion Pictures* (New York: Ungar), pp. 154-55.
12. Edmond Volpe, *A Reader's Guide to William Faulkner* (New York, 1964), p. 345.
13. Louis Daniel Brodsky, "Faulkner's Wounded Art: The Aftermath of

Hollywood and World War II," *The Faulkner Journal*, Spring 1987, p. 56.

14. Preface to *Country Lawyer and Other Stories for the Screen*, p. 10.
15. Fredrick L. Gwynn & Joseph Blotner, *Faulkner in the University: Class Conferences at the University of Virginia, 1957-1958* (Charlottesville: University Press of Virginia, 1959), p. 102.
16. Quoted by Joseph Blotner in "Faulkner in Hollywood," p. 279.
17. Quoted by Arthur Knight, *Saturday Review*, XXXVIII, June 25, 1955, p. 24.
18. *Writers at Work*, p. 125.
19. *Ibid.*
20. Quoted by Robert Coughlan, *The Private World of William Faulkner* (New York, 1954), p. 87.
21. Malcolm Cowley, ed., *The Faulkner-Cowley File: Letters and Memoirs 1944-1962* (New York, 1968), pp. 156-57.
22. *The Cinematic Imagination*, p. 167.
23. "Faulkner: Hollywood: 1943." *Faulkner: A Comprehensive Guide to the Brodsky Collection*, vol. IV, p. xiv.

Faulkner, Charlottesville and the Media

ARNOLD and MARIANNE JENSEN

FAULKNER REMEMBERED[1]

At Alderman Library, the bare little study where the late novelist William Faulkner wrote most of *The Mansion* is being used by a history professor writing a study of Southern ideology.

The battered old Remington typewriter which Faulkner pecked is back in Librarian John Cook Wyllie's office, where it had long sat before Faulkner asked for something to type on.

On the surface, little changed in the library or elsewhere around the University either before or after Faulkner died on July 6.

Great Sense of Loss

But the sense of loss here is great nonetheless, not only because a great author dies, but because many people here lost a friend, a fellow faculty member and a person who fitted in with the traditions and attitudes of the University.

In this atmosphere, Faulkner, a naturally shy and reticent man in public, "found a spiritual home," said Dr. Floyd Stovall, an English professor who was instrumental in getting Faulkner as writer-in-residence in 1957 and who knew him well.

Student and faculty members quickly learned that Faulkner preferred to be ignored. He was, from the first.

When Faulkner arrived at the University, he announced: "As far as you're concerned, I'm free game, only do flush me first, don't shoot me sitting. When I'm on the fifth floor of Cabell Hall, I'm writer-in-residence. When I'm not there, then I'm just a Mississippi citizen that likes and admires Virginia."

Perhaps because persons at the University took him at his word, Faulkner never severed his connection with the University from

1957 on, though he never took more than a nominal fee. "Enough," he said, "for tobacco and whiskey." And here, where many other persons value privacy, he made many friends.

Faulkner remained two years as writer-in-residence, then was appointed honorary consultant in American literature at the library, and in 1960 was elected Balch lecturer in American literature.

Home in Charlottesville

Until his death, he and Mrs. Faulkner maintained a second home in Charlottesville, near the University, near the fox-hunting and horse-riding country of Albemarle County, and near their daughter, Mrs. Paul Summers Jr., wife of the City Attorney, and their three children.

Faulkner himself summed up perhaps an all-inclusive reason why he liked Virginia, a statement now famous throughout the state: "I like Virginia because Virginians are all snobs and I like snobs. A snob has to spend so much time being a snob that he has little left to meddle with you and it's so very pleasant here."

FAULKNER'S WIDOW RECOUNTS MEMORIES OF COLLEGE WEEKENDS IN CHARLOTTESVILLE[2]

Barbara Hand

"I suffer dreadfully from the hardship of being Mrs. William Faulkner," said the widow of the novelist and former University writer-in-residence. "I want to be me." Though she claims to be "absolutely useless," Mrs. Faulkner paints, reads and plays the piano. She began painting while living in China in the 1920s with her first husband who was a district judge, and she now has her art studio in Charlottesville. "I used to give away most of my paintings. When someone offered to pay for them, I said to myself, 'Now there's an idea.'"...

Mrs. Faulkner plays the piano mostly by ear. Classical music is her favorite, and she said that she "can't stand country music." "Mr. Faulkner wasn't very musical. I had to punch him to stand for the Star-Spangled Banner," she commented. "I love to dance, as elderly as I am," she said. "If the music suits me, nothing holds me back," she added. Mrs. Faulkner was a student at Mary Baldwin Junior College in the early 1900s. She described it as "a small southern school for about 150 girls. We used to have a grand time in Charlottesville."...

The former Mary Baldwin student said that she does not approve of coeducation. "Boys and girls would have more of a thrill at seeing each other if they were segregated in schools," she commented.

Though she is not the accomplished novelist that her second husband was, Mrs. Faulkner did attempt to write. She related the following story: "I wrote one book in my life, and I thought it was grand. I sent it to a publisher, but it came back awfully quickly. I was so offended. It was summertime and we lived in an old frame house. I forgot the chimney had been stuffed with paper—we didn't have dampers back then. I sat down with a box of matches and I burned the manuscript page by page. Before I knew it, I had set the house on fire."

The Sound and Fury is her favorite of Mr. Faulkner's novels, and *As I Lay Dying* is her second choice. Mrs. Faulkner said: "Some people think Mr. Faulkner hated women by the way he wrote about them. When someone asked me why he dislikes them so, I said that I wasn't aware that he did. I was scared he liked women a little too much."

Mr. Faulkner sometimes enlisted his wife's help with his novels. "He would sometimes show me a few pages of his manuscript. He would tell me 'If you can understand it, anyone can.' I never figured out if it was a compliment or not," said Mrs. Faulkner. . . .

Mrs. Faulkner said that her husband used her as a model for one of his characters in his first novel and that it "hurt my feelings terribly.". . .

The Faulkners met each other in Oxford, Mississippi, when Mrs. Faulkner's family moved there from Texas. "We both had a common love of books and poetry," she added.

"I guess I was always in love with Bill [Mr. Faulkner]. The happiest years of my life were with him in Mississippi," she said.

Mrs. Faulkner claims that she is an "admirer of the younger generation." "I seem to get along much better with young people than with my contemporaries, who bore me to death," she said.

PAPPY & JILL[3]

Felicia Warburg Rogan

Jill Faulkner Summers has lived in Albemarle County for twenty-four years. She is the wife of Paul D. Summers, Jr. and the only child of William Faulkner, world famous author and his wife, Estelle. An indispensable figure to the Farmington Hunt Club, Jill, as master of foxhands, has led enthusiastic hunting members for ten years. A well-traveled woman, she has seen her father accept the Nobel Prize in Sweden and listened as a child as he told her his stories. Later these same tales would be incorporated into the books that would be an important part of our American literary heritage.

We in Charlottesville have more reason to be proud of William Faulkner than do Americans in other parts of the country. For it was here in our town that he spent his later years, working and enjoying the sporting life. It is here too, at the University Library, that is housed the greatest collection of Faulkner's printed works, a gift of his friend and literary critic Linton Reynolds Massey. The manuscripts and memorabilia reflect the career of a prolific genius as poet, artist and creator of nineteen novels and eighty short stories.

William Faulkner first visited Charlottesville in 1931, returning in 1957 to become the first writer in residence of the University of Virginia. He continued his association there until his untimely death in 1962. He will be remembered as the greatest American writer to live and die in the twentieth century. . . .

Jill Summers, his adored daughter, survives him as his literary executrix. It is her awesome responsibility to deal with the management of his papers and give permission to quote from his works. She and her husband Paul Summers live on their five hundred acre Knole farm fifteen miles outside of Charlottesville. . . .

Jill guards her privacy fiercely and much like her father, shuns the social life preferring to raise horses and fox hunt. . . .

"My father wanted a boy," Jill told me, "and I of course wasn't. When the doctor came out, he said, 'Well, Bill, you don't have a Bill, you have a Jill,' and that's how I guess I got my name. Looking back now, it seemed that I wished I could have been a boy. I never played with dolls like other girls and I didn't care about clothes. I preferred reading or riding or having fun with my pets and there were many of those. At various times, I had dogs, flying squirrels, coons and even a deer." . . .

Although Jill had Malcolm Franklin as her step-brother and Victoria as a step-sister, she was virtually brought up as an only child. . . . Although loving her father tremendously, in no way does she want to trade on his name and fame. . . . She told me she and her father had many lively discussions when she was younger. She felt a keen sense of communication with him. "Frequently, we'd argue over words and the question had to be proved before either of us would let go of it—very much like two dogs worrying away at a bone. So, in order to prove a point, we would consult an atlas or a dictionary. For that reason there was hardly a room in the house in Oxford without both of these books. We also loved to talk about mythology, arguing back and forth over some obscure figure of those times. The favorite place of these kind of talks was at the midday meal which I had with my parents. I think they felt that I should be exposed to adult conversation and ideas. Pappy would fling an idea out and I was expected to explain my position on a subject, as well as take part in most family discussions."

Jill confessed that though she loved her father very much this then to be world famous figure was a source of embarrassment for her. . . . He was sort of the black sheep of the family. Oxford was a very, very small town and rigidly conventional. We weren't really socially acceptable because Pappy didn't have a regular job and he didn't follow the good old puritan ethics of off to the office early in the morning. I had a few close friends, but some of my peers weren't allowed to play with me because we were supposed to be a little peculiar. . . .

Fox hunting and horses, in general, take up a great deal of Jill's life. . . . She obviously does not think of it as a mere sport. "It's something you have to prepare for. It has a certain amount of tradition involved in it." Jill feels that because of this, anyone who engages in hunting is serious about it and has a healthy respect for the rituals. . . . Were her father still alive, he would be following the same sport, jumping the highest fences and riding the biggest horses. Fox hunting was a way of life that William Faulkner dearly cherished. He will long be remembered by hunting compatriots who knew him as a sporting gentleman and fellow rider, for these were the modest pleasures he enjoyed most. On the evening he had been asked to dine with President Kennedy at the White House, he joined the Buck Mountain Club members on a picnic. A long-time resident of Charlottesville, Mrs. Evalyn Galban recalls that when he was asked why he declined such an illustrious invitation, Faulkner's answer was a simple one, "Well, it's one hundred and twenty five miles to Washington. That's too far to go to get something to eat."

COL. SARTORIS AND MR. SNOPES[4]
Nancy Hale

I first met William Faulkner in 1957 when he had come to Charlottesville, where I live, to be writer in Residence at the University of Virginia, where my husband is professor of English. We met at an afternoon reception the English Department gave for the Faulkners in the Colonnade Club—the faculty club on the Lawn (never called campus) which is housed in one of the original Palladian pavilions Jefferson designed. I had over the years heard some widely varying accounts of Faulkner and I was curious to meet the famous man.

I had seen him out walking alone in the suburban-type streets of Charlottesville, a dapper little figure with a neat moustache, dressed like an actor in a trench coat and fur-felt hat with an Alpine brush, swinging a stick and looking about him with a sightseer's air. It was said to be the familial tie that led him to accept the invitation from the University. He had never acted as Writer in Residence at any other university. . . .

I walked over to Mr. Faulkner. "I think we have some friends in New York in common," I said.

"Is that so, ma'am?" he said.

I mentioned a few people, writers. At each name he would nod as though giving it his considered attention. When I ran out of names, he just stood there, at ease, silent. . . .

Simple, sensuous experience was what Faulkner wanted to talk about—the taste of the first sip of whiskey, the sound of tree toads at night in summer, the way it smells when you wake up to find snow, to mention only things that came up in conversation that night. I remember the only check came when I said. "I've never been to Mississippi. I'd like to go, only I'm scared."

He stiffened. "What of, ma'am?" he said with noticeable coldness.

"The Spanish moss hanging off the trees," I said. "It looks so eerie especially at dusk."

He let his breath out. "Oh," he said , "I thought you meant *politically*."

Faulkner's simplicity was nowhere more conspicuous than in his action to being Writer in Residence. The Department had been so sure that the foremost writer in the country would not even bother to come, but now he was here it turned out he was surprised and eased to find the students really wanted to see him, and liked to talk to him and listen to him.

He would give no formal lectures, but he would answer questions of group conferences of students and staff. At the end of one of these, the presiding instructor said, "I think perhaps we've taken enough of Mr. Faulkner's time—unless, sir, you feel the wish to carry on a bit more?" to which Faulkner replied, "Well, I've told you, this is a dreadful habit to get into, where you can stand up in front of people and nobody can say, 'Shut up and sit down.'"

The readings he gave from his own work were less something to hear than a sight to behold. The audience, including townspeople, would assemble in one or another academic hall, and at last in would that tiny, set-faced man with the grey moustache, who would proceed to read, face buried in his book, in an almost inaudible tone fifteen or twenty minutes. I remember that when he read the "Spotted Houses" section from *The Hamlet*, in the McGregor Room in the Alderman Library, it was plain he himself was much amused by what he was reading but for those of us who couldn't follow his low, slurred, deep-South accent, it might almost have been a private joke.

Three or four times during his semester's work he held question and answer sessions open to the townspeople. His answers became predictable, if one went to enough of these sessions. It was as if he had worked them out to fit every conceivable question; it was as if he had constructed a carapace for himself out of set phrases. For instance he always spoke of the writer as one totally without scruples in pursuit of his art. Once when, as he often did, he spoke of himself as a "failed poet, who had to take up what he could do," the questioner then asked whether a story of his called "Carcassonne" had anything to do with a French poem of the same theme and the same title, Faulkner replied, "I don't know the poem, though if I did know it and I had needed to steal from it I'm sure I would—I wouldn't have hesitated."

Audiences often asked him about a statement he once made to the press, rating Wolfe the greatest of the modern writers precisely because he failed to achieve what he undertook. "For twenty years I've been trying to explain that," Faulkner used to reply. "I meant only that Hemingway had sense enough to find a method he could control and didn't need or didn't have to, wasn't driven by his private demon to waste himself in trying to do more than that. So, he has done consistently probably the most solid work of us all. But it wasn't the splendid magnificent bust that Wolfe made, in trying to put the whole history of the human heart on the head of a pin, you might say." When he spoke of the human heart, as he so often did, Faulkner nearly always called it "frail and fragyle."

On the whole, however, the townspeople of Charlottesville did not, to use the local phrase, pay the Nobel Prize winner much mind. There was a story current about two young women standing in the window of Timberlake's Drugstore downtown, having a Coke.

"Look there," said one. "Yonder goes Mr. Faulkner."

"Who's he?" the other said.

"You mean you don't know who Mr. *Faulkner* is?" said the first, "Why, he's Jill Summers's father, of course." . . .

Miss Estelle was charming to me. She said, "Bill gave me a message for you. I'll read you what he said."

Here is the message she gave me: "Tell the gentleman I have given up the world of literature for the world of fox hunting, but I'd be delighted to take the gentleman fox hunting." . . .

It seemed unbelievable that a man whose entire claim to fame was based on his writing should thus dismiss not only another artist but art itself. . . .

When I walked up to him feeling that I *must* talk to him, because he looked so alone—by asking whether he'd read some book I was in the middle of.

"No, ma'am," he replied. "I don't read much of any. I'm just a country boy from down Mississippi." . . .

"I hear you do a lot of fox hunting," I said, willing to play it his way.

"Well, ma'am," he said in that very slow, very soft voice, "down home we only hunt foxes on foot, with guns and dogs. Up here's the only place I ever hunted from the back of a horse, and to tell you the truth I spend right much time at it.' . . .

After Faulkner had served as Writer in Residence for the spring semester in each of two successive years, he decided to settle down in a cottage on his daughter's place in Albernarle Country and return to his farm in Mississippi only for the planting and the harvesting. The University conferred an honorary professorship on him, and in 1959 Linton Massey, a local collector, lent unique manuscripts, photographs, letters, first editions, and other records of

Faulkner's career for an exhibition which was held in the Alderman Library. The books and papers were displayed in glass cases; at the end of the room hung a portrait of Faulkner painted by his mother many years before. . . .

I remember thinking I would almost have admired Faulkner's intransigence if it had been based on the pride of an artist who knows art to be higher than politics. . . .

When Faulkner left the University, he and some friends, including his son-in-law and Mr. Massey, set up the William Faulkner Foundation, which among other benefits to young writers offers an award each year for a "notable first novel." . . . The first year it was given to John Knowles for *A Separate Peace*. . . .

Faulkner died in 1962—not at his Virginia home but on one of his visits back to Rowan Oak. Besides all the obituaries and editorials I read in the Northern papers, friends send me clippings from the Southern press about the death of America's foremost writer. One clipping that was a little different was sent to me by my husband a few weeks later.

It is from the Charlottesville *Progress*. At the top is a picture of two men and two women who are sitting, in hunting dress, on a board fence. The caption explains that the riders have just returned from a long hunt last season. Underneath, a headline reads FAULKNER MEMORIAL TROPHY ESTABLISHED. The story begins as follows:

"A William Faulkner Memorial Trophy Award has been established by the Buck Mountain Riding Club and will be awarded to a junior rider at the club's annual fall horse show.

"The award will go to the junior rider who has exhibited over the past year the keenest interest in riding to hounds, horse shows, and who has shown good sportsmanship at all times.

"Faulkner was a charter member and was director of the riding club since it was founded in 1959. Each year a junior rider will receive the memorial award—an engraved silver trophy."

MISS HALE'S FAULKNER CARICATURE EXPLAINED[5]

John Lewis Longley Jr.

As a literary critic and long-time student of American popular magazines, I want to do what I can to clarify and explain the article by Miss Nancy Hale (Mrs. Fredson Bowers) on the later William Faulkner in the current issue of a woman's fashion magazine.

The reaction of the people I have so far heard to the caricatures of themselves, their friends, and Mr. Faulkner has been one of bewilderment rather than anger. This bewilderment splits rather neatly into two parts: (1) How could Miss Hale so completely fail to understand Mr. Faulkner? (2) Why did she paint everyone as a clodhopping redneck? I believe I can answer the second question if not the first. . . .

Miss Hale explains Mr. Faulkner's refusal to attend the Kennedy dinner by his being Southern, and informs us that Mr. Edmund Wilson, the only other holdout, is also a Southerner. . . .

It all seems to come down to Miss Hale's exasperation with Mr. Faulkner's attitude toward horses and people who like them. "Vogue" magazine's attitude toward the value of great art, particularly literary art is evident. . . .

"Vogue's" standards are Miss Hale's standards. Actually, she is responsible only for what she herself wrote, signed and published in an internationally-distributed magazine. . . .

FAULKNER'S SHADOW ON THE MOON[6]

Ross Valentine

William Faulkner, speaking to a group at Mr. Jefferson's university some time ago, called Virginians "snobs." His "generalization" provided welcome grist for editorial comment and dinner table conversations.

Actually it wasn't a generalization at all. Faulkner particularized. He attributed to Virginians (at least those dyed-in-the-wool and a yard wide) an attribute common to all mankind, anywhere, with presumptive exception of saintly hermits and poetic sages like Robert Frost.

Faulkner's 25 per cent-truth may annoy, but it also stimulates. A half-truth may be believed or rejected out of hand. A 100 per cent truth (i.e. something virtually everyone believes) is ignored. . . .

But to get back to what he said of Virginia snobbery. Snobbery is not regional, but universal. . . . What we call snobbery is a craving for distinction—the kind of distinction sought by "name-droppers," the desire to be associated in the eyes of one's friends, with fame, wealth, power or aristocracy, living or dead.

Surely, this is not a quirk of human nature peculiar to Virginians!

FROM MOSCOW TO YOKNAPATAWPHA AS JULIE AND DMITRY URNOV HAVE DISCOVERED, IT'S NOT AS FAR AS YOU THINK[7]

Stuart Burlington

Both were born, brought up, and educated in the Soviet Union. They are respectively Dmitry Urnov, 55, a member of the Gorky Institute of World Literature as well as editor of a prominent Soviet journal, and his wife, Julia ("Julie") Paliyevskaya, 51, who has written a biography of William Faulkner in Russian as well as translating his famous Nobel Prize speech and Virginia lectures. . . .

Though neither Dmitry nor Julie have spent a great deal of time in the United States, American culture is a familiar milieu for both. . . . "American culture was always popular and highly esteemed in our country, though in a limited amount. The limitations were political. We were somehow made to know only those authors who were labeled progressive. That's why we couldn't read Faulkner, because he was reactionary." . . .

His wife noted of Faulkner's work, "In one of the articles in the '30s it was said 'His world is a reptile world, inhabited by spiders.'"

Faulkner was not the only reptile in the garden of Soviet censorship during the Stalinist period, as Dmitry was quick to point out: "The general trend was that any U.S. author who could be considered conservative, not just reactionary, was not allowed. Henry James, for instance, was nonexistent for years. All that set of authors, James, Edith Wharton, Willa Cather, H.L. Mencken were off-limits. Stephen Crane was always there, no problem with him."

Even classic American literature was *verboten* in the heyday of Stalinism. "We never read some of the senior American classics when I was growing up." Dmitry said. "For example, we only read Melville again in the '60s, although the first [Russian] translation of Melville appeared in 1858." . . .

"I think it is through Faulkner—by reading all his works—that is how I learned English," said Julie. Coincidentally, the first Faulkner novel she read was *The Mansion*, a novel written during the Nobel author's Charlottesville years.

Like countless bemused American students, when Julie got to

the giants of Faulknerism, *Absalom, Absalom!* and *The Sound and the Fury,* she found the going was anything but easy. . . .

Trying to translate Faulkner's Nobel speech about man enduring and prevailing despite the prospect of atomic annihilation (a very real prospect to Russians and Americans alike at the time it was given in December 1950) was more an act of faith than a trick of grammar. Julie worked at the translation "for about a year" to "render the rhythm, the pathos, and the feeling. It is very, very difficult to do in Russian." . . . Not only did Julie's translation sell 50,000 copies in the Soviet Union but, in Julie's words, "it was sold out the very day it appeared in the shops." . . . As she put it, Faulkner has such "an enormous appeal to Russians. . . . he is *the* American writer in the Soviet Union at the moment."

For one thing, Julie believes, Faulkner "is the American author who produces the impression that what he writes is not literature. It is more than literature. Faulkner is like Tolstoy in producing literature that is more than literature, in producing works that transcend to the realm of immortality. No other modern American author would produce this impression." . . .

"Your Civil War," she observed, is particularly understood by Russians who have gone through three wars in this century (World War I, the Russian Revolution, and World War II, in the latter of which alone, according to the Urnovs, "We lost at least 30 million lives; that's the official figure.") These were wars fought on our own soil, wars that divided families and disrupted countless millions of lives. Thus we can empathize with the Confederacy and the Lost Cause, however wrong that cause."

Finally, Julie said, a theme that runs throughout Faulkner strikes a resounding and responsive chord among Soviet readers—the theme of endurance. To her fellow countrymen, Julie stressed, "the idea of endurance is very, very important."

The popularity of an author like Faulkner also reflects another trait among Soviet readers, the Urnovs agree, and that is their attraction for literature that is *not* easy reading. In Julie's estimate, "The number of people [in the Soviet Union] who enjoy reading difficult literature is tremendous. . . . In any subway on the Metro you see people today reading Joyce and Proust."

Dmitry feels there is another reason why so many Soviet citizens in the days before *glasnost* and *perestroika* turned to cultural pursuits, sought refuge in what the average American would regard as highbrow reading. . . .

FAULKNER'S GENIUS—WHERE DID IT COME FROM?[8]

Anatole Broyard

"And now, at last, I have some perspective on all I have done. I mean, the work apart from me, the work which I did, apart from what I am . . . and now I realize for the first time what an amazing gift I had: uneducated in every formal sense, without even very literate, let alone literary, companions, yet to have made the things I made. I don't know where it came from."

This is William Faulkner writing to a young friend in 1953 and it expresses the feeling I get too as I look at the man himself in *Selected Letters of William Faulkner,* edited by Joseph Blotner. Where did it come from? . . . While Faulkner's prose style cannot be explained by his life, it can be related to it. A Southern accent has always struck me as an attempt, at least in part, to find and keep the music in the American language, in some cases almost to sing it. Just as in Shakespeare's time, the people at court often spoke in something like bland verse, so in Faulkner's world, there is a Southern courtliness, a royal sound, to language. The richness of African tongues—in rhythm, inflection and sonority—may also have reached him through Southern black culture.

"Oratory out of solitude" was Faulkner's own way of describing his style, and it is oratorical, an urgent attempt to talk to his fellow man, even to evangelize him.

Faulkner's experimental technique is perhaps the most surprising part of his talent, for he does not seem in these letters to be what one would call an experimental man. Quite the contrary: he was conservative, commonsensical and impatient with most forms of pretension. One can only surmise that, in his case too, we have underestimated the power of folk art. Just as some primitive American painters have anticipated Expressionism simply by exploring the materials at hand rather than through any abstract conception of art, so Faulkner seems to have whittled monuments with a penknife.

He wrote the way he did, not because he wanted to revolutionize the novel form, but because these forms simply seemed to be the best way to do what he wanted to do. One thinks of avant-garde writing as being comparatively rootless, as being the final flowering of a long evolution, but Faulkner seemed to take in the whole process from beginning to end, root to bloom. . . .

Faulkner was painfully ahead of his time. While he could write rings around Hemingway and Fitzgerald, he wrote rings around his readers, too. As a result, he was forced to grind out as many as two short stories a week to support himself, and when this was not enough, he wrote screenplays in Hollywood. America's best writer never made a decent living until he sold Intruder in the Dust to the movies for $50,000—and this was in 1948, when he was 51 years old and had been publishing novels and short stories for over 20 years.

For all the flamboyance of his style and the complexity of his structures, Faulkner worked with an astonishing rapidity. He said he finished *As I Lay Dying* in six weeks, and his early novels appeared at the rate of one a year. Most of the time, about the only feedback he had came from his editors. In his letters to them, he appears to be more tractable than one would have supposed. He never played at being a genius. And, indeed, he received very little encouragement in this direction: As late as 1947, *Partisan Review* rejected one of his stories on the ground that it "read like a rough draft." It may well have been, for Faulkner had to write to eat and he was always turning out work under extreme pressure.

As we see again and again in these letters, Faulkner was a fanatic about privacy. He knew that neither he nor anyone else could explain his accomplishment and he did not want anyone to try. Even in his letters to friends, we get only rare glimpses of the intensity that went into his books. In one letter, he confesses that he is "trying to say it all in one sentence." In another, he criticizes Hemingway for not being willing to "get out on a limb . . . to risk bad taste, overwriting, dullness, etc."

Faulkner risked just about everything, but he did not make much of a fuss about it in these letters. He once remarked that he felt he deserved "a reasonable freedom from bourgeois material, petty impediments and compulsion." It is a very modest expectation for a man who was the best novelist, and one of the most prolific, of the richest country in the world.

FAULKNER: AS HIS NEPHEW KNEW HIM[9]

David Beard

Myth and fact merge in this county. A subdivision called Tara Estates sprouts beside Jimmy Faulkner's antebellum home. Academics dig here for the roots of author William Faulkner's life and work.

Hundreds of book-length studies have been written about the Nobel Prize-winner, but many overlook William Faulkner's dry wit, his love of children, his pleasure in hunting quail and dove in the red clay hills of north Mississippi, according to family members.

That's one reason Jimmy Faulkner, his nephew, says he decided to write *Across the Creek: Faulkner Family Stories* ($12.95, University Press of Mississippi), a thin volume of reminiscences about the complex man he knew as Brother Will. . . . "If anybody was going to tell the truth about him, I'd have to do it, because I probably knew him better than any man still living," he said. . . .

Readers spotted Lafayette County in Faulkner's fictional Yoknapatawpha County, and the author came across to visitors as rude or enigmatic as he tried to preserve his privacy, his nephew said.

"He was a real quiet, private person, but he'd open up among his family and his friends. He was the funniest person I ever met. He was witty, and compassionate. Too compassionate. That's why he built that wall around himself."

In the stories, William Faulkner appears as the wise—and wisecracking—man with the droll line that puts the proper twist on any adventure.

FAULKNER REMEMBERED—TORMENTS OF AUTHOR, UVA TEACHER[10]

Julie Young

> *"A writer knows he has a short span of life, that the day will come when he must pass through the wall of oblivion, and he wants to leave a scratch on that wall."*
>
> William Faulkner
> Writer-in-residence
> University of Virginia, 1957

He passed through the wall in 1962, and left a scratch the size of the Grand Canyon on the literary world. The troubled little man, haunted by childhood demons and blessed with inner voices that inspired his novels, short stories, and poems, still has an enduring grip on the imaginations of students and academics 26 years after his death in a Mississippi sanitarium.

Stephen B. Oates, a University of Massachusetts history professor, tells Faulkner's life story in an empathetic book titled *William Faulkner: The Man and the Artist* (Harper & Row, $9.95). The book is only the second pure biography of the Nobel and Pulitzer Prize-winning author who spent his last years as a guest-lecturer at UVa.

There is not much previously unpublished information in the book, but its novelistic approach to Faulkner makes it unique, as he wrote for the reading masses instead of "a handful of Faulkner scholars.'

"It's for people who know nothing about him, who will make them go back to his fiction." . . .

Oates does, however, shed some new light on Faulkner's turbulent, but enduring marriage to Estelle Oldham, as well as his life-long bout with alcohol and his mid-life weakness for younger women. Intimate glimpses into Faulkner's marital battles and infidelity were culled from a private collection of family letters owned by Chicago poet L.D. Brodsky.

"They were startling in what they revealed about that very troubled marriage and how it impacted on Faulkner," Oates said. "I wonder how he lived at all, let alone write 30 books." . . .

Faulkner left an indelible impression on the University during the six years he spent in Charlottesville. He also wanted to flee the racial strife that was threatening to destroy his beloved South, Oates wrote in the book.

NOTES

1. Anonymous, *The Çavalier Daily*, University of Virginia, Friday, September 21, 1962, p. 2.
2. *The Cavalier Daily*, April 20, 1972.
3. *The Albemarie Monthly*, Oct.\Nov. 1978.

4. *Vogue*, August 1, 1963.
5. Letter to the Editor, *Charlottesville Daily Progress*, July 6, 1963.
6. *Richmond Times-Dispatch*, May 22, 1957.
7. *The Observer*, Oct. 10-16, 1991.
8. *Charlottesville Daily Progress*, February 19, 1977.
9. *Charlottesville Daily Progress*, October 12, 1986.
10. *Charlottesville Daily Progress*, August 28, 1988.

Contributors

AMINA AMIN was Reader in English at the School of Languages, Gujarat University, Ahmedabad. Her areas of interest are nineteenth century American literature, modern American fiction and drama, women's writing in English. Her publications include *Of Seeing Incompatibles: A Study of Evil in Herman Melville's Works, Margins of Erasure: Purdah in the Sub-continental Novel in English,* co-edited with Jasbir Jain.

NEERJA JAYAL CHAND is Reader in English at R.L.A. College, Universityof Delhi. She obtained her Master's degree from the University of Wisconsin and is currently working on her Ph. D. thesis on Nigerian writer Buchi Emecheta. She is an Associate with the Indian Insitute of Advanced Study,Shimla (1996-99) and an awardee of Shastri Indo-Canadian Fellowship (1998-99) for a project on Afro-Canadian literature at the University of Toronto.

THADIOUS M. DAVIS is Gertrude Conaway Vanderbilt Professor of English at Vanderbilt University, U.S.A. Editor of four books and the author of over forty critical essays, she has written *Nella Larsen, Novelist of the Harlem Renaissance: A Woman's Life Unveiled* as well as several works on Faulkner, including *Faulkner's "Negro": Art and the Southern Context.*

I.R. DRAXI is Reader and Head of the Department of English at Viswasrao Naik Mahavidyalaya, Shirala, Maharashtra. He also teaches American literature at K.B.P. College, Islampur. Educated at Karnatak University, Dharwad, he received his M.Phil. and Ph.D. from Shivaji University, Kolhapur working on William Faulkner.

JUDY HEN teaches English at the University of Haifa, Israel. A Hemingway scholar, she has published several articles on modern American fiction.

LOTHAR HÖNNIGHAUSEN is Professor of English in the Nordamerikaprogram at the University of Bonn, Germany. He is general editor of *Transatlantic Perspectives* and author of *William Faulkner: The Art of Stylization in His Early Graphic and Literary*

Work; and *Faulkner: Masks and Metaphors* just published by the University Press of Mississippi.

ANDREW HOOK is Bradley Professor of English Literature at the University of Glasgow. Educated at the Universities of Edinburgh, Manchester and Princeton, he taught previously at the universities of Edinburgh and Aberdeen. His publications include editions of Scott and Bronte, a collection of essays on John Dos Passos and a critical study on F. Scott Fitzgerald.

M. THOMAS INGE in Blackwell Professor of the Humanities at Randolph-Macon College, Ashland, Virginia. Among his publications are *Perspectives on American Culture: Essays on Humor, Literature and the Popular Arts* (1994), *Faulkner, Sut, and Other Southerners: Essays in Literary History* (1992). From March 3-6, 1997, he organised "The Achievement of William Faulkner: A Centennial Conference" at his college.

ARNOLD and **MARIANNE JENSEN** are senior citizens residing at Charlottesville, Virginia. Apart from hosting international students from the University of Virginia, pursuing adult degree programs, serving as interns at a local weekly newspaper, they are actively engaged in various social welfare activities.

DONALD M. KARTIGANER is William Howry Professor of Faulkner Studies at the University of Mississippi and director of the Mississippi Faulkner Conference this year. He is the author of *The Fragile Thread: The Meaning of Form in Faulkner's Novels* and, with Ann J. Abadie, of four volumes of proceedings of the Faulkner and Yoknapatawpha Conference.

RAMA KUNDU is Reader in English at Burdwan University, West Bengal. Having done her Ph.D. on Thomas Hardy, she has extensively published in various journals, including some in Bengali. Her publications include *Vision and Design in Hardy's Fiction; Wrestling with God: Studies in English Devotional Poetry; Anandamath O Sampradaikata.*

JOHN LOWE is Professor of English at Louisiana State University, U.S.A. Educated at Vanderbilt, Georgia and Columbia Universities, he also served as Senior Fulbright Professor at Munich. Among his select publications are *Jump at the Sun: Zora Neale Hurston's Cosmic Comedy; The Future of Southern Letters; Rede-*

fining Southern Culture. Among works in progress are *The Americanisation of Ethnic Humor* and *Place, Self, and the Other in Southern Fiction.*

SOMDATTA MANDAL teaches English at Vivekananda College, University of Calcutta and is guest-lecturer in English and American literature at Rabindra Bharati University, Calcutta. A Fulbright scholar at the University of Virginia, Charlottesville, she has published articles in various national and international journals and was the recipient of the Olive I. Reddick Jr. Award in 1995. She has edited a two-volume anthology *F. Scott Fitzgerald: A Centennial Tribute* (1997).

RICHARD C. MORELAND is Associate Professor of English at Louisiana State University, U.S.A. Author of *Faulkner and Modernism: Rereading and Rewriting,* he is currently at work on a project entitled "Domination and Democracy in Twain, Eliot, Ellison and Morrison."

TUTUN MUKHERJEE teaches English at Osmania University, Hyberabad. Her research interests include Critical Theory, American Studies, Film Studies and Translation. Her principal publications include *Chicago Critics: An Evaluation, Reviewing Critical Theory, Translation: From Periphery to Centrestage*, many articles and reviews in journals. She has guest-edited two special issues of *Indian Journal of American Studies* on Critical Theory and Film Studies.

MANISHA MUKHOPADHYAY is a full-time Research Scholar in the Department of English at the University of Kalyani, West Bengal. At present she is working on William Faulkner.

PRAMOD K. NAYAR teaches Modern Literature and Literary Criticism at the Department of P.G. Studies in English, Kuvempu University, Shimoga in Karnataka. His research work focussed primarily in Anglo-Indian writing. Publishing over two dozen articles, his interests include Eliot, Romantic literature, Literary Theory, Horror and Humour Fiction.

LAXMI PARASURAM is Professor of English at Burdwan University, West Bengal. Educated at Bombay and Kentucky, she was President of the Indian Association of American Studies during 1995-96. Apart from editing a book *American Literature and Culture: New Insights*, her publications include several scholarly articles and the book *Virginia Woolf: The Emerging Reality.*

DAVID PAUL RAGAN teaches English at Hammond School, Columbia, South Carolina. A great Faulkner fan, his articles have appeared in *Mississippi Quarterly* and other scholarly journals.

P.G. RAMA RAO retired as Professor of English from Utkal University, Bhubaneshwar, and served as Scholar-in-Residence at American Studies Research Centre, Hyderabad. His publications include *Ernest Hemingway: A Study in Narrative Technique.*

ASHIS SENGUPTA is Reader in English at the University of North Bengal. A winner of the Olive I. Reddick Jr. Award in 1996, he has published over a dozen articles in prestigious journals like *Indian Journal of American Studies, Indian Journal of English Studies, New Quest.* At present he is working on Arthur Miller's later plays.

ISAAC SEQUEIRA retired as Professor of English from Osmania University, Hyderabad. He is Research Consultant at the American Studies Research Centre, Hyderabad, and a distinguished scholar of Popular Culture.

AMITABHA SINHA is Reader in English at Calcutta University. He has published a number of papers, in learned journals and books, and lectured at Seminars and Refresher Courses, on English and American novels.

RANU V. VANIKAR was Professor and Head, Department of English, M.S. University of Baroda and is a Consultant in Communications. She is Visiting Professor at Jamnalal Bajaj Institute of Management Studies and at the Xavier Institute of Communications, Mumbai. She had worked on William Faulkner for her Ph.D. dissertation, on a UGC Research Fellowship. A British Council Scholar during 1977-78, she undertook postdoctoral research at University of Lancaster, UK. Recipient of the USIS Book Award and The English Speaking Union of the Commonwealth Award in 1985, she has several research publications to her credit.

HOWARD WOLF is Professor of English at State University of New York at Buffalo. Having taught abroad at Ankara University, Turkey, and University of Hongkong, as well as in India, his publications are *Broadway Serenade; The Autobiographical Impulse in America: Essays on the Crisis of Humanism in Contemporary Culture; A Version of Home: Letters from the World.*

Index

F. Scott Fitzgerald

A Centennial Tribute

in 2 vols.

Somdatta Mandal, ed.

F. Scott Fitzgerald is one of the most colourful, significant and cherished talents that brought American literature to world prominence. His career declined in tandem with the American economy and he was almost forgotten when he died at the end of the Great Depression. Interest in his work revived shortly after World War II. This wide-ranging anthology offers a critical appraisal of Fitzgerald as a novelist on the 100th anniversary of his birth. It presents Fitzgerald not as a dissolute playboy but as the literary giant of the Roaring Twenties whose works ushered in and christened the Jazz Age. The contributors to the volume comprise an august group of Fitzgerald scholars and academics of international repute.

ISBN: 81-7551-039-0, 81-7551-040-4 Rs. 600

PRESTIGE BOOKS

The Novels of Toni Morrison

A Study in Race, Gender and Class

K. Sumana

Toni Morrison is one of the foremost twentieth century African-American women novelists. In 1993, she was awarded the Nobel Prize for her outstanding contribution to literature. The book, the first of its kind by an Asian scholar, attempts to make an in-depth study of the interrelationship of race, gender, and class in her fiction. With that end in view, it examines all her six novels, namely *The Bluest Eye, Sula, Song of Solomon, Tar Baby, Beloved,* and *Jazz.* It reveals that Morrison is essentially a fictional artist combining, as she does, political consciousness with aesthetic sensibility. The book offers stimulating discussions on the much-debated contemporary issues of race and gender, placing Morrison in the literary tradition of black women's writing.

ISBN: 81-7551-048-X Rs. 400

PRESTIGE BOOKS

F. Scott Fitzgerald

Centenary Essays from India

Mohan Ramanan, ed.

F. Scott Fitzgerald, along with Ernest Hemingway and William Faulkner, is regarded as one of the "Big Three" American writers of the first half of the twentieth century. His reputation as a writer has grown the world over. In India, he is widely read and there is now a major body of Fitzgerald criticism available. The American Studies Research Centre celebrated the birth centenary of Fitzgerald in September 1996 by conducting a two-day seminar. The present volume comprises papers read at the seminar and a few which were not read but were received by the organizers. They represent a cross-section of the scholarship on Fitzgerald from India. Several of Fitzgerald's novels are discussed; the insights gained from recent theory have been put to good use in the analyses of Fitzgerald's works in these articles. A comparative approach and a self-conscious Indian dimension is evident in these essays. This volume, while offering fresh and insightful interpretations, hopefully will revive interest in a significant author.

ISBN: 81-7551-041-2 Rs. 400

PRESTIGE BOOKS